20 November 1974

For Patty and Holt,

In hopes of many
years of bliss — gustatory
and otherwise.

Love,

Patti

the seasonal kitchen
a return to fresh foods

the seasonal kitchen
a return to fresh foods

by perla meyers

Holt, Rinehart and Winston
New York Chicago San Francisco

For Bob

Published simultaneously in Canada by Holt, Rinehart and Winston of Canada, Limited.

ISBN: 0-03-003346-2
Library of Congress Catalog Card Number: 72-91567

First Edition

Designer: Corchia, de Harak Inc.
Printed in the United States of America

contents

acknowledgments

Although sincere thanks are owed to many people (marvelous chefs of many countries) who contributed their skills and knowledge to the making of this book, certain people deserve special mention: AL CORCHIA, for his brilliant and practical design; PACE BARNES, WILSON GATHINGS, ARLENE HIRST, LOUELLA STILL CULLIGAN, ANN DORE, for their strong and never-failing editorial advice and support; and SANDRA SCHOENFEIN, FRAN MANHEIMER, PEGGY GROSS, JOAN FIRESTONE, for their spirited and painstaking thoroughness in testing the recipes throughout the book.

Of all the reasons I have for writing **The Seasonal Kitchen**, the most important is to communicate an understanding of freshness and encourage a return to seasonal cooking. This is not a book for organic-food buffs, however, but for anyone willing to explore and rediscover the marvelous potential of fresh food. Cooking with fresh ingredients does not mean spending hours in the market and kitchen everyday, or in planning elaborate menus. Small daily variations such as the addition of a lemon sauce with beans, of beets sauteed in butter and cream with a touch of a seasonal herb can bring exciting new dishes to your table. An unusual combination of salad greens offers a seasonal touch and brings new life to a familiar menu.

Many dishes in this book are based on the regional cooking of Spain, Italy and France, where native cuisines have been shaped by nature's calendar. These, as well as most European countries, have a tradition of freshness that has created classics over the years. Can there be a truly great minestrone without fresh vegetables, a good paella with frozen fish?
Freshness is essential to good cooking. The total understanding of our seasons is a must if we want to re-create the great peasant dishes of Europe.

I find it ironic that, after years spent on developing the perfect peach or strawberry and when so many fresh vegetables have become supermarket staples, we pride ourselves on having the largest possible freezers, which we fill with frozen fruits or vegetables. On a recent trip to California I learned that vegetables such as broccoli or fresh peas are slowly disappearing from the markets since most people only buy the frozen variety. This in an area that produces most of the fresh vegetables in the United States and where the prices of fresh produce are lower than in any other part of the country!

Fortunately, in recent years, the attitude toward food is changing. Americans have started to realize that eating is not just something to do to survive but something to be enjoyed. Cooking is recognized as a creative outlet, and people have come to understand that the "world of food" can be as exciting as the "world of art." French food, especially, has gained enormous popularity: words like "crepe," " souffle" and "mousse" have entered our language. Unfortunately, "gourmet cooking" has also crept in, and its true meaning has been lost in the process. Any dish that is slightly more unusual and more demanding of the cook's time has become a gourmet dish. Innumerable cookbooks have been written on so-called gourmet cooking without the slightest understanding of what really makes a great dish.

Understanding ingredients and their affinities to one another is the most important key to all good cooking. This understanding must start at the market with careful shopping. I never go marketing with a preconceived idea of the day's menu, but rather let the fresh produce speak for itself. I find beauty in every fresh vegetable—a bin of new potatoes or a pile of fresh carrots can be the inspiration for a delicious meal. I strongly believe in cooking with the freshest ingredients rather than resorting to frozen foods. Even though, nowadays, I often deplore the lack of a top-quality apple or peach, I still feel that we are fortunate to have such a variety of fresh produce at hand—a variety that enables us to capture the essence of good, honest, flavorful cooking.

Techniques

Many recipes in this book are quite simple, and the method of preparation follows a pattern, which you will soon be familiar with. The steps should not be followed blindly but must be understood, since they are the basis for your own creativity. Most of the recipes are in the regional peasant tradition, which I find more suitable to our lifestyle than the French Grande Cuisine. Peasant cooking demands as much attention as any other kind of cooking, but once mastered, its techniques can be satisfactorily applied to many dishes of other countries.

The secret of success for the simplest dish lies in careful preparation. Browning the meat properly for a ragout is essential; reducing a sauce to the right consistency is a must. Steps such as seeding and draining a tomato or drying meat thoroughly before browning may seem unnecessary chores, but they are as important to the result as is careful seasoning. The first time I worked in the kitchen of a "Three Star" restaurant in France, I was overwhelmed by the intricacy of the techniques. I was convinced that each dish was a classic, not to be changed in any way. Since then, I have assisted many great French chefs and watched them give their own touch to these classics. This taught me that, above all, it is essential for a cook to understand that the techniques in cooking are the grammar of the language of food and that with this understanding any cook can be inventive and give his or her own individual touch to a dish.

Stock cooking

A full-bodied homemade stock is the most important ingredient needed to bring out the essence and flavor of many of the recipes in this book. When making a soup with canned stock, even the freshest vegetable will lose its flavor; the simplest ragout will lack body and gutsiness. When you have a good stock available, you can create an elegant dish in ten minutes. Just add a few spoonfuls of a well-concentrated brown stock to your pan after having sauteed a steak or lamb chops and you will have a delicious sauce that will give a new flavor to an all too familiar dish! A serious cook must never let anything go to waste. Chicken and veal trimmings, beef and fish bones as well as mushroom trimmings, should be saved for the stock pot. Here is where a large freezer is a blessing. Stocks can be made at any time and frozen successfully for several months.

Preparing stocks may be time-consuming, but they are not difficult to make and once you have compared the quality and substance of a soup or sauce made with a full-bodied homemade stock, you will never resort to the canned variety again.

Ingredients

Also important to a recipe is the quality of the ingredients. Seasonal cooking is catching freshness at its prime. There is no point in buying a week's supply of fresh vegetables only to let them spoil in the bottom of the refrigerator. You should only buy a one or two day supply of fruits and vegetables and use them immediately. Sweet butter, cream and especially fish should also always be fresh.

How to use this book

The recipes in this book are marked with symbols indicating whether a dish is "easy," "intermediate," or "difficult" to prepare.

Easy   **Intermediate**   **Difficult**

These symbols are especially important for the beginner in choosing a menu and will serve as guidelines for the experienced cook.

Though many of the recipes require a large quantity of ingredients, they are not always difficult to make. A dish with fourteen ingredients can often be easier to prepare than one requiring three ingredients but a more complicated technique. The easy recipes are those that require only limited experience and a basic understanding of and ability to combine ingredients. I consider a dish "difficult" when a certain amount of skill is required and when last minute preparation is involved.

None of the dishes will be hard for the cook whose kitchen is well equipped with the basic staples. A cook must be able to improvise and whisk up a souffle or a flavorful risotto at any time. To be inspired, you need the necessary equipment. Above all, cooking is a matter of experience and continuous practice. It is like speaking a foreign language: You must keep at it in order to become fluent. People who only cook for dinner parties and guests are never at ease in the kitchen, and a dish that would seem almost elementary to the everyday cook will seem difficult to the weekend or party cook. Under no circumstances should cooking become just a chore, even if you have to do it everyday. I regard my kitchen as a retreat. Cooking demands total concentration, and the results reflect my mood and that of the season. I have often heard a student comment, "I will never make this dish, it's too difficult and takes too long. . . ." To me this is inconceivable. Cooking is a challenge. When you meet it properly, you get better at it. This is what matters!

The recipes contain symbols indicating whether a dish is "inexpensive," "moderate," or "expensive."

● Inexpensive   ◉ Moderate   ✛ Expensive

I have often seen friends and students pick a recipe at random, decide they like the sound (and hopefully the taste) of it, and then proceed to the market to buy the necessary ingredients without the faintest idea of how much that recipe will cost. Then comes the surprise! Is it possible that a pound of mushrooms or a pint of strawberries can be so expensive? This is why seasonal cooking is so important: To avoid these surprises and to get better flavor for less money.

Obviously the seasons fall somewhat differently in different parts of the country and cooks in states such as California and Florida are especially fortunate to have many fruits and vegetables available to them at lower prices than on the East Coast and in the Midwest.

The symbols are based on the price of fresh produce on the East Coast and on the price of ingredients such as fish and veal, which, unfortunately, are high all over the country. Again, I must repeat that a cook must learn to understand her "local" seasons and take advantage of them to the fullest. If you live in a state such as Florida or Arizona, where avocados are cheap and plentiful in midwinter, try to use the fruit in more ways than one. If you live in the Midwest, where fresh vegetables are scarce in winter make the most of carrots, potatoes and onions. Keep in mind that many of Europe's, and indeed the world's, best regional dishes were created by the necessity of cooking with what was available locally and that many a cook has been challenged by the simplest of ingredients.

The menus

Five menus are presented for each season except in the All-Seasons chapter. To me, these menus epitomize the seasons and what is best in each one of them.

I would, however, be surprised if anybody followed these menus in every detail. All that is necessary to compose an interesting menu is a basic understanding of ingredients and the fundamental composition of a meal.

When planning a menu for entertaining, it is always wise to stick with recipes that you are already familiar with. A little bit of experimenting beforehand can save you from an embarrassing disaster in front of guests. A clever cook can build a reputation for being a great hostess simply by doing one dish extremely well, whether its an omelette or a well-flavored ragout. So many people are bound to tradition that meals often become heavy-handed and dull. Why must a salad always be served with the main course, why must a starchy vegetable always be included? These preconceived ideas of what is "right" and "elegant" leave no room for spontaneity or the individuality of each cook. A menu can consist of a bowl of soup, salad and cheese, or a plate of tender young green beans, a risotto and fruit . . . Since most cooks have no help in the kitchen these days, they must tend to last-minute preparation, which is often needed. Personally, I see no wrong in letting my guests wait a few minutes between courses, rather than sacrifice the taste of each individual dish by a rapid succession of not quite right "gourmet" dishes.

The creative cook

I have found out over the years that to be a great cook you must be a creative one.

A recipe should only be an incentive and should not have to be followed to the very last detail. Your palate is your best guide, and by continual cooking you will perfect the dishes and give them an individual flavor. Cooking is exactly like buying clothes or furnishing a house: its style lies in the individuality of each person. I have seen beautiful rooms furnished with authentic period pieces but they look dull. I feel exactly the same about an "authentic" or "classic" dish. I refuse to be bound to the concept that if a dish has been prepared in a certain way for a number of years it must always be done that way. There are innumerable great recipes that have been created by accident, and "accidents" should be allowed to happen again. This is especially true in the use of herbs and spices, where a real mystique has developed in recent years. Why must dill only be used in dishes of northern European origin or basil always go hand-in-hand with tomatoes?

Many dishes in this book are variations of classic recipes. I have tried to capture the special flavor of a regional dish and at the same time give it my own personal touch. I hope that you will add or substitute anything you like in these recipes; and where available, a space for notes is provided for your thoughts and experiences with them. Nothing would please me more than to know that one of these recipes has been the inspiration for a whole new and exciting dish.

PERLA MEYERS
January 1973

from garden to kitchen

A few years ago, standing in the Barcelona market, I wondered how I could possibly transfer that market to New York. A few days later I experienced a similar sense of frustration in Paris where, at the time, the famous Les Halles was bustling with life. I remember walking for miles from market to market, telling myself, "In New York I will never be able to cook with the fresh foods I was used to from my childhood in Europe." Then, weeks later, while looking nostalgically at the photographs I had taken of vegetable and fruit stalls, I suddenly arrived at a solution. I decided to have my own garden.

In the beginning I found gardening confusing and hard work. I was not one of those people who worked the land as a way to relax. The only reason for growing my own vegetables and herbs was to have available vegetables that were fresh and that tasted as God meant them to. I was not looking for the unusual; I was looking for quality and freshness.

The beginning was quite frustrating. I had to learn by experience. However, even that first year it was worth the effort when I popped the first tiny radishes into a salad bowl together with marvelously fresh lettuce; when I munched on the first green peas and had the first omelette with finely minced fresh herbs.

In our day and age the "real" market has all but disappeared both in the United States and in Europe where in most countries the supermarkets are taking over. Although supermarkets have many advantages, I find that the sterility of fruits and vegetables packaged in cellophane detracts from the joy of cooking. Fruits and vegetables are often shipped from thousands of miles away and in order to survive the packaging and handling they have to be picked "half-green." They never gain the full flavor and full nutritional value of fresh food.

That pretty reddish ball wrapped in tissue paper is utterly unlike a vine-ripened tomato. Supermarkets have taught us to buy by appearance instead of flavor. How can you tell what a pea tastes like if you cannot open a pod and taste one?

Fresh herbs are almost never available commercially. Italian parsley, for instance, to name the simplest of all herbs to grow, is so much tastier than the curly kind and yet is rarely found in local supermarkets. Herbs demand very little attention. They can be grown in the tiniest garden, in pots or window boxes, and will bring a whole new scope to your summer and even to your year-round cooking. In the process of growing your own herbs, you may become addicted, like me, to drying them and using them as your year's supply until the next summer comes around and you can return to your yard or terrace.

With gardening comes the desire to experiment. You will suddenly find yourself trying to grow artichokes, gray shallots, fennel or raspberries. You will enjoy a whole new world of sensations. Tiny artichokes (in which the choke has not even developed) simply eaten raw, baby zucchini poached and dressed in a lemon vinaigrette, or even served raw with an anchovy dip, are simple pleasures that can be yours as a gardener.

If you are a serious cook, I sincerely believe that growing your own vegetables and herbs will eliminate many frustrating moments in the kitchen. In a way your kitchen will become the extension of your garden. You will be cooking with what is *there*, with what is ripe and fresh. Your menus will carry the conviction possible only with fresh foods simply prepared. Even if you do not have the space for a full-scale vegetable garden, some of the most productive things—such as tomatoes, pole beans, zucchini, lettuce and radishes, with a few herbs in pots—can be grown on a very small plot or even in combination with garden flowers. You can have a nice summer-long supply of onions, beets, carrots, radishes, lettuce and a few tomatoes and beans in a plot as small as 10 by 10 feet, though a larger patch, 15 by 25 feet, gave me the opportunity to grow a larger variety of vegetables and also allowed room for successive planting of vegetables that mature quickly.

Location

A well-planned plot will make gardening relatively easy.
Consulting with the local growers and farmers gave me a great deal of professional information, the most important concerning location. Unfortunately for many people there is not much choice as to where a garden can be placed, but one thing is absolutely essential—a great deal of sunshine.

Garden plan

In my first year as a gardener, I worked in a pleasant chaos and enjoyed it, but a plan does help, especially if one's work area is limited. If, at the beginning, your garden has been well laid out, it will be fairly

undemanding. A badly planned garden is extremely hard to maintain.

Where? What? When?

These are just a few of the questions you will have during the first year. It is impossible to give all the answers in a few sentences, but here are a few tips:

• If possible—if you are not too cramped for space—try not to crowd your plants. Leave about 2 feet between rows, except for corn and tomatoes, which need more room. Try to make paths about 2 feet wide in your garden. This will enable you to maintain it with a fair degree of ease.

• Change the arrangement of your garden each year; the same vegetables should not be planted in the same space two years in a row because this exhausts fertility.

• You need not invest in a great quantity of tools, but it does pay to have the best quality. A spade, a spading fork and a trowel will help you do efficient work.

• Beware of woodchucks and rabbits. They will like your plants as much as they like your neighbor's, so put a fence around your garden if you want to be the one to enjoy the year's crop. The fence must be dug 2 feet into the ground or these burrowing animals will get past it.

• I like to plant a few rows of cutting flowers such as marigolds and zinnias among my vegetables. This gives the garden a colorful look and is also practical. Some of the nicest table arrangements I have ever made included both vegetables and flowers.

- Be sure that watering facilities are adequate. Watering is the secret to success of most gardens. Proper watering will increase your yield of new crops by 50 to 100 percent.

- Before investing in seeds and plants or doing a lot of hard work, find out from local growers what crops will do well in your area. I found gardening disappointments quite devastating.

- Do not be overambitious the first few years. If you plant a large garden, you will simply not be able to take care of it properly; it is wise to start on a small scale. After a while even your best friends will not want your surplus zucchini and tomatoes.

- Make a list of your favorite vegetables, herbs and salad plants and try a few of each according to your climate conditions. Allow room between rows for successive planting of such greens as lettuce and fast-maturing vegetables like radishes.

- Remember, in making your plan of attack, that you may want to can and preserve, in which case you will have to provide room for extra plants.

- Keep tall plants, such as corn, tomatoes and pole beans, together at the north part of your garden. This exposure gives them needed sun.

- Be careful about starting from seed, especially if you are a weekend gardener. Some things take so long to grow that you may have to start the seeds in pots or flats in a sunny window. When you plant your seeds don't plant them too deeply. This is a mistake most beginning gardeners make and it is the reason a lot of plants never come up.

- In certain sections of the country you can plant some things in the fall, but in most areas the end of March is about the earliest safe time to start working your soil.

- The preparation of the soil is of great importance. Have it tested before starting to plant; it pays to find out beforehand what fertilizers are needed and possible lime requirements.

- Take good care of your garden. Keep it free of weeds and water it regularly. Be sure to wet the soil 6 to 8 inches deep by running a sprinkler at least six hours.

Mulching will help to keep the weeds down and also to retain moisture in the soil. I, however, have never found substitutes for patience and hard work.

Herbs

Most of the kitchen herbs mentioned in this book can be grown in any section of the United States. Growing herbs is one of the most rewarding aspects of summer gardening, since these plants will thrive in almost any soil and under any system of fertilizing and manuring. You can plant them in a small section of your garden, in borders, in pots, or in window boxes. A sunny window in the city can provide some of the major kitchen herbs, such as thyme, basil, summer savory, chives and rosemary. You can fit a few herbs into a rock garden. Some have a lovely blossom and will blend well with other small flowering plants.

Two to three plants of every herb but basil will be enough for the average cook. If you are addicted to basil, as I am, you must have a dozen plants. Some herbs such as dill and chervil do require special care. They need considerable moisture and cool weather.

Here is a selection of herbs which I consider essential and which the French label "les fines herbes."

The accent herbs:

Chervil
Chives
Dill
Mint
Parsley (both flat and curly)
Summer Savory
Sweet Basil
Sweet Marjoram
Thyme

Pungent herbs (to be used in moderation):

Rosemary
Sage
Tarragon
Winter Savory

The following herbs you may add to your garden, a few at a time, as you become familiar with their culture and culinary use:

Anise
Caraway
Celery
Coriander
Cumin
Fennel
Garlic
Lovage
Shallots

Drying your herbs

The seeds, leaves, flowering tops and sometimes the roots of various plants are used for seasoning purposes. The aroma and flavor are due primarily to an oil contained in small glands in the leaves and seeds. The flavor can be prolonged by picking and drying your herbs at the proper time, usually when they begin to flower. Hang them in bunches in a well-ventilated dark room. In order to retain color herbs must dry quickly. If the leaves are dusty and gritty, they must be washed in cold water and thoroughly drained before being hung up to dry. Herbs such as basil, rosemary and tarragon must be dried far from the light in order to retain their color. Others such as sage, thyme and summer savory, can be partially dried in the sun without any effect on their color, but these too should then be placed in a dark room. Once the herbs are dry, pack them separately in well-sealed plastic bags and then grind them as needed. I make several mixtures (such as chervil, thyme and tarragon, or basil, sweet savory and oregano) for use during the winter months.

In recent years I have noticed both year-round and weekend gardeners flocking to the nurseries in search of herb plants, and I often hear the question: "What should I use this herb for?" Herb gardens have become extremely fashionable, yet many people are really at a loss as to when, how, and in what quantity, to use a given herb. Actually the use of herbs in cooking is very much a question of personal taste. In Europe, where herbs have been used for hundreds of years, their use has become so much a matter of tradition that many an herb is restricted to a particular dish and few cooks will even dare to experiment and replace one herb with another. The Italians believe that basil must go with tomatoes and that rosemary does wonders for suckling pig, while the English cannot conceive of lamb without mint sauce. The use of herbs should be as personal a matter as choosing perfume is for a woman. Although it is an area as open to experimentation as any other in the culinary field, it is nevertheless interesting to learn from tradition. Here is a list of the most usual and most popular herbs with a few words concerning their traditional use.

Basil

Basil is gaining enormous popularity in this country and is an extremely easy herb to grow. It is worth cultivating for its fragrance alone. Basil is known for its affinity to tomatoes. In southern France, Italy and Greece it is used in large quantities. France has the famous Pistou, a basil paste that is beaten into a vegetable soup. The Italians have their famous Pesto Genovese, a garlicky basil sauce used to top spaghetti or boiled potatoes. I use a basil marinade for lamb and a strong basil and anchovy sauce for grilled fish. I consider basil the most important herb of my summer garden and nothing can replace it. Once you have grown your own basil plants you will find that there can be no summer without them.

Bay leaf

Bay leaves are important in European cooking. Though a bay-leaf tree needs little care, it does not survive the cold climate of the East Coast of the United States and we are therefore mostly limited to using bay leaves in their dry form. This is a shame as there are few herbs with the marvelous fragrance of a freshly picked bay leaf. Still, California bay leaves, packaged by Spice Island, are extremely good.
To get the most out of the taste of the bay leaf, it should be finely minced before adding it to a stock. The bay leaf is an important part of a bouquet garni. When heating milk for a Bechamel Sauce or when heating cream to be used for soups or sauces, the addition of a bay leaf enhances the flavor. Bay leaves are also essential in all marinades.

Celery leaves

The celery leaves, or tops, belong to the herb family. In Europe, celery is grown essentially for flavoring purposes. A few celery sprigs, leeks, carrots and parsnip are the basic ingredients for seasoning all stocks and most soups. Celery leaves are a fine addition to a Bouquet Garni for flavoring of ragouts and braised dishes. Garden-grown celery leaves should be used in moderation because their strong, pungent flavor can easily overpower a dish. When using the leaves of store-bought celery, you can be more adventurous since their taste is mild and quite bland in comparison with the garden-grown herb.

Chives

Chives are my very favorite herb and I love both their color and their flavor. The chive plant has a delightful lavender flower and looks very pretty in pots. It is an easy herb to grow and one with limitless possibilities. It has a delicate onion flavor and is the best of summer garnishes for eggs, crepes, vegetables, salads and light sauces, either hot or cold. It is a great herb and a must in one's herb garden.

Dill

Dill, which to my taste is one of the best and most delicate herbs, is almost totally ignored in France, Italy and Spain. It is used primarily in Scandinavia, Russia and Central Europe. Scandinavians use dill the way Americans use parsley. Dill is, of course, a must for pickling, and its delicate leaves really give a delightful finishing touch to an open-faced sandwich or a poached cold salmon. It is also delicious in many cold dishes and has a natural affinity for cucumbers and radishes, as well as for shrimp or salmon.

I find it very hard to grow and prefer the hothouse dill found in good vegetable markets. Dried dill can never be a substitute for fresh dill.

Fennel

Fennel leaves are widely used in both French and Italian country cooking. They are used in stuffings for chicken and suckling pig. Fennel stalks, when dry, are the bed on which bass or red mullet are grilled in the south of France. These stalks, now sold in some specialty shops, will do wonders for fish. Incidentally, a few dry fennel sprigs with a few sprigs of rosemary, thrown onto the fire while roasting or grilling, will give your food a fantastic perfume.

The fennel bulb, with its aniseed flavor, is quite special. I like it raw and finely sliced in a salad, and it is equally good braised like endives or celery hearts. Try a little finely minced raw fennel in mayonnaise as an accompaniment to grilled or poached salmon. A touch of fennel can do wonders for the good old tuna or chicken salad and minced fennel leaves are an excellent substitute for minced parsley in garnishing a winter dish.

Only in recent years has fennel gained popularity in the United States and it is good to see it in the winter markets when the fresh vegetable selection is limited.

Marjoram

Sweet marjoram is a lovely herb and easy to dry. It is used a great deal in Middle European cooking for flavoring roasts and especially the famous Hungarian Goulash. (See also Oregano.)

Mint

Mint is a totally ignored herb in France. It is popular in England, the Middle East, and to some extent in Spain and Italy where it is used in Roman cooking. Personally I find mint almost strictly a summer herb and use it to flavor cold soups or salads and as a marinade for broiled lamb. A touch of mint in freshly cooked green peas or beans is excellent. I have never understood why anyone would smother a delicious roast leg of lamb with mint sauce —yet, again, this is a very individual matter of taste.

Oregano (wild marjoram)

Oregano is often identified in the United States with pizza. I personally am not an oregano addict and prefer to use sweet marjoram, although it is quite different in taste and much more delicate. The oregano plant has a lovely flower and should be dried while it is in blossom.

Marjoram, on the other hand, with its tiny, slightly gray leaf, will withstand the first cold days of fall, which gives the cook the possibility of using this as a fresh herb almost into the winter season.

Used in moderation, oregano is excellent in tomato dishes, with roasts and for shellfish recipes. Buy dried oregano at Italian or Greek groceries, replacing it three or four times during the year. Theirs is much better than any other store-bought prepared variety. Oregano is a definitely Italian herb and therefore adds character to recipes from the southern part of Italy.

Parsley

Parsley is the saving grace of every cook's decorative skill. That goes for the curly kind. Use the flat Italian variety if taste is what you are looking for.

Parsley has great affinity not only for garlic but for every other possible herb. I simply cannot imagine what the world of food would be without parsley and in that I am sure I am not alone. There is not a country in Europe or the Middle East that does not use it and it is so simple to grow that not having parsley in your garden or on your windowsill would really be a shame.

Rosemary

Rosemary is lovely-looking as a plant, but as a culinary ingredient I find it very powerful and therefore try to use it in moderation. Italians are extremely fond of

rosemary, especially in the southern part of Italy where this herb is used with the famous baby roast lamb and with suckling pig. The Spanish also use rosemary lavishly. In southern France rosemary is used to flavor roast lamb and pork. A sprig of rosemary can be added to the roasting pan but should be discarded before finishing the sauce. I personally have never favored the use of rosemary in stuffing chicken, although it seems to be common in American cooking. But this is an individual choice and, if not overdone, the use of this herb can be quite interesting.

Sage

Sage is an extremely popular herb in England where it is used freely in stuffings. I find it a little overpowering and therefore use it sparingly. I think the Italian use of sage is more subtle and some dishes, such as sauteed veal or calves' liver, can be flavored successfully with a sprig of fresh sage. A sprig of fresh sage buried in a risotto adds an interesting flavor. It should always be discarded before serving. Sage is an extremely easy herb to grow and will survive the first frost.

Savory

Savory is very similar in taste and fragrance to thyme but somewhat more delicate. The French use it for seasoning terrines and in stuffing for goose and turkey. Finely minced fresh summer savory is an excellent addition to a vinaigrette.

Tarragon

Tarragon is almost entirely a French herb. When you buy a tarragon plant, make sure

that you get French tarragon. There seems
to be another variety but it has no flavor.
Tarragon is the base for the famous French
Sauce Bernaise and for Chicken in Tarragon. It is also a must in Oeufs en Gelee
(Cold Poached Eggs in Aspic). It is an herb
that must be used in moderation and is
really not everybody's cup of tea. . . . In
combination with other finely minced fresh
herbs, tarragon is excellent for flavoring
a fines herbes crepe batter or omelettes.
Tarragon butter is delicious on grilled steak
or grilled fish. A few finely minced tarragon leaves go very well in a cold potato
salad and of course it is a must in Iced
Tarragon Soup. It is not a difficult herb to
grow, but it requires a lot of sun.

Thyme

Thyme is very easy to grow in a garden as
well as in pots on a windowsill. There are
several kinds of thyme plants and they are
a lovely addition to a rock garden.
Although thyme is not much used in Italian
or Spanish cooking, it gives added flavor
to dishes from these countries and I always
use it.
In winter, when one must use dried thyme,
it should be tied in cheesecloth for
easy removal from a stew or marinade.
Thyme is a strong-flavored herb and lends
itself well to preparation of "gutsy"
country stews, to soups and to pates.
In French cooking a bouquet garni consists
of a sprig of fresh thyme, a sprig of parsley
and a bay leaf. It is used to flavor most
soups, stews and marinades. It is also
excellent for flavoring the milk with which
to make a Bechamel Sauce. I usually bury a
little bouquet in a risotto for added flavor.

from market to kitchen

There is a European expression that says a good and inventive cook should be able "to cook with water." Translated it means that a clever cook should be able to get the best out of a poor piece of meat and to work creatively with leftovers and simple ingredients.

The words "simple ingredients" should not, however, bring to mind frozen and canned foods. Simplicity in food preparation is largely based on season and locality. In the summer, if you happen to live near the ocean, a simple meal could mean a Risotto a la Provencale with shellfish and peppers, or a grilled bass with a highly flavored anchovy, basil and tomato sauce. In winter you may have to make do with a broccoli puree and a well-flavored ragout of beef.

The first step towards this kind of basic and direct approach is familiarity with what the local market has to offer and an understanding of each of nature's products. They do not always have to look like "still lifes" (I refer especially to fruit, which is only too often bought for display), but they must be fresh. Wilted and tired vegetables can sometimes be refreshed to some extent, but I simply do not see the point in buying them in the first place, for they will never really regain their original flavor.

I realize that in most parts of the United States prices of raw materials have gone up so astronomically that many a beginner will shy away from the greengrocer, taking refuge in a recipe that calls for a can of this or a package of something else. This is a great mistake. The way to handle this problem is not by substituting a canned mushroom for a fresh one in a given recipe, but by being open-minded about cooking

in general, able to simplify your menus and yet, at all times, keep to freshness. A plate of sauteed and buttered spinach with a few toasted pine nuts and raisins is an excellent appetizer and certainly not expensive in its season. Once you have mastered the art of creative marketing and are familiar with local produce in each season, you will become one of those cooks who achieve marvels "with water."

Artichokes

The globe or French artichoke is by far the most interesting of the winter and early spring vegetables. It is the large unopened flower bud of a plant belonging to the thistle family, grown only in California and often shipped across thousands of miles. These artichokes sometimes have brownish streaks on their outer leaves due to frost damage. They can still be very good, but you must examine them carefully when buying them. Separate the leaves a little to see if the inner part is still bright green and fresh-looking.

Contrary to what most people think, the size of an artichoke has nothing to do with its quality. As a matter of fact, the tiny artichokes widely available in California (but on the East Coast found only in Italian markets) have almost no choke at all and can be used for innumerable marvelous dishes such as omelettes and stews. In the globe artichoke the choke is large and "feathery" and it must be removed if the artichoke is to be stuffed. The artichoke bottom or heart is a delicacy and one of the best "morsels" in the vegetable world—always enjoyed and always adding a true touch of elegance.

When buying globe artichokes, allow one per person. Cut each stem off and remove one layer of the tough outer leaves. With a sharp knife cut the top off the artichokes and immediately rub the cut part with lemon juice. Cook the artichokes in salted water for 20 to 25 minutes or until a leaf pulls out easily. Drain upside down on paper towels. Serve them hot with an herb butter, anchovy butter or simply melted sweet butter. A hot vinaigrette is also excellent served with either a hot or a cold artichoke.

Artichokes can be stuffed in a number of ways and cold artichokes can be served with various cold sauces. They can also be stuffed with many of the hors d'oeuvre salads.

Asparagus

Fresh asparagus is the first sign of spring in the market. Its peak season is April through June, although it can be found in some markets as early as mid-February. When buying asparagus, look for tightly closed tips, and bright green stalks with very little white. Try to purchase them "loose" (not tied in bundles) in order to get stalks of uniform size. When they are of different sizes, cooking time varies a great deal. Overcooked asparagus is a sad sight, and it can easily be avoided by watching carefully.

In Europe asparagus is usually served as a separate course and if this is the way you are going to treat this delicious vegetable, figure on at least ¾ pound per person. Remove the white part of the stalk and peel the rest of the stalk with a vegetable peeler. Tie the asparagus into bundles, putting stalks of the same size together. Leave one stalk loose for testing during cooking. Place the asparagus in fast-boiling salted water and cook over high heat, uncovered, for 12 to 15 minutes. Drain and run the stalks under cold water. Serve either hot or cold. If you are going to serve only the tips, reserve the stalks for soups and purees.

Avocado

Europeans regard the avocado as an exotic fruit, but it is extremely popular in the United States as a "vegetable" and is used widely in salads. Unfortunately it is often used when not fully ripe. A "green" avocado is a far cry from the rich delicious fruit it can be. Although avocados are available throughout the year, it is almost impossible to purchase a ripe one at the greengrocer's. You must therefore plan in advance and let your avocado ripen at room temperature. This can take two to three days. Once an avocado is ripe, it should be used immediately. Ripening can be slowed by refrigeration. There are several varieties of avocados; all are green when underripe, but some turn maroon, brown or purplish black as they ripen.

When buying avocados, look for fruits that yield slightly to pressure at the stem ends. In some varieties ripeness is indicated by a dark and slightly soft stem end. Avoid avocados that have cracked surfaces or dark sunken spots in irregular patches.

Do not limit the avocado to the salad bowl. An avocado soup is a real delicacy and a few avocado cubes are a lovely addition to a risotto. Pureed avocado can be used successfully as a filling for crepes.

When peeling an avocado, sprinkle the flesh immediately with lemon juice to prevent it from turning brown.

Beets

Beets are available throughout the year, but are at their best in June and July. Still, I consider them an important winter vegetable and their color adds a touch of brightness to the Winter Kitchen.
Buy firm, round beets with deep red color. It is easy to determine their freshness by the crispness of their tops. Try to select small to medium-sized beets as the large ones tend to be woody and strong-flavored. One bunch will serve 2 to 3 people.
Beets are one of the simplest vegetables to prepare. Simply wash them thoroughly under cold running water and cook them, covered, over low heat in plenty of lightly salted water until tender. Small beets will take 45 minutes to 1 hour; large ones can take up to 2 hours to cook. When tender, drain them and hold them under cold running water. The skins slip right off and the beets are ready.
There are several ways to serve beets, both hot and cold. Beets a la Creme are a marvelous accompaniment to roasts or sauteed meats. The Beet Salad in Dill Sauce is an excellent hors d'oeuvre salad for spring and summer entertaining. A well-prepared borscht is one of the world's great soups, and a herring salad mixed with tiny sliced boiled potatoes and cooked beets is a delicious summer luncheon dish.

Beans

Fava beans: These beans are a favorite country vegetable in northern Spain and Italy. When well prepared, fava beans can be absolutely delicious. They are usually cooked with a piece of smoked bacon or tiny spareribs. They are unfortunately not widely available in the United States. Buy them the same way you buy lima beans and use as soon as possible after shelling.

Green beans (string beans, snap beans): Since the green bean is almost always available and is a relatively inexpensive vegetable throughout the year, it is often treated without the care it deserves. For those who have grown their own beans and know how marvelous a raw fresh green bean can taste, the thought of an over-matured, wilted and, to top it all, over-cooked bean is unbearable.
When buying green beans, select clean, crisp, bright green beans that snap easily when bent. They should be crunchy and not too big. The smaller they are the better. Buy 1 to 1½ pounds for 4 people.
In Europe, green beans are often served as an appetizer together with sauteed smoked ham, mushrooms or shallots. You can add sauteed chicken livers or a good sprinkling of fresh herbs, including fresh mint.
Beans should never be overcooked. Drop the cleaned beans, a few at a time, into fast-boiling salted water and cook them for 12 to 15 minutes or until they are barely tender. Run them immediately under cold water to stop further cooking. Serve them with melted sweet butter or according to the recipes given in each seasonal chapter.

Lima beans: To me lima beans are very bland and I rarely use them. They can, however, be prepared in the same way as the Fava Beans a la Catalane and can be served with roast pork. They are bought in the same way as fresh peas. Figure on 3 pounds for 4 people. The pods should be crisp and not too "bulging." They are best when used soon after being shelled.

Wax beans: These beans should be bought and prepared in the same way as string beans. The two can be mixed together and served cold as a salad dressed with a lemon vinaigrette. Alone, they are a less interesting vegetable than green string beans.

Broccoli

Broccoli is considered a "new" vegetable in the United States as it has gained popularity only in the last twenty years. It has, however, been around for centuries. It belongs to the cabbage family and is a close relative of the cauliflower. Broccoli is available throughout the year, but it is at its best in the winter months. This is a gift of nature at a time of year when we lack fresh green vegetables.
When buying broccoli, look for a firm compact cluster of small flower buds that are dark green or even green with a purple tint. The stems should not be too thick or tough. Avoid woody stems and open buds. Broccoli that is too mature will have an unpleasantly strong flavor. If not to be used immediately, put the broccoli in a plastic bag and refrigerate it. It will keep for 2 or 3 days.
Broccoli, well prepared, is an excellent vegetable and can be served either hot or cold. Cut a piece of the stem off, leaving the stalk about 4 to 5 inches long. Cut large stalks in half lengthwise and peel them with a vegetable peeler, removing all leaves. Wash the broccoli under cold running water and drop the pieces into fast-boiling salted water. Cook until tender (about 8 to 10 minutes). Drain the vegetable and run it immediately under cold water to stop further cooking.
Serve either hot in a lemon sauce or cold as in a broccoli salad. You can also make a delicious broccoli soup or a puree flavored with Creme Fraiche with plenty of sweet butter and pepper. Broccoli can also be served as an appetizer. A 2-pound bunch will serve 2 to 4 people.

Brussels sprouts

This is the "miniature" member of the cabbage family. Although sprouts are available for about ten months out of the year, their peak season is during the winter months. They are usually sold in 1-quart containers covered with cellophane, which is unfortunate, because it is hard to tell how fresh each sprout is. If possible peek into the container. The sprouts should have a bright green color and tight-fitting outer leaves, free of blemishes and brown spots. Avoid sprouts with yellowish outer leaves and leaves that are loose or wilted.
When preparing Brussels sprouts for cooking, trim the base of each sprout and discard any loose or wilted leaves. Wash the sprouts well under cold running water and drop them into fast-boiling salted water for 8 minutes. Drain the sprouts, place them in a buttered baking dish, cover them with buttered foil and finish their cooking in the oven (15 to 20 minutes).
If you want to boil Brussels sprouts until they are tender, it is advisable to discard the first poaching water. Brussels sprouts

are an excellent winter vegetable and have a marvelous affinity for fresh chestnuts and other vegetables, such as small white onions.

Cabbage

Cabbage is often ignored and its importance as a versatile and flavorful vegetable is not much appreciated in the United States. It is, however, one of the very best year-round vegetables. It lends itself to soups, to braising and stuffing, not to mention raw cabbage salads, which are excellent.

There are three varieties of cabbage to be found in local markets in the United States: the smooth-leaved green cabbage, the curly-leaved Savoy cabbage and the red cabbage. The summer green cabbage is rather small and the leaves are dark green; it ranges in size from 2 to 3 pounds. In winter the cabbage called "old" cabbage is larger, with whiter leaves and the heads weigh from 4 to 6 pounds. This cabbage comes out of storage and personally I prefer using the Savoy cabbage whenever possible; it is more delicate and flavorful. Whatever you do, do not overcook green cabbage. Like all green vegetables it is better when poached until just tender, run under cold water and then dressed in butter or a sauce.

Red cabbage, which is very popular in Austria and Hungary, is also excellent both raw as a salad and braised. It should be cooked with some acid, such as vinegar or lemon juice, in order to retain its red color. A roast duck served on a bed of braised red cabbage and chestnuts is one of the best winter dishes I know.

When buying any cabbage, look for firm heads that are heavy for their size. The outer leaves should be of a fresh green or purplish-red color. They are called "wrapper leaves" and are usually discarded. There should not be many loose outer leaves on a head of cabbage. Stored in the refrigerator in a plastic bag, most cabbage will keep for a week or more. Savoy cabbage does not keep well in storage and should be used as soon as possible.

Carrots

Carrots are sold either by the package or by the bunch with their greens attached. The bunch carrots are the ones to look for, although the packaged carrot is good for soups and stocks and as part of a bed of vegetables for roasting meats. In some parts of the country it is often impossible to get carrots by the bunch and you must rely on the packaged variety. Even these can be absolutely delicious when cooked in slightly sweetened water with the addition of a good lump of sweet butter. They should be peeled with a vegetable peeler and cut either into uniform rounds or 2-inch-long matchsticks, which enables you to remove some of the hard core. When buying carrots by the bunch, look for those that are well formed, smooth, well colored and firm. Store them in a plastic bag either with or without their tops. Very young tiny carrots, generally out of your own garden, do not have to be peeled and can be cooked whole. A young carrot, braised and served with minced fresh herbs and fresh cream, is one of those simple delicacies you will remember for years. One bunch of carrots, weighing 1 pound, will serve 3 to 4 people as a vegetable.

Cauliflower

Even though cauliflower is considered a winter vegetable, its peak season being September through January, it is now available almost year round. It is usually sold in a cellophane wrapping with most of the outer leaves already removed.

When buying cauliflower, look for white, compact and clean flower clusters. Avoid heads that have brown spots or any discoloring.

A cauliflower can be cooked whole or broken into flowerets. Cooked whole, it is a handsome vegetable. Garnish the platter with cooked green beans, carrots and peas and top all the vegetables with melted sweet butter, salt and freshly ground black pepper. Personally I prefer cooking a cauliflower broken into small flowerets. It shortens the cooking time and the vegetable cooks more evenly. The cooked cauliflower should be run under cold water to stop further cooking. Then it is ready for a sauce or to be pureed for a soup or a mold.

Cauliflower is a versatile vegetable, equally good hot or cold. Raw cauliflower is delicious simply dressed in a well-flavored vinaigrette as part of an hors d'oeuvres table.

Celery

Celery, the tops of which belong to the herb family, is a marvelous year-round vegetable. European celery is very stringy and never as tender as the American variety and is therefore rarely used other than for flavoring purposes. We are very fortunate, however, to have this vegetable all year and should try to be creative with it. Most celery is the "pascal" type which is characterized by large, hearty, thick branches. Celery hearts, sold in units of two per package, should be used for braising.

When buying celery, look for fresh crisp stalks; avoid celery that has brown spots and wilted leaves. Separate the branches to see if there has been insect injury. Even though celery is mostly served as a raw vegetable to be eaten when on a diet or as a flavoring for cold meat or fish salads, these should not be its only uses.

It is a marvelous vegetable to be eaten braised with bacon and small white onions, or as a puree. It also makes a superb cream soup. Celery is, of course, with the addition of carrots and leeks, a must in almost all soups and stocks.

When preparing celery for cooking, wash it thoroughly under cold running water to remove all the sand that tends to cling to the leaves. With a vegetable peeler remove some of the "strings" on the large stalks and trim the bottoms. Celery will keep in a sealed plastic bag in the bottom of the refrigerator for several weeks. As a cooked vegetable a large bunch, weighing 1½ pounds, will serve 4 people.

Celery root or celeriac (knob celery)

The celery root is a marvelous winter vegetable, unfortunately not as popular in the United States as it should be. Celery root is, however, gaining popularity in the large cities where it is easily available from October through April. It is a round, brownish root with rough skin and green tops. It is not the root of the stalk celery as some people think. Celery root is usually sold in bunches of 3 knobs, but can sometimes be bought by the piece. Choose firm knobs about the size of an apple. The celery root's claim to fame in the United States is in a salad called Celeri Rave a la Remoulade in which the vegetable is grated and dressed with very strong mustard mayonnaise. It is one of the most popular appetizers in both France and Switzerland. Celery root's use should not, however, be limited to this dish alone. It is equally good as an addition to a chicken salad and is delicious braised or pureed. When preparing celery root, peel the knobs and immediately drop them into acidulated water as they tend to discolor. Cut them into chunks if they are large and cook them in fast-boiling salted water until just tender. They will then be ready for a puree or soup. Some salad recipes call for the root to be blanched.

Corn

A native of America, corn is a superb vegetable when it is freshly picked, quickly cooked in salted boiling water and simply served with melted sweet butter. It is available practically every month of the year, but I personally consider it a summer vegetable, at its best from July to mid-September. There are several varieties of corn. One of the best is called "8 row" corn. It has, of course, only 8 rows to an ear and is a native of Pennsylvania.
Try to buy corn directly from the grower. If this is not possible, buy it from a good greengrocer who receives his supply fresh every day while in season. Corn should be kept cool and damp. When picking your own, refrigerate it immediately after picking it. When buying corn, look for fresh husks that have a good green color and that are free from decay where the silk ends. If possible, open the ears and select the ones with kernels that are plump but not overmatured or dark yellow. Avoid ears with yellowish wilted husks in which the kernels are very large.
During the very short corn season, I prefer to serve it simply cooked. It can be used for a souffle and a Corn and Curry Soup is delicious for summer menus. You can also add some cooked corn kernels to a cold ratatouille.

Cucumbers

Although cucumbers are considered a year-round vegetable, they are really at their best, and cheapest, in the summer. Still, I cannot imagine any time of the year without this refreshing vegetable.
When buying cucumbers, chose the ones that have a good green color and are firm over the entire length. They should be well shaped, approximately 2 inches in diameter. Good cucumbers do not have to be shiny and are sometimes of a greenish white color. Do not buy overgrown cucumbers that have shriveled ends, which is a sign of toughness and bitter flavor. Although cucumbers are mostly eaten raw, they make a marvelous hot vegetable dressed with either parsley or dill. Whether you prepare them for a raw salad or for a hot vegetable, they should be seeded, salted and left to drain in a colan-

der for at least 30 minutes, then dried with paper towels and prepared in any way you wish. Cucumber Boats are a lovely "setting" for a shrimp, crabmeat or chicken salad, served as a cold hors d'oeuvre.

Eggplant

Eggplant is a beautiful purple pear-shaped vegetable that originated in China and India. It is now very popular in the United States, where unfortunately it is not prepared very imaginatively. The versatility of eggplants is enormous. Aside from sauteeing them, you can stuff them, make souffles out of them, or add them to lamb and veal ragouts. Prepare eggplants to serve cold as in the famous French Ratatouille or grill them over hot charcoal and then mix the flesh with minced onions and a little homemade mayonnaise. You can use them as appetizers and main courses and as an accompaniment to almost every meat.

When buying eggplants, look for firm and shiny fruits. Do not trust eggplants wrapped in cellophane and do not buy them by size or weight. A large and heavy eggplant usually will have more seeds and the flesh will be mushy. Avoid eggplants that are soft or of poor color, or those that have dark spots. Also avoid storing eggplants for a great length of time. They are at their best when prepared within one or two days of purchase. For stuffing, select small to medium eggplants. These are hard to get except in markets catering to people of Mediterranean origin.

When preparing eggplants for frying, slice or cube them, sprinkle them with salt and let them stand in a colander over a bowl for 30 minutes to draw out their juice. Dry the pieces thoroughly with paper towels before frying. This will remove the bitter flavor of the vegetable as well as make it absorb less oil in frying.

Fennel

Fennel looks like celery but has a delicate leaf and an aniseed flavor. The leaves are regarded as an herb and are used for flavoring sauces and soups. The fennel bulb is gaining popularity in the United States and can now be purchased at good greengrocers' from October through March. You can grow fennel in your garden, though I confess that I have never been very successful with it.

When buying fennel, choose bulbs that are crisp and fresh. Remove the tops and any wilted or brown outer leaves.

The bulb is eaten raw, finely sliced in a salad, in combination with either lettuce or cucumbers. Braised, like celery or endives, fennel is a marvelous hot vegetable. If the bulbs are large cut them in half lengthwise. One small bulb will serve 1 person. (See also page 8.)

Garlic

It is very hard for me to be really objective about garlic, since I grew up in a country that thrives on it. I personally believe that garlic is one of the best culinary discoveries of all time, although I admit that too much of a good thing can be quite devastating. Garlic is used in large quantity in all the countries around the Mediterranean as well as the Middle East and Asia. It is almost totally ignored in northern Europe.

In the United States it is often replaced by garlic powder, which has no resemblance to the taste of fresh garlic and may be the reason so many people dislike it. When buying garlic, select large firm white heads, rather than the small grayish white ones. In a cool dry place garlic will keep for weeks. When you are ready to use it, either mince the peeled cloves with a sharp knife or slice them. If you put a garlic clove through a garlic press, you will get a much stronger taste as the press releases all the volatile oils. When sauteeing with garlic, let the clove become lightly browned, then discard it; burnt garlic will give any dish a bitter flavor. There are recipes which call for whole heads of garlic; in that case the cloves are blanched first, a process which renders them quite mild and inoffensive, but does not destroy their culinary magic.

Jerusalem artichokes

The Jerusalem artichoke is a winter vegetable, native to the United States. It is used in great quantity in Pennsylvania Dutch cooking and adds an interesting note to the Winter Kitchen. The Jerusalem artichoke looks a little like a cross between a knobby potato and a fresh ginger root. Prepare Jerusalem artichokes by scrubbing them, then dropping them into fast-boiling salted water. Cook them until tender, then drain and peel them. They can be prepared in the same way as Beets a la Creme or as a soup. They can also be combined with boiled potatoes and mashed into a delicious puree. (Substitute 1 cup of Jerusalem artichoke puree for the watercress in a vegetable cream soup.)

Kohlrabi

Kohlrabi is a delicate turnip-like vegetable that is available only in large-city markets. It is, however, gaining popularity and can be used in the same way as turnips. It is available throughout summer and fall, but has its peak season in June and July. When buying kohlrabies select small to medium bulbs with fresh green leaves and rind that can easily be pierced with a fingernail. Avoid very large bulbs that are, more often than not, woody and dry. Kohlrabies can be refrigerated for several days in a plastic bag.
To cook kohlrabies, peel the bulbs, drop them into fast-boiling salted water, and cook them for 15 to 20 minutes. They are done when they are easily pierced with a fork. Drained and sliced, they are ready to be either sauteed in sweet butter or pureed. You can also place kohlrabies in a baking dish and top them with a well-flavored Bechamel Sauce. They are an excellent accompaniment to roasts and calves' liver.

Leeks

Leeks, scallions and shallots are all part of the onion family and many people seem to be confused as to when to use which. The leek is the most elegant member of the family and lends itself to many preparations both hot and cold. It is still scarce in many parts of the United States, but is gaining popularity. Leeks are available throughout the year, although they are at their peak from October to June.
When buying leeks, look for bunches with bulbs of uniform size; they should be crisp with bright green tops and firm bulbs.

Avoid wilted, yellowing or otherwise discolored tops.

When preparing leeks, discard most of the green tops. The leeks must be washed thoroughly under cold running water and then soaked in a large bowl of cold water for 30 minutes, as sand may still be within the leaves. Leeks are used in almost all soups and stocks. A cream of leek soup, the Vichyssoise, is one of the most popular cold soups in the United States and is very easy to make. Leeks are a wonderful cold vegetable simply dressed with a well-flavored vinaigrette. To serve hot, they can be braised like endives or used to replace the onions in an onion tart.

Scallions: These are green onions and both the green part and the white part can be used. They often serve to replace shallots in areas where shallots are unavailable. When growing your own green onions, let the bulbs mature fully and use them instead of the small white onions mentioned in many recipes in this book. These are much more delicate than the white onions and will cook much faster.

Shallots: The shallot found in American markets is a cross between an onion and garlic with a more refined subtle taste than either. It is not the shallot used in France, but it is nevertheless a very important part of your kitchen staples.

Legumes (dried beans, peas, lentils)

Many cooks regard "legumes" as a kitchen staple together with flour, sugar, et cetera. The world of vegetables provides these hearty foods, and peasant menus rely heavily on dishes made with dried beans, peas or lentils because they keep through the long winter months and can be eaten as a substitute for fresh vegetables. Cooking with legumes is as much an art as cooking with fresh ingredients because they are bland and depend largely on your culinary skill to turn them into a memorable dish. Some of the great dishes of the world feature dried white beans. France has its Cassoulet, a marvelous casserole of various meats and white beans. The Italians have their Pasta con Fagioli, a delicious soup, as well as innumerable other dishes that make imaginative use of the dried white bean. Holland has its famous pea soup. Lentils are a favorite in Austrian country cooking and New England has combined white beans with brown sugar and molasses and come up with a great dish, Boston Baked Beans.

When buying legumes, look for the best quality. Greek or Turkish white beans are excellent, but Great Northern beans are very good too. Personally, I do not believe in the quick-cooking kind, which are processed and need no soaking. These beans are much less flavorful than dried white beans, lentils or peas, which must be soaked in cold water anywhere from 4 to 12 hours, then drained and cooked in plenty of water with a bouquet garni, often with a piece of smoked bacon or a ham bone. Lentils and white beans can be made into delightful salads to be served at luncheon or as an accompaniment to grilled or roasted dinner meats.

Mushrooms

In Europe, some people are mushroom connoisseurs and mushroom picking is one of fall's most enjoyable pastimes. Two or three kinds of wild mushrooms are found during the fall in the local markets of Spain, France, Italy and Central Europe. In the United States only the cultivated mushroom is commercially available. This is the least interesting. However, when well prepared, it can be delicious and an important part of your repertory.

Mushrooms are good simply dressed with a vinaigrette or as an addition to various greens. They can be sauteed in sweet butter either as part of a dish or by themselves with the addition of herbs or cream. They can also be poached and used to decorate a whole fish or a roast.

When buying fresh mushrooms, look for small plump ones with caps closed around the stems or only moderately opened. The caps should be creamy white (in some areas there is a brown mushroom in which the cap is a light brown color). Avoid overripe mushrooms with wide-open and very dark discolored gills.

Do not peel mushrooms and do not soak them in water; just wipe them with a damp paper towel. As a rule, remove the stems and reserve them for soup or stock. But if the mushrooms are very fresh and the stems are white, they can be sauteed together with the caps. Cook mushrooms over high heat and do not crowd your pan. The mushrooms should saute not steam. Raw mushrooms are excellent as an addition to a green salad or marinated in oil and lemon juice and served as an appetizer.

Onions

The onion is one of the kitchen staples. There is simply no cooking without it. It adds flavor to everything from a plain broiled hamburger to a delicate ragout of veal. In some shape or form it is in almost every dish except desserts.

There are several onion varieties. Some have a strong flavor; others are quite mild. Onions are available throughout the year and can be stored in a cool dry place for several weeks.

Bermuda onion: This is a rather large, slightly flat onion. It has a mild delicate flavor and lends itself well to sauteeing and deep frying.

Globe onion: This is the most common onion and is considered primarily a cooking onion. It has a strong flavor and for best results should be used as soon as possible after being minced or chopped as its strong aroma has a tendency to permeate the entire kitchen.

Green onions: Both green onions (scallions) and shallots belong to the onion family and are discussed under Leeks (page 21).

Italian onion: This is really the prettiest of all onions and brings to mind a country kitchen with large bunches of these reddish-purple onions hanging from the ceiling. Even if you do not have a country kitchen, you can make good use of this mild delicious onion. Because of its sweet flavor the Italian onion is perfect for salads and marinades.

Spanish onion: This is a large, mild onion that can be used for baking (in the same way you would bake a potato) or for roasting on an open fire.

White onion: This familiar onion should be no larger than a large pea, but, unfortunately, it is often too large. I use these onions a great deal for flavoring meats and in combination with other vegetables. When buying them, reach into the bottom of the bin; the smallest onions usually will have settled under the larger ones. If you cannot get them very small, peel off several layers of each onion and drop them into cold water while preparing the rest. These onions are excellent for pickling and can also be served by themselves as a vegetable.

Parsnips

Parsnips are available throughout the year, but are at their best in the late winter months. They are usually sold in packages and can be refrigerated for several weeks in plastic bags. When buying packaged parsnips, open the package as soon as possible and remove any parsnips that have serious blemishes or decayed areas. These can be cut out and the whole parsnips need not be discarded. Avoid flabby and wilted-looking parsnips and those that have very large coarse roots because these will probably have "woody" centers.

Parsnips are a delicious vegetable that can be prepared in most of the ways suitable for turnips. Pureed parsnips mixed with a puree of potatoes are an excellent accompaniment to a roast. Parsnips are a "must" in most stocks and many soups to which they add great flavor.

In some parts of New England, where parsnips are used a great deal in cooking, gardeners leave them in the ground until spring. After the ground thaws, they dig up the parsnips which, cleaned, scraped and simply cooked, are extremely sweet and delicious.

Peas

For those who have at any time grown their own peas and have had the pleasure of eating them freshly cooked and buttered, the store-bought vegetable will never offer the same enjoyment. Yet even store-bought peas can be absolutely delicious and frozen or canned peas cannot be compared to them in any way. A canned or frozen pea is simply another vegetable!

Peas are available in some markets as early as the middle of January, but their peak season is from March through June. This is the time to serve them either as an appetizer as in Peas a la Venetienne or for a main course as in Duck with Fresh Peas. Shelling peas, which so many cooks shy away from, is actually a relaxing little chore that can be done even in your living room while chatting with guests. Cook the shelled peas as soon as possible in very little water with a pinch of sugar and salt. Very young and fresh peas can be cooked in sweet butter only.

When buying peas look for small shiny pods; break one open to see if the peas inside are tiny and young. Taste one to see if it is sweet. Avoid peas that are shriveled-looking or very large—indications that they are old or mature. Mature peas will always be somewhat tough and mealy.

Peppers

To appreciate the beauty of peppers one should have a chance to stroll through an

Italian or Spanish market and see the dazzling display of vegetables with piles of brilliant green, yellow and red peppers. These are not used for decorative arrangements, but for stuffing, flavoring of sauces and as a cold or hot vegetable.

The fully matured green pepper turns into a bright red pepper that is even sweeter than the green. It is unfortunately not available throughout the year and is quite perishable. It is, however, a fine vegetable and should be taken advantage of in the fall. Use it raw in salads; roast it for a pepper salad; saute it with bits of bacon as a hot vegetable; dress up an omelette with it or add it to a shellfish risotto. Its color and flavor will bring new life to many dishes.

The Italian pepper is a light green, long-shaped mild-tasting pepper that is excellent for flavoring and for salads. It does not adapt well to stuffing. Yellow peppers are not available in the United States. Select peppers which are thick-fleshed, medium to dark green and glossy. Avoid those that have punctured skins or those that are wilted or flabby. Peppers will keep for a week to two in a cool, moist place such as the bottom of the refrigerator.

Potatoes

Potatoes, like onions, are so much part of our everyday cooking that we take them for granted. They are mostly prepared without much imagination—usually either boiled, deep-fried or sauteed. For many people they are simply there to provide the meal with a "starch." This is a pity because potatoes can be made into exciting dishes and should hold their own at the dinner table. There are a great many varieties of potatoes, but they usually fall into three categories: the baking potato, the all-purpose potato and the new potato. Both the all-purpose and the baking potato are available throughout the year. New potatoes are available in late winter, early spring and throughout the summer.

Baking potato: The most famous baking potato is the Idaho. Its fame is largely due to its size. Other baking potatoes, such as the Russet and Burbank, are equally good.

All-purpose potatoes: As the name indicates, this potato can be used for general cooking purposes. It is small, rounder and also less expensive than the baking potato; it is good for boiling, sauteeing, deep-frying, mashing and for such classic potato dishes as the Gratin Dauphinois and Potatoes Anna. A good all-purpose potato lends itself to baking as well as the baking potato and I personally prefer it.

New potatoes: These potatoes come in two varieties—the red-skinned and the brown-skinned. A few tiny new potatoes, cooked in their skins and served with a lot of sweet butter and minced parsley are a simple delicacy. These potatoes, however, are not always small. They can range from a tiny ball to the size of the average all-purpose potatoes. In the summertime you can find small new potatoes at vegetable stands throughout the countryside. These may not look as attractive as the store-bought varieties, but they are absolutely delicious.

Radishes

I have never understood why some people go to all the trouble of making a radish look like a flower, when Nature has provided both color and taste in this lovely-looking vegetable that needs no improvement. A few fresh radishes, with their green tops still attached, are a delicious addition to a salad. A bowl of crisp red radishes, accompanied by a few good cheeses, French bread and sweet butter, are a marvelous spring or summer lunch. It is a pity that so many cooks limit the radish to decorative purposes. It is a vegetable that can stand on its own as a salad and is also good grated into cream cheese with some chives for breakfast.

Radishes are available throughout the year, but their peak season is from May to July. There are three varieties: the small round red radish; the white radish; and the large black radish. The black radish is not available in many parts of the United States and is only to be found in good markets. It has a sharp flavor and is at its best when grated into a Middle Eastern Salad. If you are growing your own radishes, try the long red radish that has a white tip: the French breakfast radish; this is a very popular radish in Spain, Italy and France and is delicious.

Rhubarb

Rhubarb is actually a vegetable, though it is eaten as a fruit. It is often used in compotes, in fruit sauces and for filling pies and tarts. It is available in limited supply during the winter months (in some areas through June).

When buying rhubarb, look for firm stems that have a bright glossy appearance and a large amount of pink or red color. Be sure the stems are tender and not fibrous. Avoid those that are very large and thick; they will often be tough and stringy.

Salad greens

A very important touch to a good meal is the salad. I have often wondered why many cooks take pains in preparing a delicious meal and then smother their greens with bottled dressing. Salad dressings do not have to be complicated and a green salad does not have to have various vegetables added to it. Fresh greens and a simple dressing, used in moderation and mixed into the greens only at the moment of serving, are all a salad needs to make it successful.

The first step towards a delicious salad is knowing how to select your greens and their compatibility with other vegetables. When buying greens, make sure they are fresh and crisp; avoid packaged lettuce or heads that look wilted. Wash the greens carefully under cold running water and discard any wilted or discolored leaves. Drain the greens in a colander or a wire lettuce basket. If you are not going to use them for two or three days, they will keep well in a plastic bag, which you should puncture in three or four places and refrigerate. If they are to be used within a short time, place them in a clean, dry kitchen towel and refrigerate until serving. Or you may prepare your dressing and place it in the bottom of the salad bowl; then top it with the greens gently, not mixing the two, and place the bowl in the refrigerator. At serving time mix the salad with the dressing at the table.

Belgian endive: The endive, which is considered a delicacy in the United States, is to the salad world what the raspberry is to the fruit world. It is delicious both as a raw salad ingredient and as a versatile hot vegetable. Braised Endive a la Provencale is one of my favorite winter appetizers. The Belgian endive is a compact, almost cigar-shaped vegetable; its color is creamy white and the leaves have pale yellow tips. Wrapped in tissue paper, it comes in boxes and is available only in city markets along the East Coast. Its peak season is October through May.

When buying endive, look for very firm well-bleached stalks 4 to 6 inches long. Avoid washing them. Simply wipe them with damp paper towels and remove two or three of the outer leaves. Or, if you must wash them, do it quickly under cold running water and dry them immediately in a clean towel. If endives are soaked in water, they get excessively bitter.

Raw, they combine well with all other lettuce varieties as well as with raw mushrooms and especially with beets.

When cooking endives, bring water to a boil in a large casserole and add a piece of day-old French bread to absorb the bitter flavor. Cook the endives until almost tender (8 to 10 minutes), then drain them. Saute them in browned sweet butter, salt and pepper and add a sprinkling of fresh herbs or parsley.

Bibb lettuce: Considered the king of lettuce, Bibb is certainly the most expensive green in the lettuce family. It resembles the heart of the Boston lettuce but its leaves are crisper and its flavor slightly more pungent. A most attractive lettuce, Bibb is unfortunately not always available commercially. For the sake of connoisseurs I hope the situation improves.

Boston lettuce: This is a marvelous and delicate lettuce that lends itself well to salads and serves as a bed for hors d'oeuvre salads. Use it instead of iceberg lettuce whenever possible. The heart of Boston lettuce can be cooked and served as a hot vegetable.

Chicory or **curly endives:** This lettuce resembles the escarole. The leaves have the same coloring but are slightly curlier. It has a sharp and slightly bitter taste and should be used with other greens.

Escarole: Escarole is a large fan-shaped lettuce. Its long, slender, curly leaves are yellow at the center, turning into a deep green at the edges. It is an interesting lettuce with a tangy, slightly bitter taste. It combines well with other greens or with endives.

Field lettuce (Lamb's Tongue): The field lettuce is a lovely fall green that comes in small bunches and has a tongue-shaped leaf. It does not ship successfully and therefore is not widely available. It combines well with such greens as the curly endive and romaine and gives an extremely interesting touch to a salad.

Iceberg lettuce: This is by far the dreariest and most tasteless lettuce in the salad-green family. It is the answer to the greengrocer's dream as it is much less perishable than other lettuce and can be handled without much care. This, however, is all that can be said in its favor. It is flavorless and watery and should be used only when there is no other choice.

Leaf lettuce: The leaf lettuce is a summer lettuce, not widely available because it does not ship well. You can easily grow it yourself and it is sold at roadside stands around the countryside throughout the summer. It comes in separate leaves tied into bunches and has a most delicate flavor. Leaf lettuce cannot be refrigerated for any length of time and should be washed at the very last minute. It must be very carefully dried with paper towels and should not be combined with dressing until serving time.

Romaine: This is a "Mediterranean lettuce" which is used a great deal in France, Italy and Spain. It is long and slender with deep green outer leaves. It is available throughout the year and is very tasty with a slight sharpness. Romaine must be washed carefully. The outer leaves are often coarse and should be discarded; the heart of the romaine is tender and has a lovely pale green color.

Sorrel: Sorrel is a green that must be put in a class by itself. It is by far the most interesting green of all. It has a slight lemon flavor with a refreshing sharpness that makes it one of the best spring and summer vegetables. It is really a wild grass that grows well in a sandy soil, often not far from beaches. It is, however, easily grown in any other soil and is an important plant in my garden. Sorrel is available commercially in good markets during the spring and summer months. It lends itself to soups and purees and has a special affinity for eggs. Try this marvelous vegetable and include it in your next garden plan.

Spinach: This is really not a salad green, but in recent years raw spinach salads have become extremely popular and the vegetable deserves its newfound fame. There are several greens that can be used in similar ways. These are kale, beet tops, mustard greens, Swiss chard and turnip tops. In farm areas there are several types of greens that grow wild and that are very interesting. Have a local farmer introduce you to these wild varieties and try them either raw or cooked.

Watercress: Watercress is a small round-leafed plant that grows naturally along banks of freshwater streams and ponds. It can also be cultivated easily. It is often used in decorating platters (a welcome change from the ever-present curly parsley), but it should not be limited to this use. It is a superb green, excellent in salads as well as in soups. When buying watercress, look for very crisp rich-green bunches. Watercress cannot be refrigerated. It should be used immediately.

Salsify

Salsify is an early-fall root vegetable that is unfortunately not available throughout the United States. This is a pity as salsify, when prepared with care, has a great deal of character. It looks a little like the parsnip, but the skin is darker. It is often called oyster plant due to its faint oyster taste. When buying salsify, select plump, firm, small to medium-sized roots that are free from blemishes and soft spots. You can refrigerate them for several days. To cook salsify, peel each root with a vegetable peeler and immediately drop it into a bowl of cold water to prevent it from turning brown. Drop the peeled salsify into salted boiling water to blanch for 10 to 15 minutes. Drain and saute in sweet butter and herbs or glaze in sweet butter, sugar and a little brown stock.

Spinach

I must confess that I belong to the category of people who, as a child, disliked spinach. I do not remember at what point in my life I discovered this marvelous vegetable, but today I cannot conceive of omitting spinach from my cooking repertory. Aside from being a beautiful vegetable (when it is not cooked to death) it can be used for innumerable dishes: as a bed for fish, poached eggs or meats; in tarts, molds, souffles. It can be served as an appetizer, be turned into a main course or appear as an accompaniment to meats, fish and eggs. What other vegetable can cope with such culinary responsibility? Spinach is considered a winter vegetable, but in many parts of the United States it is available throughout the year. You can buy spinach already cleaned in cellophane bags, or by the pound. I prefer buying it by the pound to be sure that it is really fresh. Look for young, tender leaves with dark green color, free from blemishes. Wash spinach thoroughly under cold running water after removing the tough stems. Soak the leaves in a large bowl of cold water for 1 or 2 minutes, then drain and repeat until the bottom of the bowl is free of grit. Do not let the leaves stand in water for any length of time. Drain the washed spinach in a colander. You can refrigerate spinach in a plastic bag for 2 or 3 days, but it is at its best when used as soon as possible after purchasing.
Very young spinach can be cooked in a little sweet butter with only the water that clings to the leaves. It is, however, advisable to blanch older spinach first by dropping it into fast-boiling salted water for 5 minutes, then draining it well. This can be done up to a day in advance, and the spinach will then be ready to be pureed, sauteed or chopped. Raw spinach, topped with a well-flavored vinaigrette and a few raw sliced mushrooms, makes a delicious salad.

Squash

There are several varieties of squash. Some are winter vegetables such as the acorn, butternut, buttercup and Hubbard. Summer varieties include the round, white, scalloped, the yellow crookneck and the zucchini, which I personally consider the best in the family.

Acorn squash: Of the winter varieties, this is the most interesting one. It is small and round with a dark green and orange skin. It is usually baked with butter and brown sugar. It can also be pureed and buttered (it must be baked first) and is a good accompaniment to roasts or grilled meats.

Scallop or **pattypan squash:** This is a disk-shaped vegetable with a scalloped edge. It is pale green when not completely mature, changing to white later. It can be sauteed, but is not a very interesting vegetable.

Summer squash: This squash has a lovely yellow color and is available from May throughout the summer. It can be used for sauteeing, in soups and mixed with other vegetables such as tomatoes and eggplant.

It does not have as fine a flavor as the zucchini and I therefore seldom use it.

Zucchini or **Italian marrow squash:** This lovely summer vegetable is at its best when picked about 6 inches long. The finest are the size of fat cigars and they can be eaten either raw or cooked. Zucchini adapts well to a variety of preparations and has great affinity for other vegetables such as eggplant, tomatoes and onions. It is combined with these in the famous French Ratatouille. The Italians are famous for their use of zucchini. It is often served poached, chilled and topped with a lemon dressing, or stuffed and baked. When buying zucchinis, look for crisp, small marrows (4 to 6 inches long). They should have dark green glossy skin and the flesh should be creamy white.

Tomatoes

The tomato is one of the great gifts the New World has given the kitchen. This beautiful vegetable was introduced in Europe at the end of the fifteenth century and was first used as a decorative plant, in both Italy and Spain. Today the cuisines of these countries are largely based on the tomato. It is equally popular in the United States and has become an almost year-round vegetable. Personally, I cannot bring myself to use the hothouse tomatoes that are available during the winter months—unless a certain dish is desired that requires tomatoes. They have a pinkish color and a mealy, tasteless flesh. It is best to use other vegetables during the winter and then, in summer, take full advantage of the ''home-grown'' tomato that has ripened on the vine and is juicy and delicious. You can grow tomatoes in a very small patch and have the pleasure of picking a vine-ripened one for a salad whenever you desire. Aside from being delicious as a raw vegetable, the tomato is used in sauces, soups, ragouts, salads and hors d'oeuvres. There are basically four kinds of tomatoes: the garden tomato, the beefsteak tomato, the Italian plum tomato and the cherry tomato. The beefsteak tomato is usually large with slightly mealy flesh. It lends itself well to salads and broiling. The cherry tomato can be sauteed and used as a garniture for a hot dish but is mostly served as an hors d'oeuvre. It can also be stuffed (raw) and served cold. The Italian plum tomato is excellent for eating and for sauces. The garden tomato is the most versatile of them all; it is also, in my opinion, the most attractive. There are four major varieties: the Patio, Ramapo, Homestead No. 24 and the Early Wonder. All are of medium size, bright red in color and have a delicious flavor. The Early Wonder, as its name indicates, is an early-maturing variety that I always include in my garden. When buying tomatoes, look for an overall rich color and a slight softness. The tomato should be well formed and free of bruises and blemishes. If you have to buy underripe tomatoes, look for firm texture and color ranging from pink to light red. Keep these tomatoes in a warm place, preferably dark, and do not refrigerate. Ripe tomatoes can be refrigerated for several days. In order to really enjoy the taste of a good tomato, it should be at room temperature or only slightly chilled. To peel tomatoes, lower them gently into boiling water, take them out after 1 minute and remove the skin with a sharp knife. To seed a tomato, cut it in half crosswise after peeling it and squeeze each half gently to extract the seeds. Sprinkle the tomato halves with salt and place them upside down in a colander; the salt will draw out much of their juice and the tomato will then be ready for cooking.

Turnips

The turnip is a delicious vegetable but one that requires careful preparation to bring out its flavor. It has great affinity for carrots, small white onions and potatoes and can be used in combination with these vegetables or by itself as an accompaniment to roasts, grilled meats and game. The most popular turnip has white flesh and a purple top; it is available off and on throughout the year. When buying turnips, look for small to medium-sized, smooth, firm vegetables. They are often sold in bunches, and the tops should be fresh with a good green color.

Rutabagas: This is a yellow turnip, much larger in size than the white turnip and not as delicate in flavor. Personally I do not find it a very interesting vegetable. When cooking these turnips, drop the peeled and cubed or sliced vegetable into fast-boiling water to blanch for 5 minutes. Drain them and they will be ready to saute in butter or to add to soups or stews.

Fruit

The art of buying fruit is very much like the art of buying vegetables. It is just as challenging, often disappointing and sometimes frustrating. Your eye tends to steer you in the direction of the perfect-looking peach, yet after a few months of careful shopping you realize that beauty will not necessarily guarantee the taste you are looking for. A small unpretentious-looking strawberry or blueberry is often much more flavorful than the large somewhat watery berry many a greengrocer will sell you with pride and conviction.

Because fruit spoils so easily during shipping and is hard to handle without bruising, many fruits are picked "green." Such fruits are still hard to the touch when they reach local markets.

A bowl of tree-ripened peaches, apricots or pears is a simple delicacy that needs no adornment, but most of us are unable to enjoy this gift of Nature for a large part of the year. With careful selection, however, a creative cook can bring out the best of any fruit and turn it into a delicious and often memorable dessert. When planning to serve a bowl of fruit with cheese for dessert, select the fruit carefully. You do not need a great variety. Do not buy according to color, but in keeping with the rest of the meal. A slice of perfectly ripe melon with a wedge of lemon can often be the right closing for your menu.

If you must buy fruit that is underripe, keep it at room temperature, out of the sun, until it reaches the right stage of ripeness. Ripe fruit should be used as soon as possible. Avoid, if you can, buying packaged fruit, but if you have no other choice, open the package at once and discard any damaged pieces. Remember, no fruit benefits by ripening in the bottom of your refrigerator. If you must refrigerate fruit for several days, keep it in an open fruit bowl where the air can circulate freely around it. Fruit compotes can be made with under-ripe fruit such as plums, pears, peaches or cherries. These can be poached in either a vanilla syrup or wine. Compotes can also be made by combining several fruits. These should not be an overcooked mush but a light and delicately flavored dessert that can grace even the most elegant dinner.

Apples

Though apples are a year-round fruit, they are at their best and most plentiful in the fall. There are a great many varieties of apples sold all over the United States. They differ in both appearance and taste. Some are suitable only for eating; others can be used for both baking and eating.
The most famous apples are the Delicious apples, both the red and golden. Admittedly a beautiful addition to the fruit bowl, they can also be used in fruit salads. Personally, I find them too sweet and lacking in character. I prefer the McIntosh and the Winesap, which have a slightly tart flavor and are good for both eating and cooking. Roman Beauties, usually sold for baking, are good apples, but often too mealy and too large. The "greening" (which, as its name indicates, is an apple that is green-skinned when ripe) is very good for compotes and other apple desserts.
When buying apples, look for firm, well-colored ones. Apples should be mature in order to be flavorful, but avoid those that are overripe and with mealy flesh and soft spots. Also avoid apples affected by freeze —easily detectable by brown and bruised areas.

Apricots

Because the apricot season is very short we should make frequent use of this delicious fruit while it is plentiful. The apricot, available in June and July, is at its best when tree-ripened. We are therefore faced with a hard, uninteresting fruit most of the time.
The apricot lends itself to a delicious mousse and a fresh apricot tart is a delightful dessert. Ripe apricots should be served fresh, possibly peeled, with the addition of sugared Creme Fraiche. Underripe fruit can be used in compotes.
When buying apricots, try to find plump, juicy-looking ones with a uniform golden-orange color. The ripe fruit will be slightly soft when tested with the fingers. Avoid both overripe fruit that looks mushy and has brown spots and the firm pale yellow or greenish apricots.

Bananas

The banana is now a year-round fruit practically all over the world, due to the fact that bananas can be harvested green and actually develop their best eating quality after being picked. This allows them to be shipped great distances. The banana, however, is sensitive to cool temperatures and should never be refrigerated. Let underripe bananas ripen at room temperature. A ripe one should have yellow skin flecked with brown. When buying bananas, avoid bruised fruit with soft dark tips and discolored skin.
Bananas are a marvelous addition to a fruit salad, and they combine well with apples and oranges. They can be served hot, either baked or sauteed in sweet but-

ter and sugar. They can also be made into delicious fritters. Once a banana has been peeled, sprinkle it with lemon juice as the flesh turns brown when exposed to the air. Do not serve bananas as part of your fruit bowl unless they have really reached the right stage of ripeness, which is the only way to appreciate this delicious fruit.

Berries

Blueberries: This is an extremely popular fruit in most parts of the United States. In Europe, where the blueberry is not available in abundance, it is a very small berry with an absolutely delicious taste. It seems to me that the larger the blueberries are the less taste they have, and I have often spent an entire summer without using them at all. You may, however, serve this fruit in an imaginative way by combining it with a cold lemon mousse or by including it in a strawberry and banana fruit salad. It is also delicious as a breakfast fruit with a bowl of sugared Creme Fraiche. When buying blueberries, look for a silvery bloom, which is a natural protective waxy coating. The fruit should be plump, firm and uniform in size. Small berries can be as good as large ones. Wild blueberries vary a great deal in size, but are more flavorful than the cultivated ones.

Boysenberries: These berries are becoming increasingly popular, although they are not available in all parts of the United States. They make a delicious compote and can also be eaten fresh, simply sugared or with Strawberry Sauce.

Gooseberries: Though less popular than they were years ago, gooseberries make

a delicious compote and I personally like their color and slightly tart flavor.

Raspberries: This is an elegant member of the berry family and many people consider it the most elegant of all. Raspberries have a beautiful color and a very unique flavor. They can be served plain with a bowl of sugar and sweetened whipped cream on the side, but you can also be more adventurous and creative and make a raspberry souffle or a raspberry mousse. Buy raspberries only when they are very ripe, which means buy them only in season. They are at their peak in May and June and then have a very short fall season from mid-September to mid-October. They are usually sold in cartons by the pint. It is good to sneak a look at the bottom of the carton to see if it contains some berries that are green or moldy. Unwrap the carton as soon as possible and discard any raspberries that have any mold, since it spreads rapidly. Raspberries should not be washed.

Strawberries: Even though strawberries are available in many parts of the country practically all year round, to me they are synonymous with spring and they are an exquisite introduction to summer. Strawberries do not have to be large to be tasty. The strawberries usually available in the eastern United States during May and June are really the juiciest and tastiest; more so than the California strawberry that looks as if it belonged in a painting. You simply cannot go wrong with good ripe strawberries. They are delicious any way you serve them: sugared, accompanied by sweetened Creme Fraiche or whipped cream, marinated in fruit liqueur or orange juice, rolled into crepes, pureed or folded into a mousse, and on and on.

When buying strawberries, be a little sneaky and peek under the berries on top of the box. You may find the bottom berries green or sometimes moldy. Look for berries with a full red color and firm flesh with the cap stem still attached. Avoid large strawberries that have extensive uncolored areas and those with soft spots. Open the carton as soon as possible and immediately discard any berries with mold, which spreads rapidly from one berry to another. Strawberries should be washed under cold running water before being hulled. Never let them soak in water as this renders them soft and soggy.

All the above berries are sold in 1-pint cartons or sometimes by the quart.

Cherries

Cherries bridge the seasons. They are available from May to August and should be taken full advantage of, since they are delicious either fresh or cooked. There are several varieties, the most popular being the Bing, the Lambert and the Royal Anne. The tart red cherry that is lighter in color and somewhat softer is used for pies or cooked desserts. I prefer using the Bing or Lambert cherry for cooking.

When buying cherries, look for a dark, firm cherry with bright glossy surfaces and fresh-looking stems. Unfortunately it is easy to overlook decayed areas in cherries, especially since most greengrocers will not let you pick out your own. Avoid, however, overmature cherries that are shriveled-looking with dried stems and look them over carefully before storing them. Wash cherries only minutes before serving

them and never let them soak in water. Serve them chilled but not ice cold because that kills most of their flavor. Better still —do not wash them at all, but serve them in a large bowl with ice water on the side and let each person dip his own cherries into the water; this way the cherries will be refreshed but will not get waterlogged.

Figs

A bowl of fresh figs served with finely sliced prosciutto is a common appetizer in Italy during the summer months. In the United States they are a luxury, since they are always expensive in most areas outside Florida and California and many people have never even had the pleasure of tasting a fresh one. This is really a pity since this exquisite fruit can be served as a dessert either plain or with cheese. A puree of fresh strawberries sugared and combined with whipped cream can be served with slightly chilled figs.

There are two types of figs. One is purple-skinned, the other white-skinned. Both should be purchased fully ripe, but firm and not mushy. Most people prefer the figs peeled; in that case you do not even have to wash them. If you are going to serve them unpeeled, allowing each person to peel his own, wipe them with a damp paper towel gently so as not to bruise them. Serve figs at room temperature or only slightly chilled.

Grapefruit

The grapefruit has become a year-round fruit, but it is at its best and least expensive from January through May. There are several varieties available, but the main distinction is one of color (one is white, the other pink). There is a variety called "seedless" while another is "seeded." As the grapefruit is picked tree-ripe, it is always ready to eat when you purchase it. When buying grapefruit, look for firm, well-shaped fruit with thin skin and choose one that is heavy for its size. If a grapefruit is pointed at the stem end, it is most likely thick-skinned and therefore not juicy. Small skin defects do not affect eating quality, but avoid grapefruit with soft spots and water-soaked areas as well as fruit with dull brownish skin.

Though the grapefruit has traditionally been limited to the breakfast table, it is an excellent addition to fruit salad and half a grapefruit, sugared and sprinkled with orange liqueur, can be a satisfactory ending to a light meal. If you have time to peel grapefruit sections in sufficient quantity, you may combine them with bananas and grapes and a few drops of fruit liqueur for an unusual salad.

Grapes

Since there are now so many varieties of grapes available, they have become basically a year-round fruit. The European varieties, which include the Thompson seedless grape, the Tokay and the Muscadet are my favorites when really ripe. The American grape—the Concord—has a very special flavor, is extremely juicy and is widely used for making grape juice. When buying grapes, look for well-colored plump ones. White or green grapes are at their best when they have turned to straw color with a touch of amber. The red varieties are at their best when deep, bright

red. Avoid soft or wrinkled grapes and leaking berries which indicate decay. When serving grapes, combine two or three varieties in a fruit bowl and serve them chilled but not icy cold because that kills their flavor. Rinse grapes quickly just minutes before serving. Grapes are an excellent accompaniment to the dessert cheese board.

Lemons

Lemons are to the fruit world what parsley is to the vegetable and herb world. They are a "must." Cooking without lemons would be limited and uninteresting. Everything about a lemon is lovely: its shape, its color and its flavor.

Lemons are available all year round and are sold either packaged or individually. Look for thin-skinned lemons that have a rich yellow color. A firm heavy lemon is good too, but it will be much less juicy. Avoid greenish lemons with coarse, rough skin. Also avoid shriveled lemons or those with soft spots and skin punctures. Keep a supply of lemons at all times; they will keep for weeks in the bottom part of your refrigerator. Having them on hand will enable you to come up quickly with an exciting dessert such as a Lemon Souffle or Mousse. If you have no time to get flowers and feel like adding a touch of brightness to your dinner-table setting, a pretty bowl simply filled with lemons will do the trick.

Limes

Limes, which belong to the lemon family, are green with a special flavor that is essential to such dishes as Mexican Seviche or Key Lime Pie (made with a very special variety of limes). Limes are available all year round and are used especially in the summer with such drinks as iced tea and gin and tonic. Look for shiny limes with glossy skins and avoid those that have soft spots, mold or skin punctures.

Melons

Melons are one of summer's most refreshing fruits and a chilled slice of ripe melon can be the perfect beginning for a Sunday breakfast or a fine ending to a light noon or evening meal. There are several varieties of melons; all have character and individuality. They can be combined into a melon salad, although I prefer to use each individually.

Cantaloupe: This is the most popular of the melons and is available from May through September. When buying a cantaloupe, look for a mature to ripe melon. A mature one will still need two to three days of ripening at room temperature. Signs of maturity are thick, coarse veining that stands out in bold relief over most of the surface and skin color which should be pale yellow, not green. A ripe cantaloupe will have a slight pleasantly distinctive aroma and will yield slightly to thumb pressure on the blossom end. Avoid overripe melons with large bruised areas. If necessary, ripen the melon at room temperature and chill it only for 4 to 6 hours before serving. A melon salad, sugared and sprinkled with lemon juice and a fruit liqueur, is a delicious dessert that takes only minutes to prepare.

Casaba: This is a sweet juicy melon that is somewhat pumpkin-shaped. The rind is hard with a light green or yellow color. The casaba season overlaps that of the cantaloupe. Casabas are available from July to November. When buying them, look for ripe melons with a golden-yellow rind and a slight softening at the blossom end. An uncut casaba has no aroma. Serve this melon chilled with a wedge of lemon.

Crenshaw: Personally I find this to be the queen of the melon family. It has a pale orange juicy flesh and a most delicate flavor. It is available in California from July through October, but is often found in Eastern markets only in August and September. When buying this melon, look for a ripe one with the rind a deep golden yellow. It should have a pleasant melon aroma and the surface should yield slightly to pressure of the thumb at the blossom end.

Honeydew: This is a very large melon and the weight can range from 4 to 8 pounds. It has generally a very smooth rind that shades from almost white to creamy yellow. A ripe honeydew has a slightly soft blossom end and a faint aroma.

Persian: This melon is very much like the cantaloupe, but usually larger with slightly finer rind. Mostly available in California, it is sometimes found in the Eastern markets during the months of August and September. When buying Persian melons, look for the same qualities as in the cantaloupe.

Watermelon: This is certainly the most refreshing of all melons, but I somehow put it in a class all by itself and do not consider it a dessert fruit. It is more of a thirst quencher to be nibbled on at any time of day during the summer. In Europe watermelons are usually bought whole, since they are small, ranging from 4 to 6 pounds. In the United States watermelons are usually sold by the piece, although you may, of course, buy a whole one. Look for firm juicy flesh with good red color and avoid melons with pale or dry and mealy-looking flesh. Do not include watermelon in a fruit salad; it loses its crispness and will make the salad watery. Serve it in thin slices thoroughly chilled.

Nectarines

This fruit looks like a cross between a peach and a plum. It has smooth highly colored reddish-amber skin. When ripe, it should yield slightly to pressure of the thumb. Though not one of my favorite fruits, nectarines lend themselves extremely well to compotes and tarts. When buying nectarines, look for bright-colored fruit with a slight softening along the "seam." Avoid shriveled or overripe fruit with cracked skin or brown soft spots. Since it is very rare to find the tree-ripened fruit, allow two or three days at room temperature for nectarines to be right for serving. Chill them for a few hours. Serve in a compote or sliced and sugared with a bowl of sweetened whipped cream.

Oranges

The orange is the most important of the winter fruits. Nothing can surpass the taste of a glass of freshly squeezed orange juice for breakfast. Sliced oranges in red wine are a delicious dessert and Duck a l'Orange is one of the great dishes of the world.

There are several varieties of oranges. Some are juice oranges and others are meant for eating. The best eating oranges are the California Navel, available from November until early May, and the Florida Temple orange, available from December until early March. Both peel easily and separate readily into segments. Both have excellent flavor. The western Valencia orange is available from April through October, but is mainly good for juicing or slicing into fruit salads. The Jaffa orange, imported from Israel, is one of the world's best oranges and is often available in large cities. It is the perfect dessert orange, since it separates beautifully into segments.

Oranges are required by law to mature on the trees before being harvested and therefore arrive fully matured at the local market. This, however, does not guarantee quality and neither does the color, since oranges are often artificially tinted to improve their appearance. When buying oranges, look for heavy bright-looking fruit with reasonably smooth skin. Avoid lightweight oranges and those with very thick skin. Also avoid oranges with soft spots on the surface and cuts or skin punctures.

Peaches

The peach is considered by many people to be the most appealing summer fruit. It is a beautiful fruit, but unfortunately it is often just that. Great quantities of peaches are shipped green across thousands of miles. Their texture is mealy and they have little or no juice. It is, therefore, best to buy local peaches in season. These will often not look beautiful but will make up for it with taste and juiciness—and this is what really matters.

Many varieties of peaches are grown, but the average person will have a hard time telling one from the other. Generally speaking, peaches fall into two categories: the clingstone peach and the freestone peach. For taste I much prefer the cling-stone and use it whenever possible both fresh and for poaching. The freestone peach is easier to eat and can also be delicious. It is perfect for certain desserts where the center is filled with a pastry cream or for a fresh peach tart.

When buying peaches, look for those that are firm but that will yield slightly to pressure. The skin color between the red areas should be yellow or creamy. Avoid peaches with a distinct green ground color; these will not ripen properly. Also avoid very soft and overripe fruit, and peaches that have even a slight pale tan spot which indicates decay.

Serve peaches slightly chilled, but never ice cold. To peel peaches drop them into fast-boiling water for 60 seconds, then run them under cold water; the skin will slip right off. For an easy and refreshing dessert serve sliced peaches sprinkled with lemon juice and sugar and a few drops of peach brandy. A bowl of sweetened whipped cream is always welcome.

Pears

Pears are one of my favorite fruits, and I like everything about them. The pear has a lovely shape and a delightful aroma. A tree-ripened pear is an excellent dessert. Unfortunately, like peaches, pears are mostly shipped green, which often prevents them from developing a juicy sweet taste. There are several varieties of pears. The Bartlett pear is available from early August through November and is good for poaching. The Anjou, Bosc, Winter Nellic and Comice are fall and winter varieties, available from November through May. The Comice is easily the finest of these pears and should be enjoyed plain, slightly chilled, with or without the addition of cheese.

When buying pears, look for mature to ripe fruit. In the Bartlett pear look for a pale yellow to rich yellow color. Anjou or Comice should be light green to yellowish green. The Bosc pear has a brown skin, which is its main characteristic and not a sign of decay. Pears that are firm but with a slight softening of the flesh near the stem will not ripen properly and should be avoided.

Pineapples

Pineapples are considered a delicacy in Europe, since they are very expensive at all times of the year. They are less of an extravagance in the United States and are available in most parts of the country all year round. The pineapple, however, does have a peak season (April and May) when it is at its best. A dead-ripe pineapple is a marvelous fruit, but when served under-ripe it is almost tasteless. Since pineapples have to be picked when still hard, they must be allowed to ripen for a few days at room temperature. In good markets you will often be able to purchase a pineapple that is completely ripe.

When buying a pineapple, test it for ripeness by its aroma, which should be strong, and by pulling at one of the leaves. If it pulls away easily, the pineapple is ripe.

The color is also important; a ripe pineapple will be either golden yellow, orange yellow or reddish brown according to the variety. The only variety that remains green even when ripe is the Sugar Loaf, seldom available in American markets. Avoid pineapples with dull yellowish green color and dried appearance. These are signs of immaturity and the pineapple will never ripen properly. Also avoid bruised fruit (which is often cheaper) as this is a sign of decay which will spread rapidly. Pineapple should be served chilled. Or it can be poached and served as a compote. It makes marvelous fritters and can also be served with a sugar and wine syrup. A whole pineapple, cubed, sugared and sprinkled with kirsch, is a simple yet delicious dessert which takes only minutes to prepare.

Plums and prunes

Plums and prunes make a lovely addition to the summer fruit bowl. They are a delicious fruit and should be bought ripe whenever possible. There are three varieties of plums: the large dark plum, the large bright red plum, and the greengage plum that has a lovely greenish yellow color. They are available from June to September. All three varieties lend themselves well to poaching—either by themselves or in combination with other fruits. Personally, I prefer the dark plum, which is juicier and makes excellent tarts.

Prunes: There are several varieties of prunes available, but they are very similar and hard to tell apart. Fresh prunes, often called Italian plums, are available from August through October. When buying either plums or prunes, look for firm yet slightly soft fruit and avoid immature fruit that is hard, poorly colored and sometimes shriveled. Also avoid overripe fruit that is excessively soft. Prunes are used a great deal in Austrian and Hungarian cooking. They make delicious compotes and, when very ripe, are good for breakfast simply sugared and served with Creme Fraiche.

On my first visit to the United States several years ago I was invited to a dinner party at which several cheeses were served with cocktails. I was quite surprised, since we spent at least an hour chatting and nibbling over cocktails. By the time we sat down to dinner, nobody was very hungry and I felt that the hostess's efforts had to some extent been wasted. "Cheese closes the stomach and should always be served at the end of a meal," I was once told by a Frenchman. At the time I did not take his comment very seriously, knowing that in many European countries cheese appears at breakfast time. Now, after years of serving cheese for dessert and still being served cheese as an appetizer, I can see the difference. Cheese should be the closing of a meal, served either with a salad or by itself. It can be followed by dessert or fruit. Pears, apples and figs have a special affinity for cheese. Cheese should be bought carefully and with thought. A platter of well-assorted cheese shows the hostess's ingenuity and culinary understanding as much as the rest of the meal. When you first venture into the world of cheese, it is advisable to buy it at a reputable delicacy shop where you can get proper help in making your selection. Sample many kinds and after a while you will be able to make your own choice according to your menu. There are over a hundred types of French cheese sold in the United States. Unfortunately, these are not available everywhere and in some areas the selection may be rather limited. Often the cheese does not have the quality the equivalent product would have in France or Italy. This is due to the processing and pasteurizing cheese has to go through before being shipped to the United States. We can, however, get the most out of many varieties by serving them properly. If cheese has been refrigerated, it must be brought back to room temperature for at least 2 to 4 hours before serving to give it a chance to breathe. Serve cheese simply, without the addition of cherry tomatoes, olives and so on. Take the cheeses out of their boxes, place them on a platter and let guests serve themselves. Crusty French bread and possibly a bowl of sweet butter are the perfect accompaniments.

French cheeses

Beaufort: The Beaufort belongs to the Gruyere-cheese family. It is slightly eyed with a smooth, rich texture. It is rather bland, which makes it an excellent accompaniment to fruits such as pears and apples. Serve a fruity white wine, such as a sauterne, with this cheese.

Beaumont: The Beaumont is a marvelous cheese made in the Haute-Savoie region. It is creamy and rich with a bright orange rind and a buttery taste. It should be served ripe but not overly ripe as its flavor tends to become very strong and overpowering. It should be served with either French bread or black bread and sweet butter. A full-bodied red wine goes well with the Beaumont.

Boursalt: There are two brands of Boursalt sold in the United States. Both are excellent. Boursalt belongs to the cream-cheese family, but is definitely more interesting than the average cream cheese. The Boursalt is delicious with all berries and can also be used for filling cherry tomatoes or cucumber boats.

Boursin (with fines herbes): This is one of the loveliest cheeses in the cream-cheese family. It is flavored with an herb and garlic mixture and can be served in innumerable ways. It is a fine complement to the dessert cheese board and can also be used for filling cherry tomatoes or thin slices of smoked ham.

Boursin (with pepper): A delicious combination! A smooth creamy cheese covered with peppercorns that give it an interesting sharp peppery taste. This Boursin should be served with either thin slices of pumpernickel or with crusty French bread and a bowl of sweet butter.

Brie: This cheese at its best is without a doubt the king of cheeses. There is an amusing story often told in France about the origin of Brie. In 1815, after the Battle of Waterloo, thirty nations participated in the Congress of Vienna. Each presented the Congress with a delicacy of its own country and the French introduced the Brie, which was immediately declared king of cheeses.
France had lost a war, but the world had gained a great cheese. . . . Unfortunately a great Brie is not easy to come by. Avoid buying one with a cakey center or one that is too runny. Brie is not really an appetizer cheese, although it is often served as such. It should be part of the dessert cheese board or served simply with crusty French bread or a well-flavored green salad.

Brie de Coulommiers or **Coulommiers:** This is really a miniature Brie. You buy a wedge of Brie, but you buy "a Coulommiers." In France the cheese is available in two stages: fresh, when it resembles cream cheese; or ripe, when its texture and flavor is similar to that of Brie. In the United States it is available in the latter stage. At the right degree of ripeness it is an excellent cheese with a velvety texture and a fine nutty flavor. Serve it as you would a Brie.

Camembert: The Camembert, like the Brie, can be an absolute marvel or a real disappointment. Camembert originated in Normandy, but even in France it is hard to find authentic Camembert. Since its name has never been legally protected, there are hundreds of so-called Camemberts all over the world, none of which comes even remotely close to the great original. Avoid buying canned Camembert or one that comes six triangles to a box. This cheese should not be overly ripe and the crust must be pure white. Serve Camembert as part of the dessert cheese board or simply accompanied by a full-bodied red wine and crusty French bread.

Carre de l'Est: This cheese is a serious rival of the Camembert. Its flavor, however, is milder. Since it is fairly easy to find this cheese at the right stage of ripeness, I often serve it instead of Camembert, accompanied by French bread and a full-bodied Bordeaux or Beaujolais.

Chabichou: The Chabichou is a young and mild goat cheese which fortunately travels well and is often available in good cheese shops. Though many people claim that one has to acquire a taste for goat cheese, I cannot imagine how anybody would hesitate to add Chabichou or any other mild goat cheese to their cheese board. Chabichou should be served with French bread and a chilled white wine such as a Pouilly-Fuisse, a Chablis or a Muscadet.

Gourmandise: This is one of the most popular French cheeses in the United States, but I personally find it bland and uninteresting. It is an extremely creamy cheese with a sweet flavor due to the addition of cherry extract. In France, it is flavored with kirsch, which gives it a certain tanginess. Even so, I consider Gourmandise one of the lesser French cheeses. It is definitely a dessert cheese and can be served with fruits such as cherries, grapes or pears.

Marc de Raisin or **Grape Cheese:** This is basically the Gourmandise in a black robe, the surface being completely covered with dark blue grape seeds. These give an interesting look but do not add to the taste, which is quite bland and too sweet. One never knows whether to eat the cheese with the seeds or remove them. If you do remove them, you are back at Gourmandise. Serve it with assorted fruits and a sauterne.

Pipo Creme: This is by far my favorite blue cheese. It is much creamier and milder than Roquefort and seldom as salty. Serve the Pipo Creme as part of the dessert cheese board or simply with crusty French bread and sweet butter. It can also be mashed with an equal amount of cream cheese and used to fill the cavities of avocado halves or lightly poached pears.

Pont l'Eveque: This is one of France's oldest and most important cheeses—of great texture, soft but not runny, and with a slightly sweet flavor. It is unfortunately extremely hard to find at its perfect stage

of ripeness in the United States. Usually the Pont l'Eveque available in cheese shops is overripe, giving it a strong flavor and a rather bitter aftertaste. This cheese is at its best from October to June and should be served with a full-bodied Bordeaux or Beaujolais. A great Pont l'Eveque does not need the adornment of fruit. Serve it as part of the dessert cheese board or simply with French bread.

Port Salut: The French Port Salut can be a delicious cheese when properly aged. At its young stage it is somewhat bland and uninteresting. At a more advanced stage it is still a mild cheese but with an interesting edge to it. The small Port Salut found in American supermarkets has no taste whatsoever and should not be given room on the cheese platter. The Port Salut is a versatile cheese that can be served with fruits such as pears, apples and grapes or with a platter of assorted sausages and a salad for lunch or a light supper.

Reblochon: Since Reblochon is my favorite cheese, I find it hard to accept the fact that it is so difficult to come by at its perfect stage. It is one of France's finest cheeses and can give a memorable finishing touch to a meal. It is a small round cheese, the color of its skin ranging from saffron yellow to deep orange and bringing to mind the colors of fall. The Reblochon is at its best from September to June and should be served at its prime but not overripe. Serve it with a white Burgundy and crusty French bread.

Roquefort: The Roquefort is the oldest of the blue cheeses and by far the most famous one. It is a cheese of great character with beautiful blue veining and very individual flavor. In France, due to the legal protection of its name, the Roquefort is almost always perfect. Unfortunately the quality of the Roquefort available in the United States varies a great deal. Often too sharp and too salty, this cheese is nevertheless an important addition to the cheese board. Serve it with a well-flavored green salad and a good red wine such as Chateauneuf-du-Pape. An excellent Roquefort may also be served with pears and a dry chilled champagne.

St. Marcellin: This is a mild and absolutely delicious goat cheese from Provence and its soft creamy texture makes it my favorite goat cheese. Serve it after a light summer lunch accompanied by a chilled white wine or use it as part of the dessert cheese board.

St. Paulin: This cheese is very similar to Port Salut in taste, but its texture is slightly different. Whereas Port Salut is smooth, St. Paulin has tiny holes. Since it is produced in several regions of France, its quality can be quite varied. Like Port Salut, St. Paulin can be served with other dessert cheeses or for lunch or light supper with assorted sausages and a salad.

Italian cheeses

There are many delicious Italian cheeses, unfortunately rarely available outside of Italy because they do not travel well. Here are a few available in the United States which will add an interesting touch to the dessert cheese board.

Bel Paese: This is an extremely popular cheese in the United States. Most Bel Paese sold in supermarkets and delicacy shops is the domestic variety—a far cry from the creamy and smooth cheese the Bel Paese can be. Try to find the imported variety and serve it with fruits such as pears, apples or fresh figs.

Fontina: This is my favorite Italian cheese. It comes from the lovely Aosta Valley in northern Italy and is one of Italy's and the world's great cheeses. Both in texture and taste it is a marvelous cheese that should be included in the dessert cheese board. It is also a very versatile cheese. With assorted sausages and a salad it can be served for lunch or for a light supper. It can also be used in melted cheese sandwiches or as a topping for sauteed scaloppine of veal. Avoid imitations of Fontina, both domestic and Danish. None can even come close to this delicious cheese.

Gorgonzola: This is Italy's contribution to the world of blue cheeses. It is a delicious and beautiful cheese with lovely green veining and a sharp tangy flavor. Serve it with crusty French bread or with thin slices of buttered pumpernickel and a well-flavored green salad. Fruits such as pears and apples go well with Gorgonzola.

Parmesan: Even though Parmesan is mostly used in the United States for cooking and seasoning, I often serve it as a dessert cheese. The younger Parmesan will be milder than the aged one, slightly whiter, with a rich and piquant flavor. Avoid buying domestic Parmesan or Parmesan from any country but Italy. None has the quality of the Italian cheese. Serve Parmesan accompanied simply by fruit such as pears, peaches or fresh figs, or as part of the dessert cheese board.

Talegio: This cheese is not as mild as the Bel Paese and I therefore prefer it. Its slight tanginess makes it an excellent dessert cheese. As the Talegio ages, it can become very sharp and biting and I prefer serving it at its young stage. Serve it with fruits such as pears or fresh figs, accompanied by a full-bodied red wine, or use it as part of the dessert cheese board.

I really find spring to be the "season of anticipation." In Europe, it is synonymous with spring lamb and duckling, fresh peas and asparagus. Even though real spring lamb is rarely available in the United States, one can still play the spring game in the kitchen and experiment with some of the famous traditional dishes as well as some of the more unusual ones I have tried to bring to you in this book. There is no doubt that great emphasis should be put on asparagus, fresh peas, the first fresh herbs and berries. These should be simply prepared since their freshness speaks its own language.

the spring kitchen

Symbols

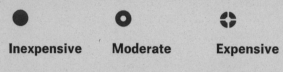

● Inexpensive   ◉ Moderate   ✪ Expensive

■ Easy   ▣ Intermediate   ⊞ Difficult

Spaghettini billi-bi
Veal don lysander
Mixed fruits in rum sauce

This menu combines some of the culinary
gems of France and Italy. The spaghetti
and veal are almost synonymous with Italy.
Mussels are used in Billi-Bi, a marvelous
French soup, and mussels in white wine is
a culinary gem.
Finish the meal with Mixed Fruits in Rum
Sauce and you have a light and exciting
spring menu.

Spaghettini billi-bi

Serves: 6
Preparation time: 20 minutes
Cooking time: 25 to 30 minutes

This dish derives its name from the traditional French mussel soup called Billi-Bi. I found that I could incorporate the essence of a French soup successfully with an Italian pasta dish—a happy combination of the flavors of France and Italy.

Ingredients

3 pounds mussels
1 cup dry white wine
2 large onions, coarsely chopped
8 to 10 peppercorns
1 large Bouquet Garni (page 397)
1 tablespoon of salt
1 pound thin spaghettini
3 tablespoons butter
2 tablespoons flour
3 egg yolks
½ cup heavy cream

Garnish:
Mixed fresh herbs, finely minced
1 tablespoon parsley
1 tablespoon fresh thyme
1 tablespoon fresh chives

Preparation

1. Scrub the mussels well under cold running water, but do not soak them.

2. Put the dry white wine in a large casserole with the onions, peppercorns and Bouquet Garni. Add the mussels, cover the casserole and steam them for 5 minutes or until they open.

3. Remove the mussels from the casserole. Drain and reserve the cooking liquid. Shell the mussels. Discard those that have not opened. Unopened mussels are not eatable and should never be used.

4. Strain the liquid from the pot through a double layer of cheesecloth to remove any sand that may have remained. Return the liquid to the pot and reduce to 1 cup.

5. Bring a large saucepan of water to boil, add the salt and cook the spaghettini until barely tender (about 8 to 10 minutes).

6. In another saucepan melt the butter. Add the flour and whisk in the mussel broth. The sauce should just coat the spoon.

7. In a small mixing bowl beat the egg yolks and the cream well together. Remove the sauce from the heat and add the egg-cream mixture. Return to low heat, but be careful not to let the sauce come to a boil or it will curdle.

8. Pour the sauce over the spaghettini. Add the mussels, garnish with minced herbs and serve immediately with French bread and a bowl of freshly grated Parmesan cheese on the side.

Remarks

This makes a hearty appetizer and when served as such, you should have a light main course such as veal cutlets or a poulet saute. Spaghettini Billi-Bi is equally excellent as the main course for a light supper.

Notes

Veal don lysander

Serves: 8
Preparation time: 10 minutes
Cooking time: 45 to 50 minutes

There are innumerable ways to prepare veal scallops (called Piccate in Italy). Every region has its own special way of preparing them. I find, however, that the fast and last-minute cooking methods used in Europe do not work well with our American veal. This recipe therefore uses a method of oven cooking that will work well with our cuts of veal and the preparation can be done well in advance of serving. You can make this a wonderful all-season dish by substituting mushrooms, sliced fresh-cooked artichoke bottoms or fresh peas for the asparagus.

Ingredients

6 tablespoons sweet butter (or Clarified Butter, page 398)
Juice of 2 lemons
8 large veal cutlets, cut ¼ inch thick
24 asparagus stalks (3 stalks per slice of veal)
Salt
1 tablespoon cooking oil
Freshly ground white pepper
Flour for dredging
8 slices boiled ham
½ cup fresh bread crumbs
2 tablespoons freshly grated Parmesan or Romano cheese
½ cup chicken stock

Preparation

1. Preheat oven to 325°.

2. In a large baking dish melt 2 tablespoons of butter. Add the juice of 1 lemon and reserve. Dry the veal slices with paper towels. In order to brown well all meats must be dry.

3. Clean the asparagus and cut off the tough bottoms, leaving the stalks almost the length of the veal scallops (about 3 inches long).

4. Bring a large saucepan of water with 1 tablespoon salt to boil. Add the asparagus and cook until almost tender (about 10 minutes). Drain and immediately run under cold water. This will keep the stalks green and prevent further cooking. Keep them warm.

5. Heat 2 tablespoons of butter and oil in a large frying pan. (If you are using Clarified Butter, you do not need the oil.) Season the veal scallops with salt and pepper and dip in the flour, shaking off any excess flour.

6. Brown the veal scallops 2 or 3 at a time in the large frying pan for 2 to 3 minutes on each side, then transfer them to the baking dish.

7. Top each scallop with 1 thin slice of ham and 3 asparagus spears.

8. In a small saucepan saute the bread crumbs in the remaining 2 tablespoons of butter for 2 minutes. Add the Parmesan, and sprinkle the asparagus with this mixture.

9. Deglaze the pan in which you have browned the veal. Add the remaining lemon juice and the chicken stock. Scrape the brown particles from the bottom of the pan and slightly reduce the stock. Pour the pan juices around the veal.

10. Cover and bake at 325° for 30 minutes. Serve directly from the baking dish.

Mixed fruits in rum sauce

Serves: 6 to 8
Preparation time: 5 minutes
Cooking time: none

■ ●

You can be totally free with this dessert. Let your own tastes be your inspiration. The recipe that follows is open-ended. It lends itself to the fruits of any season but is particularly nice in the spring when the first good melons, berries, plums and grapes appear. Use any variety of fruits you like. Leave the berries whole but cut all other fruits in small cubes.

Ingredients

Plums
Apples
Bananas
Grapes
Strawberries
5 ounces finely chopped walnuts

The rum sauce:
4 egg yolks
¾ cup sugar (superfine)
2 egg whites
2 to 4 tablespoons white rum

Preparation

1. Mix the cubed fruits, whole berries and nuts in a serving bowl and chill.

2. Beat the egg yolks with the sugar until they double in volume and are pale yellow.

3. Beat the two egg whites until they make soft peaks.

4. Add the rum to the egg yolk and sugar mixture and fold in the beaten egg whites. Serve immediately, spooning the rum sauce over individual servings of the cold fruit.

Remarks

The fruit can be assembled well ahead of time. The sauce, on the other hand, should be prepared just prior to serving.
Do not add any sugar to the fruits as the sauce is quite sweet. This sauce is also excellent served on simple poached pears or over a bowl of fresh raspberries.

Notes

Mussels in shallot mayonnaise
Spring ragout of lamb
Strawberries in liqueur

Since the main course in this menu is demanding of the cook's time, the appetizer and dessert can remain simple. The mussels may be prepared one day ahead of time (if you are really pressed for time you may substitute cooked shrimp). Follow the ragout with a crisp green salad and serve the strawberries either in liqueur or simply sugared with a bowl of sweetened Creme Fraiche on the side.

Mussels in shallot mayonnaise

Serves: 4 to 6
Preparation time: 40 minutes
Cooking time: 10 minutes

Ingredients

4 to 5 pounds fresh mussels, thoroughly
   scrubbed under cold running water
1 cup dry white wine
1 Bouquet Garni (page 397)
6 peppercorns

The sauce:
3 shallots finely minced
¼ cup tarragon wine vinegar
¼ cup white wine
1 tablespoon finely minced fresh tarragon
1½ to 2 cups Mayonnaise (page 402)
1 tablespoon small capers
1 tablespoon finely minced parsley
1 tablespoon chives
Salt and freshly ground black pepper
2 teaspoons Dijon mustard

Preparation

1. In a large saucepan combine the mussels with the wine, Bouquet Garni and peppercorns. Cook over high heat until the mussels open. When cool enough to handle, remove them from their shells. Discard any that do not open. Cool the mussels, drain them on paper towels and reserve.

2. In a small saucepan combine the shallots, vinegar, wine and tarragon. Cook the mixture until the liquid has completely evaporated.

3. Add the shallot mixture to the mayonnaise together with the capers, parsley and chives. Season with salt, pepper and Dijon mustard.

4. Add the mayonnaise mixture to the mussels and refrigerate until serving time.

Remarks

Do not add all the mayonnaise at once. The mayonnaise should bind the mussels well and you may need only 1 to 1½ cups. The mussels can also be served on the "half shell," each one topped with a little of the herb-mayonnaise mixture.

Notes

Spring ragout of lamb

Serves: 6 to 8
Preparation time: 1 hour
Cooking time: 2 hours

This is an adaptation of the famous Navarin of Lamb which calls for several spring vegetables. The secret of the dish lies in the freshness of the ingredients, and I find the combination given here very appealing. It is also an excellent recipe in which to use peas that are large and rather tough.

Ingredients

4 pounds cubed boneless shoulder of lamb
Salt
Freshly ground white pepper
5 tablespoons butter
2 tablespoons cooking oil
½ pound of bacon, cut into cubes, par-boiled for 5 minutes, then drained
2 large shallots, finely minced
2 large garlic cloves, finely minced
4 large ripe tomatoes, peeled, seeded and chopped
1 teaspoon oregano, 1 tablespoon fresh basil or 1 teaspoon dried, mixed
1 tablespoon tomato paste
¾ cup white wine
2 cups Lamb Stock (page 406)
1 Bouquet Garni (page 397)
18 small white onions
2 cups shelled peas
1 tablespoon sugar
¾ pound button mushrooms or large mushrooms, quartered

Optional:
1 tablespoon cornstarch mixed to a paste with a little stock

Preparation

1. Preheat oven to 350°.
2. Dry the meat thoroughly on paper towels. Season with salt and pepper.

3. In a large flameproof casserole, heat 3 tablespoons of butter with the oil. When the butter is very hot, add the lamb cubes a few at a time. Do not crowd the casserole. Brown all the cubes evenly on all sides. Remove and reserve them.

4. Add the bacon cubes to the casserole and cook them until they are almost crisp. Remove and reserve them.

5. Discard all but two tablespoons of fat from the casserole and add the shallots and garlic. Cook until the shallots are soft but not browned.

6. Add the tomatoes and herbs. Cook the mixture over medium heat for 2 or 3 minutes, scraping well the bottom of the casserole.

7. Add the tomato paste and wine. Bring to a boil. Add the lamb cubes, bacon and Lamb Stock. Bury the Bouquet Garni among the pieces of meat. Cover the casserole and bake in the middle of the oven for 1 hour and 15 minutes.

8. Add the onions to the casserole and return it to the oven.

9. Cover the peas with water and add the sugar and a pinch of salt. Bring the water to a boil and simmer the peas for 5 to 8 minutes. Drain them and reserve.

10. In a small skillet, heat the remaining butter and quickly saute the mushrooms for 2 or 3 minutes or until they are lightly browned. Season them with salt and pepper.

Strawberries in liqueur

Serves: 4 to 6
Preparation time: 15 minutes
Cooking time: none

11. Just before serving, add the peas and mushrooms to the casserole and cook for about 8 to 10 minutes more.

12. Remove the casserole from the oven. Bring the ragout to a simmer on the top of the stove. With a slotted spoon remove the meat and vegetables to a side dish. If the sauce seems too thin, add the cornstarch mixture a little at a time and cook until the sauce heavily coats the spoon. Taste the sauce, correct the seasoning, return the meat and vegetables to the casserole and serve.

Notes

This is a particularly good recipe for the very early strawberry season or anytime when the berries are not at their best. A liqueur brings out additional flavor in them and I find this combination of ingredients most appealing.

Ingredients

2 or 3 pints hulled strawberries
4 tablespoons granulated sugar
4 tablespoons cherry brandy
Juice of 2 oranges
Pinch of grated orange rind
1 cup heavy cream, whipped
2 tablespoons confectioners' sugar
½ cup sour cream
Finely chopped unsalted pistachios

Preparation

1. Rinse the strawberries under cold running water before you hull them. Remove the stems and place the berries in a glass serving dish. Sprinkle them with the granulated sugar.

2. Mix the cherry brandy with the orange juice and grated rind. Pour the mixture over the strawberries. Chill for 1 to 2 hours before serving.

3. Combine the whipped cream with the confectioners' sugar and sour cream and chill.

4. Serve the strawberries with the cream and sprinkle with the pistachios just before serving.

Poached eggs on asparagus
Chicken breasts in chive cream
Pears in framboise

The spring menu should bring to the table a certain light touch and the best of what the season has to offer. I find asparagus synonymous with spring and like to plan my menus around this marvelous vegetable. Here the asparagus is served in a traditional Italian way that lends itself well to our asparagus. Follow the hearty appetizer with a light main course such as Chicken Breasts in Chive Cream. As an accompaniment to the main course, serve a well-flavored risotto garnished with sliced avocados and pimiento strips. Finish the meal with the Pears in Framboise, a rich and colorful dessert—the right farewell to spring before the simpler summer desserts take over.

Poached eggs on asparagus

Serves: 4 to 6
Preparation time: 20 minutes
Cooking time: 20 to 25 minutes

■ ●

Here is a simple appetizer that must be prepared with care. The asparagus should be slightly crisp and bright green, the poached eggs not overcooked. For a variation, roll each cooked asparagus stalk in a thin slice of smoked ham or prosciutto, omitting the poached eggs. If you serve this dish for lunch or light supper, you may accompany it with a more elaborate sauce.

Ingredients

6 asparagus stalks per person
Salt
2 tablespoons sweet butter
1 cup cubed smoked ham (prosciutto)
White vinegar as needed
2 poached eggs per person
Freshly ground white pepper
2 slices white bread per person
1 cup freshly grated Parmesan cheese

The sauce:
½ cup melted sweet butter
2 tablespoons finely chopped parsley
1 teaspoon fresh chives, finely minced
Salt and pepper

Garnish:
Watercress
Bread triangles fried in Clarified Butter
   (page 398)

Preparation

1. Choose asparagus stalks of uniform size and thickness. This allows them to finish cooking at the same time. Cut off the hard bottoms, peel the asparagus spears and tie them in bundles of six. Bring a large saucepan of water to boil and add 1 tablespoon of salt. Cook the asparagus for 10 to 15 minutes or until barely tender.

Drain immediately. Run under cold water to stop the cooking and place 6 stalks in each of 6 buttered individual baking dishes.

2. In a skillet melt the butter and saute the ham cubes for 2 or 3 minutes.

3. If you do not have an egg poacher, pour water 1 inch deep into a 10-inch skillet. Add 1 tablespoon of white distilled vinegar per cup of water. Break the eggs, one at a time, into a saucer and slip each egg into the simmering water. Keep the water at a bare simmer and remove the pan from the heat. Baste the yolks with the whites 2 or 3 times. In 5 minutes the eggs should be done. Drain them. Trim the whites with a knife and reserve.

4. Place 2 poached eggs on each portion of asparagus. Season with salt and pepper. Keep warm.

5. To make the sauce, add parsley and chives to the melted butter. Heat through. Taste and season as desired.

6. Spoon the butter sauce over each dish. Serve garnished with crisp watercress and fried bread triangles.

Remarks

If you are serving this dish as an appetizer, serve only 1 poached egg per person.
To turn the recipe into an elegant first course, mince the asparagus, put it into individual tart shells, top with the poached eggs and serve with a more interesting sauce such as a mustard hollandaise.

Chicken breasts in chive cream

Serves: 4 to 6
Preparation time: 30 minutes
Cooking time: 10 minutes

■ ○

Personally I have never understood why so many people prefer to serve boned chicken breasts instead of a saute of whole chicken! They are often served overcooked and dry, and with some undistinguished sauce. However, well-prepared chicken breasts can be delicious and are especially useful in last-minute cooking.

Ingredients

8 tablespoons sweet butter
2 tablespoons chopped scallions
½ pound button mushrooms whole (or quartered large mushrooms), wiped, stems removed
Salt
Freshly ground white pepper
6 prepared chicken breasts, with skin removed, slightly flattened
½ cup concentrated Brown Chicken Stock (page 404)
Dash of lemon juice
1 cup heavy cream
1 Beurre Manie (page 397)
2 tablespoons finely chopped chives

Preparation

1. In a small skillet, heat 2 tablespoons of butter. Add the scallions and cook for 2 or 3 minutes without browning. Add the mushrooms. Season with salt and pepper and cook the mixture over high heat for 2 or 3 more minutes to brown the mushrooms lightly. Reserve.

2. Season the chicken breasts with salt and pepper and sprinkle them with lemon juice.

3. In a large chicken fryer, melt the remaining butter. When it is quite hot, add the chicken breasts and cook them for 1 minute on each side. Cover the pan with buttered wax paper and then the pan lid. Lower the heat and simmer the chicken breasts for another 8 to 10 minutes or until the juices run out pale yellow when pierced with a fork. Do not overcook or pierce every piece. Immediately remove the chicken breasts to a serving platter.

4. Pour the Chicken Stock into the fryer, raise the heat and reduce the stock until it is almost a glaze.

5. Add the heavy cream and continue cooking over high heat. Add the bits of Beurre Manie and cook until the sauce heavily coats the spoon. Add the chives and correct the seasoning.

6. Add the mushroom-and-scallion mixture. Add the chives and correct the seasoning. Pour the sauce over the chicken breasts and serve at once.

Remarks

You may vary this recipe according to the season. In the summer a touch of fresh tarragon with a puree of fresh green beans makes a marvelous dish. The mushrooms can be minced finely as a bed for the chicken breasts with the chive cream as sauce and so forth and so on!

Notes

Pears in framboise

Serves: 6 to 12
Preparation time: 45 minutes
Cooking time: 35 minutes

Ingredients

6 large underripe pears, peeled, halved
  and cored
Acidulated water
1 cup sugar
3 cups water
1 2-inch piece vanilla bean
1 3-inch piece cinnamon stick
2 cups raspberry puree (about 4 cups
  fresh raspberries plus ¾ to 1 cup
  verifine sugar beaten together in the
  blender for 3 to 5 minutes)
½ cup raspberry preserves
¼ cup framboise
6 to 12 (depending on size) almond
  macaroons soaked in kirsch

The sauce:
5 egg yolks
½ cup sugar
¾ cup sweet white wine
½ teaspoon vanilla extract
1 tablespoon grated lemon rind
Pinch of cinnamon
1 cup heavy cream
2 tablespoons confectioners' sugar

Garnish:
Macaroon Powder (page 401)
Whole raspberries

Preparation

1. Peel the pears. Cut them in half length-wise and carefully scoop out the cores. Immediately drop the pear halves into acidulated water to prevent them from turning brown.

2. In a large saucepan, combine the sugar and water. Bring the syrup to a boil and add the pears, vanilla bean and cinnamon stick. Poach the pears, a few at a time, over low heat, partially covered, until they are tender. Do not overcook. Let the pears cool completely in their syrup while preparing the rest of the dessert.

3. Pass the raspberry puree through a fine sieve and reserve.

4. Mix the raspberry preserves and the framboise in a small saucepan. Heat over a low flame until the preserves are dissolved. Pass through a fine sieve into the raspberry puree. If the puree is very thick, thin it out with spoonfuls of the syrup. Pour the puree into a glass serving dish.

5. Shape the macaroons into small balls.

6. Fill the cavities of the pear halves with the macaroon balls and place the halves on top of the raspberry puree.

The sauce:
7. Combine the egg yolks and sugar in the top part of a double boiler and beat until they are well blended and pale yellow. Add the wine.

8. Cook the sauce over simmering water, stirring constantly, until it heavily coats a spoon. Do not let it come to a boil.

9. Immediately remove from the heat. Add the vanilla extract, lemon rind and cinnamon and chill the sauce for 1 or 2 hours.

10. Whip the cream and add the confectioners' sugar. Fold the cream into the wine sauce and chill for 1 more hour.

11. Just before serving, spoon the wine sauce carefully over the pears. Decorate the top with Macaroon Powder or whole raspberries or both.

Gnocchi in basil butter
Spring duckling
Creme de cerises

This menu is your invitation to the herb
season. Here is basil in its first delicate
stage followed by one of spring's most
exciting vegetables—peas! To complement
the duck you may serve a Curry Risotto,
although good crusty French bread is really
sufficient. If you do not have the time to
pit the cherries, remember to warn your
guests.

Gnocchi in basil butter

Serves: 4 to 6
Preparation time: 20 minutes
Cooking time: 35 to 40 minutes

You can begin serving this dish in early spring as soon as the first basil plants are available at the local greengrocer's and repeat it up to late fall if you have stored some pureed basil in your refrigerator. It is a dish that has innumerable serving possibilities—excellent for lunch or supper as well as for an appetizer. It can also be served as an accompaniment to a roast leg of lamb or any barbecued meats. Other herb butters can be substituted for the Basil Butter.

Ingredients

The basil butter:
6 tablespoons softened sweet butter
2 tablespoons fresh basil leaves
2 small garlic cloves, mashed
1 tablespoon parsley

The gnocchi:
4 cups milk
2 teaspoons salt
1 cup farina (semolina)
¼ cup sweet butter
5 to 6 tablespoons freshly grated Parmesan
   cheese
Freshly ground black pepper

Preparation

1. Preheat oven to 350°.

2. To make the Basil Butter, put the butter into a mixing bowl. Place the basil leaves, garlic and parsley in a mortar and pound them into a thick paste. Add the mixture to the softened butter and chill for an hour.

3. In a large saucepan bring the milk to a boil, then lower the heat. Add the salt and slowly pour the farina into the simmering milk, stirring constantly in order to keep the farina from lumping. Cook the mixture until it is very thick.

4. Remove the saucepan from the heat and add ¼ cup of butter and 3 tablespoons of Parmesan cheese.

5. Rinse a jelly-roll pan in cold water. Spread the farina mixture in the pan and let it cool. Cover it with foil and refrigerate for 30 minutes to 1 hour.

6. Butter a large baking dish. With a cookie cutter or a small glass, cut rounds out of the farina mixture (it will be quite firm) and place the rounds in the baking dish.

7. Place bits of the Basil Butter all over the rounds and sprinkle them with the remaining Parmesan.

8. Place the dish in the preheated oven and bake for 30 minutes or until the cheese has melted and lightly browned. Sprinkle with pepper and serve.

Notes

Spring duckling

Serves: 4
Preparation time: 1 hour
Cooking time: 2½ hours

A spring duckling should be an invitation to freshness as in this recipe garnished with spring peas and small white onions. You may, of course, substitute for the onions other fresh, young vegetables such as carrots or turnip balls, with which the peas combine well. Make sure not to overcook peas. They should be slightly crisp and bright green.

Ingredients

The stock:
2 tablespoons cooking oil
1 leek, sliced
1 carrot, cubed
1 onion, chopped
Duck giblets and wing tips
1 Bouquet Garni (page 397)
Salt and freshly ground white pepper
4 cups Chicken Stock (page 404)

The duck:
1 4- to 5-pound duck
Salt and freshly ground white pepper
2 tablespoons sweet butter
1 carrot, finely minced
1 onion, finely chopped
1 stalk celery, finely chopped

The peas and onions:
1 cup water
6 tablespoons sweet butter
1½ tablespoons sugar
Salt and freshly ground white pepper
3 pounds shelled fresh peas
16 small white onions
1 cup finely cubed blanched bacon

Optional:
1 Beurre Manie or 1 tablespoon cornstarch mixed into a paste with a little
   stock

Preparation

1. Preheat oven to 400°.

2. In a saucepan heat the oil. Add the sliced leek, cubed carrot and chopped onion. Add the giblets and wings and cook the mixture until lightly browned. Add the Bouquet Garni, salt, pepper and stock. Simmer for 1 to 2 hours, covered. Then set it aside.

3. Dry the duck thoroughly with paper towels. Tie the legs and wings to the body. Prick the duck in the fatty parts. Season with salt and pepper.

4. In a roasting pan, melt the 2 tablespoons butter. Add the finely minced carrot, chopped onion and celery.

5. Place the duck on its side in the roasting pan and cook in the oven for 20 minutes. Reduce the heat to 350° and continue cooking for 1 hour and 30 minutes. It is not necessary to baste the duck or prick it with a fork as this dries it. Remove some of the pan fat from time to time with a bulb baster.

6. While the duck is roasting, combine 1 cup of water with 4 tablespoons butter and 1 tablespoon of sugar. Add salt and pepper and bring the water to a boil. Add the peas and lower the heat. Cover the pan and simmer the peas until barely tender (7 or 8 minutes). Drain the peas and keep them warm.

7. Cook the onions in salted water for 5 minutes. Drain them.

8. Heat the remaining 2 tablespoons of butter. Saute the bacon until it is almost crisp. Remove and reserve. Discard all but

2 tablespoons pan fat. Add the onions and the remaining ½ tablespoon sugar. Saute the onions for 5 minutes. Shake the pan to coat them evenly with the butter. Add ½ cup of stock, cover the pan and cook the onions for 10 to 15 minutes. Uncover the pan, add the peas and bacon and cook for 2 or 3 minutes. Place them on an oval serving platter, allowing room for the duck. Keep warm.

9. When the duck is done, cut it into quarters and place them on the serving platter. Pour all the fat from the roasting pan. Add 1½ cups of prepared stock and scrape all the brown particles loose. Strain the sauce into a saucepan and reduce it to 1 cup.

10. Add the optional Beurre Manie or cornstarch mixture if the sauce seems too thin. Cook for 1 or 2 minutes. Pour the sauce over the vegetables and duck. Serve immediately.

Remarks

Most of the steps in this recipe can be finished well in advance. You may make the duck stock the day before, cook the onions in the morning and the final assembly will only take 2 or 3 minutes. Other vegetables such as tiny cooked artichoke hearts can be substituted for the onions. A lovely and unusual combination is peas and asparagus tips.

Notes

Creme de cerises

Serves: 4 to 6
Preparation time: 35 minutes
Cooking time: 15 minutes

Ingredients

2 cups red wine
1 cup sugar
1 tablespoon lemon juice
1 3-inch piece of cinnamon
3 cloves
1½ pounds Bing cherries, pitted

The sauce:
4 egg yolks
½ cup sugar
¼ to ½ teaspoon cinnamon
Pinch of freshly grated nutmeg
¾ cup sweet white wine (sauterne)
1 teaspoon vanilla extract
½ cup heavy cream, whipped

Optional for garnish:
½ cup Macaroon Crumbs (page 401)

Preparation

1. In a large enamel saucepan, combine the red wine, sugar, lemon juice, cinnamon stick and cloves. Bring the mixture to a boil and as soon as the sugar is dissolved, add the cherries.

2. Poach the cherries over low heat for 8 to 10 minutes or until they are tender. Remove the saucepan from the heat and let the cherries cool completely in the wine.

3. To make the sauce: In the top part of an enamel double boiler combine the yolks and sugar. Whisk the mixture until it is pale yellow and smooth.

4. Add the cinnamon, nutmeg and white wine and blend well.

5. Place the pan over simmering water and cook the sauce, whisking constantly for about 5 minutes. Then switch to a spoon and cook until the sauce heavily coats the spoon. Be sure not to let the sauce come to a boil or the yolks will curdle.

6. Remove the sauce from the heat, and add the vanilla. Pour the sauce into a clean bowl and chill.

7. Just before serving fold the whipped cream into the sauce.

8. Drain the cherries and place them in individual fruit bowls. Pour sauce over each bowl and garnish with Macaroon Crumbs.

Notes

Beet and endive salad primavera
Salmon steaks suedoise
Lemon souffle with strawberry sauce

Spring brings to my mind the thought of fresh salmon, an exquisite fish that should be simply prepared and given the opportunity to stand out in your menu. Start off with a crisp Beet and Endive Salad. (You may serve finely sliced prosciutto on the side.) Finish the meal with Lemon Souffle. Together with the Strawberry Sauce, the refreshing taste will be the final complement to your meal.

Beet and endive salad primavera

Serves: 6
Preparation time: 20 minutes
Cooking time: 1 to 1½ hours

Ingredients

2 cups beets, fresh-cooked, cubed
2 cups small new potatoes, cooked until
   barely tender, sliced
⅔ cup Vinaigrette (page 408–409)
Salt and freshly ground black pepper
3 to 4 Belgian endives, cleaned and cut in
   half lengthwise
Juice of ½ lemon

Optional:
4 ounces tuna in olive oil
Rolled filets of anchovies
A platter of finely sliced prosciutto

Garnish:
2 hard-boiled eggs, quartered
Chopped parsley

The dressing:
1 egg yolk
¼ cup Creme Fraiche or sour cream
½ cup Vinaigrette (page 408–409)
¾ cup Mayonnaise (page 402)
1 tablespoon parsley, finely minced
1 tablespoon chives, finely minced
1 teaspoon lemon juice
Salt and freshly ground black pepper

Preparation

1. In a salad bowl combine the beets with
the potatoes. While the vegetables are still
warm pour ½ of the Vinaigrette over them
and season with salt and black pepper.
Chill.

2. Place the endives in a separate salad
bowl and sprinkle with lemon juice.

3. Just before serving add the remaining

Vinaigrette to the endives and toss them
lightly. Arrange the endives around the
beet and potato salad.

4. Garnish with the hard-boiled eggs and
sprinkle the salad with parsley.

5. Top the salad with tuna fish chunks and
anchovy filets or serve a platter of finely
sliced prosciutto and the following sauce
on the side:

The dressing:
1. Place the egg yolk in a small bowl. Add
the Creme Fraiche or sour cream and
whisk the mixture until it is smooth.

2. Add the Vinaigrette a little at a time
until it is completely blended into the egg
and cream mixture.

3. Add the Mayonnaise, parsley and chives.

4. Season with lemon juice, salt and black
pepper and serve well chilled.

Remarks

Watercress or raw mushrooms may be
added to the salad.

Notes

Salmon steaks suedoise

Serves: 6
Preparation time: 25 minutes
Cooking time: 11 minutes

It is hard to keep from combining salmon with dill. It is a perfect "marriage" and therefore I feel there is really no reason to separate these friends.

Ingredients

6 salmon steaks, cut into ¾-inch slices
3 large sprigs of fresh dill
¾ cup olive oil
Juice of 1 lemon
1 teaspoon salt
½ teaspoon white pepper, freshly ground
½ cup melted sweet butter
Additional lemon juice

The sauce:
1 small cucumber, peeled, seeded and cubed
Coarse salt
2 cups Creme Fraiche (page 398)
1 tablespoon scallions, finely minced
3 tablespoons fresh dill, finely minced
1 to 2 tablespoons white vinegar
Salt and freshly ground white pepper

Optional:
1 teaspoon well-drained prepared horseradish

Garnish:
Boiled parslied potatoes

Preparation

1. Preheat the broiler.

2. In a large porcelain, enamel or glass baking dish place the salmon steaks. Bury the dill sprigs among them. (Taste the dill and if its flavor is not strong enough, add 2 or 3 more sprigs.)

3. Mix the olive oil, juice of 1 lemon, salt and pepper in a mixing bowl and pour it over the salmon steaks. Cover well with Saran Wrap and place in the bottom part of the refrigerator. Marinate for 4 hours, turning the fish steaks once.

4. Place the cucumber cubes in a sieve over a bowl and sprinkle with coarse salt. Let them drain for at least 30 minutes.

5. For the sauce combine the Creme Fraiche, scallions, minced dill and the well-drained cucumber in a mixing bowl. Add the optional horseradish and vinegar. The amount of vinegar needed will depend on the sourness of your Creme Fraiche. Season the sauce with salt and pepper and chill.

6. Drain the salmon steaks and dry them thoroughly with paper towels. Put a little of the melted butter in the bottom of a baking dish, place the salmon steaks in the dish and dribble with a little more of the butter.

7. Place the dish about 3 inches from the broiler flame and broil the steaks for 3 minutes, after which dribble the remaining melted butter over them.

8. Broil the fish for 2 or 3 more minutes, then carefully turn the steaks to the other side. Broil for another 5 minutes. Be sure not to overcook the salmon or it will be dry and tasteless.

9. Remove the salmon steaks from the broiler, sprinkle with a little lemon juice and serve garnished with the potatoes and the cold sauce.

Lemon souffle
with strawberry sauce

Serves: 4 to 6
Preparation time: 35 minutes
Cooking time: 15 to 18 minutes

■ ●

In the world of souffles the lemon is king. Its fresh and tangy flavor makes it a year-round favorite. Served with the Strawberry Sauce it is one of the best possible ways to finish a delicious spring meal.

Ingredients

6 egg whites
4 tablespoons butter
4 tablespoons flour
¾ cup milk, hot
Juice of 2 large lemons
½ cup sugar
4 egg yolks
1 teaspoon vanilla extract
1 tablespoon grated lemon rind
Pinch of salt
Powdered sugar
2 cups Strawberry Sauce (page 116)

Preparation

1. Preheat the oven to 450°.

2. Butter a six-cup souffle mold and sprinkle it with sugar, shaking out the excess. Set it aside. Bring the egg whites to room temperature and set aside.

3. In a large heavy-bottomed saucepan heat the butter over low heat. Add the flour and whisk the mixture until the flour and butter are well blended. Add the hot milk all at once and beat the mixture until it is very thick and quite smooth.

4. Add the lemon juice and sugar. Cook this souffle base for 2 or 3 minutes until the sugar is dissolved.

5. Remove the saucepan from the heat. Add the yolks one by one, beating to in-corporate each one completely before adding the next. Add the vanilla extract and the lemon rind. Return the saucepan to the stove and reheat the souffle base over very low heat until a very light steam rises from the mixture. Immediately take the saucepan off the heat and set aside.

6. Add a pinch of salt to the egg whites and beat them with a wire whisk until they form soft peaks.

7. Add a little of the beaten egg whites to the souffle base and gently fold them in. Pour this mixture into the egg whites, using your hands to fold it in.

8. Pour the souffle mixture into the souffle mold and set in the middle part of the oven. Cook the souffle for 12 to 15 minutes. Serve immediately sprinkled with powdered sugar and serve the cold Strawberry Sauce on the side.

Remarks

For a variation, make the sauce with fresh raspberries and decorate the souffle with some choice berries.

Notes

Marinated mackerel

Serves: 6
Preparation time: 25 minutes
Cooking time: 45 to 50 minutes

This is an excellent spring and summer appetizer. It can be made one or two days in advance and can be part of your hors d'oeuvre table. You can serve it for lunch together with one or two hors d'oeuvre salads. Mackerel is an oily full-bodied fish that is excellent either hot or cold. Use the smallest mackerel you can find and always choose Boston—not Spanish—mackerel.

Ingredients

6   small whole mackerel or 3 large ones, fileted
Salt and freshly ground white pepper
2   tablespoons olive oil
2   medium-sized onions, finely sliced
2   carrots, finely sliced
1/3 cup white wine vinegar
1/3 cup white wine
3/4 cup water
1   large Bouquet Garni (page 397)
10 peppercorns
2   bay leaves
1/2 teaspoon celery seeds
3   garlic cloves, whole
Dash of Tabasco
Juice of 1 large lemon

Garnish:
4 to 6 lemon wedges
Black olives
2   tablespoons minced parsley

Preparation

1. Preheat oven to 350°.

2. Wash the mackerel under cold running water, leaving the heads on. Season with salt and pepper.

3. In a saucepan heat the olive oil. Add the onions and carrots and cook them, covered, for 3 to 5 minutes without browning.

4. Add the vinegar, wine, water, Bouquet Garni, peppercorns, bay leaves, celery seeds and garlic. Bring the bouillon to a boil, then simmer partially covered for 20 minutes.

5. Place the mackerel in a large enamel or stainless steel baking dish and pour the bouillon over them. Cover the baking dish with buttered wax paper and place in a 350° oven for 20 to 25 minutes. Do not overcook the fish. Test it with a fork and, if it flakes easily, it is done. Remove from the oven.

6. Let the fish cool in the bouillon at room temperature. Add a dash of Tabasco and then place in the refrigerator, covered, for at least 12 hours before serving.

7. Remove fish to serving plates just before serving. Sprinkle with fresh lemon juice and spoon the bouillon over the fish. Garnish with lemon wedges, olives and parsley.

Notes

Salmon trout bellevue

Serves: 4 to 6
Preparation time: 35 minutes
Cooking time: 1 hour 10 minutes

The salmon trout is one of the most delicate of spring fish and this recipe brings out its full flavor. If you cannot get salmon trout, use a small whole fresh salmon. (Most salmon recipes can be used to prepare salmon trout and the fish should always be used whole.) Serve it with tiny boiled potato balls sprinkled with dill or serve it simply with buttered asparagus.

Ingredients

1½ cups heavy cream
Juice of 1 large lemon
2   pounds fish trimmings (preferably lean white fish)
2   cups dry white wine
2   cups water
1   large Bouquet Garni (page 397)
6   peppercorns
1   whole onion, stuck with 2 cloves
1   carrot
Salt
1   4-pound salmon trout, whole and cleaned, with head on
Freshly ground white pepper
4   tablespoons sweet butter
4   shallots, finely minced

Garnish:
Lemon wedges, quartered
Watercress

Preparation

1. Preheat oven to 375°.

2. In a bowl mix the heavy cream with the lemon juice and let it stand at room temperature for 2 or 3 hours.

3. In a large casserole, place the fish trimmings, wine, water, bouquet, pepper-corns, onion, carrot and salt. Simmer uncovered for 35 minutes. Strain this stock and reserve 2 cups. Return them to the casserole and reduce to 1 cup. Set aside and keep warm.

4. Season the fish with salt and pepper.

5. In a large baking dish, melt butter. Add the shallots and place the fish on top of them in the dish.

6. Add the reduced stock. Cover the dish with buttered wax paper. Place the fish in the oven and cook for about 35 minutes. Test with a fork for doneness. The fish should flake easily. Remove it to a serving platter.

7. Strain the pan juices and return them to the pan together with the lemon cream. Cook the sauce over high heat until it is thick and creamy and heavily coats a spoon. Correct the seasoning and pour the sauce over the fish.

8. Garnish with lemon wedges and watercress. Serve immediately.

Remarks

Before spooning the sauce over the fish, dry the platter around it with paper towels. If there is any liquid left on the plate, it will thin the sauce. The stock can be made a day in advance and kept in the refrigerator. The trout should be served as soon as it is cooked and it is best to use it as an appetizer. If you wish to serve it as a main course, however, you can keep the dish warm over a pan of simmering water for a short while.

Cold artichoke bottoms with salmon mousse

Serves: 6
Preparation time: 45 minutes to 1 hour
Cooking time: 45 minutes

■ ◔

Here is a dish that calls on your supply of leftover poached salmon. It is an elegant and simple-to-prepare appetizer, but the right ingredients are a must. If you do not have leftover cooked salmon, turn to page 93 for information on how to poach a small piece. If canned artichoke bottoms and canned salmon are substituted, the dish will be a far cry from the "real thing."

Ingredients

The artichoke bottoms:
6   very large artichokes or 12 medium ones
2   tablespoons flour
½ lemon plus 1 tablespoon lemon juice
4   cups cold water
Salt
¾ cup Lemon Vinaigrette (page 408)

The salmon mousse:
2   cups flaked, poached salmon (page 93)
3   tablespoons Mayonnaise (page 402)
Salt and freshly ground white pepper
Pinch of cayenne pepper
1 to 2 teaspoons lemon juice
1   tablespoon finely minced fresh dill

Optional:
3   tablespoons Creme Fraiche (page 398)
     or whipped cream

Garnish:
Sprinkle of paprika
A few large capers
Dill sprigs
Black olives

Preparation

1. Cut the stems off the artichokes as close to the base as possible. Remove the first few layers of outer leaves. When the leaves become light green and bend forward, cut them off with a sharp knife close to the base. Rub the cut parts immediately with the cut side of ½ lemon.

2. In a large enamel saucepan combine the flour, 1 tablespoon lemon juice and water.

3. Bring the mixture to a boil, add a pinch of salt and the artichoke bottoms. Cook them for 20 to 30 minutes or until tender. Do not overcook. Cool them and dry well on paper towels. As soon as they are cool enough to handle, remove the choke with a grapefruit spoon and trim the artichoke bottoms with a sharp knife.

4. Make a Lemon Vinaigrette and pour it over the artichoke bottoms. Cover the bowl and let the bottoms marinate for 2 hours.

5. Puree the salmon in a blender or put it through the fine blade of a meat grinder.

6. Add the mayonnaise, salt, white pepper, a touch of cayenne, lemon juice and dill. Chill the mixture for 1 hour. If it seems too thick, thin it out with a little Creme Fraiche or whipped cream. The mixture must be quite thick in order to stay on the artichoke bottoms.

7. Drain the artichoke bottoms and dry well on paper towels. Top each one with a dome of salmon mousse.

8. Sprinkle lightly with paprika. Make a little circle of capers on each dome and top each one with 2 tiny sprigs of dill and a black olive. Chill again and serve cold with buttered pumpernickel.

Mushrooms a l'italienne

Serves: 4
Preparation time: 20 minutes
Cooking time: 30 minutes

Here is a simple appetizer that takes only minutes to prepare and for which the small button mushrooms are perfect. Garnish the dish with sauteed French bread slices or serve the mushrooms as an accompaniment to an omelette or poached eggs.

Ingredients

6 tablespoons sweet butter, softened
2 to 4 anchovies, rinsed and mashed
2 large garlic cloves, mashed
4 tablespoons chopped parsley
1 cup Brown Stock or Beef Stock
    (pages 403, 405)
1½ pounds button mushrooms (reserve
    stems for stock)
2 tablespoons sweet butter
1 tablespoon oil
Salt and freshly ground black pepper
Juice of 1 lemon

Optional:
1 tablespoon minced fresh chives

Preparation

1. Preheat oven to 350°.

2. In a bowl combine the softened butter, anchovies, garlic, 2 tablespoons of parsley and chives (if used). Chill the mixture for 30 minutes or until it is firm.

3. In a 1-quart saucepan combine the Brown Stock with some of the mushroom stems. Let the mixture simmer for 20 to 30 minutes or until the stock is reduced by ⅓. Strain the stock, pressing down on the stems to extract all their juice, and reserve.

4. Wipe mushrooms with damp paper towels. In a large skillet, heat the 2 tablespoons of butter and the oil. When the mixture is very hot, add a few mushrooms at a time. Do not crowd the pan. Cook the mushrooms over high heat, shaking the pan to brown them evenly. Transfer these mushrooms to a large buttered baking dish. Add more mushrooms to the skillet and continue sauteeing them, adding a little more butter if necessary.

5. When all the mushrooms have been browned, add the stock to the skillet. Bring it to a boil and cook over high heat until it is reduced to ⅓ cup. Pour the stock over the mushrooms.

6. Cut the anchovy and herb butter into tiny pieces and sprinkle them over the mushrooms. Sprinkle the mushrooms with salt, pepper and lemon juice.

7. Place baking dish in the oven until the mushrooms are hot and the butter melted and bubbly.

8. Serve garnished with the remaining parsley and thin slices of French bread sauteed in Clarified Butter (page 398) or olive oil.

Notes

Peas a la venetienne

Serves: 4 to 6
Preparation time: 30 minutes
Cooking time: 12 to 15 minutes

Fresh peas are one of my favorite vegetables. When they are young, they are sweet and tender, requiring only a few minutes of cooking.
This is a lovely spring dish. The peas are not presented in their usual role as accompaniment to a main course but are introduced as an appetizer or a simple supper. For supper you may serve a good homemade pate as an appetizer and for dessert a tray of cheese with a seasonal fruit.

Ingredients

3 pounds fresh peas, shelled
Salt
1 pound small shrimp
4 tablespoons sweet butter
4 finely minced shallots (2 tablespoons)
1 cup cubed prosciutto (use ¼-inch-thick slices for cubing)
Freshly ground white pepper

Optional:
1 to 2 teaspoons sugar

Garnish:
Chopped parsley and grated Parmesan cheese

Preparation

1. In a large saucepan, bring 4 cups of salted water to boil. Add the peas and simmer uncovered for 5 to 7 minutes or until barely tender. (If you are using large peas, add a little sugar to the water.) Drain the peas and run them under cold water. This stops the cooking and retains the color.

2. In a 2-quart saucepan bring salted water to a boil. Add the shrimp and when the water returns to a boil, cook them for 3 to 5 minutes. The shrimp should be pink. Run them immediately under cold water and peel.

3. In a large skillet melt the butter and add the shallots. Cook for 2 or 3 minutes until tender but not browned. Add the shrimp and shake the pan to coat them evenly with the butter. Add the peas and the prosciutto and heat through.

4. Correct the seasoning. Sprinkle with parsley and serve immediately with a bowl of Parmesan cheese on the side.

Notes

Crepes primavera

Serves: 6 to 8
Preparation time: 45 minutes
Cooking time: 45 minutes

Spinach crepes add an interesting touch to the spring table. Serve them either as an appetizer or unfilled and folded into triangles as an accompaniment to a roast or veal scallops.

Ingredients

The batter:
2 cups fresh spinach
2 cups milk
1½ cups sifted flour
3 whole eggs
Pinch of salt
Pinch of nutmeg
3 tablespoons melted sweet butter

The filling:
2 tablespoons sweet butter
1 pound fresh mushrooms, cleaned and finely minced
2 shallots, finely minced
¼ cup Creme Fraiche (page 398)
Salt and freshly ground white pepper
½ cup finely minced prosciutto or Westphalian ham

The topping:
2 tablespoons sweet butter
1½ cups heavy cream
4 tablespoons finely grated fresh Parmesan cheese

Preparation

1. Preheat the oven to 350°.

2. Place the well-washed spinach in a saucepan and cook over high heat until it is completely wilted. Drain. When cool enough to handle, squeeze it into a small ball.

3. Mince the spinach ball finely and place it in the top part of a blender with a little milk. Puree it until completely smooth.

4. Add the rest of the batter ingredients and let the mixture relax for 2 hours.

5. Make the crepes as described on page 400. Reserve 12 to 14 crepes and freeze the rest.

6. To make the filling, in a skillet heat 2 tablespoons of butter. Add the mushrooms and shallots and cook the mixture over high heat until all the juice has evaporated.

7. Add the Creme Fraiche, salt and pepper and continue cooking until the mixture is very thick.

8. Puree the mixture in a blender or pass it through a food mill.

9. Add the prosciutto. Correct the seasoning and reserve.

10. For the topping, melt the 2 tablespoons of butter in a heavy 10-inch skillet. Add the cream and cook over high heat until it is reduced to 1 cup. Season lightly with salt and pepper and reserve.

11. Fill the crepes with the mushroom mixture, roll them up, and place them in a buttered baking dish. Pour the topping over them and sprinkle with Parmesan.

12. Bake the crepes for 20 to 30 minutes or until the cheese is melted and the sauce is hot and bubbly. Serve immediately.

Cold baked tomatoes

Serves: 6
Preparation time: 25 minutes
Cooking time: 20 minutes

Baked tomatoes are equally good warm or cold. They can be filled with a variety of fillings such as spinach, sorrel or mushrooms.

Ingredients

6 medium-sized tomatoes
Salt
¼ pound fresh mushrooms
½ cup olive oil
2 tablespoons finely chopped green onions
2 tablespoons finely chopped parsley
½ cup bread crumbs (unflavored)
1 tablespoon finely minced chives
Freshly ground black pepper
Large pinch of oregano

Preparation

1. Wash the tomatoes, cut off their tops, gently scoop out the center flesh and discard the seeds. Sprinkle the tomato "shells" with salt and turn them upside down on a plate to drain.

2. Wipe the mushrooms with paper towels and mince them finely. You may include the stems if they are perfectly fresh and white.

3. Heat 4 tablespoons of olive oil in a heavy skillet. Add the finely diced mushrooms and green onions. Cook for 3 to 5 minutes until the mushrooms are soft and lightly browned.

4. Add the parsley, bread crumbs, chives and seasoning and blend the mixture thoroughly. Remove from the heat. If the mixture seems too dry, add a little finely diced tomato pulp.

5. Fill the tomato shells with the mushroom mixture. Arrange the tomatoes in an oiled baking dish and dribble a little of the remaining olive oil over each one. Bake the tomatoes for 10 to 15 minutes and serve either warm or cool.

Remarks

These tomatoes can be served as an appetizer or as an accompaniment to a roast or grilled fish.
To serve the tomatoes cold let them stand in a cool place until serving time. Avoid refrigerating.

Notes

Cold stuffed zucchini

Serves: 3 to 6
Preparation time: 15 minutes
Cooking time: 5 to 8 minutes

This is an unpretentious little appetizer that is attractive and delicious. When growing your own zucchini, you will find yourself in great need of recipes that call for this vegetable. Be inventive and fill zucchini boats with other fillings such as Rice Salad.

Ingredients

3 medium-sized zucchini
Lemon juice
Olive oil
4 tablespoons tuna fish in olive oil
½ cup finely sliced black Greek olives
1½ cups Mayonnaise (page 402)
1 tablespoon tiny well-drained capers
1 garlic clove, mashed
2 teaspoons anchovy paste or 2 anchovy filets, finely minced
Salt and freshly ground black pepper

Garnish:
1 small red onion, finely sliced
2 tablespoons minced parsley
2 tablespoons minced pimientos

Preparation

1. Drop the zucchini into fast-boiling water and poach them for 5 to 8 minutes. Drain them and cut them in half lengthwise. Carefully scoop out the seeds without breaking the shell. Sprinkle the zucchini with a little lemon juice and olive oil.

2. In a mixing bowl mash the tuna fish, adding a dash of lemon juice, the olives and 1 tablespoon of mayonnaise.

3. Fill the zucchini boats with the tuna fish mixture.

4. In a mixing bowl combine the remaining mayonnaise, capers, garlic and anchovy paste. Taste and season with salt and pepper.

5. Pour the mayonnaise mixture over the zucchini boats and place a row of red onion slices along each zucchini. Sprinkle with parsley and pimientos and chill until serving time.

Remarks

Finely flaked crabmeat or leftover poached salmon can be substituted for the tuna. The platter can be garnished with quartered hard-boiled eggs, whole cherry tomatoes, radishes and on and on and on. . . .

Notes

Spring cream of curried asparagus soup

Serves: 4 to 6
Preparation time: 20 minutes
Cooking time: 50 minutes to 1 hour

■ ○

A simple yet marvelous way to mark the change of the seasons in your menu is with the preparation of soups. These can be as important as any other elaborate first course. For a great soup you must use good homemade stock. Once you have the "soup base," which can be refrigerated or frozen for several weeks, you may vary the seasonal vegetables used to flavor the soup.

Ingredients

1 pound fresh asparagus
5 cups Chicken Stock (page 404)
Salt
4 tablespoons sweet butter
4 tablespoons flour
1 to 2 teaspoons curry powder
¾ cup heavy cream
Freshly ground white pepper
3 egg yolks
Dash of lemon juice

Preparation

1. Remove the woody ends from the asparagus stalks. Clean the stalks with a vegetable peeler, cut off the tips and reserve.

2. Place the Chicken Stock and asparagus stalks in a 3-quart casserole. Bring the stock to a boil, reduce the heat and simmer covered for 40 to 45 minutes.

3. While the soup is simmering, drop the asparagus tips into fast-boiling lightly salted water and cook them for 3 to 5 minutes or until tender. Drain and reserve.

4. Puree the stock and asparagus stalks in the blender and reserve. Keep warm.

5. In a heavy-bottomed saucepan melt the butter, add the flour and cook for 2 minutes without letting it brown.

6. Add the pureed stock all at once and bring the soup to a boil. Cook over low heat until it thickens and lightly coats a spoon.

7. Mix the curry powder with a little cream in a small mixing bowl and add it to the soup together with the asparagus tips. Taste for seasoning, adding salt and pepper as needed.

8. Just before serving, mix the remaining cream and egg yolks in a small bowl and add the mixture to the soup with a dash of lemon juice. Reheat the soup without letting it come to a boil and serve it very hot.

Remarks

The soup can be kept hot in the top part of a double boiler.
For a variation, omit the curry and add 2 tablespoons of finely minced fresh herbs, such as chives, chervil or dill.

Notes

Potage vert pre

Serves: 4 to 6
Preparation time: 15 minutes
Cooking time: 50 minutes to 1 hour

A soup that can be served either hot or cold is an important part of any cook's repertory. Hot soups are perfect for elegant entertaining and cold ones can be served at lunch or supper. This is a most versatile soup. You may add diced cooked shrimp to the cold soup and with the addition of 1 tablespoon of finely minced fresh herbs you will enjoy an early touch of summer.

Ingredients

3   tablespoons sweet butter
½ cup finely minced scallions
3   tablespoons flour
4   cups fresh peas
1   cup fresh spinach leaves, washed
1   head Boston lettuce, shredded
1   tablespoon sugar
6   cups Chicken Stock (page 404)
Salt
1   cup heavy cream
3   egg yolks
Freshly ground white pepper

Optional:
1   tablespoon minced fresh mint

Preparation

1. In a large casserole melt the butter over medium heat. Add the scallions and cook until tender (about 5 minutes) without letting them brown. Add the flour and continue cooking over low heat for 2 or 3 minutes.

2. Add 3 cups of peas, spinach leaves, lettuce and sugar. Cover the vegetables with the Chicken Stock and bring to a boil. Reduce the heat, cover the casserole and cook the soup for 45 to 50 minutes.

3. In the meantime, put the remaining peas in a small saucepan with water to cover. Season with a pinch of salt and cook until barely tender. Drain them immediately and reserve.

4. Puree the soup in a blender or pass it through a food mill. Return to the casserole over low heat.

5. In a bowl mix the cream and egg yolks. Add this mixture to the soup without letting it come to a boil or the yolks will curdle.

6. Add the whole peas, pepper and optional mint to the soup and serve.

Remarks

If the soup is to be served cold, it may need thinning out with additional cream or milk. Soups that have been thickened with yolks and cream cannot be brought to a boil. Keep this soup warm over simmering water.
When you make the Chicken Stock, reserve one breast of chicken. Cut it into fine julienne strips and garnish each bowl of soup with a few strips. This makes a lovely change. Serve the soup with thin slices of pumpernickel or black bread and a bowl of sweet butter.

Notes

Viennese cream of chicken soup

Serves: 6
Preparation time: 40 minutes
Cooking time: 25 minutes

■ ●

Here is a velvety soup that is a far cry from the pasty one restaurants so often serve as "cream of chicken." The soup must be made with a well-flavored chicken stock. When you make the soup at other times of the year, you may add or substitute other finely diced fresh vegetables, such as cubed avocados, carrots or celery.

Ingredients

3   chicken livers
6   tablespoons sweet butter
Salt and freshly ground white pepper
¼ pound fresh mushrooms, cubed
½ cup water
1 or 2 teaspoons lemon juice
1   cup very fresh tiny peas
Large pinch of sugar
4   tablespoons flour
6   cups warm Chicken Stock (page 404)
2   egg yolks
¾ cup heavy cream
Freshly ground black pepper
Dash of white pepper

Preparation

1. Clean the chicken livers very carefully, removing all dark and green spots. Dice the livers.

2. In a small skillet melt 2 tablespoons of butter. Add the chicken livers and saute them over high heat until they are lightly browned. Season with salt and pepper and place on paper towels to drain.

3. Wipe the mushrooms well with paper towels and remove the stems. (Reserve these for stock.) Combine the mushrooms with ½ cup of water, 1 teaspoon of lemon juice, salt and pepper in a small saucepan

and poach them for 3 to 5 minutes, partially covered. Let the mushrooms cool in the poaching liquid.

4. Cook the peas for 3 to 5 minutes in a small saucepan with water to cover and the sugar. Do not overcook them. Drain and reserve.

5. In a large heavy saucepan melt the remaining butter. Add the flour and stir for 2 or 3 minutes without browning. Add the Chicken Stock all at once and cook the soup until it is lightly thickened.

6. While the soup is cooking, combine the egg yolks with the cream in a small bowl.

7. Drain the mushrooms and add them to the soup along with the chicken livers and peas. Reserve the poaching liquid.

8. Whisk in the cream and egg yolk mixture. Do not let the soup come to a boil. Taste for seasoning and add a little more lemon juice and a good dash of white pepper. Serve hot with crusty French bread.

Remarks

If the soup gets very thick, beat in the mushroom poaching liquid. Be sure to include some peas, mushrooms and chicken livers in each individual serving.

Notes

Fried eggs a l'espagnole

Serves: 4
Preparation time: 25 minutes
Cooking time: 30 to 40 minutes

Ingredients

7 tablespoons olive oil
2 tablespoons finely minced shallots
1 small minced onion
2 large garlic cloves, finely minced
1 red pepper, roasted, peeled, seeded and chopped, or ½ cup minced pimientos
1 green pepper, roasted, peeled, seeded and chopped
1 cup finely cubed prosciutto
6 large tomatoes, peeled, seeded and chopped
Salt and freshly ground black pepper
1 small crumbled bay leaf
2 cups finely sliced Chorizo (Spanish sausage) or Italian spicy sausage
8 large eggs
12 thin asparagus stalks, cooked until barely tender
1 cup fresh peas, cooked until just tender

Garnish:
Finely minced parsley
Pimiento strips

Preparation

1. Preheat oven to 375°.

2. Oil a large baking dish with 3 tablespoons of olive oil.

3. In a heavy skillet heat the remaining olive oil.

4. Add the shallots, onion and garlic and cook over medium heat until soft but not browned.

5. Add the peppers and prosciutto and simmer the mixture for 5 more minutes.

6. Add the tomatoes, salt, pepper and bay leaf. Partially cover the skillet and cook the mixture until it is reduced to a thick puree.

7. Add the sausage and heat it through.

8. Pour the puree into the baking dish. Spread the mixture and make 8 "pockets" in it.

9. Break an egg into each "pocket" and place the dish in the oven.

10. Bake the eggs until they are almost set, then remove the dish from the oven.

11. Place the asparagus stalks in the dish in a decorative crisscross pattern.

12. Surround the eggs with the cooked peas and return the dish to the oven.

13. When the eggs are done, sprinkle them with minced parsley and decorate the asparagus stalks with strips of pimientos. Serve immediately with crusty bread and sweet butter.

Notes

Poached eggs escona

Serves: 6
Preparation time: 45 minutes
Cooking time: 20 minutes

Every season brings with it some vegetables that can be used in purees—winter broccoli, spring asparagus, summer green beans, for example. Purees are a wonderful accompaniment to roasts, grilled meats and fish. They also offer a fine way to use a vegetable when it is not at its best either at the beginning or end of a season.

Ingredients

2 cups water
Salt
1 tablespoon sugar
3 pounds fresh peas, shelled
8 tablespoons sweet butter, softened
6 tablespoons flour
Freshly ground white pepper
6 eggs at room temperature
2 cups warm milk
Dash of nutmeg
Dash of cayenne
½ cup grated Swiss or Gruyere cheese

Optional:
3 tablespoons heavy cream or Creme
   Fraiche (page 398)

Preparation

1. In a saucepan bring to a boil 2 cups of water with 1½ teaspoons salt and 1 tablespoon sugar. Add the peas and simmer gently until they are barely tender. Drain very well.

2. Put the peas through a food mill or an electric blender.

3. In a heavy-bottomed 2-quart saucepan, melt 3 tablespoons of butter. Add 3 tablespoons of flour and cook slowly until it turns chestnut brown. Do not burn it.

4. Add the pea puree to the flour mixture and mix well. Season with salt and pepper. Add 2 more tablespoons of butter and beat in the cream if used.

5. Spread the puree in an oval au gratin dish large enough to hold the eggs in one layer.

6. Bring salted water to a boil in a large casserole. Carefully add 6 large eggs one at a time and cook slowly for 6 minutes. Run them under cold water immediately and peel carefully. Place the whole eggs on the puree of peas and coat with the following sauce:

7. In a heavy-bottomed saucepan melt the 3 tablespoons of butter over low heat. Add 3 tablespoons of flour and cook slowly, stirring constantly for 2 or 3 minutes without letting it brown.

8. Add the milk all at once, beating constantly to blend with the flour. The sauce will thicken considerably. If it gets too thick, thin it out with a little milk. Remove from the heat and season to taste with salt, pepper, nutmeg and cayenne.

9. Add all but 2 tablespoons of the cheese and blend until it is melted. Pour this sauce over the eggs. Sprinkle with the remaining grated cheese.

10. Place the dish under a very hot broiler and brown. Serve immediately.

Remarks

If your sauce is lumpy, pass it through a fine sieve or blend it in the blender at high speed. This sauce can be made in advance. If it is not to be used right away, cover it.

Rice a la catalane

Serves: 6
Preparation time: 35 minutes
Cooking time: 1 hour 30 minutes

Northern Spain and Italy make good use of rice as an appetizer or as a simple main course. This rice, accompanied by fried eggs with a well-seasoned tomato sauce on the side, is often served as a hot lunch or supper dish.

Ingredients

1 pound spareribs, cut into small pieces
Salt and freshly ground white pepper
3 tablespoons olive oil
6 small pork sausages
2 large garlic cloves, minced
1 large onion, finely minced
2 red peppers, charred, peeled and diced
4 large ripe tomatoes, peeled, seeded and chopped
Pinch of cayenne and of saffron
1½ cups raw rice (not converted)
3 cups White Stock (page 405) or water
2 tablespoons sweet butter
¼ pound fresh mushrooms, cubed

Garnish:
Pimiento strips
Hard-boiled eggs, quartered

Preparation

1. Preheat the oven to 350°.

2. Season the spareribs with salt and pepper.

3. Heat the olive oil in a large heavy casserole. Add the spareribs and brown them on all sides over medium heat so as not to burn the oil. Remove the spareribs from the casserole and reserve.

4. Quickly brown the sausages in the pan fat until they are nice and crisp. Remove the sausages and reserve. Discard all but 2 tablespoons of fat from the pan.

5. Add the garlic and onion to the pan and cook until lightly browned but not burnt.

6. Add the peppers and tomatoes, salt, pepper and cayenne. Return the spareribs to the casserole, cover the pan and cook the mixture over low heat for 45 to 50 minutes.

7. Uncover the casserole and cook the mixture for 10 more minutes.

8. In the meantime wash the rice thoroughly and drain.

9. Add the rice to the casserole together with the saffron and a good pinch of salt. Cover with White Stock or water. Bring to a boil, cover the casserole and place in the oven. Bake the rice without stirring for 25 minutes.

10. While the rice is baking, melt the butter in a small skillet. Add the mushrooms and cook them for 3 minutes until they are evenly browned. Season with salt and pepper. Uncover the rice and add the mushrooms, peas and beans if desired. Toss the vegetables with the rice, using two forks. If the rice is not tender and the liquid has not completely evaporated, bake the rice uncovered for 5 to 10 more minutes.

12. In the last few minutes add the sausages to the casserole and heat them through.

13. Remove the rice from the oven, garnish with hard-boiled eggs and pimiento strips and serve directly from the casserole.

Spaghettini primavera

Serves: 4 to 6
Preparation time: 30 minutes
Cooking time: 30 minutes

In springtime, in homes and little restaurants where this dish is popular, individual portions of spaghetti are served simply buttered, then topped with 2 or 3 tablespoons of the peas, prosciutto and mushroom mixture, which each person mixes into his own spaghetti.

Ingredients

1 pound thin spaghetti (Ronzoni No. 9)
Salt
10 tablespoons sweet butter
1½ pounds fresh peas
1 whole onion
Pinch of sugar
1 cup finely diced prosciutto
½ pound mushrooms, cubed
Freshly ground black pepper
1 cup freshly grated Parmesan cheese

Preparation

1. In a large casserole, bring 3 quarts of salted water to a boil. Add the spaghetti and cook over high heat for 8 to 10 minutes, stirring occasionally to prevent it from sticking to the bottom of the casserole.

2. While the spaghetti is cooking, melt 6 tablespoons of butter in a skillet. Add the peas and the onion and season with a pinch of salt and sugar. Cover the skillet and cook the peas over low heat for 10 minutes or until they are almost tender.

3. Add the prosciutto and heat it through.

4. In another small skillet heat 2 tablespoons of butter. Add the mushrooms and cook them over high heat until they are browned. Season with salt and pepper and add them to the peas and prosciutto mixture.

5. As soon as the spaghetti is cooked (be sure not to overcook it), drain and run under cold water. Return the spaghetti to the casserole. Add the remaining butter. Discard the onion and pour the peas, prosciutto and mushroom mixture over the spaghetti.

6. Season with additional black pepper and ½ cup of the grated Parmesan. Serve the remaining Parmesan on the side.

Notes

Poulet fontainebleau

Serves: 4
Preparation time: 25 minutes
Cooking time: 1 hour 30 minutes

Spring can be brought to the table by the presentation of the simplest of dishes, such as a well-roasted chicken served on a bed of peas and sauteed cherry tomatoes. At any other time of the year, be inventive and serve the chicken with a garniture of the freshest seasonal vegetables.

Ingredients

1 whole roasting chicken (3 to 3½ pounds)
Salt and freshly ground white pepper
1 teaspoon paprika
1 teaspoon dried marjoram
1 garlic clove, mashed
1 teaspoon Dijon mustard
10 tablespoons sweet butter
1 large carrot, finely diced
1 large onion, finely diced
1 celery stalk, finely diced
2 cups Chicken Stock (page 404)
1 to 2 tablespoons sugar
2 pounds fresh peas
½ cup heavy cream
1 Beurre Manie (page 397)
3 tablespoons olive oil

Garnish:
1 pint sauteed cherry tomatoes

Preparation

1. Preheat oven to 400°. Season the chicken's cavity with salt and pepper.

2. Truss the chicken. Dry it thoroughly with paper towels and season with salt, pepper and paprika. Sprinkle with marjoram and rub the skin with garlic and mustard.

3. In a large oval baking dish, melt 4 tablespoons butter and add the finely diced

vegetables. Place the chicken on its side in the baking dish and set the dish in the oven. Allow the chicken to brown lightly for about 10 minutes. Reduce the heat to 375° and baste the chicken with a little hot stock about every 10 minutes. After 35 minutes turn the chicken on the other side and continue basting. The chicken is done when the juices run pale yellow when pierced with a fork (1 hour and 20 minutes to 1 hour and 30 minutes).

4. While the chicken is roasting, heat 2 tablespoons of butter in a heavy saucepan and add the sugar and the peas. Cook for 2 or 3 minutes until the peas are well coated with butter and the sugar is dissolved. Add ½ cup of boiling water, cover the saucepan and cook the peas for 8 to immediately under cold water. Place them on a large serving platter. Keep warm.

5. Remove the chicken from the baking dish. Cut away the trussing string and place the chicken on the bed of peas.

6. Add remaining stock to the baking dish and scrape loose any brown particles that may have stuck to the bottom. Strain into small saucepan. Add the cream and reduce the sauce by ⅓ over high heat.

7. Slowly whisk bits of Beurre Manie into the sauce. It should lightly coat a spoon. Correct seasoning. Off the heat, beat in the remaining butter.

8. Coat the chicken with a little of the sauce and reserve the rest to be served on the side in a sauceboat. Surround the platter with sauteed cherry tomatoes and serve immediately.

Roast squab
a la danoise

Serves: 4
Preparation time: 15 to 20 minutes
Cooking time: 55 minutes

■●

Squabs are delicious little birds,
but they must never be overcooked as the
meat is lean and easily becomes dry. A
slightly soured cream sauce flavored with
chives or dill gives squabs an elegant
touch.

Ingredients

4 small whole squabs
Salt and freshly ground white pepper
Pinch of rosemary
2½ tablespoons lemon juice
12 tablespoons sweet butter
4 small whole onions
1 tablespoon oil
8 slices of blanched bacon
1 to 1½ cups Brown Chicken Stock (page
    404)
2 tablespoons finely minced shallots
½ cup dry white wine
1 cup Creme Fraiche (page 398)
1 pound button mushrooms
2 tablespoons finely minced parsley
2 tablespoons minced dill or chives

Optional:
1 Beurre Manie (page 397)

Garnish:
Sprigs of fresh watercress

Preparation

1. Preheat the oven to 350°.

2. Dry the squabs thoroughly with paper
towels. Season with salt, pepper, rosemary,
2 tablespoons lemon juice. Place 1 tablespoon of butter and 1 whole onion in the
cavity of each squab.

3. Heat 2 tablespoons butter and the oil
in a large flameproof baking dish and
brown the squabs on all sides over medium
heat.

4. Place 2 slices of bacon on the breast of
each squab and tie it with kitchen string.

5. Place the squabs on their sides in the
baking dish and pour a little of the stock
around them. Cover the dish with foil and
set in the oven. Braise the birds for 50
minutes. During roasting time, baste them
with the pan juices, adding a little more
stock if necessary.

6. While the squabs are roasting, heat 2
tablespoons of butter in a small saucepan.
Add the shallots and cook until they are
soft, but not browned.

7. Add the wine, bring it to a boil and cook
it over high heat until it is reduced to 2
tablespoons.

8. Add the Creme Fraiche and cook until
the mixture is reduced by ⅓. Season with
salt and pepper. Strain and reserve.

9. Wipe the mushrooms with a damp paper
towel. Do not wash.

10. Heat the remaining butter in a large
skillet and add the mushrooms. Do not
crowd the pan. The mushrooms should not
steam but brown very quickly. Shake the
pan to cover the mushrooms with the
butter.

11. Season the mushrooms with salt and
pepper, sprinkle with parsley and reserve.

12. When the squabs are done, remove the
bacon, take the onions from the cavities
and place the squabs on a serving platter.

13. Degrease the pan juice and add any
remaining stock to the pan. Place over high

heat and reduce the pan juices to 1 cup. The sauce should lightly coat a spoon.

14. Add the Creme Fraiche mixture and the dill or chives and 1 teaspoon of lemon juice. Heat the sauce and correct seasoning. Add the optional Beurre Manie if the sauce seems too thin.

15. Pour the sauce into a sauceboat and serve on the side. Surround the squabs with the sauteed mushrooms, garnish the platter with watercress and serve.

Remarks

If you like the squabs crisp, braise them for only 40 minutes and for the last few minutes run them under a hot broiler, turning them once.

Notes

Lamb chops
a la catalane

Serves: 4
Preparation time: 35 minutes
Cooking time: 25 to 30 minutes

■ ◑

Come spring, many Spaniards take to the hills for an outdoor picnic. The most popular meal is still the paella made on a wood fire, but tender young chops of spring lamb broiled on a wood fire are a close second. The sauce is usually brought along in a large jar, reheated on the fire and poured over the grilled chops. Each cook has her own version of this sauce. . . . Here is one of my favorites.

Ingredients

8 rib lamb chops, cut 1 inch thick
Salt and freshly ground white pepper
2 garlic cloves, mashed
1 cup diced smoked bacon, blanched and drained
2 tablespoons olive oil
1 tablespoon minced shallots
1 large garlic clove, minced
1 tablespoon tomato paste
6 large ripe tomatoes peeled, seeded and finely chopped
Pinch of thyme
Pinch of oregano
½ teaspoon saffron
1 bay leaf
4 tablespoons sweet butter
12 small white onions
1 teaspoon sugar
1 cup Brown Stock (page 403)
½ pound fresh mushrooms, quartered
1 teaspoon lemon juice
Freshly ground black pepper

Optional:
1 cup fresh peas cooked until barely tender

Garnish:
Sprigs of fresh parsley

Preparation

1. Season the chops with salt and pepper and rub with mashed garlic. Reserve.

2. Drop the bacon into boiling water and cook for 5 minutes. Drain well on paper towels.

3. Heat the olive oil in a large skillet. When the oil is hot, add the bacon and cook it until it is almost crisp. Remove it to a side dish and reserve.

4. To the fat remaining in the pan, add the shallots and minced garlic and cook without browning for 2 or 3 minutes.

5. Add the tomato paste and the chopped tomatoes, and season with thyme, oregano, saffron, salt and pepper. Add the bay leaf. Simmer the mixture until juices have evaporated.

6. While the tomato mixture is cooking, heat 2 tablespoons of butter in a small saucepan. Add the onions and roll them in the butter for 2 or 3 minutes. Season with salt, pepper and sugar and continue to cook them until they are glazed and nicely browned. Be sure not to burn them.

7. Add ¾ cup of stock and bring it to a boil. Then reduce the heat and simmer the onions for 15 minutes or until they are tender.

8. Remove the onions from the heat and reserve.

9. Heat the remaining butter in a small skillet. Add the mushrooms, season with salt and pepper and sprinkle with lemon juice. Cook the mushrooms over high heat for 2 or 3 minutes until lightly browned.

10. Add the mushrooms to the onions.

11. Broil the lamb chops under a very hot broiler or grill them over a charcoal fire. They may also be pan-fried until done to your taste.

12. While the chops are cooking, add the mushroom and onion mixture to the tomato sauce together with the bacon and optional cup of fresh peas. Correct the seasoning and heat through. Remove the bay leaf. If the sauce seems too thick, add a little more stock.

13. Place the grilled chops on a platter and pour the sauce around them. Season with lots of freshly ground black pepper and garnish with parsley.

Remarks

For a variation you may add 1 to 2 dried hot chilies to the tomato mixture and add 1 large minced clove of garlic to the finished sauce.

Notes

Veal in basil sauce

Serves: 6
Preparation time: 30 minutes
Cooking time: 40 to 45 minutes

This is a refreshing dish that should be made as soon as the first basil plants are available in the spring. It is a cheerful introduction to your spring and summer kitchen.

Ingredients

The basil butter:
4 tablespoons sweet butter, softened
3 tablespoons finely minced fresh basil
2 cloves of garlic, mashed

The veal:
12 to 14 veal scallops, cut ¼ inch thick
Salt and freshly ground white pepper
Flour for dredging
2 tablespoons sweet butter
2 tablespoons oil
3 tablespoons finely minced shallots
½ cup white wine
1 cup Brown Stock (page 403)
Dash of lemon juice
1 teaspoon cornstarch mixed with a little water or stock

Optional:
1 teaspoon meat glaze

Garnish:
2 tablespoons sweet butter
2 tablespoons olive oil
2 cups cherry tomatoes
Salt and freshly ground white pepper
2 tablespoons finely minced parsley

Preparation

1. Preheat the oven to 325°. Butter a large flameproof baking dish and set aside.

2. In a bowl combine the softened butter with the basil and garlic and beat the mix-ture with a wooden spoon until it is well blended and smooth. Chill.

3. Dry the veal slices with paper towels. Season with salt and pepper and slightly dredge the slices in flour, shaking off the excess.

4. In a large heavy skillet melt the butter and oil. When the mixture is very hot, add the veal, a few slices at a time, and cook for 2 minutes on each side or until they are very lightly browned. Remove the veal slices to a buttered baking dish and con-tinue sauteeing until all the slices are done.

5. Add the shallots to the skillet and cook until they are tender but not browned.

6. Add the wine, bring it to a boil, and re-duce to 2 tablespoons.

7. Add the Brown Stock. Bring it to a boil and scrape well the bottom of the pan.

8. Pour the sauce over the veal and cover the baking dish with buttered foil. Place in the oven and bake for 25 minutes.

9. While the veal is cooking prepare the garnish as follows:

10. Heat the butter and oil in a large skillet.

11. When the mixture is very hot, add the cherry tomatoes. Roll them in the hot butter and oil, sprinkle them with salt and pepper and cook them for 3 minutes or until they are just heated through. Sprinkle with the minced parsley and set aside.

12. When the veal is done, remove it to a serving platter. Sprinkle with lemon juice, and surround it with the cherry tomatoes.

13. Set the baking dish over high heat, add the meat glaze, and reduce the sauce. Whisk in the cornstarch mixture little by little, cooking until the sauce coats a spoon.

14. Remove the pan from the heat, add the Basil Butter and whisk the sauce until the butter is just melted. Correct the seasoning and spoon the sauce over the veal and tomatoes.

Notes

Roast veal
a la fermiere

Serves: 6
Preparation time: 45 to 50 minutes
Cooking time: 2 hours

■ ◑

Casserole-roasted veal garnished with seasonal vegetables is the perfect main course for a party of 6 or more. Vary the garniture with the seasons to make the dish always fresh and exciting.

Ingredients

1 3½- to 4-pound veal roast, boned and tied
Salt and freshly ground white pepper
1 garlic clove, mashed
1 teaspoon imported paprika
1 teaspoon marjoram
4 slices bacon
6 tablespoons sweet butter
2 tablespoons oil
2 cups Brown Stock (page 403)
2 small whole onions
1 Bouquet Garni (page 397)
1 pound carrots, peeled and cut into 1½-inch-long matchsticks
1 teaspoon sugar
2 tablespoons finely diced shallots
½ pound mushrooms, quartered
1 Beurre Manie (page 397)

Optional:
2 cups cooked fresh peas

Garnish:
Watercress
Whole poached mushrooms

Preparation

1. Preheat the oven to 350°.

2. Rub the veal roast with salt and pepper, the mashed garlic, paprika and marjoram.

3. Drop the bacon slices into fast-boiling water and cook for 10 minutes, then dry

well on paper towels and reserve.

4. In a large heavy flameproof baking dish, melt 2 tablespoons of butter and the oil. When the butter is very hot, brown the veal over medium heat on all sides.

5. When the veal is well browned, cover it with the bacon strips. Pour ½ cup of Brown Stock into the pan and add the onions and the Bouquet Garni. Cover the pan with a lid or foil and place in the oven.

6. Baste the roast every 10 minutes with a little of the stock. The roast will be ready in 1 hour and 45 minutes to 2 hours. The juices should run clear when the meat is pierced with a fork.

7. While the veal is roasting, combine the carrots with 1 cup of water, salt, 1 teaspoon of sugar and 2 tablespoons of butter in a saucepan. Bring the mixture to a boil, reduce the heat and simmer the carrots covered for 20 minutes or until barely tender. Be sure not to overcook. Drain the carrots and keep warm.

8. In a large skillet, melt the remaining butter. Add the shallots and cook until they are soft but not browned.

9. Add the mushrooms and saute them for 5 minutes until browned and well covered with butter. Season with salt and freshly ground pepper.

10. Add the carrots and cook the vegetables together for 2 or 3 more minutes. Remove from the heat and reserve.

11. As soon as the veal is done, remove it from the pan, cut the roast into thin slices and place the slices in the center of a serving platter.

12. Degrease the pan juices. Remove the onions and the Bouquet. Pour ½ cup of the pan juices into the vegetables. Add the optional fresh peas and simmer the mixture for 2 or 3 more minutes to blend the flavors. Place the vegetables around the sliced veal.

13. Pour any remaining stock into the baking dish. Reduce the pan juices over high heat. Slowly beat in bits of Beurre Manie until the sauce heavily coats a spoon.

14. Pour the sauce over the veal slices and garnish the platter with watercress and a few whole poached mushrooms.

Remarks

You may substitute for the peas 2 cups of cooked green beans cut into 2-inch-long pieces.

Notes

Veal scallops a la danoise

Serves: 4 to 6
Preparation time: 20 minutes
Cooking time: 40 to 45 minutes

■ ✪

Scandinavian cooking makes greater use of the cucumber than any other national cuisine I know. I personally find hot cucumbers one of the most delicious vegetables, especially suited to the United States, where cucumbers are a supermarket staple.

Ingredients

6   tablespoons sweet butter
Juice of 1 lemon
12 to 14 veal scallops
Salt and freshly ground white pepper
Flour for dredging
2   large cucumbers, peeled, seeded and cut into 1½-inch-long matchsticks
Coarse salt
1   tablespoon white wine vinegar
1   tablespoon oil
1   cup White Stock or Chicken Stock (pages 404–405)
3   tablespoons finely minced scallions
2   tablespoons finely chopped parsley, or 1 tablespoon finely chopped fresh dill plus 1 tablespoon parsley

Preparation

1. Preheat the oven to 350°.

2. Butter a large baking dish with 2 tablespoons butter, add the juice of ½ lemon and reserve.

3. Dry the veal thoroughly on paper towels. Season it with salt and pepper and dredge lightly in flour on both sides, shaking off the excess.

4. Sprinkle the cucumbers with coarse salt and wine vinegar and let them stand in a colander for at least 30 minutes to drain.

5. In a large frying pan, melt 2 tablespoons of butter and the oil. When the mixture is hot, add the veal scallops a few at a time (do not crowd the pan) and saute for 2 or 3 minutes on each side until they are just lightly browned. Remove the scallops to the baking dish. Add the stock to the pan and bring it to a boil. Pour it over the veal.

6. In another skillet, heat the remaining butter. Add the scallions and cook over medium heat until they are soft but not browned. Add the well-drained cucumbers and toss them in the butter until well coated (2 or 3 minutes). Add the cucumbers and scallions to the baking dish.

7. Cover the baking dish with buttered foil and bake for 25 to 30 minutes.

8. When the veal is done, remove it to a serving platter and top it with the cucumbers and scallions. Set the baking dish over high heat and reduce the sauce until it lightly coats a spoon. Add the remaining lemon juice, parsley (or parsley and dill) and pour over the veal. Sprinkle with a good dash of pepper. Serve immediately.

Remarks

Most of the above recipe can be prepared well in advance. You can saute the veal with the cucumbers and scallions in the morning and have the dish ready for the oven. The finished dish cannot wait.

The pan juices will not need thickening if the cucumbers have been well drained.

Serve with buttered new potatoes boiled with a large sprig of dill and add a salad made with Lemon Vinaigrette (page 408).

Clams orleans

Serves: 6
Preparation time: 15 minutes
Cooking time: 20 to 25 minutes

Here is a clever way to prepare clams and the recipe is equally good made with fresh oysters. When clams are used, I prefer Little Necks or "steamers," which do not get chewy; but whichever clams you choose, the dish will still be delicious.

Ingredients

30 clams (Little Necks)
½ cup white wine
1 Bouquet Garni (page 397)
4 tablespoons olive oil
1½ cups homemade white bread crumbs
½ cup finely chopped parsley
1 tablespoon finely minced chives
Salt and freshly ground black pepper
2 small tomatoes, peeled, seeded, chopped and well drained
½ to 1 cup heavy cream
2 to 4 tablespoons sweet butter

Preparation

1. Preheat oven to 350°.

2. Wash the clams thoroughly in cold water to remove all sand.

3. In a large saucepan combine the wine, Bouquet Garni and clams and cook them covered, over medium heat, until they are all open.

4. Discard any clams that have not opened and reserve the others.

5. In a skillet heat the olive oil; add the bread crumbs, parsley and chives. Cook the mixture for 1 or 2 minutes or until the crumbs are just coated with oil. Season with salt and pepper.

6. Add the tomatoes and cook the mixture for 2 or 3 minutes.

7. Remove the clams from their shells, being careful not to break them. Discard the shells and strain the clam juice through a double layer of cheesecloth.

8. Flavor the heavy cream with 2 or 3 teaspoons of the clam broth. Do not use too much of the broth for it may be quite salty.

9. Place a layer of the bread-crumb mixture in individual baking dishes or scallop shells. Place 5 clams in each dish. Top with another layer of bread crumbs and dot each one with ½ tablespoon butter. Pour a little of the clam broth and cream mixture into each dish.

10. Bake the clams for 10 minutes and serve immediately.

Remarks

The tomatoes must be well squeezed or else the bread-crumb mixture will become too soggy.
If you like the combination of bacon and clams, you may add ½ cup of finely minced crisp bacon to the bread-crumb mixture. The baking dishes should be ¾ filled with the cream mixture, so you may need a little more than the ½ cup according to the size of the baking dish.

Notes

Steamed clams
a la provencale

Serves: 4
Preparation time: 20 minutes
Cooking time: 20 minutes

Here is a simple yet delicious way to prepare either clams or mussels. Serve right out of the casserole in which they have steamed. An earthenware casserole is particularly attractive. The clams can also be steamed in the oven.

Ingredients

4 quarts small clams or mussels
½ cup olive oil
2 hot chili peppers, dry
3 large garlic cloves, finely minced
2 tablespoons finely minced shallots
2 tablespoons finely minced fresh
    oregano, or 1 teaspoon dried
1 cup finely minced parsley
Freshly ground black pepper

Preparation

1. Put the clams or mussels in a colander and rinse them well under cold running water. Scrub them with a stiff brush to remove all sand that may cling to the shell, then soak them for 30 minutes in ice water.

2. Combine the olive oil and chili peppers in a large kettle or earthenware casserole.

3. Add the garlic and shallots. Cook until they are soft but not browned.

4. Add the clams, oregano and ¾ cup of minced parsley. Shake the kettle to coat the clams well with the oil and herbs.

5. Cover the kettle and cook the clams over low heat for 10 to 12 minutes or until they have all opened. Discard any that have not opened. Sprinkle with salt and pepper.

6. Sprinkle with the remaining parsley and serve right from the pot with crusty bread.

Poached salmon

Serves: 2 to 4
Preparation time: 15 minutes
Cooking time: 50 minutes

When poaching a small cut (1½ to 2 pounds) of salmon or halibut, you do not have to use a Fish Stock though it does enhance the flavor of the fish.

Ingredients

1 tablespoon white wine vinegar
1 large Bouquet Garni (page 397)
1 onion, stuck with a clove
5 white peppercorns
Pinch of salt
1 carrot, sliced
1 celery stalk with leaves
4 cups of water
1 cup wine
2 to 2½ pounds center cut of salmon

Optional:
1 large sprig of dill

Preparation

1. Combine all the ingredients (except the fish) in a large enamel casserole. Bring to a boil, then reduce the heat and simmer, partially covered, for 45 minutes.

2. Wrap the fish in a cheesecloth and lower it into the simmering liquid.

3. Bring the bouillon to a boil and cook exactly 2 minutes over high heat. Immediately remove the casserole from the heat.

4. Let the fish cool completely in the bouillon, then drain and chill.

Remarks

Serve the salmon with a herb-flavored mayonnaise or mince it to be used for dishes such as Cold Artichoke Bottoms with Salmon Mousse (page 71).

Salmon and mushroom quiche

Serves: 4 to 6
Preparation time: 30 minutes
Cooking time: 45 minutes

■ ●

A salmon quiche lightly flavored with dill is one of the best luncheon or appetizer dishes in my spring repertory and it takes advantage of leftover salmon. When poaching a whole salmon there is a good chance that you may end up with some leftovers. As a matter of fact, you should! Serve them with Cucumber Salad as a light main course or by itself as an hors d'oeuvre.

Ingredients

1   9-inch Pastry Crust (page 407)
1   cup heavy cream
3   eggs
Salt and freshly ground white pepper
Nutmeg, freshly grated
3   tablespoons butter
2   tablespoons finely minced scallions
¼ pound finely diced, cleaned mushrooms
1   cup cooked, flaked salmon (page 93)
Dash of lemon juice
2   teaspoons finely minced fresh dill
2   tablespoons finely grated Gruyere or
    other imported Swiss cheese

Preparation

1. Preheat the oven to 375°.

2. Partially bake the crust.

3. While it is baking, mix the cream and eggs in a mixing bowl. Season with salt, pepper and a pinch of nutmeg and reserve.

4. In a skillet melt the butter. Add the scallions and mushrooms and cook the mixture for 5 or 6 minutes or until all moisture has evaporated. Add the flaked salmon and heat through, adding a dash of lemon juice and the dill. Spread mixture into the partially baked crust.

6. Pour the cream and egg mixture over the salmon and top with grated cheese.

7. Bake the quiche for 35 to 40 minutes or until lightly browned. Test with a toothpick, which should come out dry. Serve the quiche as soon as possible. It can be reheated in a 250° oven for 25 to 30 minutes.

Remarks

When using a deep porcelain quiche pan, you will need more mustard. Use 2 cups of heavy cream blended with 4 whole eggs. If you do not have leftover salmon, turn to page 93 for instructions on poaching a small cut of salmon. It is always worthwhile to poach enough salmon to insure leftovers for making a salad or filling hard-boiled eggs or artichoke bottoms.

Notes

Salmon steaks zingara

Serves: 6
Preparation time: 45 minutes
Cooking time: 40 minutes

Spring brings the best of salmon and the first cravings for a cold dish. The sauce can be served with other fish, a cold veal roast or as a dip for raw vegetables.

Ingredients

3 tablespoons butter
1 medium onion, finely chopped
1 carrot, finely sliced
1 celery stalk, chopped
6 cups water
1 lemon, cut in half
1 Bouquet Garni (page 397)
6 peppercorns
3 tablespoons white wine vinegar
6 salmon steaks, cut ¾ to 1 inch thick
Salt and freshly ground white pepper

The sauce:
2 small zucchini
1 tablespoon olive oil
3 tomatoes, peeled, seeded and chopped
1 green bell pepper, minced
2 garlic cloves, minced
1 tablespoon curry powder (mild)
2 hard-boiled eggs, chopped
2 tablespoons minced fresh chives
3 cups Mayonnaise (page 402)
Juice of 1 lemon

Garnish:
3 hard-boiled eggs, halved
Rolled anchovy filets and watercress

Preparation

1. In a flameproof baking dish, melt 2 tablespoons of butter and add the sliced and chopped vegetables. Saute them without browning for 5 minutes.

2. Add the water, lemon, Bouquet Garni, peppercorns and vinegar. Bring to a boil, then simmer, covered for 12 minutes.

3. Season the salmon steaks, wrap each one in cheesecloth and place them in the bouillon. Cover and bring to a boil. Then reduce the heat and simmer for 12 minutes. Cool the steaks in the bouillon.

4. Remove the salmon carefully from the bouillon, unwrap and place on a serving platter. Chill; top with the following sauce:

The sauce:
5. In a casserole, bring 4 cups salted water to a boil. Add the zucchini and parboil for 5 minutes or until they are barely tender. Remove them from the water and, as soon as they are cool, cut them into ¼-inch slices and reserve.

6. Heat the olive oil in a small skillet and add the tomatoes, green pepper, garlic and curry powder. Cook the mixture until all the moisture has evaporated.

7. Remove it from the fire. Add the chopped hard-boiled egg and the chives. Bind the mixture with mayonnaise.

8. Add lemon juice and the sliced zucchini. Correct the seasoning and chill again until serving time.

9. To serve, pour the sauce over the salmon steaks, garnish with the halved hard-boiled eggs, anchovy filets and watercress.

Remarks

Additional whole poached zucchini can be marinated in a Lemon Vinaigrette (page 408) and served around the salmon steaks.

Whole poached salmon in champagne sauce

Serves: 4 to 6
Preparation time: 30 minutes
Cooking time: 45 to 50 minutes

■ ◑

Ingredients

The mushrooms:
½ pound button mushrooms
½ cup water for poaching
½ teaspoon salt
1 tablespoon lemon juice
2 tablespoons sweet butter

The salmon:
4 tablespoons sweet butter
2 carrots, finely diced
1 onion, finely diced
1 celery stalk, finely sliced
3 shallots, finely chopped
1 3- to 4-pound whole salmon, cleaned
  with head left on
Salt and freshly ground white pepper
1 large Bouquet Garni (page 397)
3 cups dry champagne

The sauce:
4 egg yolks
1 tablespoon cornstarch

Optional:
½ cup heavy cream
1 to 2 teaspoons lemon juice
2 to 4 tablespoons sweet butter

Preparation

1. Preheat the oven to 350°.

2. Combine the cleaned mushrooms with the water, salt and lemon juice in a small saucepan. Add the 2 tablespoons of butter and poach the mushrooms over low heat until tender (about 5 minutes). Reserve them in their liquid while preparing the fish.

3. In a large flameproof baking dish, melt the 4 tablespoons of butter. Add the vegetables and shallots and cook them over low heat for 5 minutes without browning.

4. Season the fish with salt and pepper. Place it on the bed of vegetables, add the Bouquet Garni and pour the champagne around it. Cover the dish with buttered wax paper and place it in the oven.

5. Cook the fish for 35 minutes or until it flakes easily when tested with a fork. Remove it carefully to a serving platter and keep it warm.

6. Strain the cooking liquid into a saucepan and reduce it over high heat to 1 cup.

7. Meanwhile mix the egg yolks and cornstarch in the top of a double boiler, place over medium heat. Add the reduced bouillon slowly and whisk the sauce until it heavily coats a spoon. Be sure not to let the sauce come to a boil or it will curdle. If the sauce is too thick, thin it out with heavy cream and lemon juice. The sauce should have the consistency of a thin mayonnaise.

8. Off heat, whisk the sweet butter into the sauce and spoon it over the fish. Surround it with the well-drained poached mushrooms and serve.

Notes

Coquilles saint-jacques printanier

Serves: 6
Preparation time: 35 minutes
Cooking time: 35 to 40 minutes

■ ⬥

This dish is most often prepared with sea scallops. In Europe the coral is always added to the finished dish. Its orange color together with the fresh vegetables make a lovely "color story." Unfortunately in America scallops are sold without the coral. Nevertheless this superb dish is perfect as a light main course with French bread and a crock of sweet butter.

Ingredients

The bouillon:
1 cup white wine
1 cup water
1 carrot
1 celery stalk
1 whole peeled onion stuck with a clove
1 large Bouquet Garni (page 397)
6 to 8 peppercorns
2 whole garlic cloves, peeled
½ teaspoon salt
Pinch of freshly ground white pepper
1½ pounds scallops, bay or sea

The sauce:
2 egg yolks
1 teaspoon dry English mustard
2 teaspoons Dijon mustard
1 cup heavy cream
6 tablespoons sweet butter
3 tablespoons flour
Juice of 1 large lemon
Salt and freshly ground white pepper

The vegetables:
1 cup carrots, cut into ⅛-inch slices and cooked until tender
1 cup fresh peas, cooked until barely tender and drained
1 cup small white onions, cooked until tender and drained

Optional:
2 tablespoons finely chopped mixed herbs (fennel, parsley and chervil)

Preparation

1. Combine the wine, water, vegetables, Bouquet Garni and seasonings in an enamel casserole. Bring the mixture to a boil, reduce the heat and simmer covered for 20 minutes. Add the scallops, cover the casserole and simmer for 5 minutes.

2. With a slotted spoon, remove the scallops to a side dish. Keep them warm in a little bouillon. Strain rest of bouillon and reduce it over high heat to 1½ cups.

The sauce:
3. In a mixing bowl, combine the egg yolks with the dry mustard and Dijon mustard. Add the heavy cream and whisk until the mixture is well blended.

4. In a heavy saucepan, heat 4 tablespoons butter. When it is very hot, add the flour and cook it for 2 or 3 minutes, stirring constantly. Be sure not to brown it. Add the 1½ cups hot bouillon (reserved above) and whisk the mixture until it thickens. Simmer the sauce for 8 to 10 minutes, whisking it several times. Add the egg and cream mixture; do not let the sauce come to a boil or it will curdle. Off the heat, add the lemon juice, salt and pepper, and beat in 2 tablespoons butter.

5. Place the scallops in a serving dish together with the cooked, well-drained vegetables. (Reserve a few peas for garnish.) Pour the sauce over the entire dish.

6. Sprinkle the dish with finely chopped mixed herbs and a few peas and serve immediately.

Remarks

The vegetables (except for the few peas) are not a garnish and should be inter-mixed with the scallops. The carrots should not be too thinly sliced as this is a gutsy peasant dish. Serve it with plain boiled potatoes and a dry white burgundy. You may add other shellfish such as mussels and shrimp to this dish, but they should, of course, be poached separately.

Notes

Sea scallops a la creole

Serves: 6 to 8
Preparation time: 15 minutes
Cooking time: 35 minutes

Even though sea scallops have a less deli-cate flavor than bay scallops, they are excellent when prepared with a strong marinade such as the one given here. This dish is at its best if it is prepared the day before it is to be served. In the sum-mer, the addition of 1 or 2 tablespoons of finely chopped fresh herbs will give it a whole new zest.

Ingredients

1 cup dry white wine
1 cup water
1 large Bouquet Garni (page 397)
2 celery stalks
6 peppercorns
1 onion stuck with a clove
1 teaspoon salt
2 pounds fresh sea scallops

The marinade:
Juice of 2 lemons
1 tablespoon wine vinegar
6 tablespoons olive oil
1 teaspoon dry mustard
1 teaspoon Dijon mustard
1 small red onion, thinly sliced
1 bay leaf
½ cup sliced olives (preferably Greek olives)
1 whole unpeeled lemon, thinly sliced
3 tablespoons finely chopped pimientos
2 tablespoons finely chopped parsley
1 garlic clove, finely minced
Salt and freshly ground black pepper
Pinch of cayenne

Preparation

1. In a large enamel saucepan, combine the wine, water, Bouquet Garni, celery

stalks, peppercorns, onion and salt. Bring the mixture to a boil, then simmer partially covered for 30 minutes.

2. Add the scallops and cook for 5 minutes over low heat. Drain and cool.

3. In a serving bowl combine the lemon juice, vinegar and oil. Add the dry mustard and Dijon mustard and whisk the dressing until it is very smooth.

4. Add the scallops, sliced onion, bay leaf, olives, lemon slices, pimientos, parsley, garlic, salt, black pepper and cayenne. Carefully blend the scallops in the dressing and chill until serving time.

5. Serve with crusty bread and a bowl of sweet butter.

Remarks

For a variation you may add ¼ pound of sliced fresh raw mushrooms to the dressing. Instead of 2 pounds of scallops, you may use 1 pound of scallops and 1 pound of cooked shrimp.

Notes

Baked trout zurichoise

Serves: 4
Preparation time: 45 minutes
Cooking time: 20 minutes

Trout is a particularly delicate fish and should therefore be served "meuniere" (sauteed in butter) or "au bleu" (poached and served in brown butter). The following combination is somewhat unusual, yet the cheese souffle in no way overpowers the subtle taste of the fish.

Ingredients

The trout:
4   trout, about 1½ pounds each, fileted
1   cup milk
Flour for dredging
Salt and freshly ground white pepper
4 to 6 tablespoons Clarified Butter
     (page 398)

The souffle:
4   tablespoons sweet butter
3   tablespoons flour
1   cup warm milk
Salt and freshly ground white pepper
Pinch of nutmeg
4   egg yolks
¾ cup grated Gruyere or other imported
     Swiss cheese
5   egg whites

Garnish:
½ cup finely slivered toasted almonds

Preparation

1. Preheat oven to 375°.

2. Dip the trout filets in milk. Dry them well on paper towels and dip into flour seasoned with salt and pepper. Shake off excess flour.

3. In a large heavy skillet melt 4 tablespoons of Clarified Butter. When it is very

hot, add the filets and saute until golden brown on one side (2 or 3 minutes). With 2 spatulas, carefully turn the filets and saute for 2 or 3 minutes on the other side. Remove the filets carefully to a buttered rectangular baking dish.

The souffle:
4. Melt the butter in a saucepan over low heat. Add the flour and cook slowly for 2 or 3 minutes without letting it brown.

5. Add the warm milk all at once. Raise the heat and whisk the mixture constantly until it becomes very thick and smooth. Add salt, pepper and a good pinch of nutmeg. Remove the saucepan from the heat.

6. Add the egg yolks one at a time and beat the mixture well to incorporate them completely. Add the cheese and mix well.

7. Beat the egg whites until they are stiff and stand in soft peaks. (Always beat the egg whites for a souffle by hand.) Gently fold the cheese mixture into the beaten whites. This, too, is best done by hand to maintain the air pockets.

8. Cover the trout filets completely with the souffle mixture and place in the oven. Bake for 12 to 15 minutes or until the top is lightly browned.

9. While the trout are baking, heat the remaining 2 tablespoons of Clarified Butter in a small skillet, and saute the almond slivers until they are lightly browned.

10. Remove the baking dish from the oven and sprinkle the souffleed trout with the almond slivers. Serve immediately.

Remarks

Though trout is one of the best fish to treat in this way, you can make this dish with filets of sole or even flounder. If you want to use it as a main course, complement it with sauteed whole mushrooms or hot dilled cucumbers.

Notes

Trout in cream and dill sauce

Serves: 4
Preparation time: 30 minutes
Cooking time: 20 minutes

■ ◓

Trout is a delicate fish and is really at its best when simply prepared. However, I find myself a little bored with menus in which trout is either poached or a la meuniere. Here is an elegant and more interesting dish that brings out its delicate flavor.

Ingredients

2   tablespoons sweet butter
2   tablespoons finely minced scallions
1   cup dry white wine
1   cup water
1   large Bouquet Garni (page 397)
4   whole trout (1 to 1½ pounds each), cleaned, heads left on
Salt and freshly ground white pepper
1 to 2 Beurre Manie (page 397)
1   cup Blender Hollandaise (page 402)
Dash of lemon juice
1 to 2 tablespoons finely minced fresh dill

Garnish:
Parslied cucumbers
Sprigs of fresh dill

Preparation

1. In a large flameproof baking dish melt the butter. Add the scallions and cook them for 2 minutes until they are soft but not browned.

2. Add the wine, water and then the Bouquet Garni.

3. Season the fish with salt and pepper, place it in the baking dish, and cover the dish with buttered wax paper. Simmer the trout on the lowest possible heat for 15 minutes, or until the flesh flakes easily when tested with a fork. The poaching liquid should just tremble and never boil.

4. When the trout are done transfer them to a serving platter and keep warm over simmering water.

5. Strain the pan juices into a saucepan and reduce them over high heat to 1 cup.

6. Bit by bit beat the Beurre Manie into the pan juices until the sauce becomes thick and very smooth.

7. Remove the saucepan from the heat and whisk a little of the sauce into the Hollandaise, then pour the Hollandaise into the rest of the sauce. Be sure to whisk all the time and keep the saucepan off the heat or the sauce will curdle. Season the sauce with salt, pepper and lemon juice to taste and add the minced dill.

8. With paper towels remove any cooking liquid that may have accumulated around the trout.

9. Carefully take the skin off the top of the fish and coat with the sauce.

10. Garnish the platter with Parslied Cucumbers and dill and serve immediately.

Remarks

In summer you may substitute for the dill other fresh herbs such as tarragon or a mixture of chives and chervil.

Notes

Artichokes a la nicoise

Serves: 4
Preparation time: 25 minutes
Cooking time: 40 to 50 minutes

The globe artichoke is certainly one of the most exciting of the winter-spring season. It is a shame that it is mostly limited to two preparations—either hot with melted butter or cold with French dressing—when it can be stuffed, sauteed and even made into a delicious soup!

Ingredients

4 large artichokes
½ lemon
7 tablespoons sweet butter, softened
1 garlic clove, finely minced
1 tablespoon minced parsley
1 large shallot, finely diced
Salt and freshly ground white pepper
2 cups Chicken Stock (page 404)
1 Bouquet Garni (page 397)
1 onion, sliced in half
Juice of 1 lemon
1 Beurre Manie (page 397)

Preparation

1. Cut the stems off the artichokes and with a sharp knife cut off the tips of the leaves. Immediately rub the cut parts with the cut side of half a lemon. Drop the artichokes into boiling salted water and cook for 10 minutes. Drain them upside down on paper towels and as soon as they are cool enough to handle, gently spread the leaves apart and with a sharp knife or a grapefruit spoon scoop out the chokes.

2. In a small mixing bowl combine 6 tablespoons of the butter, garlic, parsley and shallots. Season with salt and pepper. Fill the artichokes with the herb butter.

3. In an oval casserole, large enough to hold the artichokes upright, close together, melt the remaining butter. Add the Chicken Stock, Bouquet Garni, onion and artichokes. Cover the casserole with buttered wax paper and then the lid. Simmer the artichokes over low heat for 20 minutes.

4. Uncover the casserole and sprinkle the artichokes with the lemon juice. Test for doneness by pulling off one of the leaves and tasting it. If necessary, cover the artichokes again and cook for 10 more minutes.

5. As soon as the artichokes are done, transfer them carefully to a serving platter. Remove the Bouquet and the onion.

6. Raise the heat and reduce the stock by ⅓. Beat in a Beurre Manie bit by bit until the sauce lightly coats a spoon. Pour the sauce around the artichokes and serve.

Remarks

These artichokes are also excellent cold, but it is a shame to forgo the delicious sauce.

Notes

Artichokes valeuris

Serves: 4
Preparation time: 10 minutes
Cooking time: 30 minutes

This recipe of Roman origin originally called for the small artichokes found only in Italy and California. These artichokes are no larger than eggs and are so tender they do not have to be parboiled. But I found a way to duplicate this recipe with the artichokes available in most markets.

Ingredients

4 artichokes
1 tablespoon salt
4 tablespoons olive oil
½ cup dry white wine
4 anchovies
2 tablespoons finely minced parsley
2 garlic cloves, finely minced
1 tablespoon capers
½ teaspoon freshly ground black pepper

Preparation

1. Place the artichokes in a large saucepan with 2 quarts of water and 1 tablespoon of salt. Cover the pan and cook over medium heat for 15 minutes.

2. Drain the artichokes well on paper towels. Cut off the tips of the leaves and remove the stems.

3. Cut the artichokes lengthwise into 3 or 4 slices each. Thoroughly scrape out the chokes without breaking the slices.

4. Heat the olive oil in a large frying pan. Add the artichokes and 3 tablespoons of white wine. Cover the skillet and cook over low heat until the artichokes are tender (about 10 minutes).

5. Mix together the anchovies, parsley, garlic and capers. Add to the artichokes and just heat through. If the mixture seems too thick, add 2 more tablespoons of wine.

6. Sprinkle with pepper and serve immediately.

Remarks

This makes a lovely appetizer but can also be served as a vegetable with roast leg of lamb.
For a richer sauce you may add 2 to 4 tablespoons of butter before serving. But I prefer the entire cooking to be done in olive oil so that the Provencale flavor of the dish will be retained.

Notes

Asparagus chantilly

Serves: 6 to 8
Preparation time: 35 to 40 minutes
Cooking time: 15 minutes

Asparagus Chantilly is good both hot or cold. I like the Austrian way of using asparagus as a "centerpiece" on a platter surrounded by hard-boiled stuffed eggs, ham cornucopias and possibly other poached cold vegetables.

Ingredients

2 pounds fresh asparagus
Lemon juice to taste
Salt and freshly ground white pepper
1/3 cup heavy cream
2 teaspoons Dijon mustard
1 1/4 cups Mayonnaise (page 402)
1 tablespoon minced chives or dill

Garnish:
3 to 4 hard-boiled eggs
2 tablespoons sweet butter, softened
1 tablespoon minced parsley
2 teaspoons minced chives
Salt and freshly ground white pepper
Pinch of curry
Pinch of cayenne
1 tablespoon chopped parsley

Optional:
6 to 8 slices of smoked ham or prosciutto
    rolled into cornets
Whole radishes
Black olives

Preparation

1. Choose thick asparagus stalks, peel each one with a vegetable peeler and cut off a piece of the bottom, leaving the stalks about 7 to 8 inches long. Wash them well under cold running water and tie into bundles, leaving one stalk loose for testing during the cooking process.

2. Bring 3 quarts of salted water to a boil in a large casserole, add the asparagus and cook over medium heat for 12 to 15 minutes. The asparagus should be tender but still somewhat crisp.

3. Drain the asparagus as soon as it is done, place the bundles on paper towels, cut the strings and let the stalks cool.

4. Arrange the cooled asparagus on a serving platter, sprinkle with lemon juice, salt and pepper, then chill.

5. Whip the cream and add the mustard.

6. Add the cream and mustard mixture to the mayonnaise; add 1 tablespoon of very finely minced chives or dill and correct the seasoning. Coat the asparagus with 1 cup of the mayonnaise mixture, leaving the tips exposed.

7. Slice the eggs in half lengthwise. Carefully remove the yolks to a bowl, add the softened butter, remaining mayonnaise and herbs and beat into a paste.

8. Add salt, pepper, curry and cayenne. Correct the seasoning. Chill for 1/2 hour.

9. Fill a pastry bag with the mixture and pipe it into the egg whites.

10. Garnish the eggs with chopped parsley and place them around the asparagus.

11. Decorate the platter with the ham cornets, radishes and black olives and serve chilled, but not icy cold, with thinly sliced, buttered black bread.

Asparagus in lemon and herb sauce

Serves: 4 to 6
Preparation time: 25 minutes
Cooking time: 20 minutes

Ingredients

20 to 30 stalks of asparagus, 6 inches long
3 egg yolks
1 teaspoon cornstarch
Juice of 1 lemon
1 cup warm Chicken Stock (page 404)
Salt and freshly ground white pepper

Optional:
1 tablespoon finely minced chives
1 tablespoon finely minced dill

Preparation

1. Clean the asparagus, removing the tough ends. Tie the stalks in bundles. Bring 3 quarts of salted water to a boil in a large casserole. Drop the asparagus into the boiling water and cook until tender; be sure not to overcook. The stalks should still be slightly crisp. As soon as the asparagus is done, run it under cold water. Keep warm while making the sauce.

2. In a small heavy saucepan, combine the egg yolks and cornstarch. Add the lemon juice and whisk until the mixture is quite smooth.

3. Add the warm stock and place the saucepan over medium heat. Cook the sauce until it is quite thick, whisking vigorously all the time. As soon as the sauce has the consistency of a custard, remove the saucepan immediately from the heat and continue whisking until the sauce has cooled.

4. Season the sauce with salt and pepper and add the chives and dill. Place the asparagus on a serving platter and spoon the sauce over it without covering the tips. Serve immediately.

Green beans in lemon sauce

Serves: 4
Preparation time: 15 minutes
Cooking time: 20 minutes

Here is a simple way to prepare creatively a relatively common vegetable. Other vegetables, such as asparagus or poached whole mushrooms, also lend themselves to this preparation. Serve as an accompaniment to a simple roast, braised chicken or veal scallops. Toward summer you may add 1 or 2 tablespoons of finely mixed fresh herbs to the sauce.

Ingredients

1½ pounds of fresh green beans
Salt
3 egg yolks
2 tablespoons finely grated Parmesan cheese
Juice of 1 lemon
4 tablespoons sweet butter
¾ cup hot Chicken Stock (page 404)
Freshly ground white pepper

Optional:
1 tablespoon finely minced parsley (or a mixture of parsley and chives, or dill)

Preparation

1. Snap off the tips of the green beans. Drop the beans into 3 quarts of fast-boiling salted water and cook them until just tender. As soon as the beans are done, run them under cold water. Keep them warm while making the sauce.

2. In the top of the blender combine the egg yolks, Parmesan and lemon juice. Blend for 1 minute at top speed.

3. Add 2 tablespoons butter and then, still at top speed, blend the Chicken Stock into the egg yolk mixture which should become smooth and creamy. Reserve.

4. Melt the remaining 2 tablespoons of butter in a large heavy skillet. Toss the beans in the butter for 2 or 3 minutes; reduce the heat and add the sauce. Blend the mixture and cook until the sauce becomes very thick. Do not let it come to a boil because the yolks will curdle.

5. Season to taste, add the parsley and pour the beans into a serving dish. Serve immediately.

Remarks

The sauce can be made in a heavy saucepan over direct heat. It should be whisked vigorously to prevent curdling. You may also serve the beans chilled. Sprinkle them with lemon juice and olive oil. Serve the warm sauce on the side.

Notes

Braised beans a la bresse

Serves: 4 to 6
Preparation time: 30 minutes
Cooking time: 20 minutes

This is an excellent brunch or light supper dish when accompanied by poached or fried eggs. Place the eggs on a serving platter and surround them with the bean mixture and sauteed bread triangles.

Ingredients

½ pound chicken livers
1½ pounds green beans
5 tablespoons chicken fat or sweet butter
2 tablespoons finely minced green onions
Salt and freshly ground black pepper
½ pound small mushrooms, quartered
   (cleaned with damp paper towels)
2 tablespoons finely chopped mixed herbs
   (parsley, chervil, summer savory, pinch
   of rosemary) or parsley only

Optional:
2 tablespoons sweet butter

Preparation

1. Clean the chicken livers, removing any dark or green spots. Cut the livers into small pieces. Dry with paper towels.

2. Clean the green beans and remove the tips. Cut the beans into 2-inch-long pieces.

3. Bring 3 quarts of salted water to a boil and drop the beans into it a few at a time. As soon as the water comes back to a boil, lower the heat and cook the beans until just tender (12 to 15 minutes).

4. While the beans are cooking, melt 3 tablespoons of chicken fat or butter in a large skillet. Add the chicken livers and cook them over high heat until they are nicely browned. Add the onions, salt and pepper and cook the mixture for 3 more

minutes. Remove from the heat and reserve.

5. Melt the remaining fat in another skillet and saute the mushrooms until they are nicely browned (3 to 5 minutes). Do not overcook them. Season the mushrooms and add them to chicken liver mixture.

6. When the beans are done, drain them and immediately run them under cold water to stop further cooking. Pour the beans into the skillet with the chicken livers and mushrooms and toss them lightly. Cook the mixture for 5 more minutes, shaking the pan.

7. Add the herbs and 2 tablespoons of butter if desired. Season with additional salt if necessary and a large dash of pepper.

8. Serve directly from the skillet or on a serving platter.

Notes

Cherry tomatoes in chive cream

Serves: 4 to 6
Preparation time: 10 minutes
Cooking time: 5 to 7 minutes

Some of the tastiest vegetables are often the simplest to prepare. This excellent spring vegetable dish takes only minutes. It makes a colorful accompaniment to roast chicken and is especially good with roast veal. Other herbs such as dill or fresh chervil can be used.

Ingredients

2 pints cherry tomatoes
4 tablespoons sweet butter
1 teaspoon salt
Freshly ground white pepper
1 cup heavy cream
2 tablespoons plus 1 teaspoon finely minced fresh chives

Preparation

1. Clean the tomatoes and remove the stems.

2. In a large skillet heat the butter. Add the tomatoes, salt and a large dash of pepper. Cook the tomatoes for 2 minutes, shaking the pan constantly to coat them evenly with the butter.

3. Add the cream and 2 tablespoons of chives and continue cooking for 2 more minutes. With a slotted spoon remove the tomatoes to a serving dish.

4. Raise the heat and continue cooking the cream until it is reduced by half. Pour it over the tomatoes and sprinkle the top with the remaining chives and a grinding of white pepper. Serve immediately.

Cold broccoli salad

Serves: 4 to 6
Preparation time: 20 minutes
Cooking time: 10 minutes

With the first warm days of spring comes the desire for a refreshing salad. Broccoli, one of the few reliable year-round vegetables, is first on my list for just such a day. Serve it as a cold appetizer or as an imaginative accompaniment to poached or grilled fish.

Ingredients

2   pounds fresh broccoli
Salt
Dash of lemon juice
Freshly ground black pepper
1½ to 2 cups Mayonnaise (page 402)
3   shallots, finely minced
½ cup white wine
1   tablespoon finely chopped chives

Garnish:
2   hard-boiled eggs
Rolled filets of anchovies

Preparation

1. Rinse the broccoli under running cold water, then cut it into even pieces. Slice the thick ones in half lengthwise. Remove all but 3 inches of each stem. Peel the broccoli with a vegetable peeler. Drop the prepared pieces into boiling salted water for 8 to 10 minutes. The vegetable should be just tender and still a little crisp. Drain and spread on paper towels to dry. Place in a serving dish. Sprinkle with lemon juice and black pepper.

2. In a small saucepan, combine the shallots and wine and cook the mixture until the wine has completely evaporated. Incorporate the shallots into the mayonnaise. Add the chives.

3. Pour the mayonnaise over the broccoli and refrigerate for 2 or 3 hours before serving.

4. At serving time garnish the salad with hard-boiled eggs and anchovies.

Notes

Danish crab salad

Serves: 6 to 8
Preparation time: 25 minutes
Cooking time: none

Here is a refreshing and delicious salad. If you cannot get good crabmeat, use fresh shrimp instead, for the success of the salad depends mostly on the quality of the crabmeat you use. Serve the salad elegantly by lining coquille shells with a Bibb or Boston lettuce leaf and placing the salad on the leaf.

Ingredients

1   pound lump crabmeat
2   cucumbers
Salt
2   cups sliced radishes
Lemon juice to taste
Freshly ground white pepper
¾ cup Mayonnaise (page 402)
½ cup sour cream
2   tablespoons finely chopped chives
1   teaspoon horseradish

Garnish:
3   hard-boiled eggs, sliced
Whole radishes
Watercress

Preparation

1. Pick over the crabmeat to remove bones.

2. Peel the cucumbers, halve them lengthwise and scrape out the seeds. (This is best done with a grapefruit spoon or a melon-ball cutter.) Cut the cucumbers into fine 1-inch matchsticks and put them in a colander. Sprinkle with salt and let them drain for 1 hour. Dry them with paper towels.

3. Put the crabmeat into a salad bowl. Add the radishes and cucumbers. Sprinkle with lemon juice, salt and pepper.

4. Combine the mayonnaise, sour cream, chives, horseradish. (Squeeze the liquid out of the horseradish in the corner of a napkin.) Carefully combine the dressing with the salad.

5. Chill well before serving. Garnish the bowl with sliced eggs, radishes and watercress. Serve with thin-sliced buttered black bread.

Notes

Spring zucchini salad

Serves: 4
Preparation time: 10 minutes
Cooking time: 5 to 8 minutes

This simple little salad will come as a welcome change after many meals served with the usual winter lettuce. A zucchini salad can be served as an accompaniment to veal, chicken or fish dishes, as part of an hors d'oeuvre table or served as an appetizer with some finely sliced prosciutto.

Ingredients

4 to 5 medium-sized crisp zucchini
3   tablespoons lemon juice
8   tablespoons olive oil
1   teaspoon Dijon mustard
1   small garlic clove, mashed
2 to 3 tablespoons of Creme Fraiche (page 398)
Salt and freshly ground white pepper
1   small red onion, finely sliced
3   tablespoons finely grated radishes
1   tablespoon minced parsley

Preparation

1. Drop the zucchini into boiling water and poach them over medium heat for 5 minutes. Drain them thoroughly and while they are still warm, cut them in half lengthwise and then into ¼-inch slices. Place the zucchini in a serving bowl and sprinkle the slices with 1 tablespoon lemon juice and 2 tablespoons olive oil.

2. In a small mixing bowl, combine the remaining lemon juice, olive oil, mustard, garlic and Creme Fraiche and whisk the mixture until it is perfectly blended. Add a pinch of salt and pepper and pour this dressing over the zucchini.

3. Add the onion slices, and toss. Chill the salad for 2 or 3 hours.

4. Before serving, sprinkle the salad with the grated radishes and minced parsley. Let it come to room temperature and serve.

Remarks

This salad can be made a day ahead of time. When making it in the summer with tiny baby zucchini, you need not poach them. Just cut them raw into very thin slices and marinate them in the dressing.

Notes

Fresh apricot mousse

Serves: 4 to 6
Preparation time: 30 minutes
Cooking time: 20 to 25 minutes

Apricots are certainly one of the best of the late spring fruits. They should be fully ripe and served simply with slightly whipped cream or marinated in port. For those who love apricots and want to serve them in a more elaborate way, here is a superb recipe.

Ingredients

1   pound fresh apricots, peeled
1   cup sugar
4   eggs, separated
1   cup warm milk
2   teaspoons vanilla
3   tablespoons apricot liqueur
Few drops almond extract
1   envelope unflavored gelatin
1   cup heavy cream

Preparation

1. Puree the apricots in the blender and strain them through a sieve. Sprinkle the puree with ½ cup sugar and set it aside.

2. In the top of a double boiler beat the remaining sugar and egg yolks until the mixture is pale yellow.

3. Pour in the warm milk and cook the custard over simmering water (medium heat), stirring continuously until it coats a spoon. Add the vanilla, apricot liqueur and almond extract. Remove from the heat.

4. In a small saucepan combine the gelatin with 3 tablespoons of water. Heat to dissolve the gelatin completely. Beat the gelatin into the warm custard.

5. Place the egg whites in a large mixing bowl, add a pinch of salt and beat them until they are stiff. Fold the beaten whites into the still warm custard.

6. Chill the mixture, whisking it from time to time until it starts to set.

7. Whip the cream and fold it into the custard together with the apricot puree.

8. Pour the mousse into individual parfait glasses or into a crystal bowl and chill for 3 or 4 hours before serving.

Remarks

A lovely way to serve the mousse is to garnish it with whole poached apricots that have been marinated for 1 hour in apricot brandy. You can, of course, make the mousse with peaches, but apricots have a unique flavor and their short season should be taken full advantage of.

Notes

Banana beignets with apricot sauce

Serves: 4
Preparation time: 15 minutes
Cooking time: 3 to 4 minutes

Ingredients

3 to 4 bananas (slightly underripe), cut
    into 1-inch-thick slices
Juice of ½ lemon
Sugar
¼ cup white rum

The batter:
1 cup sifted flour
Pinch of salt
2 teaspoons sugar
⅓ cup warm beer
A little water
2 tablespoons melted sweet butter
Vegetable oil for deep frying
2 egg whites
Apricot Sauce (pages 119–120)

Garnish:
Confectioners' sugar

Preparation

1. Place the banana slices in a bowl and
sprinkle with lemon juice, sugar and rum.
Toss lightly. Cover and marinate for 40
or 50 minutes.

The batter:
2. In a bowl combine the flour, salt and
sugar.

3. Add the beer and incorporate it into the
flour. Do not overbeat, just blend it in. Add
just enough water to give the batter the
consistency of heavy cream.

4. Add the melted butter and let the batter
stand for 40 minutes to 1 hour.

5. Heat the oil (to the depth of 3 inches)
in a large skillet. You do not need a deep
fryer.

6. While the oil is getting hot, beat the egg
whites and add them to the batter.

7. Drain the banana slices and dip them
into the batter. Drop 4 to 6 at a time into
the hot fat and fry them until they are
nicely browned.

8. Drain the beignets on paper towels and
sprinkle with lots of confectioners' sugar.
Serve immediately with the Apricot Sauce
on the side.

Remarks

Apple slices can be fried in the same manner and served with the Apricot Sauce.

Notes

Cherry crepes praline

Serves: 6 to 8
Preparation time: 45 minutes
Cooking time: 20 minutes

The filling for these crepes can actually be served as a dessert all by itself.
Just omit the cornstarch thickening and serve the cherries with a side dish of whipped cream flavored with sugar and cognac.

Ingredients

2 cups water
1 cup sugar
1½ pounds pitted cherries
1 2-inch piece vanilla bean
1 piece of lemon peel
2 teaspoons cornstarch
⅓ cup cherry brandy
12 to 16 Dessert Crepes (page 399)
½ cup Praline Powder (page 402)
Verifine sugar

Optional:
8 cracked cherry pits, wrapped in cheesecloth
Dash of lemon juice
¼ cup cherry brandy mixed with ⅓ cup
   cognac

Preparation

1. In a saucepan, combine the sugar and water and cook over medium heat, stirring from time to time, until the sugar is dissolved. Raise the heat and cook the sugar syrup for 10 minutes without stirring until a candy thermometer reads 220 degrees.

2. Reduce the heat and add the cherries, the optional cherry pits, vanilla bean and lemon peel. Cook the cherries over low heat for 5 minutes or until tender.

3. When the cherries are done, remove

them with a slotted spoon to a bowl. Discard the cherry pits, the vanilla bean and the lemon peel.

4. Stir the cornstarch into the cherry brandy and add it to the syrup. Cook until the syrup has thickened. Taste the syrup and add a dash of lemon juice if you like a certain tanginess.

5. Pour the hot syrup over the cherries and cool.

6. Butter a large baking dish. Fill the crepes with the cherry mixture and place them in the baking dish.

7. Sprinkle the crepes with the Praline Powder and verifine sugar and run the dish under the broiler until the sugar is lightly glazed. Remove the dish from the oven and serve immediately.

8. If you wish to flame the crepes, warm the optional cherry brandy and cognac in a small saucepan, bring the pan to the table and pour the warm liqueur over the crepes; ignite and shake the dish until the flames subside. If you are not sure you can do this gracefully, flame the crepes in the kitchen. They will taste the same.

Remarks

The whole dish can be prepared well in advance.
The cracked cherry pits add a light almond flavor to the syrup. All fruit compotes made with pitted fruits, such as apricots, peaches and plums, benefit immensely by adding a few cracked pits to the sugar syrup.

Spring strawberry crepes

Serves: 6 to 8
Preparation time: 25 minutes
Cooking time: 5 minutes

When strawberries are in season, it is hard to get away from them since they are such a delicious fruit. One does, however, tire of plain sugared strawberries or strawberries in cream so here is a refreshing change.

Ingredients

2 cups finely sliced strawberries
Verifine sugar

The filling:
3 egg yolks
⅓ cup sugar
3 tablespoons cornstarch
1 cup warm milk
1 teaspoon vanilla extract
¼ cup Grand Marnier
12 to 16 small warm Dessert Crepes
   (page 399)

Garnish:
Confectioners' sugar
¼ cup Grand Marnier plus ¼ cup Cognac
   or Strawberry Sauce (page 116)

Preparation

1. Place the sliced strawberries in a small bowl and sprinkle them with sugar. Let them stand for 30 minutes to 1 hour.

2. Preheat the broiler.

3. In a mixing bowl combine the egg yolks and sugar and whisk the mixture until it is pale yellow. Add the cornstarch and blend it thoroughly. Add the warm milk and whisk until the mixture is well blended. Pour it into a heavy-bottomed saucepan and cook over medium heat, stirring constantly, until the sauce is very thick (1 or 2 minutes). Be careful not to scorch the bottom of the pan. Pour it into a bowl, and add the vanilla extract and the Grand Marnier. Chill the sauce for 2 hours.

4. Drain the strawberries thoroughly and fold them into the chilled sauce.

5. Butter a large baking dish. Fill each warm crepe with a little of the strawberry mixture and place them in the baking dish.

6. Sprinkle heavily with confectioners' sugar and run under the broiler to carmelize the sugar.

7. Heat the liqueurs together in a small saucepan. Pour the mixture over the crepes and ignite. Serve flaming.

Notes

Lemon roulade

Serves: 6 to 8
Preparation time: 35 to 40 minutes
Cooking time: 25 to 30 minutes

Ingredients

The lemon butter cream:
1½ cups sugar
½ cup water
4 egg yolks
2 teaspoons vanilla
Juice of 1 large lemon
2 teaspoons grated lemon rind
2 sticks sweet butter, softened

The sponge roll:
4 large eggs
½ cup sugar
½ teaspoon baking powder
¾ cup sifted cake flour
Pinch of salt
1 teaspoon grated lemon rind
1 teaspoon vanilla extract
2 tablespoons confectioners' sugar

Preparation

1. Preheat the oven to 400°.

2. Butter a jelly-roll pan, then sprinkle it with flour, shaking out the excess. Place a sheet of wax paper in the pan. Cut the paper a little larger than the pan. Butter the wax paper and set aside.

3. In a heavy saucepan combine the sugar and water. Place a candy thermometer in the pan and cook the mixture over high heat, without stirring, until the thermometer reads 238°. Check by dropping a little of the sugar syrup into cold water. It should form a soft ball.

4. While the sugar is cooking, whisk the egg yolks until they are pale and fluffy.

5. When the sugar has reached the right stage, remove it from the heat. Pour the hot syrup by droplets into the egg yolks, whisking constantly until the mixture is thick and cool. This is best done with a small electric hand beater.

6. Add the vanilla, lemon juice and rind to the mixture and set it aside until it is completely cooled.

7. When cool, fold in the softened butter and beat until the butter is completely incorporated and the cream is smooth and thick. Chill for 2 hours.

8. For the sponge roll, place the eggs and sugar in a bowl. Whisk until well blended.

9. Place the bowl over a pan with hot water. The water should be hot but should not be boiling. Warm the egg mixture, stirring from time to time for 15 minutes, or until the mixture feels tepid.

10. Remove the bowl and beat the mixture with a wire whisk or electric beater until it doubles in volume and is pale yellow.

11. Combine the baking powder, flour and salt. Fold it gently into the egg mixture.

12. Add the lemon rind and vanilla.

13. Pour the mixture into the pan and spread it evenly with a spatula.

14. Place the pan in the preheated oven and bake for 13 to 15 minutes.

15. While the cake is baking, dust a clean towel heavily with confectioners' sugar.

16. When the cake is done, place it upside down on the towel and carefully remove the pan and the wax paper. Cover the cake with a moist towel and cool.

17. As soon as the cake is completely

cool, spread it with a heavy layer of the lemon butter cream (1½ cups). Roll the roulade either lengthwise or the short way. Carefully remove it from the towel to a serving platter and chill until serving time.

18. Put the remaining lemon butter cream in a pastry bag and decorate the roulade with rosettes of cream. If the cake has cracked, sprinkle it heavily with confectioners' sugar. Serve very well chilled but not cold.

Remarks

For a variation you may use only ½ the amount of cream for filling the cake, then cover the entire roll with the remaining butter cream smoothing it with a knife dipped in hot water.

Notes

Melon in strawberry sauce

Serves: 4 to 6
Preparation time: 25 minutes
Cooking time: 3 to 5 minutes

4 cups fresh strawberries
¾ cup sugar
½ cup currant jelly
2 tablespoons Grand Marnier
¼ cup kirsch
1 large ripe Casaba or Spanish melon
Juice of 1 lemon

Preparation

1. Wash and hull the strawberries. Reserve 1 cup of the most perfect berries. Place the remaining berries in the top part of the blender together with the sugar and blend at high speed for 3 minutes or until the sugar is completely dissolved. Pass the mixture through a fine sieve and reserve.

2. Combine the currant jelly with the liqueurs in a small saucepan and heat until the jelly is completely dissolved. Beat the mixture into the strawberry puree and reserve.

3. Cut the melon into small cubes or balls with a melon-ball cutter. Sprinkle with lemon juice and a little sugar and marinate for 30 minutes.

4. Add the strawberry puree, fold lightly and top with the whole strawberries. If you wish, sprinkle the whole strawberries with a little sugar and dribble a little Grand Marnier on them. Chill for 2 hours before serving.

Remarks

A mixture of melons may be used except watermelon, which does not lend itself well to fruit salads.

Oranges a la valenciana

Serves: 6 to 8
Preparation time: 15 minutes
Cooking time: 15 to 20 minutes

Whole oranges sugared and served with a liqueur-flavored strawberry sauce are the perfect introduction to spring when we are ready for a certain lightness in our desserts.

Ingredients

6 to 8 large navel oranges
2 tablespoons Grand Marnier
2 tablespoons sugar

The strawberry sauce:
2 pints fresh, very ripe strawberries
¾ cup currant jelly
¼ cup Grand Marnier
Few drops of lemon juice

Optional:
2 tablespoons confectioners' sugar

Preparation

1. Remove the orange part of the skin of two oranges. Be careful not to include the white part. Cut the peel into fine strips 2 inches long and about ⅛ of an inch thick. Place the strips in a small saucepan, cover with boiling water, and simmer for 10 minutes. Then drain and reserve.

2. Marinate the strips in the 2 tablespoons of Grand Marnier for 2 or 3 hours.

3. Carefully peel all the oranges, removing all the white membrane and exposing the orange flesh. Cut a slice off the bottom of each orange and stand it up in a serving bowl. Sprinkle with sugar and chill while making the sauce.

4. Puree the strawberries in the blender. (Reserve 6 to 8 perfect ones for garnish.)

Pass the puree through a fine sieve into a bowl and reserve.

5. In a small saucepan heat the currant jelly over very low heat until it is completely dissolved. Add the Grand Marnier and lemon juice. Cool the mixture slightly and then whisk it into the strawberry puree

6. Taste the sauce and if it is not sweet enough, add 1 or 2 tablespoons of confectioners' sugar.

7. Pour the strawberry sauce around the oranges. Top each orange with one perfect strawberry and sprinkle with the orange strips and their Grand Marnier liqueur.

8. Chill again until serving time.

Remarks

If the oranges are to be served whole, you must provide each guest with a knife and fork as well as a dessert spoon. You may prefer to slice the oranges. It is not as attractive a presentation but certainly easier to eat.

Notes

Pineapple a la brezilienne

Serves: 4
Preparation time: 15 minutes
Cooking time: 20 minutes

Ingredients

2 cups water
1 cup sugar
3-inch piece vanilla bean
1 large pineapple, peeled and cubed
1 tablespoon lemon juice
1 piece lemon peel
¼ cup apricot preserves
3 tablespoons white rum

Optional:
1 cup small whole strawberries, slightly
   underripe

Preparation

1. In a saucepan combine the water, sugar and vanilla bean. Bring the water to a boil, reduce the heat and simmer the syrup for 5 minutes.

2. Add the pineapple, lemon juice and peel. Partially cover the saucepan and simmer for 5 to 8 minutes.

3. If you wish to use strawberries, add the washed, unhulled berries to the pineapple and poach them for 1 minute. With a slotted spoon remove the fruit to a bowl.

4. Raise the heat; reduce the syrup by ⅓.

5. While the syrup is cooking, combine the apricot preserves with the rum in a small saucepan and heat.

6. Strain the preserves through a sieve into the pineapple syrup, remove the lemon peel and taste the sauce for sweetness, adding more sugar if needed. Pour it over the pineapple and strawberries and chill.

7. Serve very cold with champagne biscuits or sweetened whipped cream.

Raspberries in lemon whipped cream

Serves: 6 to 8
Preparation time: 15 minutes
Cooking time: 10 minutes

Even though fresh raspberries usually need no adornment, a cold lemon sauce gives them a delicate finishing touch.

Ingredients

3 pints fresh raspberries
Verifine sugar
2 to 4 tablespoons kirsch or framboise

The sauce:
4 egg yolks
1 cup sugar
3 to 4 tablespoons lemon juice
2 tablespoons cornstarch
2 cups water
1 teaspoon vanilla
2 teaspoons grated lemon rind
4 tablespoons sweet butter
1 cup heavy cream, whipped

Preparation

1. Place the raspberries in a large serving bowl. Sprinkle them with verifine sugar and kirsch or framboise. Marinate for 2 to 3 hours.

The sauce:
2. In a mixing bowl combine the egg yolks, ½ cup of sugar and the lemon juice. Whisk the mixture until it is light and pale yellow. Set aside.

3. In a heavy saucepan combine the remaining ½ cup of sugar and the cornstarch dissolved in a little cold water. Add the remaining water, place the saucepan over high heat and cook the mixture until it is very thick and clear.

4. Remove the saucepan from the heat and beat in the lemon and egg yolk mixture.

Place the pan over a very low flame and heat the mixture, whisking constantly, until a very faint steam rises. Remove the saucepan from the heat.

5. Add the vanilla, lemon rind and butter and cool the sauce completely.

6. Whip the cream and fold it into the cooled sauce. Chill until serving time.

7. Serve the raspberries with the lemon sauce on the side or fill individual parfait glasses with berries, topping them with lemon sauce just before serving.

Notes

Souffle creole with apricot sauce

Serves: 4 to 6
Preparation time: 30 minutes
Cooking time: 35 to 40 minutes
■ ●

The world of souffles is without limits. For those who really love them, any combination is a culinary delight. Personally I like few dessert souffles, but this is one that I do like. Since bananas are available year round, this souffle is excellent for a time when fresh fruit is scarce.

Ingredients

The souffle:
½ cup sugar plus 2 tablespoons
½ banana, finely sliced
2 tablespoons banana liqueur
3 tablespoons sweet butter
3 tablespoons flour
¾ cup milk, hot
4 egg yolks
1 tablespoon vanilla extract
2 tablespoons white rum
1 banana, mashed
6 egg whites

The sauce:
1 cup apricot preserves
¼ cup water
1 teaspoon lemon rind
Juice of ½ lemon
3 tablespoons apricot brandy

Preparation

1. Preheat the oven to 450°.

2. Butter a 1½-quart souffle mold, then sprinkle it with 1 tablespoon of sugar, shaking out the excess. Place a 3-inch collar of foil around the dish. Butter the collar and tie with a string.

3. Sprinkle the banana slices with the banana liqueur and 1 tablespoon of sugar. Reserve.

4. Melt the butter in a heavy saucepan. Add the flour and cook the mixture for 1 or 2 minutes without browning.

5. Add the hot milk all at once and beat until the mixture gets smooth and thick. Remove it from the heat.

6. Add ½ cup sugar and incorporate it well.

7. Add the egg yolks, one at a time. When all have been incorporated, return the mixture to the stove and heat carefully for a minute or 2. Do not let it come to a boil or the yolks will curdle. Remove from heat.

8. Add the vanilla, rum and mashed banana. Taste the souffle for flavor. You may like more rum.

9. Beat the egg whites until they form soft peaks. Carefully incorporate them into the souffle mixture. For the best results use your hands!

10. Pour half the mixture into the prepared mold. Top with the sliced bananas. Then pour in the remaining souffle mixture. Place in the oven and immediately reduce temperature to 375°. Bake for 30 to 35 minutes without opening the oven door. While it is baking prepare the sauce.

11. In a small saucepan combine the apricot preserves, water, lemon rind and lemon juice. Bring the mixture to a boil and reduce the heat. Simmer the sauce until the apricot preserves are completely dissolved, then add the brandy. Serve the sauce warm.

Remarks

Use two small bananas, mashed, if you like a strong fruit flavor. This should make a full cup of pulp. In that case omit the sliced banana.

Rum raisin ice cream is also a delicious accompaniment to this souffle. You can make it by adding 2 tablespoons of parboiled, well-drained raisins and 2 tablespoons white rum to softened vanilla ice cream.

Notes

Fresh grape tart

Serves: 6
Preparation time: 35 minutes
Cooking time: 35 minutes

Ingredients

1   9-inch Tart Shell (page 407)
3 to 4 cups seedless Thompson grapes

The pastry cream:
6   egg yolks
½ cup sugar
½ cup sifted flour
1½ cups warm milk
1   tablespoon vanilla
3   tablespoons rum
4   almond macaroons, toasted and
    crumbled

The glaze:
1   cup apricot preserves
3   tablespoons sugar
1   tablespoon lemon juice
2   tablespoons apricot brandy

Preparation

1. Make a tart shell according to directions on page 407.

2. Wash the grapes well, dry them with paper towels and set them aside.

3. Preheat the oven to 350°.

The pastry cream:
4. In a bowl combine the egg yolks and sugar and beat the mixture until it is pale yellow and fluffy.

5. Add the flour and stir until it is completely incorporated into the yolks.

6. Add the warm milk and whisk again. Pour the mixture into a heavy-bottomed saucepan. Set the pan over medium heat and cook the mixture, whisking constantly with a wire whisk, until it becomes very thick and smooth.

7. Pour the cream immediately into a bowl and add the vanilla and rum.

8. Fold in the macaroon crumbs and chill the filling for 1 or 2 hours.

9. Fill the baked tart shell with the pastry cream and place the grapes very closely together on top of the cream.

The apricot glaze:
10. In a small saucepan combine the apricot preserves with the sugar and lemon juice. Heat until the sugar is completely dissolved.

11. Add the apricot brandy and pass the glaze through a fine sieve.

12. While the apricot glaze is still hot, brush it over the grapes. Serve the tart the same day.

Remarks

For a more interesting color effect, use both white and dark grapes. The dark grapes should be seeded.
You can substitute fresh blueberries for the grapes in the summer. In that case, omit the macaroons from the pastry cream, and instead of an apricot glaze, make a red-currant-jelly glaze flavored with kirsch instead of apricot brandy.

Notes

Many fruits and vegetables are at their natural peak of perfection during the summer and are cooked best by cooking them least. The emphasis is on letting them be.

Summer is so rich with fresh produce that the season is total excitement to me—a never-ending discovery of what Nature has to offer: fresh herbs, fantastic fruit, young and tender vegetables and flowers rich in color. It is not necessary in summer to work out an elaborate menu; you should rather feel your way through your garden or local market. Look for ingredients with which to make several salads. Serve these with a platter of cheese and one or two good sausages. A cold soup followed by simply grilled fish and a platter of fruit for dessert can be the perfect supper.

The only things to keep in mind are that simplicity requires perfection; that the overcooked green bean is not simple but a sad failure; that salads should not be refrigerated beyond recognition and that barbecues can get to be pretty dull, unless the menu has been well thought out and features some detail that proves your familiarity with the season and its potential. There is such incredible room for creativity in summer, and it would be a shame not to take full advantage of the few months when Nature provides such a wealth of ingredients.

the summer kitchen

Symbols

● **Inexpensive**

◉ **Moderate**

✦ **Expensive**

■ **Easy**

▫ **Intermediate**

⊞ **Difficult**

Scandinavian cold cucumber soup
Grilled lamb chops in mint butter
Middle eastern summer salad
Plums in white wine

When the cook gets ready for outdoor barbecuing, she obviously cannot be in two places at one time. Therefore, as much as possible, the menu must be prepared in advance so that complete attention can be given to the grilling of the meat. As with all grills, the meat has to be watched carefully, for there is nothing less appealing than a burnt chop tasting of charcoal. The advantage of outdoor grilling is that it leaves time for the hostess to be creative with appetizers, salads and desserts. Another excellent accompaniment to this main course is Sicilian Rice with Peppers followed by a green salad (dandelion greens would be perfect) dressed in an anchovy vinaigrette. Vary the dessert by adding other fruits such as peaches and apricots to the compote.

Scandinavian cold cucumber soup

Serves: 8
Preparation time: 5 minutes
Cooking time: none

This cucumber soup is extremely easy to prepare. It requires no cooking and therefore is ideal for summer entertaining.

Ingredients

5 cucumbers
Salt
½ cup chopped parsley
6 scallions, chopped
2 tablespoons freshly chopped dill
¼ cup lemon juice
1 quart buttermilk
1 pint sour cream or Creme Fraiche (page 398)
Freshly ground white pepper

Garnish:
½ cup finely sliced radishes
½ cup cucumber, finely cubed
Fresh mint leaves

Remarks

1. Peel the cucumbers, cut them in half lengthwise and remove the seeds.

2. Sprinkle them with salt and let them stand for 30 minutes. Drain off the accumulated water; chop the cucumbers coarsely and place them in blender with the parsley, scallions, dill, lemon juice, buttermilk and sour cream. Blend at high speed.

3. Add salt and pepper and chill. Pour the soup into a large tureen and garnish it just before serving.

Remarks

For variation, garnish the soup with tiny, freshly poached shrimp or finely minced lobster meat.

Grilled lamb chops in mint butter

Serves: 4
Preparation time: 15 minutes
Cooking time: 10 minutes

Lamb has a natural affinity for mint. Since this dish in itself is extremely simple, it gives the cook time to elaborate on an imaginative accompaniment such as a casserole of sauteed eggplant, peppers and onions, or a gratin of potatoes a la provencale.

Ingredients

The herb butter:
8 tablespoons sweet butter, softened
2 tablespoons finely minced fresh mint
1 tablespoon finely minced parsley
2 to 3 garlic cloves, mashed

The marinade:
½ cup chopped mint
1 garlic clove, finely minced
Juice of 1 lemon
½ to ¾ cup olive oil
8 double loin lamb chops
Salt and freshly ground black pepper

Garnish:
A bed of fresh watercress

Preparation

1. For the herb butter, combine in a small bowl the butter, minced mint and parsley and mashed garlic. Beat until thoroughly blended. Chill the herb butter until firm and reserve.

2. For the marinade, puree the ½ cup of chopped mint in the blender. Add the minced garlic, lemon juice and enough olive oil to make a smooth puree.

3. Place the lamb chops in an enamel dish. Cover them with the marinade and let them

stand at room temperature for 2 to 4 hours.

4. Dry the chops well with paper towels. Broil or grill them to the degree of doneness you prefer. Season with salt and pepper.

5. Garnish a round serving platter with a bed of watercress. Top each chop with a tablespoon of the herb butter, and serve immediately.

Remarks

A bed of fresh mint can be used instead of the watercress.

Notes

Middle eastern summer salad

Serves: 4 to 6
Preparation time: 15 minutes
Cooking time: none

■ ●

The secret of a delicious salad is not one of "outlandish" combinations, which restaurants have on their menus! It is, rather, a fine blending of perfectly fresh vegetables or greens topped with a simple dressing! Here is what I mean . . .

Ingredients

1   garlic clove
1   head romaine lettuce torn into bite-size
    pieces (use only the "heart")
1   green pepper, seeded and cubed
1   cucumber, diced (seeds removed)
2   tomatoes, quartered
1   cup radishes, thinly sliced
1   red onion, thinly sliced
12 green pimiento-stuffed olives
6   tablespoons olive oil
Juice of 1 large lemon
2   tablespoons finely chopped parsley
Salt and freshly ground black pepper
1   cup crumbled Feta cheese (fresh goat
    cheese), or fresh French goat cheese
½ cup fresh grated carrot

Preparation

1. Rub a large salad bowl with the cut side of a large clove of garlic. Combine all the salad ingredients in the salad bowl. In a small mixing bowl combine the oil, lemon juice, parsley, salt and pepper. Blend the dressing thoroughly, add to the salad and toss it lightly. Top the salad with the crumbled goat cheese and grated carrot. Serve immediately.

Remarks

For variation, add ½ cup sour cream to the dressing.

Plums in white wine

Serves: 6
Preparation time: 10 minutes
Cooking time: 8 to 10 minutes

Fruit compotes are the perfect finish to a summer meal. They can be prepared well in advance and offer a good way of using slightly imperfect or underripe fruit.

Ingredients

1½ cups sugar
2 cups sauterne wine
1 3-inch piece of cinnamon stick
3 whole cloves
2 pounds fresh purple plums, washed but not peeled or stoned
2 slices lemon
3 tablespoons white rum

The sauce:
1 cup Creme Fraiche (page 398) sweetened with 2 tablespoons powdered sugar
Lemon rind (1 teaspoon, finely grated)

Preparation

1. In a large saucepan combine the sugar, wine, cinnamon stick and cloves. Bring to a boil and cook over high heat until the sugar is dissolved.

2. Add the plums and lemon slices. Reduce the heat and cook, partially covered, until the plums are tender but not mushy (5 to 8 minutes).

3. Remove the lemon slices and let the plums chill completely in the syrup. Just before serving add the rum.

4. Combine 1 cup Creme Fraiche with powdered sugar and grated lemon rind. Serve the plums in a glass bowl with the Creme Fraiche on the side.

Remarks

You may substitute sweetened whipped cream for the Creme Fraiche. However, the tartness of Creme Fraiche goes particularly well with fruit compotes.

Notes

Eggplant provencale
Grilled bass in basil sauce
Peaches and champagne sabayon

Summer around the Mediterranean is very
much like ours, and this menu brings the
essence of the Mediterranean to our table.
Whether you are spending the summer at
the beach or near a lake, don't hesitate
to experiment with other fish such as red
snapper, lake trout or mullet.
The sauce, appetizer and dessert can be
prepared well in advance, leaving only the
grilling of the fish for the last minute. You
may, however, roast the fish in the oven
and still enjoy this dish to its fullest.
The dessert is rather elaborate. You may
vary the menu by serving a bowl of
carefully picked fresh fruit and a few well-
selected dessert cheeses.

Eggplant provencale

Serves: 4 to 6
Preparation time: 15 minutes
Cooking time: 30 to 40 minutes

Here is a delightful dish that can be served as an appetizer or as a salad. It is an excellent accompaniment to grilled meats or fish. Roast the eggplants and peppers directly over the coals while they are readying for the grilling of the main course.

Ingredients

4   medium eggplants
1   red bell pepper
1   green bell pepper
3 to 4 tablespoons Mayonnaise (Page 402)
3   tablespoons finely minced red onion
1   garlic clove, mashed
Salt and freshly ground black pepper
¼ teaspoon cayenne

Garnish:
Black olives
Tomato wedges
2   tablespoons finely chopped parsley
1   teaspoon lemon juice

Preparation

1. Place the whole eggplants and peppers on a grate 1 inch from the fire and grill them until both vegetables are well charred on the outside. Or place them under the broiler flame until well charred (20 to 30 minutes). Keep turning the eggplants and peppers until they are evenly charred, but do not prick with a fork.

2. When the peppers are ready, remove the stems and seeds and peel off the charred skin. Cut the peppers into small cubes.

3. Mix the peppers in a bowl with the mayonnaise, onion, cayenne and garlic.

4. Place the roasted eggplants on a cutting board, slice them in half and carefully scoop out the soft white centers. Taste the seeds. If they are bitter, discard them.

5. Chop the eggplant and add it to the pepper and onion mixture. Season the salad with salt and pepper. Mix well and garnish with olives, tomato wedges and parsley. Just before serving stir in the lemon juice. Serve at room temperature.

Notes

Grilled bass
in basil sauce

Serves: 4 to 6
Preparation time: 20 minutes
Cooking time: 40 to 50 minutes
■ ●

Grilling a fish is somewhat tricky since it breaks easily when it is turned. It is therefore best to use small whole fish for outdoor grilling. If, however, you are grilling a large fish (2½ to 3 pounds), I suggest placing it in well-oiled foil on a bed of finely sliced vegetables such as onions and celery plus a Bouquet Garni. Season the fish with salt and pepper, close the foil tightly and place it on the grill. The fish will take 40 to 50 minutes. For the last few minutes open the foil and throw a few pine twigs onto the fire. These will give the fish the desired smoky flavor.

Ingredients

4   1- to 1½-pound small freshwater bass
    or 3½- to 4-pound striped bass
Salt and freshly ground black pepper
7   tablespoons olive oil
1   tablespoon lemon juice
1   cup fresh basil leaves
2 to 3 garlic cloves
4   large shallots, finely chopped
6   fresh ripe tomatoes, peeled, seeded and
    chopped
4   anchovies, finely chopped
1   tablespoon capers
2   tablespoons parsley

Garnish:
Basil leaves
Black olives
Lemon wedges
Sprigs of watercress

Preparation

1. Sprinkle the fish with salt and pepper. Brush with olive oil and sprinkle with lemon juice. Grill 4 inches away from the coals for 5 minutes on each side. Do not char the fish. Remove it to a serving platter.

The sauce:
2. Puree the basil leaves with the garlic and 4 tablespoons of olive oil in the blender.

3. In a large skillet heat the remaining olive oil and saute the shallots. Cook until they are soft and transparent but not browned.

4. Add the tomatoes and cook this mixture until thick and all the juices have evaporated.

5. Add the basil puree, anchovies, capers and parsley and just heat through. Correct the seasoning.

6. Pour the sauce around the fish and decorate with basil leaves, black olives, lemon wedges and sprigs of watercress.

Remarks

This sauce is usually served warm, but it is also excellent cold as an accompaniment to cold poached salmon or bass.

Notes

Peaches
and champagne sabayon

Serves: 6 to 8
Preparation time: 10 minutes
Cooking time: 5 minutes

■ ◕

Since fresh peaches have a short season, you should, while they are at their best, strive to use them in a variety of ways. They can be served simply chilled with a pitcher of cream and sugar or poached in red wine. However, if you want to try something more elaborate for family or guests, this dessert, with its light champagne sauce, is perfect.

Ingredients

6 fresh large peaches
Juice of 1 lemon
Rind of 1 lemon, grated
4 egg yolks
⅓ cup sugar
¾ cup champagne
1 to 3 tablespoons kirsch

Garnish:
Finely chopped toasted almonds

Preparation

1. Plunge the peaches into boiling water for 60 seconds, then peel. The skin should slip right off. Cut the peaches into ½-inch-thick wedges and place in a serving bowl.

2. Sprinkle the peaches with the lemon juice and rind. Chill for 1 to 2 hours.

3. In the top of a double boiler, whisk the egg yolks with the sugar and champagne. Keep the water in the bottom of the double boiler at a simmer. Whisk the mixture until it is thick and creamy and coats a spoon heavily. Do not let it come to a boil or the sauce will curdle. Add the kirsch and cool.

4. Drain the lemon juice from the peaches and pour the champagne sauce over them.

Cover and refrigerate until ready to serve.

5. Just before serving sprinkle with the toasted almonds.

Remarks

Other fruits, such as fresh strawberries, blackberries or blueberries, may be served with the same sauce. You may add a cup of whipped cream to the sauce, turning it into a lovely dessert all by itself. Spoon it into parfait glasses and serve with champagne biscuits.

Notes

Stuffed eggplant a l'italienne
Saute of chicken tropezienne
Cherries in meringue

There is no question that the main course will dominate this entire menu. The use of herbs is generous, but it is your personal taste that should guide you. Do not be afraid to experiment, substituting other herbs such as rosemary, chervil, thyme or summer savory for those I have used here. You must, however, keep the herbs in balance! Some, such as rosemary or summer savory, have to be used with care. They can easily overpower any dish.

Serve a light dessert such as the Cherries in Meringue. For a variation follow the main course with a sliced tomato and minced chives salad, crusty French bread, a good soft cheese and the cherries simply poached in red wine without the meringue topping.

Stuffed eggplant
a l'italienne

Serves: 6
Preparation time: 30 minutes
Cooking time: 1 hour 15 minutes

Ingredients

6   very small eggplants (4-inch), or 2 to 3
    medium-sized
Salt
½ cup olive oil
4   tomatoes, peeled, seeded and finely
    chopped
1½ cups homemade bread crumbs
1   7-ounce can of tuna (preferably in olive
    oil)
2   tablespoons finely chopped parsley
2   garlic cloves, finely minced
½ cup minced green olives
1   tablespoon finely chopped basil
6   anchovy filets, finely minced
2   tablespoons minced capers
Freshly ground black pepper

Garnish:
Chopped parsley

Preparation

1. Preheat the oven to 375°.

2. Cut the eggplants in half lengthwise;
with a melon-ball scoop take out the flesh
gently, being careful not to damage the
skin. Mince the pulp well. Sprinkle it with
salt and place in a colander for 30 minutes.
Sprinkle the inside of the eggplant shells
with salt and place them upside down on
paper towels to drain.

3. Heat 4 tablespoons of olive oil in a large
skillet. Add the well-drained eggplant pulp
and cook until lightly browned.

4. Add the tomatoes and cook the mixture
over high heat until all the liquid has
evaporated.

5. Add the bread crumbs, tuna, parsley,

garlic, olives, basil, anchovies and capers
and cook the mixture for 2 more minutes.
Season.

6. Fill the eggplant halves with the mixture.
Dribble the remaining olive oil on each
half, place in a baking dish and bake for
1 hour.

7. Sprinkle with additional parsley and
serve warm or at room temperature.

Remarks

A fresh Tomato Sauce (page 400) is excellent with this dish. For variation, substitute
1 cup finely minced cooked shrimp for
the tuna.

Notes

Saute of chicken tropezienne

Serves: 6
Preparation time: 35 minutes
Cooking time: 2 hours 45 minutes

■●

A tender chicken, sauteed with fresh herbs and finished with a lovely creamy sauce, can bring the essence of southern France to your table. You may want to change your selection of herbs, but remember that no dish should ever be completely taken over by herbs. The chicken, not the herbs, should dominate.

Ingredients

2　egg yolks
½ cup heavy cream
2　2- to 2½-pound chickens, cut into serving pieces (use the wings and giblets for stock)
2　carrots
1　leek
1　Bouquet Garni (page 397), including 1 large celery stalk with leaves
Salt
5　peppercorns
Basil leaves
1　large sprig fresh tarragon
1　large sprig fresh rosemary
Freshly ground white pepper
4　tablespoons sweet butter
1　tablespoon oil
¾ cup dry white wine
4　whole garlic cloves, peeled
2　tablespoons finely chopped fresh herbs (parsley, chives and chervil)

Preparation

1. In a small bowl combine the egg yolks and cream. Blend the mixture and reserve.

2. In a saucepan, combine giblets and wings with the carrot, leek and Bouquet Garni. Cover with 4 cups of cold water, season with salt and the peppercorns.

Bring the mixture to a boil, reduce the heat and simmer, partially covered, for 1 hour to 1 hour and 30 minutes. Strain the stock, reduce it to 1 cup and reserve.

3. Dry the chicken pieces well on paper towels and place basil leaf, 2 tarragon leaves and 2 rosemary leaves under the skin of each piece. Season with salt and pepper.

4. In a large chicken fryer, heat the butter and oil. Saute the chicken pieces a few at a time until evenly browned. Remove them to a side dish; continue sauteeing.

5. Add the wine to the pan, bring it to a boil and scrape the bottom of the pan well.

6. Return the chicken pieces to the pan. Add the stock and garlic cloves. Reduce the heat and simmer the chicken covered for 45 to 50 minutes, or until tender.

7. With a slotted spoon remove the chicken pieces to a serving platter. Raise the heat and reduce the pan juices by ⅓.

8. Take the frying pan off the heat and beat in the cream and egg yolk mixture. Return the pan to very low heat and whisk it constantly until it thickens. Do not let it come to a boil.

9. Taste the sauce and correct the seasoning. Spoon it over the chicken and sprinkle with the fresh herbs. Serve with tiny buttered potato balls, simply cooked young green beans, followed by salad and a bowl of fresh fruit or the Cherries in Meringue.

Remarks

The chicken can be kept warm in its sauce in a 200° oven for 20 minutes.

Cherries in meringue

Serves: 6
Preparation time: 35 minutes
Cooking time: 10 to 15 minutes

Here is a gem of a summer dessert. The cherries are poached in wine and topped with meringue. Other fruits, such as small whole peaches and pears, can be treated in the same way, but I find cherries extremely refreshing and like to take advantage of their short season.

Ingredients

3 cups red wine
1½ cups sugar
1 3-inch piece of cinnamon
2 cloves
2 pounds fresh pitted Bing cherries

The meringue:
4 egg whites
10 tablespoons verifine sugar
1 teaspoon powdered cinnamon
2 tablespoons Praline Powder (page 402)

Preparation

1. Preheat oven to 350°.

2. In a large saucepan combine the wine, sugar, cinnamon and cloves. Bring the mixture to a boil. Reduce the heat. Cover the saucepan and cook over low heat for 5 minutes.

3. Add the cherries a few at a time and cook for 5 to 7 minutes or until just tender.

4. Remove the cherries to individual earthenware bowls. When all the cherries have been poached, cook the syrup over high heat until it thickens. Pour a little into each bowl. Chill the cherries for 2 to 4 hours.

5. Beat the egg whites. Add the sugar a tablespoon at a time until the meringue is stiff and glossy.

6. Put the meringue into a pastry bag and pipe it onto the cherry bowls, covering the top of each one entirely.

7. Sprinkle the meringues with cinnamon and Praline Powder. Place in the oven for a few minutes until the top is lightly browned. Serve immediately.

Remarks

You may substitute powdered macaroons for the Praline Powder.
The cherries can be poached a day or two ahead of time and refrigerated. They are an excellent dessert by themselves.
The bowls for this dessert should be the size of individual souffle dishes. Other ovenproof dishes can be used. You may also put the poached fruit in one large souffle dish and top with meringue. It will look spectacular but be harder to serve.

Notes

Iced parsley and tarragon soup
Scotch poached salmon
Radish salad lugano
Westphalian leeks in sauce ravigote
Blueberries in lemon mousse

This is a menu planned for a buffet party. Cold salmon should be accompanied by two or three salads. You may serve several others such as the Cucumbers and Mint (page 181). Thus the salmon becomes the centerpiece of an exciting summer menu. In serving this soup, you are being creative with the most common herb, displaying indeed a real touch of ingenuity in this use of parsley and tarragon. The Blueberries in Lemon Mousse give this menu a finishing touch of freshness that spells "summer."

Iced parsley and tarragon soup

Serves: 6 to 8
Preparation time: 20 minutes
Cooking time: 45 minutes

Cold soups dominate the summer scene. Indeed they should, since they require little effort, minimum cooking and can be made well in advance. In addition, they offer the cook an opportunity to use all the season's vegetables. Here is a soup to which you may add any of your garden herbs. Since parsley is generally abundant in most gardens, it inspired this recipe.

Ingredients

1   large bunch parsley (preferably the Italian flat-leaf type)
2   tablespoons sweet butter
2   large leeks, finely sliced
1   pound new potatoes, peeled and cubed
6   cups Chicken Stock (page 404)
Salt and freshly ground white pepper
2   cups light cream
2   tablespoons fresh tarragon, finely chopped

Garnish:
Freshly ground black pepper
Minced parsley
Radish slices

Preparation

1. Wash the parsley. Remove and discard the coarse stems. Chop the leaves. This should yield about 3 cups. Reserve 2 tablespoons for garnishing.

2. In a large heavy-bottomed casserole melt the butter. Add the leeks and cook over moderate heat until they are soft but not browned.

3. Add the potato cubes and the Chicken Stock. Bring to a boil. Season with salt and pepper.

4. Turn the heat down and simmer the stock, covered, until the potato cubes are quite soft (about 35 minutes). Add the chopped parsley and simmer for 10 minutes more.

5. Puree the soup in a blender or rub it through a sieve. Add the cream and tarragon. Taste the soup and correct the seasoning. Chill until serving. Just before serving add a dash of freshly ground black pepper. Garnish with sliced radishes and the remaining parsley.

Remarks

The soup may thicken considerably in the refrigerator, especially if you use home-made stock. If so, just add more cream or even milk. You may also beat in 1 cup of sour cream and garnish with finely minced fresh herbs. Do not try to make this soup with dry tarragon.

Notes

Scotch poached salmon

Serves: 6
Preparation time: 10 minutes
Cooking time: 15 minutes

One of the best light summer meals is a cold salmon surrounded by fun salads such as the Radish Salad Lugano, or a green bean salad with a touch of mint and a cold caper sauce. I learned the following foolproof method of cooking salmon in Scotland where the salmon is simply marvelous. It can be used with any size salmon.

Ingredients

Fresh salmon (3 to 4 pounds, center cut, in 1 piece)
1 tablespoon salt
1 small bunch fresh dill
3 tablespoons vinegar
1 large onion, stuck with a clove
2 bay leaves
10 peppercorns

Garnish:
Watercress
Unpeeled lemon slices

Preparation

1. Fill a large casserole (or fish poacher) in which the fish will fit comfortably with enough water to cover it. Add all ingredients except the fish. Bring to a boil and simmer for 10 minutes.

2. Add the salmon and bring the water back to a boil. Cook for exactly 2 minutes.

3. Take the casserole off the heat. Cover with a tight lid and let the fish cool in the liquid for a few hours. When completely cool, drain the fish, place it on a serving platter and chill.

4. Take the salmon out of the refrigerator 20 minutes before serving. Serve garnished with watercress and lemon slices.

Radish salad lugano

Serves: 6 to 8
Preparation time: 30 minutes
Cooking time: none

Slicing radishes is certainly one of the most boring of chores. All the same, this salad is worth the effort. There is something very refreshing about radishes and it is sad to see their use limited to decorating other foods. Here is a chance for them to be "center stage" so take advantage of it.

Ingredients

5 cups radishes, sliced
1 cup finely cubed Swiss cheese
2 tablespoons tarragon vinegar
6 tablespoons olive oil
1 teaspoon anchovy paste
1 teaspoon Dijon mustard
1 small garlic clove, mashed
2 tablespoons minced scallions (both green and white part)
Salt and freshly ground black pepper

Garnish:
Sprigs of parsley
Black olives
Rolled filets of anchovies

Preparation

1. Place the sliced radishes in a large serving bowl and sprinkle them with Swiss cheese.

2. In a flour shaker or a small covered jar mix the vinegar, oil, anchovy paste, mustard, garlic and scallions. Cover tightly and shake. The dressing will become thick and creamy. Pour it over the radishes and blend well. Season with salt and pepper.

3. Garnish with parsley, black olives and anchovy filets. Serve chilled but not cold, the flavor will be lost if "frozen" in.

Remarks

You may slice the radishes one or two days in advance and keep them in iced water. They must be thoroughly drained and dried on paper towels. Once the dressing has been poured over them, they should be served within 3 to 4 hours.

Notes

Westphalian leeks in sauce ravigote

Serves: 6
Preparation time: 30 minutes
Cooking time: 15 minutes

Cold leeks are a marvelous vegetable. They lend themselves to all sorts of sauces and are particularly good in combination with Westphalian ham. I realize, however, that it is not always available. When it isn't, the leeks are just as delicious wrapped in thin slices of baked ham.

Ingredients

12 leeks
1 teaspoon salt
12 thin slices Westphalian ham or baked ham
1 teaspoon Dijon mustard
1½ cups Mayonnaise (page 402)
2 small dill gherkins, finely minced
1 tablespoon capers
1 tablespoon finely chopped scallions

Garnish:
Cherry tomatoes
Sprigs of watercress
Hard-boiled eggs

Preparation

1. Select leeks of uniform size so that they will cook evenly.

2. Trim the leeks, leaving the green parts 5 to 6 inches long. Wash them thoroughly under cold water (leeks tend to retain a lot of sand). Even better, leave them in a bowl of ice water for a few hours.

3. Drain the leeks and place them in a saucepan large enough to keep them in 1 layer. Cover with water. Add the salt and set the saucepan over high heat. As soon as the water comes to a boil, turn the heat down to simmer and cook the leeks, par-

tially covered, until just tender. Drain them on paper towels.

4. Wrap each leek in a slice of Westphalian ham and place on a serving platter.

5. Mix the Dijon mustard with the mayonnaise. Then add the gherkins, capers and scallions. Correct the seasoning and pour the sauce over the leeks.

6. Garnish the platter with cherry tomatoes, watercress and hard-boiled eggs.

Remarks

The leeks can be poached a day ahead of serving, but they should be wrapped in the ham no more than 2 or 3 hours before serving. The sauce can also be made ahead of time, but should not be poured over the leeks until just prior to serving.

Notes

Blueberries in lemon mousse

Serves: 6
Preparation time: 15 minutes
Cooking time: 7 to 10 minutes

This simple mousse is excellent with all kinds of berries. Blackberries and blueberries tell the best color story, but strawberries and raspberries may also be prepared this way. The mousse can even be served by itself or over plain sponge cake, if this appeals to you.

Ingredients

1   quart blueberries
1   cup sugar
5   eggs, separated
Juice of 2 large lemons
1   cup whipped cream
2   teaspoons grated lemon rind

Preparation

1. Wash blueberries and remove their stems. Pour them into a glass serving bowl and sprinkle with ¼ cup sugar.

2. In the top of a stainless steel or enamel double boiler beat the egg yolks with the rest of the sugar until the mixture becomes a light lemon color. Add the lemon juice and cook the mixture over simmering water, whisking constantly until it heavily coats a spoon. Do not let it come to a boil. Immediately remove from the heat and cool.

3. Beat the egg whites until they are stiff but not dry and fold them gently into the lemon mixture.

4. Fold in the whipped cream and lemon rind. Incorporate them well and make sure the mousse is very smooth. Chill, and just before serving cover the berries with the mousse.

Remarks

Do not garnish the mousse with additional
berries. Your guests will have the surprise
of discovering the fruit during serving.
Do not cook the lemon mixture in an alumi-
num double boiler as it affects the flavor
and color of the mousse.

Notes

Stuffed tomatoes bergerette
Tournedos sautes fines herbes
Strawberries imperiale

Pan-frying involves last-minute cooking and even an experienced cook can become frustrated when watching over three or four dishes at the same time. This is especially true in the summer when kitchens tend to be hot and when you want to be outdoors. I find it easier therefore to prepare an appetizer well in advance. The dessert, too, can be made a day ahead. This leaves me with only 10 final minutes in the kitchen yet still able to serve a quality meal.

In this menu, keep in mind that the tomatoes should be brought back to room temperature for 15 to 30 minutes before serving. The baked Potatoes Aioli (page 383) are a perfect accompaniment to the Tournedos. For a more elaborate meal follow the main course with a mixed green salad, dressed in a vinaigrette that has been flavored with 2 tablespoons of Creme Fraiche, and a platter of cheese.

The strawberries can be marinated in sugared fresh orange juice flavored with 1 or 2 tablespoons of orange liqueur. This gives a lighter touch to the menu, but is somewhat less exciting then the Strawberries Imperiale.

Stuffed tomatoes bergerette

Serves: 6
Preparation time: 25 minutes
Cooking time: 20 minutes

A cold stuffed tomato is one of summer's most attractive appetizers. It is a marvelous way to use leftovers creatively and even with a simple filling such as this one you can create a refreshing and delicious hors d'oeuvre. You may vary the filling by adding to it finely minced poached salmon, a few poached mussels or even flaked tuna.

Ingredients

6   medium-sized tomatoes
Salt
¾ cup Vinaigrette (pages 408–409)
½ cup Italian rice
⅓ cup heavy cream
1   teaspoon Dijon mustard
Freshly ground white pepper
2   tablespoons finely minced scallions
2   tablespoons finely minced parsley
2   tablespoons finely minced green pepper
2   tablespoons finely minced pimientos
4   anchovy filets

Garnish:
6   whole cooked peeled shrimp or 6 whole
    rolled anchovy filets
Black olives
Bed of watercress
Juice of ½ lemon
2 to 3 tablespoons olive oil

Preparation

1. Cut a slice off the top of the tomatoes. Gently loosen the flesh with a small knife and remove it. Discard the seeds but reserve the pulp. Sprinkle the tomato shells with salt and place them cut side down on a plate for 30 minutes.

2. After 30 minutes, sprinkle the tomato shells with ¼ cup of the Vinaigrette and let them marinate while you prepare the rice.

3. In a saucepan, bring to a boil 1½ cups of water seasoned with ½ teaspoon salt. When the water comes to a boil, add the rice, reduce the heat and simmer, covered, until it is tender (about 20 minutes). Then remove the rice to a mixing bowl and cool completely.

4. Whip the cream. Add the Dijon mustard, salt and pepper and reserve.

5. When the rice is quite cold, add the minced vegetables and anchovies. Bind the rice salad with the whipped cream mixture and add the remaining Vinaigrette. The tomato pulp, finely chopped, may be added to the rice too. Be sure not to include any of the seeds. Refrigerate the rice for 30 minutes to 1 hour.

6. Drain the tomato shells and fill them with the rice. Top each shell with 1 whole shrimp, anchovy filet or black olive. Put the tomatoes on a bed of watercress seasoned with lemon juice and olive oil. Serve chilled but not cold.

Notes

Tournedos sautes fines herbes

Serves: 4
Preparation time: 45 minutes
Cooking time: 15 minutes

■ ✛

Here is an inspired way to prepare filet steaks or pan-fried shell steaks. It is a method often used for meat of medium quality. The butter and herbs will seep through the beef and give it unusual flavor and tenderness. If you want to serve these steaks at any other time of the year when you do not have all the herbs available, try it with just parsley, shallots and a finely minced garlic clove. If you use shell steaks, you will have to use two pans in order to serve more than two people at a time.

Ingredients

8   tablespoons sweet butter
1   tablespoon finely minced fresh parsley
½ tablespoon chopped fresh chervil
½ tablespoon finely chopped summer
     savory
2   tablespoons finely minced shallots
4   slices day-old white bread, cut ½ inch
     thick
4   tablespoons Clarified Butter (page 398)
4   filet steaks, cut ¾ inch thick
Salt and freshly ground black pepper
1   tablespoon oil

Optional:
Sprigs of watercress
2 or 3 summer vegetables (such as green
     beans, sauteed cherry tomatoes or
     carrots) braised in sweet butter

Preparation

1. Cream 6 tablespoons of butter with the finely chopped herbs and shallots.

2. Fill a saucepan with water; bring it to a boil. Reduce the heat; set a dinner plate on top and place the herbed butter on it.

3. Cut the crusts off the bread and saute the slices in the Clarified Butter until lightly browned. Place them on a serving platter.

4. Dry the filets well with paper towels. Season them with salt and pepper.

5. In a large heavy skillet melt the remaining butter, add the oil and when very hot, saute the filets for 3 or 4 minutes on each side. They should be well browned but still rare. Make sure you do not crowd your pan.

6. Place the four filets on the melted herb butter and cover with another plate or with foil. Keep the water simmering. Let the steaks "steam" for 5 to 7 minutes, then place them on the bread slices.

7. Pour the herb butter from the plate onto the steaks.

8. Garnish the platter with watercress and braised vegetables. Serve the steaks immediately.

Notes

Strawberries imperiale

Serves: 4 to 6
Preparation time: 45 minutes
Cooking time: 10 to 12 minutes

Ingredients

5 egg yolks
¾ cup sugar
1½ cups warm milk
1 tablespoon vanilla extract
3 tablespoons Grand Marnier
1 tablespoon unflavored gelatin
1 cup heavy cream, whipped
3 pints fresh strawberries
2 tablespoons kirsch
6 tablespoons currant jelly

Preparation

1. In the top of a double boiler combine the egg yolks and ½ cup of sugar. Beat the mixture until it is pale yellow and forms a ribbon when dropped from a spoon. Add the warm milk and cook the custard over simmering water until it thickens and lightly coats the spoon. Add the vanilla extract and the Grand Marnier. Stir well and then pour the custard into a mixing bowl.

2. In a small saucepan over moderate heat, melt the gelatin in 3 tablespoons of water. Whisk the melted gelatin into the custard and place the bowl in the refrigerator. Stir the custard from time to time.

3. When the custard begins to set, add the whipped cream and pour the custard into a serving bowl.

4. Wash and then hull the strawberries. Top the custard with 2 cups of the most perfect berries.

5. Puree the remaining strawberries in a blender together with the remaining sugar and the kirsch. Force this mixture through a fine sieve to remove all the seeds.

6. In a small saucepan heat the currant jelly. When it is well dissolved, add it to the strawberry puree. Chill until ready to serve.

7. Just before serving, pour the strawberry sauce over the strawberries and serve immediately.

Remarks

Raspberries can be used instead of strawberries to top the custard. Do not wash the raspberries.

Notes

Salad of beets in mustard sauce

Serves: 6 to 8
Preparation time: 30 minutes
Cooking time: none

■ ●

Beets are an important part of the summer hors d'oeuvre table. This recipe can be made well in advance and kept for several days in a covered jar in the refrigerator. Serve on a bed of lettuce as an appetizer or as part of a cold vegetable platter with marinated sardines and deviled eggs.

Ingredients

4 cups cooked beets, cut into ½-inch matchsticks
1 tablespoon white cider vinegar
2 tablespoons lemon juice
2 teaspoons sugar
¼ cup Dijon mustard
⅓ cup olive oil
1 tablespoon finely chopped parsley
3 tablespoons finely chopped fresh dill
Salt and freshly ground black pepper

Garnish:
2 hard-boiled egg yolks, finely minced
Sprigs of fresh dill

Preparation

1. Place the beets in a salad bowl.

2. In a small bowl combine the vinegar, lemon juice and sugar. When the sugar has dissolved, add the mustard and olive oil. Whisk the dressing until it is well blended and creamy.

3. Add the parsley and dill and blend well.

4. Pour the dressing over the beets and season with salt and pepper. Cover the bowl and refrigerate for at least 4 hours before serving.

5. Just before serving, sprinkle with minced hard-boiled egg yolks and sprigs of dill.

Green beans bonne femme

Serves: 6
Preparation time: 20 minutes
Cooking time: 20 minutes

■ ●

In Europe many vegetable dishes are served as an appetizer or first course. This enables the cook to spend time elaborating on other dishes. Here is a recipe that is simple and tasty. It can be served either as an appetizer or as an accompaniment to steaks and roasts.

Ingredients

2 pounds green beans
Salt
1 cup finely cubed bacon
2 tablespoons olive oil
2 garlic cloves
2 cups finely sliced onions
Freshly ground black pepper

Optional:
1 tablespoon finely minced fresh herbs (chervil or mint)

Garnish:
1 tablespoon finely chopped parsley
Bread triangles fried in olive oil

Preparation

1. Snap off the tips of the beans.

2. In a large saucepan, bring salted water to a boil. Add the beans a few at a time in order to bring the water back to a boil as fast as possible. Boil uncovered for 10 to 12 minutes or until barely tender. Drain the beans and run them under cold water to stop further cooking.

3. In a large skillet, saute the cubed bacon until it is crisp. Remove from the skillet and drain on paper towels.

4. Pour out all but one tablespoon of fat from the skillet. Add the olive oil. When

it is hot, add the garlic clove and let it brown. Then discard it.

5. Add the onion slices and cook them over medium heat until they are lightly browned and soft.

6. Add the beans and the bacon. Shake the pan to coat all the beans with the onions and bacon. Season with salt and pepper. Cover the pan and simmer for 2 or 3 minutes.

7. Transfer the beans to a serving dish. Sprinkle with parsley and the optional herbs. Arrange the bread triangles around the platter and serve immediately.

Notes

Cold tomatoes a la creme

Serves: 6 to 8
Preparation time: 15 minutes
Cooking time: none

Ingredients

6 ounces cream cheese
3 tablespoons finely minced chives
2 tablespoons finely minced chervil
1 cup thick Creme Fraiche (page 398)
Salt and freshly ground white pepper
6 to 8 small whole firm tomatoes (not
    overly ripe)

Garnish:
Boston lettuce
Lemon Vinaigrette (page 408)

Preparation

1. Put the cream cheese in a small mixing bowl. Let it come to room temperature, then blend it with the chives and chervil until the mixture is smooth and creamy.

2. Add the Creme Fraiche, salt and pepper and let the mixture develop flavor in the refrigerator for 1 hour.

3. Cut the tops off the tomatoes, but do not discard them. Scoop out the seeds and flesh gently so as not to break the skins. Salt the tomatoes and let them drain upside down on a platter for 1 hour.

4. Just before serving, fill the tomatoes with the cream cheese mixture and top each one with its cap. Place the tomatoes on a bed of crisp Boston lettuce and serve the Lemon Vinaigrette on the side.

Remarks

The platter may also be garnished with radishes, black olives, sliced cucumbers and thinly sliced green pepper rings. Thinly sliced and buttered pumpernickel is the perfect bread to serve.

Pate au fines herbes

Serves: 6 to 8
Preparation time: 45 minutes
Cooking time: 10 to 12 minutes

Here is a pate that has in its flavor the essence of Provence. It is easy to prepare and can be successfully frozen. This enables you to carry a little of the taste of summer's herbs into the late fall or winter.

Ingredients

1½ pounds fresh chicken livers
Salt and freshly ground white pepper
3   tablespoons sweet butter
1   tablespoon oil
4   large shallots, finely minced
3   tablespoons cognac, warmed
½ cup Concentrated Brown Stock (page 403)
2 to 3 tablespoons finely ground fresh herbs, mashed (chervil, parsley, rosemary and thyme)
1   large garlic clove
½ pound (2 sticks) sweet butter, softened
½ cup Clarified Butter (page 398), or 1 cup clear aspic

Preparation

1. Clean the chicken livers thoroughly removing all green and black spots. Slice each chicken liver in half. Season them well with salt and pepper.

2. Melt the butter and oil in a large skillet. When hot, add the chicken livers together with the shallots and saute over medium heat until the livers are nicely browned. Shake the pan several times to insure the even cooking of the chicken livers and do not let the shallots burn.

3. When the chicken livers are done, pour the warm cognac over them and ignite. Shake the pan to spread the cognac evenly.

When the flames die down, remove the chicken livers to the top part of the blender.

4. Pour the Brown Stock into the skillet, scraping the bottom well and cook over high heat until the liquid is reduced to 2 tablespoons. Add the reduced stock to the chicken livers.

5. Puree the mixture at high speed until it is very smooth (you may have to do it in 2 or 3 batches). Correct the seasoning and transfer to a bowl. Cool for 30 minutes.

6. While the chicken livers are cooling, combine the herbs and garlic in a mortar and pound them into a smooth paste. (This can also be done in the blender.) With a wooden spoon, cream the sweet butter in a mixing bowl until it is smooth and pliable. Add the herb paste and blend thoroughly.

7. Beat the herb butter into the completely cooled chicken liver puree. It should be completely incorporated and smooth.

8. Spoon the mixture into individual ramekins or a pate mold. Or, if you have a nice earthenware crock, use that. Refrigerate the pate for 2 hours.

9. Warm the Clarified Butter in a small saucepan. Pour a little of it onto each cold ramekin or if you are using one crock pour all of it over the cold pate.

10. Refrigerate for 12 hours before using. Serve with crusty French bread and a bowl of tiny dill gherkins (French Cornichons).

Remarks

For a more elegant presentation, top the pate with clear aspic.

Sardines montelemar

Serves: 6
Preparation time: 35 minutes
Cooking time: broiler—15 minutes; open
  fire—8 to 10 minutes

Grilled fish, served cold, can be delicious. Grilling can be done on the barbecue, but the charcoal flavor usually dominates the delicate flavor of the fish. However, grilling on twigs, especially pine twigs, is excellent, for it will give the fish a smoky flavor. For those who like this dish and do not want to go to all the trouble of starting a fire, oven grilling is almost as good.

Ingredients

20 small sardines or 10 medium-sized
    herring
Salt and freshly ground black pepper
1 large sprig thyme
1 large sprig fresh rosemary
3 red onions, thinly sliced
3 lemons
¾ to 1 cup olive oil
5 tablespoons wine vinegar
2 large garlic cloves, finely minced
1 tablespoon finely minced fresh thyme
2 bay leaves
2 tablespoons minced Italian parsley
Coarse salt
Juice of 1 lemon

Preparation

If you are grilling on the barbecue, be sure that the coals are completely white before adding the sardines.

1. Season the fish with salt and pepper and grill for 2 or 3 minutes on each side. Just before they are done, throw a sprig of thyme and rosemary on the fire. This will give the fish a most wonderful herb bouquet. (In the oven. Preheat the oven to 400°. Place the sardines in a large baking pan that has been well oiled. Dribble with olive oil and bake the sardines for 15 minutes or until they flake when tested with a fork.)

2. In a large earthenware dish, put a layer of onion slices.

3. Cut 2 lemons in thin slices. Do not peel them. Add 1 lemon to the onion layer, sprinkle with olive oil and vinegar and top with ½ of the sardines placed close together.

4. Season the sardines with vinegar, pepper, garlic and minced thyme.

5. Top with a bay leaf and make another layer of onions, lemon slices and sardines with vinegar, garlic, thyme and bay leaf. Finish with 2 tablespoons of chopped parsley. Sprinkle the lemon juice and 2 tablespoons olive oil on the sardines. Cover the dish with foil and refrigerate overnight.

6. Serve as an appetizer with crusty bread or as part of an hors d'oeuvre table.

Remarks

Smelts, grilled in the oven, can be the winter substitute for this dish. Dry herbs can be used, though there is no comparison to the fresh thyme and rosemary that give this dish its distinctive flavor. In southern France, the sardines are washed in sea water. It is supposed to give them extra flavor. If you are near a beach, try it.

Notes

Summer basil soup

Serves: 6 to 8
Preparation time: 40 to 45 minutes
Cooking time: 20 to 25 minutes

Basil, the most aromatic of the summer herbs, is one of the simplest to grow. It is mostly known for its natural affinity to tomatoes, but I use it in many other dishes. Here is a simple summer soup that is delicious either hot or cold. Seasonal vegetables other than zucchini—leeks, turnips or cauliflower flowerettes, for instance—can be finely diced, parboiled and added to this soup.

Ingredients

1   cup fresh basil leaves
2   garlic cloves, minced
1   tablespoon pine nuts
2 to 3 tablespoons finely grated
     Parmesan cheese
Olive oil
6 to 8 cups Chicken Stock (page 404)
1   cup broken-up spaghetti or other thin
     pasta (vermicelli)
2   small zucchini, cut into ¼-inch slices
Salt and freshly ground white pepper

Preparation

1. In a mortar, pound the basil leaves together with the garlic, pine nuts and Parmesan. Add enough olive oil so that the mixture will turn into a smooth, thick paste.

2. In a large casserole heat the Chicken Stock. Add the spaghetti and cook, covered, until barely tender (about 10 minutes).

3. Add the zucchini and cook for 10 more minutes or until it is tender.

4. Season the soup with salt and pepper. Whisk in the basil paste and serve it immediately.

Soup menton

Serves: 6
Preparation time: 25 minutes
Cooking time: 35 to 40 minutes

This is an excellent summer soup which allows you to take full advantage of your garden. A few shelled peas or several tiny cauliflower flowerettes may be added to it.

Ingredients

8   tablespoons olive oil
2   onions, finely minced
1   pound fresh ripe tomatoes, peeled,
     seeded and chopped
2   cups new potatoes, cut into small cubes
2   cups young green beans, cut into 1-inch
     pieces
Salt and freshly ground white pepper
3   small zucchini, cut into cubes
½ cup broken-up spaghetti
1   cup fresh basil leaves
4   garlic cloves, minced
3   tablespoons freshly grated Parmesan
     cheese

Optional:
3   egg yolks

Preparation

1. In a large casserole heat 3 tablespoons olive oil. Add the onions and cook without browning for 3 to 5 minutes.

2. Add the tomatoes, potatoes and beans. Season with salt and pepper and cover with 6 to 8 cups of water. Bring the mixture to a boil and reduce the heat. Simmer the soup partially covered for 15 minutes, or until the potatoes are almost tender.

3. Add the zucchini and spaghetti and continue simmering the soup for 12 to 15 minutes more or until all the vegetables are tender. Do not overcook. The soup must retain its freshness.

Cold zucchini soup

Serves: 6
Preparation time: 10 minutes
Cooking time: 25 minutes

4. While the soup is simmering, combine the basil, garlic and Parmesan in the top part of a blender. Add enough olive oil to make a smooth paste. You will need about 5 tablespoons.

5. Just before serving, whisk the basil paste into the soup. Correct the seasoning and serve.

Remarks

For a more refined soup, mix the egg yolks with a little of the broth, and whisk the egg-yolk mixture into the soup. In this case the soup must not come to a boil again or the yolks will curdle.
A firm tomato, peeled, seeded and cut into tiny cubes, is a lovely addition to the soup just before serving.
When including peas in the soup, they should be added no more than 5 to 8 minutes before the soup is done. Cauliflower flowerettes can be added together with the zucchini.

Notes

Ingredients

6 small zucchini, cut into 1-inch cubes (with a few slices reserved for garnish)
Salt
2 tablespoons olive oil
2 tablespoons sweet butter
2 onions, finely minced
1 garlic clove, finely minced
5 cups Chicken Stock (page 404)
2 tablespoons mixed fresh herbs, finely chopped (parsley, chives, oregano, basil)
1 to 2 teaspoons lemon juice
Freshly ground black pepper

Optional:
1 cup sour cream mixed with 1 tablespoon finely chopped chives for garnish
½ to ¾ cup heavy cream or milk

Preparation

1. Salt the zucchini cubes, and place them in a sieve over a bowl for at least 30 minutes to drain.

2. In a large casserole, heat the olive oil and butter. Add the onion and the garlic and cook over low heat for 5 minutes without browning.

3. Dry the zucchini cubes very well on paper towels. Add them to the skillet and continue cooking over low heat for 5 minutes.

4. Add Chicken Stock and let the soup simmer for 15 minutes. Turn off the heat and as soon as the soup is cool enough, puree it in the blender.

5. Add the herbs and lemon juice. Season with salt and pepper and chill the soup until serving time.

6. You may garnish the cold soup with sour cream mixed with chives or grated raw zucchini which will give the soup an interesting texture.

Remarks

All cold soups should be made with rich homemade stock. It gives the soup a texture that cannot be achieved by using canned stock. If the soup thickens too much during refrigeration, thin it out with spoonfuls of heavy cream or milk. This soup is equally good served hot in the early fall.

Notes

Crepes aux fines herbes a la mexicaine

Serves: 6
Preparation time: 45 minutes
Cooking time: 20 minutes

Ingredients

12 to 14 Crepes Fines Herbes (page 399)

The filling:
1　large ripe avocado, peeled and cubed
4　ounces cream cheese
Dash of lemon juice
Salt and freshly ground white pepper
Drops of Tabasco
2　tablespoons finely minced chives
4 to 6 finely minced cooked shrimp

Optional:
1　tablespoon finely minced tarragon (or dill)

The sauce:
½ cup melted sweet butter
1　garlic clove, mashed
Dash of lemon juice
Salt and freshly ground black pepper

Preparation

The filling:
1. In a mixing bowl combine the avocado, cream cheese, lemon juice, salt, pepper and Tabasco. Mash together with a fork until smooth. Add the chives, optional tarragon (or dill) and the shrimp. Correct the seasoning. Cover well and chill until serving time.

2. Make the crepes according to instructions on page 399 and cool them slightly.

3. Fill the crepes with the avocado and cream cheese mixture and place them in a baking dish or on a serving platter.

The sauce:
4. Combine the warm melted butter with the mashed garlic clove and lemon juice.

Season lightly with salt and fresh black pepper and dribble a little of the warm sauce over the crepes. Serve warm.

Remarks

You may garnish the platter with avocado slices and a few whole cooked shrimp.

Notes

Eggs mollets with fines herbes

Serves: 6
Preparation time: 20 minutes
Cooking time: 10 to 12 minutes

This is an extremely simple dish to prepare, yet somewhat demanding. The eggs must not be overcooked or the dish loses its character.

Ingredients

1   pound chicken livers
Salt and freshly ground white pepper
6   tablespoons sweet butter
2   tablespoons minced scallions
2   tablespoons dry sherry
½ cup Brown Stock (page 403), or beef bouillon
Pinch of fresh sage, minced
6   large eggs
2   tablespoons finely minced fresh herbs (chervil, parsley, chives and tarragon)
6   oval toast slices

Garnish:
2 to 3 tablespoons minced parsley

Preparation

1. Clean the chicken livers and remove any greenish spots. Cut each liver in half and dry them on paper towels. Season with salt and pepper.

2. In a heavy skillet, melt 2 tablespoons of butter. When it is very hot, add the scallions and cook them until they are soft but not browned.

3. Add the chicken livers and cook them over high heat until they are nicely browned. When they are done, remove them to a side dish.

4. Add the sherry and Brown Stock to the pan, scraping the bottom of the pan well. Reduce to about 2 tablespoons.

5. Remove from the heat, add the sage and pour over the chicken livers. Keep them warm over warm water while preparing the eggs.

6. Lower the eggs carefully into fast-boiling water and cook them for 5 minutes over medium heat. Run the eggs under cold water to stop the cooking and carefully peel them.

7. In a large skillet, melt the remaining butter over low heat. When hot, add the minced herbs together with the eggs.

8. Season with salt and pepper and roll the eggs gently in the herb butter for 1 or 2 minutes.

9. Place each egg on a piece of toast. Pour the herb butter over the eggs and place the chicken livers around them. Sprinkle with parsley and serve immediately.

Remarks

To make the toast, cut bread into ½-inch-thick slices, then cut out ovals with an oval-shaped cookie cutter. Saute the slices in Clarified Butter (page 398) or butter them and toast them in the oven.

Notes

Quiche nicoise

Serves: 8 to 10
Preparation time: 1 hour
Cooking time: 50 minutes

■ ●

"Quiche" is rapidly becoming a household word in the United States. When well prepared, the traditional Quiche Lorraine, with bacon and cheese, can be excellent. Unfortunately, it is often a soggy, bland concoction. Many different fillings can be used for a quiche. Here is one that I find interesting and the perfect dish for a simple summer lunch.

Ingredients

1   9-inch Tart Shell (page 407)

The filling:
1   small eggplant, peeled and cut into small cubes
6   tablespoons olive oil (or more if needed)
1   cup onions, finely minced
1   garlic clove, mashed
1   green pepper, seeded and finely cubed
3   ripe tomatoes, seeded, peeled, chopped and drained
Salt and freshly ground white pepper
2   tablespoons finely minced fresh basil
1   teaspoon oregano

The sauce:
3   tablespoons sweet butter
4   tablespoons flour
2   cups warm milk
Salt and freshly ground white pepper
Pinch of nutmeg
2   egg yolks
4   tablespoons finely grated Parmesan cheese

Preparation

1. Sprinkle the eggplant cubes with salt and put them in a colander over a bowl. Let them drain for at least 1 hour.

2. Heat 2 tablespoons of olive oil in a heavy skillet. Add the onion and garlic and cook the mixture until the onions are quite soft and very lightly browned. Add the minced green pepper and cook the mixture until the pepper is soft.

3. Add the tomatoes, and continue cooking the mixture until it is a thick puree. Season with salt and pepper and add the minced basil and oregano.

4. Heat 4 tablespoons oil in another skillet. Dry the eggplant cubes thoroughly on paper towels and saute them until nicely browned on all sides. You may need a little more oil. Season the eggplant cubes lightly with salt and pepper.

5. When the eggplant cubes have all been sauteed, dry them thoroughly on paper towels and then add them to the onion and tomato mixture. Reserve.

The sauce:
6. In a heavy saucepan, melt the butter, add the flour and cook for 1 or 2 minutes, stirring constantly without letting it brown.

7. Add the warm milk all at once and continue stirring until the mixture comes to a boil and is very thick.

8. Season with salt, pepper and nutmeg. Remove the pan from the heat and whisk in the egg yolks.

9. Fill the pastry shell with the eggplant mixture.

10. Top the filling with the sauce and sprinkle heavily with the grated Parmesan.

11. Bake the quiche for 30 minutes or until nicely browned. Let stand for 10 minutes before serving.

Remarks

You may add minced anchovy filets to the filling as well as flaked tuna or finely cubed crabmeat.
The shell can be made in advance and will freeze well. If you are a quiche fan, make several crusts at a time and freeze them one on top of the other. This will enable you to make a quiche on the spur of the moment.

Notes

Tomatoes and eggs a la nicoise

Serves: 6
Preparation time: 15 to 20 minutes
Cooking time: 6 to 8 minutes

This is a breakfast dish for those days when you are tired of the usual fried or scrambled eggs. It may also be part of a brunch buffet table.

Ingredients

6 slices beefsteak tomatoes, ½ inch thick
Salt
Freshly ground white pepper
2 tablespoons sweet butter
2 tablespoons olive oil
6 poached eggs or 6 Eggs Mollets (page 400)
⅓ cup heavy cream
1 cup Hollandaise (page 402)
2 tablespoons finely minced fresh herbs, including parsley, chives and tarragon

Preparation

1. Season the tomato slices with salt and pepper and let them drain on a large plate for 30 minutes.

2. Heat the butter and oil in a large skillet. When very hot, add the tomatoes and cook for 1 or 2 minutes or until they are just heated through. They should still be crisp. Remove the tomatoes carefully to a serving dish.

3. Top each tomato with a poached egg.

4. Whip the cream and just before serving combine with the Hollandaise and herbs. Spoon the sauce over the eggs and serve.

Remarks

If you do not have time to make the Hollandaise, substitute melted butter flavored with minced herbs.

Omelette a l'espagnole

Serves: 4
Preparation time: 10 to 15 minutes
Cooking time: 30 to 40 minutes

Open-faced omelettes are an important part of peasant cuisine in southern Europe. There are innumerable variations and I very seldom make the same one twice. You can use any kind of seasonal vegetables, or leftovers such as cooked chicken, poached salmon or seafood. These omelettes make excellent first courses for brunch, lunch or simple supper.

Ingredients

1½ pounds baby clams
½ cup finely cubed bacon
6 whole eggs
Salt and freshly ground white pepper
1 tablespoon finely chopped parsley
1 tablespoon finely chopped mixed fresh herbs (thyme, tarragon, chives)
1 tablespoon sweet butter
2 tablespoons olive oil

Preparation

1. Preheat oven to 375°.

2. Wash the clams thoroughly in cold running water. Place them in an empty kettle in the oven and steam them until they open—about 7 to 10 minutes. Discard any unopened ones.

3. Remove the clams from the shells and drain them thoroughly on paper towels.

4. In a 10-inch skillet saute the bacon until it is almost crisp. Remove it from the pan and discard all the fat. Then set the skillet aside.

5. While the bacon is cooking, beat the eggs well. Do not overbeat. Add the clams, salt, pepper, parsley and herbs.

6. In the same skillet used to cook the bacon, heat the butter and oil. Pour the egg mixture into the skillet and cook over a low heat until the underside is set and lightly browned and the top is creamy. Then sprinkle the bacon cubes onto the eggs. Place another hot and well-oiled 10-inch skillet on top of the skillet containing the eggs and turn it over upside down. Continue cooking in the second skillet until the bottom is brown and set. Serve immediately.

Remarks

Open-faced omelettes are not served "runny" as French omelettes are. Rather, they are like a very thick pancake and should be cut into wedges like a pie. You may serve a bowl of fresh Tomato Sauce (page 400) on the side.

Notes

Tarragon duckling
Serves: 4
Preparation time: 30 minutes
Cooking time: 2 hours

Slow braising is an excellent method for cooking ducks found in supermarkets. The meat remains moist and the fat under the skin dissolves. If you like crisp skin, you can always run the duck under the broiler for a few minutes before serving. Green beans sauteed with shallots or White Beans Bretonne are an excellent accompaniment.

Ingredients

1 5-pound duck
Salt and freshly ground white pepper
1 large sprig fresh tarragon
4 tablespoons Clarified Butter (page 398)
1 small carrot, sliced
1 medium onion, sliced
1 Bouquet Garni (page 397)
1½ cups Brown Duck Stock (page 405)
1 tablespoon cornstarch
¼ cup white port wine
2 to 3 teaspoons finely minced fresh tarragon
3 tablespoons cold sweet butter
1 tablespoon finely chopped parsley

Preparation

1. Preheat the oven to 350°.

2. Season the duck with salt and pepper. Place the sprig of tarragon in the cavity. Truss the duck.

3. In a large casserole heat the Clarified Butter. When it is very hot, brown the duck lightly on all sides, then remove it to a side dish.

4. Add the sliced vegetables to the casserole and cook until they are soft. Add the Bouquet Garni and return the duck to the pan. Cover the casserole with buttered

wax paper and then with its cover. Place in the middle of the oven and roast the duck for 1 hour and 30 minutes to 1 hour and 45 minutes. (The duck is done when the juices run pale yellow when the meat is pierced with a fork.)

5. Remove the duck from the oven. Remove the trussing thread and place the duck on a serving platter (or if you want the skin crisp, brown it quickly on both sides under the broiler). Cut the duck into quarters.

6. Remove all but 1 tablespoon of fat from the casserole. Pour in the Brown Stock. Bring to a boil and scrape the bottom of the pan. Strain the stock and return it to the casserole.

7. Reduce the stock by 1/3, then add the cornstarch mixed into a paste with the wine. Stir the sauce until it is smooth and correct the seasoning.

8. Add the minced tarragon, a little at a time, tasting as you go, for it should not overpower the sauce.

9. Off the heat, add 2 or 3 tablespoons of cold butter, stirring constantly until it is just melted. Add the chopped parsley, pour the sauce over the duck and serve.

Notes

Ham rolls a la basquaise

Serves: 8 to 10
Preparation time: 15 minutes
Cooking time: 30 minutes

■ ●

Red, green and yellow peppers can be found in European markets during the summer. In the United States we mostly find the green bell peppers and sometimes the red. Peppers are excellent in so many dishes both hot and cold that they are worth the effort of roasting and peeling. They are also usually inexpensive, which enables the cook to be creative on a low budget.

Ingredients

2   red bell peppers
1   green bell pepper
2   tablespoons fruity olive oil
1   red onion, finely sliced
4 to 6 medium tomatoes, peeled, seeded and chopped
1   tablespoon tomato paste
Salt and freshly ground white pepper
4 to 6 green olives, chopped
4 to 6 Greek black olives, chopped
1   tablespoon finely chopped mixed fresh herbs (thyme, summer savory, chervil, chives)
1   tablespoon finely chopped parsley
8 to 10 slices cooked ham (either smoked or baked, 1/8 inch thick)

Garnish:
Fresh watercress
Quartered hard-boiled eggs
Black and green olives

Preparation

1. Roast the peppers by holding them on a long fork over an open flame until their skin begins to char and blister. This can also be done under a hot broiler, turning them to roast evenly.

2. Peel off the thin outer skin. Remove the core and the seeds, then cut the peppers into thin strips.

3. In a heavy 10-inch skillet, heat the olive oil. Add the onions and saute them over medium heat until they are soft and lightly browned.

4. Add the tomatoes, tomato paste and seasoning. Raise the heat and cook until the mixture becomes a thick puree.

5. Add the chopped olives to the skillet together with pepper strips. Simmer the mixture for 5 more minutes and then add the mixed herbs and parsley.

6. Cool the tomato mixture completely. Correct the seasoning.

7. Place 1 heaping tablespoon of this filling on each slice of ham and roll up the slices. Place the rolls on a serving platter and garnish with watercress, hard-boiled eggs and olives.

Remarks

I usually roast 2 or 3 additional red and green peppers, leave them whole and marinate them in olive oil and vinegar for 2 or 3 hours. These, too, may be used to garnish the platter.
Any leftover tomato puree makes an excellent filling for an omelette or crepe.

Notes

Lamb chops portugaise

Serves: 6
Preparation time: 15 minutes
Cooking time: 25 minutes

A bed of seasonal vegetables offers one of the most attractive ways to serve grilled or roast meats. You can be imaginative and change the "bed" with each season as long as you keep in mind the affinity of certain vegetables for certain meats.

Ingredients

12 rib lamb chops, cut ¾ inch thick
18 small white onions
Salt
1½ to 2 cups finely diced bacon
7 tablespoons olive oil
3 to 4 green bell peppers, seeded, cored and cut into ¼-inch strips
3 to 4 red bell peppers, seeded, cored and cut into ¼-inch strips
Freshly ground black pepper
2 tablespoons finely chopped parsley
4 garlic cloves

Garnish:
Rolled filets of anchovies
Pimientos (24 strips)

Preparation

1. Dry the chops thoroughly on paper towels.

2. Peel the onions. Drop them into salted boiling water for 10 minutes, then drain and set aside.

3. In a large skillet saute the bacon until it is lightly crisp. Remove it from the skillet and discard all the fat.

4. Add 3 tablespoons of olive oil to the skillet and when it is hot add the onions and cook them until they are nicely browned. Be sure not to burn them. Add the pepper strips and cook the mixture over

high heat for 5 to 7 minutes. They should retain their crispness. Season with salt and pepper. Sprinkle with parsley and 2 cloves of garlic, finely minced, and pour the vegetables onto a round platter. Put aside and keep warm.

5. In a large skillet, heat the remaining olive oil. Add the remaining garlic cloves and when brown, discard them. Add the chops a few at a time. Do not crowd the pan. Saute them over very high heat until they are nicely browned on both sides. Season with salt and pepper.

6. Place the chops on top of peppers and onions in an attractive round pattern.

7. Make a design with 2 pimiento strips on each chop and top with an anchovy filet. Serve at once.

Notes

Ragout of lamb a la portugaise

Serves: 6 to 8
Preparation time: 1 hour
Cooking time: 2 hours 30 minutes

■ ●

Summer casseroles are a great help to the cook since they can be prepared in advance and, as a matter of fact, are improved when prepared even 2 or 3 days before serving. Serve this country dish simply with crusty bread followed by a salad and an assortment of cheese.

Ingredients

4-pound shoulder of lamb, cubed
Salt and freshly ground white pepper
6 tablespoons olive oil
4 medium onions, finely minced
4 garlic cloves, finely minced
1 tablespoon tomato paste
1 teaspoon meat glaze
6 fresh ripe tomatoes, peeled, seeded and finely chopped
3 cups Lamb Stock (page 406)
1 large Bouquet Garni, including 1 large sprig fresh oregano (page 397)
2 green peppers, finely cubed
1 red pepper, finely cubed
2 tablespoons minced parsley
1 tablespoon minced capers
½ cup minced basil
1 Beurre Manie (page 397)
Freshly ground black pepper

Garnish:
Green and red pepper rings cooked in olive oil until tender
Chopped parsley

Preparation

1. Preheat the oven to 350°.

2. Dry the meat thoroughly on paper towels. Season with salt and pepper. In a large casserole heat 4 tablespoons of olive oil.

Add the meat, a few pieces at a time. Saute well on all sides over medium heat so as not to burn the fat. Remove the browned cubes to a side dish and continue browning until all are done.

3. Add the minced onions and ½ of the minced garlic and brown lightly without burning them.

4. Add the tomato paste, meat glaze and about ¾ of the chopped tomatoes. Bring the mixture to a boil, add the Lamb Stock and Bouquet Garni and scrape well the bottom of the casserole.

5. Return the meat to the casserole and place the casserole in the preheated oven. Cook the lamb covered for 1½ to 1¾ hours or until it is tender but not falling apart.

6. While the lamb is braising, heat the remaining olive oil in a skillet. Add the peppers and cook them over medium heat for 5 minutes or until they are cooked through but still slightly crisp.

7. Add the remaining chopped tomatoes and cook the mixture until all the juice has evaporated.

8. While the pepper mixture is cooking, combine the parsley, capers, remaining garlic and basil in a small bowl. Add this mixture to the peppers. Do not cook; just heat through and reserve. Season with salt and pepper.

9. When lamb is cooked, remove it with a slotted spoon to a serving platter and keep hot. Discard the Bouquet.

10. Place the casserole over high heat and reduce the pan juices ½. You should have about 2 cups of sauce. Slowly whisk in the Beurre Manie bit by bit. You may not need an entire "ball."

11. As soon as the sauce heavily coats a spoon, add the pepper and parsley mixture. Heat the sauce through, and correct the seasoning, adding a good dash of black pepper. Pour the sauce over the lamb and garnish the ragout with pepper rings and chopped parsley.

Notes

Saddle of lamb
a l'orientale

Serves: 4
Preparation time: 50 minutes
Cooking time: 1 hour

■ ◐

A rack of lamb is always an impressive dish for summer entertaining. It is simple to prepare and gives the cook the chance to experiment with some unusual vegetables.

Ingredients

18 new potatoes, cut into 1-inch balls
4   tablespoons olive oil
¾ cup fresh homemade bread crumbs
½ cup finely chopped parsley
1   rack of lamb (weight about 4 pounds)
Salt and freshly ground white pepper
3   large garlic cloves, 1 mashed, 2 halved
3   tablespoons sweet butter
1   onion, coarsely chopped
Chicken fat
2   tablespoons coarsely chopped toasted almonds
½ cup Brown Stock (page 403)

Preparation

1. Preheat oven to 450°.

2. Drop the potato balls into fast-boiling salted water and cook for 8 to 10 minutes. Drain and reserve.

3. In a small skillet heat 3 tablespoons of olive oil. Add the bread crumbs and parsley. Brown the mixture and reserve.

4. Season the lamb with salt and pepper and rub it with 1 clove of mashed garlic.

5. Melt the butter with the remaining oil in a roasting pan. Turn the saddle upside down in the pan and brown it lightly. Turn again and place under it the remaining garlic cloves and the chopped onion. Roast in the 450° oven for 15 minutes. Reduce the

heat to 400° and cook for 35 minutes more.

6. Melt the chicken fat in a baking dish. Saute the potato balls for 3 to 5 minutes on top of the stove and then place them in the oven. Bake the potatoes for 55 minutes. They should be ready at the same time as the lamb. Baste them often with the fat in the pan.

7. Ten minutes before the lamb is done, take it out of the oven and spread the saddle with the parsley and bread crumb mixture, pressing down with your hands. Add the Brown Stock to the pan. Return the saddle to the hot oven and cook for 10 more minutes. Remove to a serving platter.

8. Five minutes before the potatoes are done, sprinkle them with the chopped almonds and bake for 5 more minutes. Be sure not to burn the almonds. Surround the saddle with the potatoes, pour the pan juices over both. Serve with the following sauce on the side:

Mint and butter sauce

Ingredients

½ cup white vinegar
2   tablespoons finely minced mint
2   tablespoons finely minced shallots
4   egg yolks
1   cup melted Clarified Butter (page 398)
1   tablespoon finely chopped parlsey
Pinch of salt
Large pinch freshly ground white pepper

Preparation

1. In a saucepan combine the vinegar, 1 tablespoon of mint and the shallots. Cook

over high heat until the mixture is reduced to 2 tablespoons. Transfer it to the top of a blender.

2. Add the egg yolks. Blend at low speed, then turn the speed slightly higher and add the melted butter by droplets until the sauce starts to get thick. Then pour in the rest of the butter in a slow stream.

3. Pour the sauce into a warm sauceboat, add the remaining mint and the parsley. Season with salt and pepper and serve.

Notes

Saute of veal lucarno

Serves: 6
Preparation time: 25 minutes
Cooking time: 40 minutes

Ingredients

2 medium-sized eggplants
Salt
½ cup olive oil plus 2 tablespoons
12 small veal scallops
1 freshly ground white pepper
Flour for dredging
2 tablespoons sweet butter
½ cup Chicken or Brown Stock (page 403–404)
2 finely minced garlic cloves
1 tablespoon tomato paste
5 large tomatoes peeled, seeded and chopped
Large pinch of sugar
2 tablespoons minced fresh basil
6 pitted green olives
6 pitted black olives
½ cup finely grated Parmesan or Romano cheese

Preparation

1. Preheat the oven to 375°.

2. Cut the unpeeled eggplants into ½-inch slices, sprinkle with salt and let them stand in a colander to drain for 1 hour.

3. Dry the slices well on paper towels. Heat the ½ cup olive oil in a large skillet and when it is hot, saute the eggplant slices on both sides until they are lightly browned. Remove and reserve on paper towels.

4. Dry the veal and season it with salt and pepper. Dredge lightly in flour, shaking off the excess.

5. In a large skillet, heat the butter with the 2 tablespoons of oil. When very hot, add the veal and saute on both sides for

2 or 3 minutes. Place the veal in one layer in a 14-inch-long buttered baking dish and reserve.

6. Pour the stock into the skillet, scrape the bottom of the pan well and reduce the stock to 2 tablespoons.

7. Add the garlic and cook for 1 or 2 minutes until it is soft. Add the tomato paste and the tomatoes. Season with salt, pepper and sugar. Cook until the mixture becomes a fairly thick puree.

8. Add the basil and olives and remove the tomato mixture from the heat.

9. Place a slice of eggplant on top of each veal scallop. Pour the tomato mixture around the veal. Cover the baking dish and place in the oven for 25 minutes.

10. Uncover the baking dish and sprinkle with the grated cheese. Cook for a few more minutes until the cheese is melted and slightly browned. Serve immediately directly from the baking dish.

Notes

Clams galicia

Serves: 6 to 8
Preparation time: 25 minutes
Cooking time: 25 minutes

■ ✤

In northern Spain, where this dish originated, it is served right out of a large kettle and with plenty of crusty bread. I find it perfect for informal summer entertaining and serve it as an appetizer or as a light main course, followed by a Salade Nicoise and some cheeses.

Ingredients

6 to 8 dozen small to medium-sized clams
1¼ cup dry white wine (preferably Muscadet)
1 Bouquet Garni (page 397)
3 shallots, finely minced
3 tablespoons sweet butter
3 tablespoons flour
½ to ¾ cup heavy cream
3 garlic cloves, finely chopped
2 tablespoons finely chopped parsley
Salt and freshly ground black pepper

Preparation

1. Wash the clams thoroughly under cold running water.

2. Place the clams in a large kettle together with ¾ cup wine and the Bouquet Garni. Cover the kettle and steam the clams over medium heat until they open (about 5 minutes). Strain the liquid through a fine sieve lined with a triple layer of cheesecloth. Reserve 1½ cups. Keep warm over low heat.

3. Pull off half the shell of each clam and place the other half (with the clam in it) on a large round serving platter. Cover and keep warm.

4. In a small saucepan, combine the shallots with the remaining wine and cook over

high heat until the wine is reduced to 1 tablespoon. Remove from heat and reserve.

5. In a heavy-bottomed 2-quart saucepan, melt the butter, add the flour and cook without browning for 3 or 4 minutes. Add the 1½ cups hot clam stock all at once and whisk continuously until the sauce thickens and is very smooth. Thin it with cream and let it simmer for 5 minutes. Add the shallots, garlic and parsley. Season with salt and lots of pepper.

6. Pour the sauce over the clams. Serve immediately with French bread and lots of napkins.

Remarks

Do not hesitate to make this dish because it sounds difficult to eat. Anything so delicious is worth a few extra napkins. You may, of course, go a step further and offer a finger bowl for each person.

Notes

Steamed clams a la catalane

Serves: 6 to 8
Preparation time: 30 minutes
Cooking time: 1 hour 15 minutes

I keep a large jar of fresh tomato sauce in the refrigerator during summer and fall. It is certainly one of the most versatile sauces and easy to make, though it needs slow, long cooking. It can be frozen quite successfully. Here is a peasant dish perfect for summer lunches or suppers. Serve it with crusty white French bread. Follow with a salad and fruit.

Ingredients

The tomato sauce:
4   tablespoons olive oil
1   large onion, diced
1   carrot, finely sliced
4   garlic cloves, mashed
1   celery stalk, finely minced
1   tablespoon tomato paste
2   pounds coarsely chopped tomatoes
½ cup fresh basil, minced
1   tablespoon chopped fresh thyme or
     ½ teaspoon dried thyme
Sprig of Italian parsley
1   Bouquet Garni (Page 397)
Salt and freshly ground white pepper

The clams:
6 to 8 dozen small clams
4   tablespoons olive oil
2   onions, finely sliced
2   large cloves garlic, finely chopped
½ cup dry white wine
1   teaspoon oregano
2   hot dried red peppers
2   tablespoons finely chopped parsley

Preparation

The tomato sauce:
1. In a large heavy saucepan, heat the olive oil. Add the onion, carrot, garlic and

celery. Cook the mixture for a few minutes until the vegetables are soft but not browned. Add the tomato paste, tomatoes, herbs, Bouquet Garni and seasoning.

2. Cover the saucepan and simmer the sauce for 45 minutes. Strain it through a fine sieve and correct the seasoning.

The clams:
3. Thoroughly wash the clams under cold running water and scrub with a stiff brush to remove all the sand.

4. In a large casserole, heat the olive oil. Add the onions and cook until they are soft and lightly browned. Add the garlic, tomato sauce, wine, oregano, and peppers.

5. Add the clams to the casserole and simmer for 10 minutes, covered, or until the shells have opened.

6. Sprinkle with parsley and serve right from the casserole or in deep soup plates.

Remarks

You may, of course, serve mussels in the same way. The sauce should be quite spicy and in Spain it is used for all shellfish. It is the specialty of every region in one form or another.
Remember to serve plenty of napkins as one should use one's fingers for this dish.

Notes

Steamers in herb and lemon butter

Serves: 4
Preparation time: 35 minutes
Cooking time: 15 minutes

When I think of summer at the beach, I look forward to one dish—steamers! Here is a simple and light way of preparing them. The herb butter adds a marvelous, aromatic final touch. The dish is equally good made with fresh sardines or small whole perch.

Ingredients

3   pounds fresh steamers
¾ cup flour
2   tablespoons olive oil
¾ cup warm water
Salt
Oil for deep frying
2   egg whites

The sauce:
10 tablespoons sweet butter
1   large garlic clove, mashed
1   tablespoon finely chopped parsley
1   tablespoon finely chopped chives
1 to 2 tablespoons lemon juice

Garnish:
2   quartered lemons
Sprigs of mint
Bread triangles fried in sweet butter

Optional:
1   teaspoon finely chopped mint
Dash of Worcestershire sauce

Preparation

1. Preheat oven to 375°.

2. Wash the steamers carefully under cold running water. Place them in a large pan in the oven or on top of the stove over medium heat until they open. Remove them from the shells; dry on paper towels and reserve.

Frogs' legs valeuris

Serves: 6
Preparation time: 25 minutes
Cooking time: 30 minutes

3. Sift the flour into a bowl and add the olive oil. Stir until smooth then add the warm water. As soon as this mixture is smooth, stop stirring. Add a pinch of salt and let the batter stand uncovered for 2 hours. The batter must have the consistency of heavy cream.

4. While the batter is standing, melt the butter for the sauce in a small saucepan; add the garlic, parsley, chives and lemon juice. Start by using 1 tablespoon of lemon juice, then add more if you like. Add optional mint and Worcestershire if desired. Keep the sauce warm until the steamers are done.

5. Heat the oil (to the depth of 3 to 4 inches) in the deep fryer.

6. While the oil is heating, beat the egg whites until stiff and lightly fold them into the batter.

7. Dip a few steamers into the batter and drop them into the hot oil. As soon as they are brown and crusty (this should only take a minute), remove them to a platter lined with paper towels and place in a 200° oven while you finish the rest of the steamers.

8. Serve in individual ramekins or on a serving platter garnished with lemon quarters, sprigs of fresh mint and bread triangles. Pour some of the herb-butter sauce on the steamers and serve the rest in a little copper saucepan.

Remarks

As a garnish you may deep-fry eggplant and zucchini slices. For this you will have to make a double batch of the batter.

Even though frogs' legs are considered a delicacy, very few restaurants serve them properly and very few cooks attempt their preparation at home. The frogs' legs usually available in the United States are very large and do not lend themselves well to quick sauteeing. Here is a recipe which takes little time to prepare and should make a frogs'-legs buff out of many a dinner guest.

Ingredients

3 dozen frogs' legs
2 cups milk
Flour for dredging
Salt and freshly ground white pepper
3 tablespoons sweet butter
4 shallots, finely chopped
8 large garlic cloves, finely minced
½ cup tomato puree
6 tomatoes, peeled, seeded and chopped
½ cup dry white wine
1 sprig fresh thyme
1 bay leaf
6 filets of anchovies
1 tablespoon parsley, minced
2 tablespoons fresh basil, minced
1 teaspoon fresh sage
1 tablespoon fresh oregano
4 tablespoons olive oil

Garnish:
Slices of French bread fried in olive oil
2 tablespoons finely minced parsley

Preparation

1. Place the frogs' legs in a large bowl and cover them with milk. Soak for 2 hours. Dry them well on paper towels and dredge them in flour seasoned with salt and pepper.

2. In a small skillet, melt the butter. Add the shallots and garlic and cook until they are soft but not browned. Add the tomato puree, tomatoes, wine, thyme, bay leaf, and a pinch of salt and pepper. Let the mixture come to a boil. Partially cover the skillet and cook for 10 minutes or until the tomatoes are reduced to a thick puree.

3. In a small mixing bowl mash the anchovies together with the remaining herbs and add to the tomato mixture.

4. In a large frying pan, heat the olive oil and add the frogs' legs. Don't crowd the pan. Saute until the legs are crisp and golden brown on all sides.

5. When all the frogs' legs have browned, pour the tomato puree over them. Cover the pan and cook the legs over very low heat for 10 to 15 minutes. Season with additional pepper.

6. Serve the frogs' legs on a round platter surrounded with slices of French bread sauteed in olive oil and sprinkled with minced parsley.

Notes

Halibut steaks
a l'indienne

Serves: 6
Preparation time: 25 minutes
Cooking time: 35 to 40 minutes

■ ✦

I find the discreet use of curry in French cooking more interesting than in Indian cooking, where this spice often overpowers a sauce. Here is a substantial dish, yet its flavor remains quite delicate. Serve the fish with the Pilaf a l'indienne (page 179).

Ingredients

1 cup Creme Fraiche (page 398)
2 tablespoons curry powder
Pinch of ground cumin
4 to 6 fresh halibut steaks (¾ inch thick)
Salt and freshly ground white pepper
4 tablespoons sweet butter
2 tablespoons olive oil
2 onions, very finely minced
2 large garlic cloves, finely minced
4 ripe tomatoes, peeled, seeded and finely chopped
½ cup tomato puree
1 large Bouquet Garni (page 397), including a large sprig of basil
1 cup dry white wine
1 Beurre Manie (page 397)

Optional:
2 tablespoons sweet butter

Garnish:
2 tablespoons pine nuts sauteed in 1 tablespoon sweet butter until golden

Preparation

1. In a small bowl combine the Creme Fraiche, curry powder and cumin. Reserve.

2. Dry the fish steaks well on paper towels and season them with salt and pepper.

3. Heat the butter and oil in a large skillet. When very hot, add the fish steaks and

brown them lightly on both sides. Carefully remove them to a side dish and reserve.

4. Remove all but 2 tablespoons of fat from the skillet. Add the onion and garlic and cook without browning for 2 or 3 minutes.

5. Add the tomatoes, tomato puree and the Bouquet Garni. Season the mixture with salt and pepper, bring it to a boil and add the wine. As soon as the liquid starts to boil, reduce the heat.

6. Return the fish steaks to the pan, cover the pan, reduce the heat and cook the fish for 30 minutes. Test the fish. It is done when it flakes easily when pierced with a fork.

7. Carefully remove the fish steaks to a serving platter and keep them warm over simmering water.

8. Strain the sauce into a 2-quart saucepan, pressing down on the tomato pulp to extract all its juice.

9. Place the saucepan over high heat and reduce the sauce by ⅓.

10. Add the cream-and-curry mixture and continue cooking the sauce over high heat. Bit by bit, beat in a Beurre Manie until the sauce heavily coats a spoon.

11. Taste the sauce for seasoning. If you wish a stronger curry flavor, add 1 teaspoon of curry powder mixed into a paste with a little cream.

12. Pour the sauce over the fish steaks. Sprinkle with the sauteed pine nuts and serve immediately.

Lobster valdosta

Serves: 4
Preparation time: 30 to 35 minutes
Cooking time: 20 minutes

There are many exciting ways to prepare lobsters, some quite easy once you get over your hesitation about splitting a live lobster. The fastest and easiest way: plunge a knife into the head between the eyes, then proceed with the recipe. For a variation you may use large prawns. These will need a shorter cooking period.

Ingredients

4 1½- to 2-pound lobsters
Salt and freshly ground white pepper
1 stick of sweet butter, melted
3 tablespoons olive oil
2 teaspoons lemon juice
1 teaspoon finely chopped fresh oregano
1 tablespoon finely minced parsley
2 shallots, finely chopped
1 small garlic clove, minced
1 teaspoon Dijon mustard
Few drops Worcestershire sauce

The sauce:
1½ cups Hollandaise (page 402)
Lobster coral
1 tablespoon finely chopped parsley
1 tablespoon finely chopped fresh tarragon
2 teaspoons finely chopped fresh thyme
Salt and freshly ground white pepper

Preparation

1. Preheat the broiler.

2. Slit open the lobsters lengthwise. Remove the claws, discard the stomach sack and reserve the coral (roe).

3. Place the lobsters cut side up in a large baking dish; sprinkle with salt and pepper.

4. In a small saucepan heat the butter and

oil. Add the lemon juice, oregano, parsley, shallots, garlic, Dijon mustard and Worcestershire sauce.

5. Spoon the mixture over the lobsters and broil them for 15 minutes, basting them several times with the butter mixture.

The sauce:
6. In a bowl combine the Hollandaise and coral with the chopped herbs. Add a pinch of salt and pepper. Spoon a little of the sauce on each lobster. Return them to the broiler and broil them until their tops are lightly browned. Serve immediately.

Notes

Grilled shrimp a la mallorquina

Serves: 4 to 6
Preparation time: 15 minutes
Cooking time: 5 to 7 minutes

■ ◆

Ingredients

⅔ cup olive oil
Juice of 1 large lemon
1 or 2 hot chili peppers, crumbled
1 Italian onion, finely sliced
2 tablespoons finely chopped fresh basil (or 1 teaspoon dried)
1 large sprig fresh oregano (or 1 teaspoon dried)
1 teaspoon dry mustard
4 large garlic cloves, finely minced
2 pounds large raw peeled shrimp or scallops
Salt and freshly ground black pepper
2 tablespoons finely minced parsley

Preparation

1. In a large enamel bowl combine ⅓ cup olive oil, lemon juice, chili peppers, onion, basil, oregano, mustard, and ½ of the garlic.

2. Place the peeled shrimp in the marinade and coat them well with it. Cover the dish and let it stand at room temperature for 2 to 4 hours or place in the bottom of the refrigerator overnight.

3. Just before serving, drain the shrimp and dry them well on paper towels.

4. Heat the remaining olive oil in a large skillet until it is smoking hot. Add the shrimp and cook them over high heat for about 5 minutes or until they turn bright pink.

5. Season the shrimp with salt and pepper; sprinkle them with parsley and the remaining garlic. Serve immediately.

Shrimp in dill sauce

Serves: 6
Preparation time: 20 minutes
Cooking time: 5 to 7 minutes

The Scandinavians have a wonderful way with shellfish and this is an adaptation of a dish usually prepared with small crayfish, unavailable in the United States. However, small shrimp can be prepared successfully this way.

Ingredients

1½ pounds raw small shrimp
¼ cup Dijon mustard
½ cup fresh lemon juice
½ cup olive oil
1 tablespoon sugar
2 tablespoons wine vinegar
4 tablespoons chopped fresh dill
Salt
2 tablespoons chopped parsley

Garnish:
1 cup finely sliced radishes

Preparation

1. In a large saucepan bring salted water to a boil.

2. Add the shrimp and bring the water back to a boil. Cook the shrimp for 2 minutes or until they turn bright red. Immediately remove from the heat. Drain and run them under cold water. Peel the shrimp and chill until ready to use.

3. Make the following sauce: In a small bowl mix the mustard with the lemon juice. Beat in the olive oil slowly. The mixture should be thick and creamy.

4. Mix the sugar with the vinegar until the sugar is completely disolved.

5. Add the vinegar to the lemon and mustard mixture. Add the dill and parsley.

6. Season the sauce with salt and pour it over the shrimp. Marinate for at least 4 hours. Half an hour before serving time bring the shrimp back to room temperature and sprinkle them with radish slices.

Remarks

Shrimp do not have to be deveined, especially when they go into a salad. This makes it easier for the busy housewife to prepare a recipe like this one without having to buy frozen or already cooked shrimp.

This dish requires fresh dill; frozen dill or dry dill will not do. If you can't get fresh dill, just turn the page to another recipe.

Notes

Sorrel sea trout

Serves: 4
Preparation time: 35 minutes
Cooking time: 40 minutes

Sorrel is also called "sourpress" and is unfortunately rarely available commercially. It is, however, one of the simplest vegetables to grow and needs little care. It belongs to the spinach family, but the flavor is entirely different and absolutely delicious. Sorrel has a special affinity for fish and eggs.

Ingredients

1 whole sea trout, 3 to 3½ pounds
2 tablespoons sweet butter
2 tablespoons finely minced shallots
Salt and freshly ground white pepper
2 cups good full-bodied Fish Stock (page 406)
1 large Bouquet Garni (page 397)
1 to 2 Beurre Manie (page 397)

The sorrel:
3 pounds fresh sorrel
5 tablespoons sweet butter
Salt and freshly ground white pepper
2 egg yolks
1 teaspoon Dijon mustard
⅓ cup cream
2 teaspoons minced tarragon
2 mashed garlic cloves
1 teaspoon sugar

Garnish:
Lemon slices
Few tarragon leaves
2 tablespoons finely chopped fresh sorrel leaves

Preparation

1. Have the fishmarket clean the sea trout, leaving the head and tail on.

2. Preheat oven to 350°.

3. In a large baking dish in which the fish will fit properly heat the 2 tablespoons of butter. Add the shallots. Cook for 1 or 2 minutes over low heat without browning. Season the fish with salt and pepper and place it in the baking dish.

4. Add the Fish Stock and Bouquet Garni. Cover the dish with buttered wax paper. Prick the wax paper with a sharp knife in 2 or 3 places and place the dish in the oven. Bake for 30 to 35 minutes or until it flakes easily when tested with a fork.

The sorrel:
5. While the fish is baking, wash the sorrel thoroughly under cold running water. Snap off the stems and put the sorrel, together with 2 tablespoons of butter, salt and pepper, in a saucepan over low heat. Cook, covered, for 10 minutes. Cool, drain and puree in a blender until smooth.

6. Mix the egg yolks with the mustard and cream and beat the mixture into the sorrel. Add the remaining 3 tablespoons butter, the tarragon, garlic and sugar. Correct the seasoning. Heat the puree, but do not let it come to a boil.

7. Pour the puree onto a serving platter. Remove the fish from the baking dish and place it on top of the puree.

8. Strain the Fish Stock into a saucepan and reduce it to 1 cup. Bit by bit beat in the Beurre Manie until the sauce is thick and smooth. Correct the seasoning and coat the fish with some of the sauce. Serve the rest on the side.

9. Garnish with lemon slices, tarragon and chopped sorrel leaves.

Fava beans a la catalane

Serves: 6
Preparation time: 25 minutes
Cooking time: 1 hour 30 minutes

Fava beans have a wonderful and some-what unusual flavor. This hearty dish from northern Spain is a peasant dish at its best. I often serve it as an accompaniment to cold leftover roast lamb or pork.

Ingredients

1 cup finely cubed bacon
2 tablespoons olive oil
2 large onions, thinly sliced
2 garlic cloves
6 ripe tomatoes, peeled, seeded and chopped
½ cup tomato puree
Salt and freshly ground white pepper
2 tablespoons finely chopped fresh sage
1 bay leaf
3 pounds fava beans
1 small fresh red chili pepper (or 1 dried)
1 pound small bones of fresh pork or
    1 small ham bone

Optional:
½ cup Brown Stock (page 403)
1 garlic sausage, cut into ½-inch-thick slices

Preparation

1. In a large skillet, saute the bacon cubes until they render all fat. They should not be crisp, however. Remove them from the pan and reserve.

2. Remove all the fat from the pan and add the olive oil. When hot, add the onions and garlic. Cook, covered, over low heat until they are soft and lightly brown. This will take about 15 to 20 minutes.

3. Add the chopped tomato, tomato puree, salt, pepper, sage and bay leaf. Simmer for about 5 minutes.

4. Add the fava beans, chili, pork bones and bacon cubes. Cover the pan tightly and simmer on top of the stove for 45 minutes to 1 hour or until the beans are very tender. Do not add water. If the mixture seems to get dry, add a little good Brown Stock. If the skillet has a tight-fitting cover, you will not need to add any liquid.

5. Ten minutes before the beans are ready, add the sausage slices and continue simmering for 10 more minutes. Correct the seasoning. Discard the pork bones and serve directly from the skillet.

Remarks

The whole dish can be baked in a 350° oven in a casserole with a tight lid. An earthenware casserole out of which you can serve at the table is excellent.
Small whole pork sausages fried in olive oil can be substituted for the garlic sausage.

Notes

Eggplant a la basquaise

Serves: 4 to 6
Preparation time: 30 minutes
Cooking time: 20 minutes

One of the most versatile of vegetables, the eggplant has everything going for it: its color, shape and, of course, its taste, which will almost never disappoint you. Serve this dish warm, as an accompaniment to a roast leg of lamb or shish kebabs, or cold, as part of an hors d'oeuvre table.

Ingredients

3 medium eggplants
Salt
Olive oil for frying
3 onions, finely sliced
4 tomatoes, peeled, seeded and chopped
2 garlic cloves, mashed
1 teaspoon fresh thyme
1 tablespoon fresh basil
Freshly ground white pepper
4 anchovy filets, finely chopped
1 cup fresh Feta cheese, crumbled

Garnish:
Whole anchovy filets for garnish
2 tablespoons chopped parsley mixed with
   1 clove garlic, minced

Preparation

1. Do not peel the eggplants. Cut them crosswise into ½-inch slices. Place the slices in a colander and sprinkle with salt. Let them drain for 30 minutes to 1 hour.

2. Dry the eggplant slices well with paper towels. Heat 3 to 4 tablespoons of olive oil in a large skillet and saute the eggplant over medium heat until the slices are lightly browned. Transfer them to a large lightly oiled baking dish.

3. Pour the remaining oil out of the skillet and add 3 tablespoons of fresh olive oil. (Do not cook in the oil which has developed black specks and is burnt.) Saute the onions over low heat until they are lightly browned.

4. Add the tomatoes, garlic and herbs and cook until most of the liquid has evaporated and the mixture is thick. Add a large pinch of pepper. Add the anchovies. Taste them before using as certain brands are very salty and require 10 minutes of marination in milk to draw out the salt. Add the Feta.

5. Spoon the tomato mixture over the eggplant slices and sprinkle with parsley and garlic. If you wish, top each slice with a rolled anchovy.

6. Serve hot or cold.

Remarks

If you can get fresh Greek Feta, mix a cup of this cheese with the tomato mixture. (The Basques use a fresh goat cheese called "Manchego," which is very similar to the Feta but much less salty. Always keep Feta in water; it will take out some of the saltiness.)

Notes

Frito misto of vegetables

Serves: 6
Preparation time: 30 minutes
Cooking time: 10 minutes

One of the pleasures of summer gardening is being able to pick your vegetables when they are young and tender. Here is a lovely way to enjoy your own "crop." Choose vegetables such as beans, eggplants, zucchini, green peppers and tender scallions. Dip them in a light batter, quickly deep-fry them, and serve immediately as a light appetizer or with cocktails.

Ingredients

The sauce:
2 to 2½ cups Mayonnaise (page 402)
1 hard-boiled egg, finely minced
2 tablespoons minced parsley
2 tablespoons finely minced dill gherkins
2 tablespoons minced, well-drained capers
1 tablespoon chili sauce
1 tablespoon finely minced green olives
Lemon juice to taste
Salt and freshly ground black pepper

The batter:
1 cup sifted flour
¾ to 1 cup warm water
1 teaspoon salt
3 tablespoons olive oil
2 to 3 beaten egg whites
Oil for deep frying

The vegetables:
3 small zucchini, sliced into ½-inch slices
1 or 2 small eggplants, sliced into ½-inch slices
2 to 3 green peppers, seeded and cut into quarters
12 whole scallions (5 to 6 inches long)
2 dozen tender young whole green beans
Flour for dredging
Salt

Garnish:
Lemon wedges
Minced parsley

Optional:
4 small cooked artichokes cut in half, choke removed

Preparation

1. In a bowl combine the Mayonnaise and the remaining sauce ingredients. Season to taste. Chill until serving time.

2. In a large mixing bowl combine the flour with just enough water to make a batter the consistency of heavy cream. Do not overbeat. Add the salt and let the batter stand unrefrigerated for 2 hours.

3. Sprinkle the zucchini and eggplant with salt; let them drain in a colander for 2 hours.

4. Preheat the oven to 200°.

5. Five minutes before frying fold 2 beaten egg whites gently into the batter.

6. Heat the oil in a deep fryer. Test by dropping a little batter into the oil. If it sizzles, the oil is ready for the frying. Be sure to regulate the temperature of the oil so that the vegetables do not burn.

7. Dry the eggplant and zucchini slices on paper towels. Dredge all the vegetables lightly in flour, dip them into the batter and drop them into the hot oil a few at a time. Do not crowd your deep fryer. Turn the vegetables gently with a pair of tongs and when nicely browned on all sides, transfer them to a clean napkin.

8. You may keep the napkin-wrapped vegetable fritters warm in the 200° oven.

9. When all the vegetables have been fried, place them on a round serving platter, sprinkle with salt and decorate with lemon wedges and minced parsley. Place the sauce in a separate dish in the center of the platter. Serve immediately.

Remarks

If, after a while, the batter loses its fluffiness, add the third beaten white to the batter.

Notes

Stuffed peppers a la tropezienne

Serves: 6 to 8
Preparation time: 45 minutes
Cooking time: 1 hour 20 minutes

■ ●

It is often impossible to re-create a dish one has eaten while on a trip because one tends to remember the atmosphere of the restaurant as well as the actual flavor of the food. Many dishes, however, are worth experimenting with and adding to one's own repertory. Here is one of them.

Ingredients

8 medium-sized green bell peppers
2 medium eggplants, peeled and cubed
Salt
Olive oil
1 onion, finely minced
2 garlic cloves, finely minced
2 large tomatoes, peeled, seeded and chopped
½ cup finely chopped black olives
2 tablespoons pine nuts
1 tablespoon tiny capers
2 tablespoons finely chopped parsley, chervil and basil
½ cup homemade white bread crumbs
Freshly ground white pepper

Preparation

1. Preheat the oven to 375°.

2. Clean the peppers, removing their tops and seeds. Reserve.

3. Sprinkle the eggplant cubes with salt and let them drain in a colander for 1 to 2 hours. Dry them well with paper towels.

4. In a large skillet, heat 4 tablespoons of olive oil. When very hot, saute the eggplant cubes until they are browned. Do not crowd your pan. You may need more oil.

5. When the eggplant is done, remove it to a mixing bowl.

6. Add a little more oil to the pan. Add the onion and garlic and cook until the mixture is tender but not browned.

7. Add the tomatoes and cook until the mixture becomes a fairly thick puree. Add the olives, pine nuts, capers and herbs.

8. Return the eggplant cubes to the pan together with the bread crumbs. Season with salt and pepper.

9. Fill the peppers with the mixture. (If there is any of it left, reserve it for filling an omelette or a crepe.) Place the peppers in an oiled baking dish. Dribble them with olive oil and bake for 1 hour. Serve warm or at room temperature.

Remarks

You may serve the peppers as an accompaniment to a roast leg of lamb or as part of your hors d'oeuvre table. In that case, slice the cool peppers in half lengthwise and dribble a little wine vinegar and olive oil over them. Do not refrigerate.

Notes

New potatoes in herb butter

Serves: 6 to 8
Preparation time: 10 minutes
Cooking time: 25 minutes

This is one of my favorite summer dishes. Basic, simple and delicious. Use only new potatoes, very fresh herbs and sweet butter. Serve as an accompaniment to grilled steak or roast leg of lamb.

Ingredients

20 to 24 tiny new potatoes
½ cup sweet butter
2 tablespoons finely minced shallots
2 cloves of garlic, finely minced
2 tablespoons finely minced parsley
1 tablespoon finely minced chervil
Salt and freshly ground black pepper

Preparation

1. Scrub the potatoes with a stiff brush but do not peel them. Drop them into fast-boiling salted water and cook uncovered over high heat for 10 minutes. Drain and reserve.

2. In a saucepan, just large enough to hold the potatoes snugly, melt the butter and add the shallots, garlic and herbs. Add the potatoes and shake the skillet to cover them well with the butter-herbs mixture. Season with salt.

3. Cover the saucepan tightly, braise the potatoes in the butter for 15 to 20 minutes, or until tender.

4. Check from time to time to make sure the potatoes are not sticking to the pan. If necessary, add a little water and cover the pan again.

5. Serve the potatoes very hot with a good sprinkling of pepper.

Pilaf a l'indienne

Serves: 6
Preparation time: 15 minutes
Cooking time: 35 minutes

Most American cooks ignore the creative
potential in rice dishes, yet entire countries
must rely on this grain and do so with
great versatility. Here is a simple pilaf
that is a superb accompaniment to
curry dishes, but will go equally well with
roast duck or a roast loin of pork.

Ingredients

3   tablespoons sweet butter
2   tablespoons finely minced onion
1½ cups raw rice
3   cups Chicken Stock (page 404) or
    bouillon
Salt
2   tablespoons finely sliced blanched
    almonds
2   tablespoons white raisins

Optional:
2   tablespoons sweet butter

Preparation

1. Preheat the oven to 350°.

2. In a heavy saucepan, heat 2 tablespoons
of butter. Add the onion and cook it, without browning, for 3 minutes.

3. Add the rice and stir to cover it well
with the butter.

4. Add the stock and let it come to a boil.
Reduce the heat to its lowest. Season with
salt. Cover the saucepan and simmer for
20 to 25 minutes without stirring.

5. While the rice is cooking, melt the remaining butter in a small skillet, add the
almonds and brown them lightly. Remove
them from the heat and reserve.

6. Put the raisins in a small saucepan and
cover them with water. Let the water come
to a boil, then remove from heat. Let the
raisins "plump" for 10 minutes. Drain and
reserve.

7. After 20 minutes, add the raisins and
almonds to the rice. Fluff the rice up with
2 forks. Cover the pan and place it in the
oven in a baking dish. Pour boiling water
around the saucepan to come halfway up
the sides and bake the rice for 10 minutes.

8. Add the optional butter and again fluff
the rice up before serving.

Remarks

The rice will keep warm in a 200° oven in
the pan of hot water for 30 to 40 minutes.
If you are serving the rice as an accompaniment to roast duck, you may add 1 to
2 teaspoons of finely grated orange rind.
Toasted pine nuts can be substituted for
the almonds.

Notes

Zucchini a l'italienne

Serves: 6
Preparation time: 10 minutes
Cooking time: 25 minutes

This recipe calls for fresh "baby" zucchini the size of fat cigars. These are unfortunately not available in most markets. I have grown my own and find great satisfaction in picking my day's supply of fresh zucchini. If you do not grow your own, find the smallest ones possible and blanch them in salted water for 8 to 10 minutes and bake them an additional 10 minutes.

Ingredients

1   cup finely diced bacon
6   tablespoons sweet butter
3   shallots, finely minced
¾ cup finely diced prosciutto
1   teaspoon fresh oregano, minced, or ½ teaspoon dried
3   tablespoons finely chopped Italian parsley
12 baby zucchini, or 4 to 6 small ones
Salt and freshly ground white pepper
2   cups Tomato Sauce (page 400)

Preparation

1. Preheat oven to 350°.

2. In a skillet, saute the bacon until all the fat is rendered. Do not get the bacon crisp. Remove it from the pan, discard all the fat and add the butter to the pan.

3. When the butter is melted, add the shallots. Cook until they are soft but not browned.

4. Add the prosciutto, oregano and bacon and continue cooking over low heat for 1 or 2 minutes. Remove the pan from the heat and mix in the parsley.

5. Cut the zucchini in half. Season with salt and pepper. Butter a large baking dish and in it place the zucchini halves, cut side up. Sprinkle with the parsley, bacon and prosciutto mixture, cover the baking dish and bake in the oven for 20 minutes. Serve with a bowl of Tomato Sauce.

Remarks

For a nice change, substitute finely chopped blanched spinach for the parsley. For 3 tablespoons you will need 8 ounces of spinach, thoroughly drained, squeezed into a ball and then chopped.

Notes

Cucumber and mint salad

Serves: 4 to 6
Preparation time: 10 minutes
Cooking time: none

Cucumbers have a natural affinity to dill, but why confine them to this combination? For a change of pace use mint!

Ingredients

1 tablespoon lemon juice
½ cup heavy cream or Creme Fraiche
3 to 4 cucumbers
Salt
1 tablespoon finely minced mint
1 tablespoon finely chopped parsley
Freshly ground white pepper

Preparation

1. In a bowl, combine the lemon juice and cream and let the mixture stand for 2 to 3 hours.

2. Peel the cucumbers and cut them in half lengthwise. Remove the seeds with a spoon or melon-ball cutter. Cut the cucumbers into ¼-inch slices. Sprinkle with salt and let them stand in a colander for at least 30 minutes.

3. Drain the cucumbers and dry well with a paper towel. Combine with the cream. Sprinkle with the mint and parsley. Season with additional salt and pepper. Serve well chilled.

Remarks

The salad can be made several hours ahead of time. If prepared the day before, the cucumbers will lose some of their crispness, but they will still be delicious. You can combine cucumbers and sliced radishes for a variation and use fresh dill instead of mint.

Green beans tivoli

Serves: 6 to 8
Preparation time: 15 minutes
Cooking time: 10 to 12 minutes

This is an unusual salad highly flavored with dill. It can be served in innumerable ways and leaves great room for the cook's own ingenuity. Fresh dill is a must and the green beans should be young and tender. With the addition of radishes, ham or Gruyere or a combination of all three, you can serve this dish as a luncheon salad.

Ingredients

1½ pounds green beans
Salt
¾ cup scallions, finely minced
4 tablespoons finely chopped parsley
4 tablespoons finely minced fresh dill
4 tablespoons cider vinegar
9 to 12 tablespoons olive oil
3 ounces coarsely chopped walnuts

Garnish:
½ cup finely cubed Gruyere and/or ½ cup finely sliced radishes and/or ½ cup finely cubed smoked ham

Preparation

1. Snap off both ends of the green beans. Bring 3 quarts of salted water to a boil in a large casserole. Add the beans a few at a time. The water should not stop boiling. Cook the beans until just tender. Drain and immediately run them under cold water. Place them in a salad bowl and chill.

2. Combine the remaining ingredients (not including garnishes) and puree in the blender. If the mixture seems too thick, add 1 or 2 tablespoons of olive oil and puree again. The sauce should be smooth. Pour it over the beans and toss the salad. Chill for at least 2 hours. Garnish before serving.

Marinated eggplant

Serves: 6
Preparation time: 15 minutes
Cooking time: 30 minutes

This salad, with its sweet and sour taste, is somewhat more unusual than the stewed eggplant and tomato salad that has become quite popular during the last few years. You may serve it as an appetizer on a bed of Bibb lettuce or as part of an hors d'oeuvre table. It goes well with all grilled meats and especially complements grilled fish or shrimp.

Ingredients

2 to 3 medium-sized eggplants
¼ teaspoon salt
6 tablespoons olive oil
2 to 3 medium-sized onions, thinly sliced
2 stalks celery, diced
1 cup tomato puree
1 tablespoon capers
½ cup green olives
Freshly ground black pepper
4 teaspoons sugar
⅓ cup red wine vinegar

Garnish:
Finely minced parsley
1 teaspoon finely grated lemon rind

Preparation

1. Cube the unpeeled eggplants, sprinkle with salt and place in a colander over a bowl for at least 1 hour. Then dry well on paper towels.

2. In a large skillet, heat 3 tablespoons of olive oil and add the eggplant cubes a few at a time. Saute until light brown. Don't crowd your pan. Remove these cubes to a side dish and continue sauteeing, adding a little more olive oil when needed. When all the eggplant has been cooked, add a little more oil, the onions and celery. Cover and cook the mixture for 5 or 10 minutes without browning. Add the tomato puree and cook for 5 more minutes. Add the eggplant cubes together with the capers and olives. Add ¼ teaspoon salt and freshly ground black pepper. Cover the skillet and simmer for 5 more minutes.

3. In a small bowl, combine the sugar and vinegar. When the sugar is completely dissolved, add it to the eggplant and tomato mixture. Cook, uncovered, for 5 more minutes.

4. Pour the mixture into a bowl. Cover and refrigerate overnight.

5. Garnish with parsley and grated lemon rind before serving.

Notes

Palermo salad

Serves: 4 to 6
Preparation time: 30 minutes
Cooking time: 20 minutes

Young string beans, one of the most versatile of summer vegetables, are perfect for all kinds of exciting salads. Here is a recipe that can be prepared well in advance or at the very last minute. You do not have to use two kinds of beans, although this makes the salad more attractive.

Ingredients

¾ pound wax beans
¾ pound green beans
Salt
1   7-ounce can tuna fish (prepared in olive oil)
1   red onion, finely sliced
3   whole roasted red peppers or pimientos
2   tablespoons olive oil
½ cup pine nuts
¾ cup Sauce Vinaigrette (pages 408–409)
Freshly ground black pepper

Garnish:
2   tablespoons finely chopped parsley
2   hard-boiled eggs, quartered

Preparation

1. Snap off the tips of the beans and wash them under cold water. Drop them a few at a time into fast-boiling salted water. The water should return to a boil as fast as possible. Cook the beans uncovered for 15 minutes or until tender. Drain them and immediately run them under cold water. This stops the cooking and the beans will conserve their fresh bright color.

2. Cut the beans into 2-inch pieces and place them in a salad bowl.

3. Drain the tuna and break it up. Add to the beans together with the onion. Cut the peppers (or pimientos) into strips and add to the bowl.

4. In a small skillet, heat the oil. Add the pine nuts and saute until lightly golden. Drain the nuts and add them to the salad bowl.

5. Add the Vinaigrette and toss the salad carefully. Sprinkle with parsley. Season with salt and pepper and garnish with hard-boiled eggs. Serve with French bread and a bowl of sweet butter.

Remarks

If you cannot get pine nuts, you may substitute toasted sliced almonds, although the texture and taste are not at all the same. Pine nuts will keep for a long time in a covered jar in the refrigerator, so be practical and keep a supply of them year round.

Notes

Fresh cherry compote

Serves: 6
Preparation time: 10 to 20 minutes
Cooking time: 20 minutes

Cherry pitters are available in good specialty stores. They are a great gadget to have as they remove pits from both cherries and plums without breaking the fruit. The French often serve cherry compotes without pitting the fruit. If you do, warn your guests when serving the compote.

Ingredients

2 pounds fresh cherries
1½ cups sugar
2 cloves
3 cups water
1 3-inch piece of cinnamon stick
1 2-inch piece lemon peel

Garnish:
1 cup Creme Fraiche (page 398)
1 to 2 tablespoons confectioners' sugar

Preparation

1. For an elegant (and simple to eat) presentation, pit the cherries. This is best done with a cherry pitter.

2. In a 2-quart enameled casserole, combine the sugar, cloves, water, lemon peel and cinnamon stick. Let the syrup cook, covered, over low heat for 5 minutes.

3. Add the cherries a few at a time and poach for 10 minutes or until just tender. Remove them to a serving bowl. Continue adding the cherries to the syrup until all are poached.

4. Cook the syrup for about 5 minutes more until it thickens slightly. Pour it over the cherries and chill.

5. Serve with a side dish of Creme Fraiche sweetened with confectioners' sugar.

Peaches in apricot sauce

Serves: 6 to 8
Preparation time: 35 minutes
Cooking time: 50 minutes

Ingredients

1 cup dried apricots
6 to 8 freestone peaches
1½ cups sugar
3 cups water
1 2-inch-stick cinnamon
4 tablespoons apricot brandy
Juice of ½ lemon
1 teaspoon grated lemon rind

Optional:
1 to 2 tablespoons confectioners' sugar

Preparation

1. Soak the apricots in water to cover for 2 hours.

2. Drop the peaches into boiling water for 60 seconds, remove and peel them. Carefully cut them in half and remove the pits.

3. In a large saucepan, combine 1 cup of sugar, the water and cinnamon stick. Bring the syrup to a boil, then simmer for 5 minutes. Add the peach halves and simmer them for 5 minutes or until they are just tender.

4. Remove the peaches to a serving bowl and reserve the syrup.

5. Drain the apricots. Place them in a saucepan, cover them with fresh water and add the remaining sugar. Cook for 30 to 40 minutes or until the apricots are very soft.

6. Cool the apricots, drain them and pour them into the top part of a blender. Pour in some of the peach syrup and puree the apricots. Continue adding syrup until the mixture becomes a thick sauce.

7. Add the apricot brandy, lemon juice, and lemon rind. Taste the sauce. If it does not seem sweet enough, add 1 or 2 additional tablespoons of confectioners' sugar.

8. Cool the sauce; pass it through a fine sieve and pour over the peaches. Chill for 2 to 4 hours before serving.

Remarks

If fresh apricots are available, substitute 1 pound of very ripe apricots for the dried ones. Fresh apricots do not have to be soaked and they may need more or less sugar.
Leftover sauce may be used to top ice cream or a plain sponge cake. It can also be frozen and will keep for several months.

Notes

Peaches au caramel

Serves: 6
Preparation time: 40 minutes
Cooking time: 10 minutes

■ ●

A fresh peach is one of summer's best and most versatile fruits. But after a while we tire of the usual fresh fruit bowl. That is when a dessert like this is a welcome change. Fall fruits such as pears can also be prepared in this manner.

Ingredients

6   freestone peaches
2   cups water
1   cup sugar
1   2-inch-stick cinnamon

The cream:
3   egg yolks
½ cup sugar
2   tablespoons cornstarch
1   cup hot milk
2   tablespoons sweet butter
1 or 2 tablespoons kirsch
¼ teaspoon almond extract
2   teaspoons vanilla extract
½ cup blanched toasted almonds

The syrup:
1   cup sugar
½ cup water
½ cup warm water

Preparation

1. Drop the peaches into boiling water for 60 seconds. Drain and peel. Slice the peaches in half and remove the pits, being careful not to break the fruit.

2. In a large saucepan, combine the water, sugar and cinnamon stick. Cook for 5 minutes or until the sugar has melted.

3. Add the peach halves and poach over low heat for 5 to 8 minutes. Remove the

saucepan from the heat and let the peaches cool in the syrup.

The cream:
4. In a heavy-bottomed saucepan combine the yolks and sugar and whisk until the mixture is pale yellow. Add the cornstarch and blend it thoroughly into the yolks. Add the hot milk all at once and blend well. Place the saucepan over direct heat and cook the sauce, whisking constantly, until it is very thick and smooth. Do not scorch the bottom of the pan. Pour the sauce immediately into a bowl and add the butter, kirsch, vanilla and almond extracts.

5. Put the almonds in the top of a blender and blend at high speed until they are reduced to a paste. Incorporate this paste into the cream sauce and chill for 1 to 2 hours. Fill a pastry bag with the almond cream.

6. Remove the peach halves from the syrup. Place them on a serving platter or in a shallow bowl. Pipe cream into each peach half. (Leftover cream can be used for filling small tart shells or poached pears.)

The syrup:
7. Combine the 1 cup of sugar and ½ cup water in a small saucepan and cook, stirring until the syrup turns a light brown color. At this point, add the warm water and simmer for 2 or 3 minutes.

8. Cool the syrup; pour over the peaches.

Remarks

You may keep caramel syrup in a covered jar in the refrigerator. It is delicious on ice cream and on various fruits.

Poached fruit compote

Serves: 6
Preparation time: 15 minutes
Cooking time: 10 to 15 minutes

The secret of a good compote lies in the cooking and fine blending of the fruits. Whether dried or fresh, the fruits should be poached until barely tender. They must never become a thick pulp.

Ingredients

3 large or 6 small ripe peaches
6 small plums
3 pears
3 cups water
1½ cups sugar
1 2-inch vanilla bean
¼ cup lemon juice (or 3 slices of unpeeled lemon)
1 cup heavy cream
2 tablespoons confectioners' sugar
1 tablespoon cognac
2 tablespoons peach liqueur

Preparation

1. Drop peaches and plums into boiling water for 2 or 3 minutes. Remove and peel. If the peaches are large, cut them in half. Otherwise, keep them whole. Keep the plums whole.

2. Peel the pears and cut them in half. Remove the cores.

3. Combine the water, sugar, vanilla bean and lemon juice in a saucepan. Bring the mixture to a boil; reduce it to simmer. Place all the fruit in the syrup and simmer until tender. Some pieces may be ready before others and will have to be removed to a side dish.

4. When all the fruit is ready arrange it in a glass bowl.

5. Remove the vanilla bean from the syrup and reduce it by ⅓ over high heat. Remove it from the heat and cool it slightly.

6. Pour the syrup over the fruit and chill the compote for 2 to 4 hours.

7. Just before serving, whip the cream gradually adding the confectioners' sugar. Do not whip until stiff. The cream should still have a pouring consistency. Add the cognac and peach liqueur.

8. Pour some of the cream on the fruit and serve the rest in a bowl on the side.

Remarks

Other fruits, such as apricots and grapes, can be included in the compote. If you have Creme Fraiche, it can be substituted for the cream. Whip the Creme Fraiche lightly. Add the liqueurs and sugar and serve.

Notes

Cherry flan tart

Serves: 6 to 8
Preparation time: 35 minutes
Cooking time: 45 minutes

■ ●

Ingredients

1   9-inch baked Tart Shell (see page 407)

The cherries:
3   cups pitted Bing cherries
Sprinkling of sugar
Juice of ½ lemon
⅓ cup sweet port wine

The custard:
2   whole eggs
2   egg yolks
1   cup heavy cream
⅓ cup sugar
1   teaspoon vanilla
1   teaspoon lemon rind

The meringue:
3   egg whites
Pinch of salt
8   tablespoons sugar

Preparation

1. Preheat the oven to 350°.

2. Pit the cherries and place them in a bowl. Sprinkle with sugar, lemon juice and wine and marinate for 30 minutes to 1 hour.

3. In another bowl combine the whole eggs with the yolks, cream, sugar, vanilla and lemon rind and whisk until the mixture is very well blended. Set it aside.

4. In a large bowl combine the egg whites with the salt and beat, adding the sugar a little at a time, until the meringue is stiff and glossy. Set it aside.

5. Drain the cherries thoroughly and place them in the baked tart shell. Top them with the egg and cream mixture.

Peach meringue tart

Serves: 6 to 8
Preparation time: 35 minutes
Cooking time: 25 minutes

6. Return the tart to the oven and bake until the custard is set (about 30 to 40 minutes).

7. Remove the tart again and spoon the meringue on it, covering it completely.

8. Turn the oven to 450°. Return the tart to the oven for 3 or 4 minutes or until the meringue is lightly browned. Remove the tart and let it cool.

9. Carefully unmold the tart and slide it onto a serving platter. Serve the same day at room temperature.

Notes

Ingredients

1   9-inch baked Tart Shell (page 407)

The pastry cream:
6   egg yolks
⅔ cup sugar
⅔ cup sifted flour
2   cups hot milk
1½ tablespoons vanilla
2   tablespoons peach brandy

The peach filling:
4   freestone peaches
2   tablespoons peach brandy
3   cups water
1   cup sugar
Juice of ½ lemon
1   3-inch piece vanilla bean

The meringue:
3   egg whites at room temperature
Pinch of salt
8   tablespoons verifine sugar
½ cup finely sliced blanched and toasted almonds

Preparation

The pastry cream:
1. In a bowl combine the yolks and sugar and beat until the mixture is light and fluffy.

2. Add the flour and stir until it is completely incorporated into the yolks.

3. Add the hot milk and whisk the mixture. Pour it into a heavy-bottomed 3-quart saucepan and cook over medium heat, whisking constantly with a wire whisk, until the cream becomes very thick and smooth. Be careful not to scorch the bottom of the saucepan.

Raspberry roulade

Serves: 6
Preparation time: 30 minutes
Cooking time: 15 minutes

4. When the cream is done, pour it into a bowl and add the vanilla and peach brandy.

5. Chill the cream for 1 or 2 hours or until it is very thick and cold.

The peach filling:
6. Drop the peaches into boiling water for 1 or 2 minutes. Remove them, peel them and cut them in half carefully. Remove the pits.

7. Place the peach halves in a bowl, sprinkle them with a little peach brandy and marinate for 30 minutes to 1 hour.

8. In a 3-quart saucepan combine the water and sugar. Bring to a boil and add the lemon juice and vanilla bean to the pan. Add the peach halves and poach over low heat for 5 to 7 minutes or until barely tender. Drain the peach halves on paper towels.

9. Fill the shell with the cold pastry cream.

10. Drain the peaches thoroughly and place them cut side down on the cream.

The meringue:
11. Preheat oven to 400°.

12. Add the salt to the egg whites and beat them, adding the sugar a little at a time, until they are stiff and glossy.

13. Spoon the meringue into a pastry bag and make a decorative circle around the peach halves.

14. Sprinkle the tart with the almonds.

15. Place the tart in the oven for 3 or 4 minutes or until the meringue is lightly browned. Remove the tart and serve the same day.

A roulade is a simple yet elegant dessert to make out of any seasonal berries—blackberries, blueberries and raspberries can all be used. It is an excellent dessert for a buffet dinner and for a large party I sometimes make 2 or 3 with different fillings. Decorate the platter at the last minute with additional fresh fruits such as tiny bunches of grapes and whole strawberries.

Ingredients

1   tablespoon flour
5   eggs, separated
2/3 cup granulated sugar
1/2 teaspoon grated lemon rind
1/2 cup sifted cake flour
1/4 teaspoon baking powder
2   cups fresh raspberries
1/3 cup confectioners' sugar, sifted
1 1/2 cups whipped cream
2   tablespoons seedless raspberry preserves

Garnish:
Small bunches of seedless grapes
2 to 3 tablespoons confectioners' sugar

Preparation

1. Preheat oven to 375°.

2. Butter a jelly-roll pan (16" x 11") and line it with wax paper, letting it extend over the edge of the pan. Butter the paper thoroughly and sprinkle with 2 tablespoons flour. Shake out the excess flour.

3. In a mixing bowl, combine the egg yolks and granulated sugar and beat the mixture until it is pale yellow and quite thick.

4. Add the lemon rind, flour and baking powder. Continue beating until the mixture is smooth.

5. Beat the egg whites until they are stiff and stand up in peaks. Fold them into the yolk mixture. This is best done by hand so as not to break the air pockets in the egg whites.

6. When the batter is thoroughly blended, pour it into the jelly-roll pan. Spread it well into the corners and bake for 15 minutes. The top should be lightly browned.

7. As soon as the cake is done, remove it from the oven. Place a dry linen towel over it and gently turn it upside down onto the towel. Remove the pan and wax paper. Slowly roll up the cake into a cylinder. Keep it covered with the towel until ready to fill.

8. Clean the raspberries by rinsing them quickly under running water. Drain on paper towel. Remove any dry or bruised ones. Sprinkle them with the 1/3 cup confectioners' sugar and let them stand for 15 minutes.

9. Combine the berries with the whipped cream.

10. Unroll the cake and gently spread it with raspberry preserves. Spread the raspberry cream mixture over the preserves and sprinkle with confectioners' sugar. Carefully roll up the cake.

11. Place the roulade on a silver or glass serving platter. Sprinkle heavily with confectioners' sugar. Surround the cake with small bunches of green and dark seedless grapes and chill until ready to serve.

Remarks

If you cannot find seedless raspberry preserves, put any other good preserves through a fine sieve. You may need 3 tablespoons instead of 2.
You can make the roll 3 to 4 hours ahead of time, but if you do be sure to keep it covered completely with the towel until serving time or it will dry out.

Notes

Schwartzwalder roulade

Serves: 6 to 8
Preparation time: 35 minutes
Cooking time: 15 minutes

Switzerland's famous Schwartzwalder Kirsch Torte is a delicious cake that unfortunately involves lengthy preparation for which most cooks have little time. I decided to combine the flavor of cherries, chocolate and whipped cream in a simple roulade. This produced a happy combination that is easy to prepare.

Ingredients

The cake:
8 ounces semisweet chocolate
4 tablespoons strong coffee
2 teaspoons vanilla
8 eggs, separated
¾ cup sugar
Pinch of salt

The filling:
2 cups pitted fresh Bing or black cherries, sliced in half
3 tablespoons confectioners' sugar
4 tablespoons kirsch
2½ cups whipped cream
⅓ cup confectioners' sugar
½ cup unsweetened cocoa
4 tablespoons black cherry preserves

Garnish:
3 tablespoons confectioners' sugar
Fresh Bing or black cherries

Preparation

1. Combine the cherries, 3 tablespoons confectioners' sugar and kirsch in a bowl and marinate for 1 to 2 hours.

2. Preheat oven to 375°.

The cake:
3. Grease the bottom of a jelly-roll pan and line it with wax paper. Set the prepared pan aside.

4. Combine the chocolate and coffee in a small saucepan and cook over low heat until chocolate is melted. Add vanilla.

5. In a large bowl, beat the egg yolks with the ¾ cup sugar until thick and creamy and almost doubled in volume. Add the melted chocolate. Fold the mixture gently with a rubber spatula.

6. Beat the egg whites with a pinch of salt until they form soft peaks. Fold them into the chocolate mixture. Spread the batter evenly in the pan and bake for 15 minutes.

7. While the cake is baking, whip the cream for the filling. Gradually add the ⅓ cup confectioners' sugar.

8. Drain the cherries thoroughly and fold into the whipped cream. Add 1 tablespoon of the marinade.

9. Cover a clean dish towel with 2 tablespoons confectioners' sugar (for garnish) and when the cake is done, turn it onto the towel. Peel off the wax paper, being careful not to damage the cake. Cover it with a moist towel; cool for 30 minutes.

10. Unroll the cake, spread it with the cocoa and black cherry preserves, then with a thick layer of whipped cream and cherries and roll the cake up again.

11. With two spatulas, transfer the cake carefully to a serving dish. Serve at once or refrigerate until serving time. Then sprinkle with the remaining 1 tablespoon of confectioners' sugar and garnish the platter with bunches of fresh cherries.

The fall kitchen reflects the full ripeness of foods at the high point of maturity. Temperamentally fall is a time of renewed energy for working in your kitchen. Colors are rich, tastes are overripe if anything. There is a sense of excitement; you are eager to use ingredients before they have passed their prime. Meats regain the center place in your menu planning. Use of herbs and spices can be proportionately richer and heavier.

There is also the additional excitement of canning and preserving, the preparation of game and the marvelous aroma of roasted chestnuts over an open fire. There is excitement in drying your own herbs, preparing your favorite blends for winter use. Fall, to me, is somehow full of frantic energy induced by the first cool days of the changing season.

the fall kitchen

Symbols

 Inexpensive

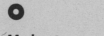 **Moderate**

Expensive

 Easy

Intermediate

Difficult

Potage polonaise
Poulet de bayonne
Mousse au chocolat souffle

In the early days of fall menus often reflect the anticipation of a new season and nostalgia for the abundant, carefree summer kitchen. Fall is the time for the first hearty soups. Start with a rich and delicate soup that traditionally is made with wild mushrooms, but is just as delicious when prepared with dried imported ones. Follow with the Poulet de Bayonne, a dish that makes lavish use of ripe tomatoes—the very essence of hearty Basque-country cooking.
Finish the meal with a bang! After a long "fruity" summer it is time again for chocolate desserts such as souffles and crepes. The simple souffle of this menu will be an easy introduction to the marvelous world of fall desserts.

Potage polonaise

Serves: 4
Preparation time: 10 minutes
Cooking time: 45 minutes

It is unfortunate that we cannot get commercially in the United States the variety of mushrooms that are available in Europe in the fall. But the dried mushrooms, particularly the Polish variety, lend themselves well to this simple soup which can be served at an elegant dinner party as well as for a late fall brunch with black bread and a crock of sweet butter.

Ingredients

4 cups Beef Stock (page 405) or beef
    bouillon
1 ounce imported dry mushrooms
1 large bunch scallions
3 tablespoons sweet butter for sauteeing
1 garlic clove, mashed
3 tablespoons flour
1 cup warm heavy cream
Salt and freshly ground white pepper

Optional:
2 egg yolks mixed with the cream
3 tablespoons cold sweet butter

Garnish:
1 tablespoon finely chopped parsley
2 tablespoons finely sliced raw mush-
    rooms

Preparation

1. In a large saucepan heat the Beef Stock.

2. Rinse the mushrooms, break them into small pieces and add them to the broth. Simmer for 20 to 30 minutes.

3. While this is heating, chop the scallions finely, using both white and green parts.

4. In a heavy-bottomed 6-cup saucepan melt the butter over low heat.

5. Add the scallions and garlic and cook for 5 minutes until tender but not browned.

6. Add the flour and cook for 3 minutes without browning. The flour must cook, otherwise the soup will have a pasty flavor.

7. Add the broth to the saucepan all at once. Don't worry if at this point the soup seems a little lumpy. It will smooth out in 2 or 3 minutes of cooking.

8. Simmer for another 5 minutes and then add the cream (with the egg yolks, if desired).

9. Reheat the soup. Season with salt and pepper and beat in the optional cold butter. Keep warm.

10. Serve garnished with chopped parsley and sliced mushrooms.

Remarks

Combining the egg yolks with the cream results in a more "velvety" soup, but if the yolks are used, the soup should never come to a boil or they will curdle. You can keep it warm over simmering water.

Notes

Poulet de bayonne

Serves: 4 to 6
Preparation time: 15 minutes
Cooking time: 1 hour 15 minutes

This dish derives its name from the Bayonne ham, a smoked ham very much like the Italian prosciutto. I prefer using the boiled smoked ham instead of the prosciutto, which is a little salty for this dish. Exercise your own creativity in adding your favorite seasonal vegetable to the dish. A few black olives will give the Poulet a Provencale touch.

Ingredients

2   small chickens, cut up into serving
    pieces
Salt and freshly ground white pepper
3   tablespoons sweet butter
4   tablespoons olive oil
4   shallots, finely chopped
2   garlic cloves, finely chopped
4 to 6 ripe tomatoes, peeled, seeded and
    finely chopped
1 to 2 tablespoons tomato paste
½ cup dry white wine
½ cup Chicken Stock (page 404)
1   tablespoon fresh basil or ½ teaspoon
    dry basil
1   bay leaf
12 to 16 small white onions
1   cup finely diced ham, preferably smoked

Optional:
1   Beurre Manie (page 397)

Garnish:
2   tablespoons finely chopped parsley
½ cup finely sliced toasted almonds

Preparation

1. Dry the pieces of chicken with paper towels. If damp, they will not brown well.

2. Season with salt and pepper.

3. In a large casserole (or frying pan with cover) melt the butter and 1 tablespoon olive oil. Saute the chicken pieces, a few at a time, until nice and evenly browned. Make sure that the butter and oil do not burn. Transfer the finished pieces to a side dish and reserve.

4. Add the shallots and garlic to the butter and oil remaining in the pan and saute for a couple of minutes. Add the tomatoes and the tomato paste. Cook this mixture for 5 minutes, stirring constantly.

5. Add the wine, Chicken Stock and herbs to the tomato mixture. Season with salt and pepper but do not oversalt as the smoked ham will add its own saltiness.

6. In the meantime, heat the remaining 3 tablespoons olive oil in a separate skillet and saute the onions for 6 to 8 minutes until lightly brown. Add them to the tomato mixture, then return the chicken pieces to this pan.

7. Cover and simmer for 40 to 50 minutes or until the chicken is tender.

8. Remove the chicken pieces with a slotted spoon to a serving dish. Place the onions around the chicken.

9. Raise the heat and reduce the sauce by half until it heavily coats a spoon and the flavor is concentrated. Beat in bits of the optional Beurre Manie to give the sauce the proper consistency. Add the diced ham and just heat through. Pour over the chicken and onions. Correct the seasoning.

10. Garnish with parsley and almonds and serve.

Mousse au chocolat souffle

Serves: 4 to 6
Preparation time: 10 minutes
Cooking time: 12 to 15 minutes

Here is your chance to be ingenious. A happy combination of the traditional chocolate mousse and the souffle, it is elegant yet simple and practically a must for chocolate lovers.

Ingredients

4   egg yolks
½ cup granulated sugar
3   tablespoons rum
6   ounces bittersweet chocolate
4   tablespoons sweet butter, softened
6   egg whites
Confectioners' sugar

Optional:
Vanilla ice cream

Preparation

1. Preheat oven to 475°. Butter the inside of a 4-cup souffle mold and sprinkle with sugar. Shake out the excess sugar.

2. In a large mixing bowl beat the egg yolks with ½ cup of sugar until the mixture is pale yellow. Add the rum and reserve.

3. In a heavy-bottomed saucepan melt the chocolate over very low heat. Beat in the butter 2 tablespoons at a time. Remove from heat and add the egg yolk mixture.

4. With a wire whisk beat the egg whites until they form soft peaks but are not dry.

5. Add a little of the beaten egg whites to the chocolate mixture, then reverse the procedure, folding the chocolate mixture lightly into the whites. It is best to use your hands. Do not worry if the egg whites are not entirely incorporated into the chocolate.

6. Pour the mixture into the souffle dish, place it in the oven and bake for 12 to 15 minutes. The center should still be a little runny.

7. Sprinkle the top with confectioners' sugar and serve immediately. A side bowl of vanilla ice cream can be served with the souffle.

Remarks

Instead of using only confectioners' sugar, sprinkle the souffle with Praline Powder (page 402) and confectioners' sugar.
If there is some souffle left over, serve it cold the next day with whipped cream. It will taste like a delicious chocolate brownie.

Notes

Souffleed eggplant
Roast leg of lamb
Tuscan white bean casserole
Pears al vino

The kitchens of France and Italy both contribute to this traditional menu. It brings to mind cozy country kitchens permeated with the aroma of good cooking, and it is a perfect proof that some of the great dishes are essentially quite simple. The harmony of lamb with white beans, of pears with red wine always enchants me. This is one of my favorite fall and—actually—year-round menus. It spells tradition and substance, a marvelous transition from the light meals of summer.

Both eggplants and peppers have a special affinity for lamb. Here they are combined with a light cheese souffle mixture that gives the appetizer a touch of elegance. Follow the lamb with Watercress Salad a la Bernoise or a well-seasoned fresh spinach salad and finish with the wine-and-cinnamon-flavored pears, well chilled and served in a crystal bowl. A few champagne biscuits are the ideal accompaniment to the dessert.

Souffleed eggplant

Preparation time: 45 minutes
Cooking time: 40 minutes

Eggplants stuffed with a souffle lightly flavored with peppers and cheese is an unusual appetizer. They are simple to prepare and are a welcome change after a long season of salads and grills.

Ingredients

4   medium-sized eggplants
Salt
6   tablespoons olive oil
1   red pepper, finely minced
1   green pepper, finely minced
Freshly ground white pepper
2/3 cup finely grated Gruyere or Comte
    cheese

The souffle mixture:
3   tablespoons sweet butter
3   tablespoons flour
1   cup hot milk
4   egg yolks
Salt and freshly ground white pepper
Pinch of nutmeg
4   egg whites at room temperature

Preparation

1. Preheat the oven to 400°.

2. Butter a large baking dish and set it aside.

3. Cut the eggplants in half lengthwise. Do not peel them. With a sharp knife scoop out the eggplant flesh leaving the shells 1/4-inch thick. Be careful not to break them. Cube the eggplant pulp and place it in a colander. Let it drain for 30 minutes to an hour. Sprinkle the eggplant shells with salt and place them upside down on paper towels.

4. While the eggplants are draining, heat 2 tablespoons of oil in a small skillet. Add the red and green peppers and cook them, covered, over low heat for 10 minutes, or until they are very tender. Set them aside.

5. The souffle mixture: In a heavy saucepan, melt the butter, add the flour and cook, stirring constantly, for 2 or 3 minutes without letting it brown. Add the hot milk all at once and whisk the mixture over medium heat until it is thick and completely smooth.

6. Remove the saucepan from the heat. Add the yolks, one at a time, incorporating each yolk completely before adding the next. Season the mixture with salt, pepper and nutmeg and reserve.

7. Dry the eggplant cubes thoroughly with paper towels. Heat the remaining olive oil in a large skillet and saute the eggplant for a few minutes until it is soft and lightly browned. (You may need more oil.)

8. Remove the eggplant cubes and place on a double layer of paper towels and dry them thoroughly. Remove the pulp to a chopping board. Remove all the seeds and chop it finely.

9. Add the pulp to the pepper mixture and heat over low flame. Season it with salt and pepper.

10. Fold the pepper and eggplant mixture into the souffle base and add 1/3 cup of cheese. Set it aside.

11. Beat the egg whites until they form soft peaks. Fold the souffle base into the egg whites by hand in order not to break the air pockets.

Roast leg of lamb

Serves: 6 to 8
Preparation time: 30 minutes
Cooking time: 1 hour 30 minutes

12. Place the scooped-out eggplant shells in the baking dish. Spoon the souffle mixture into each half (it can overflow the shells).

13. Sprinkle with the remaining cheese and place the dish in the preheated oven. Immediately turn the heat down to 375° and bake the stuffed eggplants for 12 to 15 minutes. Serve immediately.

Notes

Ingredients

6- to 7-pound leg of lamb
Salt and freshly ground black pepper
½ teaspoon marjoram
¼ teaspoon oregano
2 large garlic cloves, mashed
1 teaspoon imported paprika
2 teaspoons Dijon mustard
3 tablespoons olive oil
1 onion, finely minced
1 carrot, finely minced
1 celery stalk, finely minced
1 small sprig of fresh rosemary
Flour
2 to 3 cups warm Lamb Stock (page 406)
1 Beurre Manie (page 397)

Garnish:
Sprigs of fresh watercress

Preparation

1. Preheat the oven to 375°.

2. Dry the lamb thoroughly with paper towels. Season with salt, pepper, marjoram and oregano. Make tiny slits in the meaty part of the leg and insert little bits of mashed garlic. Rub the lamb with paprika and Dijon mustard and let stand at room temperature for 30 minutes to 1 hour.

3. In a large baking dish, heat the oil, add the minced onion, carrot, celery and rosemary sprig. Cook the mixture without browning for 2 or 3 minutes and set aside.

4. Sprinkle the lamb with a layer of flour and place it in a baking dish. Roast the lamb for 1 hour and 30 minutes, basting every 30 minutes with warm stock. When done, remove to a serving platter and reserve.

5. Add any remaining stock to the pan, bring it to a boil over direct heat, scraping well the bottom of the pan. Strain the pan juices into a small saucepan and cook over high heat, whisking the Beurre Manie a little at a time until the sauce heavily coats the spoon. Taste the sauce and correct the seasoning. Spoon some of the sauce over the white beans and serve the rest on the side.

6. Garnish the lamb with sprigs of fresh watercress and serve immediately.

Remarks

For a more traditional presentation, place the lamb on an oval serving platter and surround it with the beans. Garnish the platter with sauteed Tomatoes a l'Italienne (page 386).

Notes

Tuscan white bean casserole

Serves: 6 to 8
Preparation time: 30 minutes
Cooking time: 1 hour 30 minutes

European peasant cooking during the fall and winter months relies heavily on dry vegetables such as peas and beans. When well prepared, a casserole of white beans can be as delicious as a fresh vegetable. This casserole is traditionally an accompaniment to a roast leg of lamb.

Ingredients

2 cups dry white beans, soaked overnight
1 onion, stuck with 1 clove
1 large Bouquet Garni (page 397)
Salt
1 cup finely cubed, blanched salt pork
2 tablespoons olive oil
2 onions, finely sliced
2 large tomatoes, peeled, seeded and chopped
Pinch of dried oregano
Pinch of dried basil
1 green pepper, seeded and cubed
2 tablespoons finely minced parsley
Freshly ground white and black pepper

Preparation

1. Preheat oven to 300°. Drain the soaked beans thoroughly.

2. In a large casserole place the beans, whole onion and Bouquet Garni. Add 1 tablespoon of salt and cook the beans covered over moderate heat for 45 minutes or until soft but not mushy. Drain them. Discard the Bouquet.

3. In a skillet saute the salt pork. When it is crisp, remove it to paper towels. Discard the fat and in the same skillet heat the olive oil.

4. Add the sliced onions and cook them for

a few minutes until they are soft but not browned. Add the tomatoes, oregano, basil and the green pepper. Cook for 10 minutes or until the mixture is a thick puree. Season and add the salt pork.

5. Place the cooked beans in a large oval baking dish. Add the tomato puree and mix it gently into the beans making sure not to break them. Cover the dish with foil and bake in a 300° oven for 30 minutes. Sprinkle before serving with parsley and black pepper. The beans can be prepared well ahead of time and reheated before serving.

Remarks

Since beans and lamb have a natural affinity to each other, you can also serve the bean casserole with sauteed or broiled lamb chops or grilled butterflied leg of lamb. Diced leftover roast lamb can be added to the casserole and served for simple family suppers.

Notes

Pears al vino

Serves: 8
Preparation time: 30 minutes
Cooking time: 20 to 30 minutes

This is a classic dessert that is popular in both France and Italy. If small pears are used, leave them whole with their stems attached. Large pears should be sliced in half and the core removed with a melon-ball cutter or sharp knife. If the pears are not to be poached immediately, keep them in acidulated water.

Ingredients

2   oranges
¼ cup Grand Marnier
8   whole pears
3   cups good Bordeaux wine
1   3-inch piece cinnamon stick
1½ cups sugar
3   cloves
1   2-inch piece lemon peel
½ cup currant jelly
1   teaspoon lemon juice

Preparation

1. With a very sharp knife, remove the peel from the oranges. Do not include the white membrane, which is bitter. Cut the peel into very fine strips, drop them into boiling water and cook for 10 minutes. Drain the strips and place them in a small mixing bowl. Cover with Grand Marnier and reserve.

2. Peel the pears without removing the stems. Drop them into acidulated water as soon as they are peeled to prevent discoloration. Reserve.

3. In a large enamel saucepan combine the wine, cinnamon, sugar, cloves and lemon peel. Bring to a boil and as soon as the sugar is dissolved add the pears. Cook

over low heat, partially covered, until tender.

4. When the pears are done, remove them to a serving bowl. Raise the heat and reduce the cooking liquid by $\frac{1}{3}$ or until it very lightly coats a spoon and is somewhat syrupy.

5. Beat in the currant jelly and as soon as it is dissolved completely, taste the syrup, adding the lemon juice to give it a little tartness. Pour it over the pears.

6. Sprinkle the pears with the orange peel as well as the Grand Marnier in which they have been marinating. Chill until served.

Remarks

A bowl of freshly whipped cream may be served on the side. You may also garnish the pears with finely sliced dates and finely slivered toasted almonds instead of using the orange peel.

Notes

Spinach crepes bernoise
Roast duck au calvados
Mocha roulade

This is a late fall menu, one that moves toward winter and more formal entertaining. Start the meal with a spinach crepe that has a light mushroom-and-chicken-liver filling. The bright green color of the crepe is reminiscent of summer freshness and suggestive of the spring to come. Follow the crepes with the Duck au Calvados. The duck's affinity to fruits has influenced me in creating this recipe. It is, however, unusual as the duck is not surrounded by the familiar oranges, peaches or cherries. The dish has a certain formality that makes it a perfect prelude to the rich Mocha Roulade. Do not serve a salad following the main course. Simply move your guests to the living room for dessert and coffee a la Viennese.

Spinach crepes bernoise

Serves: 6 to 8
Preparation time: 45 minutes
Cooking time: 30 minutes

Crepes are really food for all seasons. They lend themselves to innumerable variations. They should not, however, be used to "doctor up" some unappealing leftovers and should never be heavily sauced. Here they are served simply with melted butter, which is the way I like them best.

Ingredients

12 to 14 Spinach Crepes (page 400)

The filling:
4   tablespoons sweet butter
4   chicken livers, cleaned and dried on
    paper towels
Salt and large pinch freshly ground white
    pepper
¼ pound mushrooms, cleaned and finely
    minced
2   tablespoons minced scallions
8   ounces cream cheese
1   stick sweet butter, melted

Optional:
1 to 2 teaspoons minced dill

Preparation

1. Preheat the oven to 325°.

2. For the filling, in a heavy skillet melt 2 tablespoons of butter. Add the chicken livers and saute them until they are nicely browned on all sides. Season with salt and pepper. As soon as they are cool enough to handle, mince them with a sharp knife and place them in a mixing bowl.

3. Melt the remaining butter in another skillet, add the mushrooms and scallions and cook until they are lightly browned (about 2 minutes). Season lightly with salt

and pepper and add them to the bowl.

4. Cream the cream cheese together with the optional dill.

5. With a wooden spoon blend cream cheese, mushroom-and-chicken-liver mixture together and correct the seasoning.

6. Fill the crepes with the mixture. Roll them and place them in a buttered baking dish.

7. Pour the melted butter over the crepes and heat in the oven for 20 minutes or until heated through. Serve immediately.

Remarks

Any remaining crepes can be frozen according to instructions on page 399. The entire dish can be prepared well in advance and reheated just before serving.

Notes

Roast duck au calvados

Serves: 6 to 8
Preparation time: 45 minutes
Cooking time: 2 hours 30 minutes

Fall brings to my mind fruit stands filled with apples, delicious cider and the urge to return to the kitchen with an elaborate menu. Here is a dish that is simple yet elegant, the perfect opening to your fall repertory.

Ingredients

2   roasting ducks (4½ to 5 pounds)
Salt and freshly ground white pepper
2   whole onions, each stuck with a clove
2   tablespoons sweet butter
1   finely minced carrot
1   finely sliced onion
½ cup finely diced celery
1   Bouquet Garni (page 397)
2   cups Brown Duck Stock (page 405), or Chicken Stock (page 404)

The apples:
6 to 8 firm medium-sized baking apples
6   tablespoons sweet butter
½ cup sugar
1   cup white wine

The sauce:
3   tablespoons Calvados
½ cup heavy cream
1   tablespoon cornstarch mixed to a paste with a little stock plus 1 Beurre Manie (page 397)
2 to 4 tablespoons sweet butter, cold

Preparation

1. Preheat the oven to 450°. Dry the ducks well both inside and out. Season with salt and pepper. Put a whole onion inside each cavity. Tie the legs and wings (reserve the wing tips for the stock) to the body. Stab the ducks' breasts and thighs with a fork.

2. In a large flameproof baking dish, melt 2 tablespoons of butter. Strew the vegetables and Bouquet Garni in the bottom of the dish.

3. Place each duck on its side on top of the vegetables and put the dish in the oven. Turn the heat down to 350° and roast the ducks for 2 hours to 2 hours and 30 minutes, turning them once. During the cooking time, remove accumulated fat from the dish with a bulb baster.

4. Baste the ducks a few times with hot stock, using about 1 cup of it.

5. While the ducks are roasting, peel the whole apples, carefully removing the cores with an apple corer. Melt 6 tablespoons butter in an enameled casserole. Add the apples, sprinkle with sugar and wine. Cover the casserole and place in the oven for 30 to 35 minutes. Do not overcook or the apples will fall apart. Keep the apples warm.

6. When the ducks are cooked, remove them to a baking sheet. Turn on the broiler and broil the ducks for 3 to 5 minutes on each side to crisp the skin.

7. While the ducks are broiling remove any remaining fat from the baking dish. Put the dish over high heat, pour in the rest of the stock and the Calvados, scraping the bottom of the pan well. Strain the pan juices into a smaller saucepan.

8. Place the saucepan over high heat, add the cream and reduce the sauce slightly. Beat in the cornstarch paste and Beurre Manie and continue cooking until the sauce heavily coats a spoon. Beat in 2 to 4 tablespoons cold butter. Correct the seasoning and reserve.

Mocha roulade

Serves: 6 to 8
Preparation time: 35 to 40 minutes
Cooking time: 25 to 30 minutes

9. Carve each duck into four pieces and place them on a round serving platter. Place the apples in the center. Spoon the sauce over both ducks and apples and serve.

Remarks

Both the ducks and the sauce can be made ahead of time and reheated separately. The apples may be stuffed with prunes that have been soaked in white wine.

Notes

Ingredients

The mocha cream:
¾ cup granulated sugar
¼ cup water
2 egg yolks
8 tablespoons sweet butter, softened
    and whipped
1 to 2 teaspoons instant coffee diluted
    in 2 tablespoons of water

The cake:
4 large eggs
½ cup granulated sugar
¾ cup sifted cake flour
1 teaspoon baking powder
1 teaspoon vanilla
Pinch of salt

Optional:
Chocolate shavings

Garnish:
2 to 3 tablespoons confectioners' sugar
Mocha Cream rosettes

Preparation

1. Preheat the oven to 400°.

2. Butter a jelly-roll pan. Sprinkle the pan with flour, shaking out the excess. Line the pan with wax paper, cut 2 inches larger than the pan on both ends. Butter the wax paper and set the pan aside.

The mocha cream:
3. In a heavy saucepan combine the ¾ cup sugar and water. Place a candy thermometer in the pan and cook the mixture without stirring until it registers 238°. Check by dropping a little bit of the sugar syrup into a pan of cold water. It should form a soft ball.

4. While the syrup is cooking beat the egg yolks in a bowl until they are pale yellow.

5. As soon as the syrup has reached the right degree, add it by droplets to the egg yolks, whisking constantly as if you were making mayonnaise. Whisk until the mixture is thick and cool.

6. Fold the softened whipped butter into the egg and sugar mixture, incorporating it completely.

7. Add the instant coffee and chill the cream.

The cake:
8. Combine the 4 eggs with the ½ cup sugar in a bowl and beat until well blended.

9. Set the bowl over a saucepan of very hot water (it should not be boiling). Warm the egg mixture until it feels tepid when tested with a finger. Whisk it from time to time. This will take about 15 minutes.

10. Remove the bowl and beat the egg and sugar mixture with a wire whisk or a small electric hand beater until it is doubled in volume and pale yellow.

11. Combine the flour and baking powder and gently fold it into the egg mixture. Do not overbeat.

12. Add the vanilla and salt and pour the mixture into the prepared pan. Spread it evenly with a spatula and set it in the preheated oven. Bake for 13 to 15 minutes.

13. While the cake is baking, sprinkle a clean towel heavily with 2 tablespoons confectioners' sugar. As soon as the cake is done, place it upside down on the towel, remove the pan and carefully peel off the wax paper. Place a damp towel over the cake. Let it cool completely.

14. As soon as the cake is cool, spread it heavily with the Mocha Cream. Reserve 3 tablespoons for garnish.

15. Roll the cake either lengthwise or the short way and carefully transfer it to a serving platter. Sprinkle with additional confectioners' sugar and chill until 5 minutes before serving.

16. Garnish the cake with rosettes of Mocha Cream (piped through a pastry tube) and chocolate shavings.

Notes

Fennel mushrooms
Beef a l'arlesienne
Apple mousse with apricot sauce

To many people, a filet of beef immediately brings to mind elegance. I find that this cut of meat usually needs a hearty and flavorful preparation, not limited to roasting or pan frying. In this menu the main course has great character. The rest of the meal should therefore be light and unassuming. The fennel mushrooms are a simple yet delicate and refreshing appetizer. For a more elaborate touch you can fill the Crepes Fines Herbes (page 399) with the mushrooms, sprinkle them heavily with melted butter and freshly grated Parmesan cheese and run them under a hot broiler for a few minutes.

Since apples are the essence of fall they should be used lavishly during their peak season. A bowl of apples with a platter of dessert cheeses could be the perfect ending to this meal, but if you want to go a step further, here is a delicate mousse that captures the flavor of this delicious fruit. When preparing this menu, the dessert should be made a day in advance.

Fennel mushrooms

Serves: 8
Preparation time: 15 minutes
Cooking time: 10 minutes

This is an unusual combination of two of fall's most prevalent vegetables. You may serve this dish as an appetizer garnished with bread triangles fried in butter or as a vegetable accompanying a roast.

Ingredients

2   pounds fresh mushrooms
6   tablespoons sweet butter
1   cup fresh fennel, cut into fine strips
1½ cups sour cream
2 to 3 tablespoons fresh dill
2   tablespoons fresh chopped chives
Salt and freshly ground black pepper

Optional:
Watercress
Bread triangles fried in Clarified Butter
    (page 398)

Preparation

1. Wipe the mushrooms with wet paper towels. Avoid washing them because they tend to absorb water and will release it during cooking.

2. Quarter large mushrooms; cut the smaller ones in half.

3. In a large skillet heat the butter until it foams. Add the mushrooms, making sure that you do not crowd the pan. Saute over high heat for 3 to 5 minutes. Add the fennel and cook for 2 more minutes.

4. Mix the sour cream with the herbs and add to the mushrooms and just heat through without letting it come to a boil. Add seasoning; be generous with pepper.

5. Serve immediately garnished with watercress and fried bread triangles.

Beef a l'arlesienne

Serves: 6 to 8
Preparation time: 30 minutes
Cooking time: 1 hour 30 minutes

Fall is the time to get away from the simple meats of summer. This recipe is marvelous for year-round entertaining, but it is especially good in late summer and early fall when fine, ripe tomatoes abound. It is an elegant dish, perfectly suited to fall entertaining.

Ingredients

2   cups salt pork, cut into 1½-inch strips
2   tablespoons Clarified Butter (page 398)
24 small white onions
6   large ripe tomatoes
4   pounds filet of beef in one piece
¼   cup Armagnac
1   cup Brown Stock (page 403)
3   tablespoons olive oil
4   shallots, finely minced
2   garlic cloves, mashed
1   tablespoon fresh basil
½   teaspoon oregano
1   large Bouquet Garni (page 397), tied in
    cheesecloth
Salt and freshly ground white pepper
½   cup white wine
15 green pitted olives

Optional:
1   tablespoon cornstarch mixed with 2
    tablespoons white wine
2   tablespoons sweet butter

Garnish:
2   pimientos, sliced
2   tablespoons minced parsley

Preparation

1. Preheat oven to 325°. Cut the salt pork into strips called "lardons." Blanch them in boiling water for 5 minutes, then drain

the lardons well on paper towels.

2. In a large oval casserole heat the butter. Add the "lardons" and saute until crisp. Remove them from the casserole and reserve. Add the onions. Cook for 7 or 8 minutes or until nicely browned.

3. While the onions are cooking, peel the tomatoes by putting them in boiling water for 1 or 2 minutes. Remove immediately and peel. Squeeze them gently to extract the juice and seeds. Chop the pulp coarsely and reserve.

4. When the onions have finished browning, remove them from the casserole and set aside. Add the beef and brown it quickly on all sides. (If the butter has burned, discard it and add 2 more tablespoons of butter to the casserole.) Pour the Armagnac over the meat and ignite it. As soon as the flames die down, remove the meat from the casserole.

5. Add the Brown Stock, bring to a boil. Return the beef to the casserole together with the lardons and onions, cover it and place it in the oven for 60 minutes for rare beef or 70 minutes for medium rare. (You may use a meat thermometer and cook the beef until it reads 135° for rare and 145° for medium rare.)

6. In a large skillet heat the olive oil. Add the shallots and garlic. Cook until tender (about 5 minutes). Add the tomatoes, herbs, Bouquet and seasoning. Add the white wine and cook over high heat until the mixture thickens and most of the juices have evaporated. Strain the sauce through a fine sieve and reserve.

7. Bring a small saucepan of water to boil and blanch the olives for 5 minutes. Drain them and add them to the tomato sauce.

8. When the beef is ready, remove it to a serving platter together with the lardons and onions. Keep warm while you finish the sauce. Skim the extra fat from the surface of the casserole meat juices and reduce the juices by 1/3 over high heat. Add the tomato mixture and simmer for a few minutes. If the sauce does not seem thick enough, beat in the cornstarch mixture and the optional butter. Correct the seasoning.

9. Slice the beef, spoon a little sauce over each slice and garnish with pimientos and parsley.

Notes

Apple mousse
with apricot sauce

Serves: 6 to 8
Preparation time: 35 minutes
Cooking time: 20 minutes

This is a simple dessert that will delight those who look forward to fall's abundance of apples. You may prefer to serve the mousse completely unadorned since even this light sauce may take away from it.

Ingredients

4   medium-sized apples (McIntosh or other firm cooking apples), peeled, cored and quartered
½ teaspoon cinnamon
¼ cup apricot preserves
Pinch nutmeg
Pinch grated lemon rind
4   egg yolks
1   teaspoon cornstarch
¾ cup sugar
1½ cups warm milk
1   tablespoon unflavored gelatin
½ cup orange juice
1   teaspoon vanilla extract
1   cup heavy cream, whipped

The sauce:
1   cup apricot preserves
2   tablespoons lemon juice
1   teaspoon grated lemon rind
¼ to ½ cup apricot brandy
1½ to 2 tablespoons confectioners' sugar
¼ cup kirsch

Preparation

1. In a heavy-bottomed saucepan, combine the quartered apples, cinnamon, apricot preserves, nutmeg and lemon rind. Cook over low heat until the apples are very soft and the mixture can easily be mashed with a fork. Be careful not to scorch the bottom of the pan. As soon as the apples are done, pass them through a sieve and reserve the puree.

2. In the top part of a double boiler, combine the egg yolks, cornstarch and sugar and beat until the mixture is light, fluffy and pale yellow.

3. Add the warm milk and place the pan over simmering water. Stir constantly until the custard coats a spoon. Do not bring it to a boil or it will curdle. Remove the custard from the heat and reserve.

4. Heat the gelatin with the orange juice in a small saucepan. Whisk the melted gelatin into the still hot custard.

5. Pour the custard into a clean bowl and chill for 2 hours, whisking occasionally until it starts to set.

6. Remove the custard from the refrigerator and whisk in the vanilla, the apple puree and the whipped cream.

7. Chill. Pour the mousse into individual dessert cups or a glass bowl and chill for at least 4 hours before serving with the following sauce:

8. In a small saucepan, combine the apricot preserves, lemon juice, lemon rind, apricot brandy and confectioners' sugar. Heat the mixture until the preserves are completely dissolved.

9. Pass the sauce through a fine sieve and add the kirsch.

10. Taste the sauce. You may want to add more sugar or a little more apricot brandy.

11. Chill the sauce and serve it with the apple mousse.

Remarks

This sauce is delicious with a variety of fruits, such as poached pears, poached bananas or a simple apple compote as well as on ice cream and crepes.

Notes

Shrimp and eggs nantua
Veal birds a la florence
Souffle normand

After the informality of summer entertaining, it is exciting to spend some time in the kitchen on a rather elaborate menu. Even though the dishes are a little more time consuming than those of summer, most of the preparation can be done in advance. The elegant appetizer is French in feeling. Follow it with the delicate veal birds in a rich brown sauce. You may serve them with a well-flavored risotto and a chilled white burgundy wine. Follow the main course with an endive salad dressed in a lemon vinaigrette. Do not serve cheese.

Since apples are synonymous with fall, the Souffle Normand gives this elegant dinner the stamp of the Fall Kitchen.

A delicious cup of espresso coffee served with a chilled liqueur glass of Calvados will be the right finishing touch.

Shrimp and eggs nantua

Serves: 6
Preparation time: 30 minutes
Cooking time: 15 minutes

In peasant cooking eggs play a very important role. They are often served simply on top of a seasonal vegetable. This dish, however, can stand up to any sophisticated appetizer and can even be served as a main course at an elegant brunch.

Ingredients

1 cup Fish Stock (page 406)
1 pound fresh shrimp
5 tablespoons sweet butter
3 tablespoons flour
¾ cup heavy cream
Salt and freshly ground white pepper
Juice of ½ lemon
6 slices day-old bread, cut ½ inch thick
½ cup Clarified Butter (page 398)
6 eggs at room temperature

Optional:
1 tablespoon finely chopped fresh tarragon
Freshly ground black pepper

Preparation

1. In a saucepan bring the Fish Stock to a boil. Add the shrimp and poach them until they just turn pink (3 to 5 minutes). Strain the stock and keep it warm. Peel the shrimp, reserving 6 of the best ones for garnish. Mince the rest and reserve.

2. In a heavy-bottomed saucepan, melt 3 tablespoons of butter and add the flour. Cook over low heat for 2 or 3 minutes without letting it brown. Add the fish stock all at once and whisk the sauce until it is smooth and thick. Thin it out with heavy cream (the sauce should heavily coat a spoon), and add seasoning.

3. Add the minced shrimp and lemon juice. Beat in the remaining butter. Keep the mixture warm.

4. With a cookie cutter cut the bread slices into oval shapes the size of the eggs.

5. Heat the Clarified Butter in a large skillet. Add the bread slices and saute them on both sides. Arrange them on a serving platter.

6. Place the eggs carefully into boiling salted water and cook them over medium heat for 5 minutes. Immediately run them under cold water to stop further cooking. Carefully peel the eggs and cut a thin slice lengthwise off each.

7. Place an egg on each bread slice and pour the sauce over them. Garnish with the whole shrimp and sprinkle with tarragon and black pepper.

Remarks

You can make the sauce ahead of time and keep it warm in the top of a double boiler over simmering water. In this case add the final butter flavoring just before serving. Fish stock can be made in advance and stored in the refrigerator for several days. If you do not have fresh tarragon, do not substitute any other herb.

Notes

Veal birds a la florence

Serves: 6
Preparation time: 1 hour
Cooking time: 2 hours 30 minutes

Ingredients

The sauce:
4 tablespoons sweet butter
2 shallots, finely minced
½ carrot, finely minced
½ celery stalk, finely minced
3 tablespoons flour
2½ cups hot Brown Stock (page 403)
1 Bouquet Garni (page 397)
Salt and freshly ground white pepper

The stuffing:
2 cups fresh spinach, cleaned and washed
¼ pound lean pork, ground
¼ pound lean veal, ground
2 eggs
Salt and freshly ground white pepper
2 tablespoons sweet butter
2 finely minced shallots
1 teaspoon minced garlic
2 to 3 slices of white bread (soaked in milk
    and well squeezed)
Pinch of sage
Pinch of allspice

The veal:
12 veal scallops, cut ¼ inch thick
Salt and freshly ground white pepper
Flour for dredging
4 tablespoons sweet butter
2 tablespoons oil
1 teaspoon meat glaze
½ cup dry white wine

Optional:
1 tablespoon cornstarch mixed with a little
    white wine

Garnish:
½ pound Poached Mushrooms

Preparation

The sauce:
1. Butter a large flameproof baking dish
and reserve.

2. In a heavy saucepan melt the 4 tablespoons of butter. Add the minced vegetables and cook them over low heat for 5 to
6 minutes or until they are soft but not
browned.

3. Add the flour and stir to blend it well
with the vegetables. Cook over medium
heat until the mixture turns hazelnut
brown. Be careful not to burn the mixture
or scorch the bottom of the pan. As soon as
the mixture has turned brown, add the
hot stock all at once and stir until there
are no lumps in the sauce.

4. Add the Bouquet Garni, mushroom stems,
and salt and pepper. Do not add too much
salt, for the sauce gets saltier as it
reduces. Partially cover the saucepan and
simmer the sauce for 1 hour and 30 minutes,
stirring it from time to time.

5. Strain the sauce and reserve.

The stuffing:
6. Drop the spinach into fast-boiling
water. Cook for 3 minutes and drain in a
colander. As soon as the spinach is cool
enough to handle squeeze out all the
remaining moisture with your hands. It
should be reduced to a small, firm ball.
Place the spinach ball on a chopping board
and mince it finely.

7. Place the spinach, ground meats, eggs,
salt and pepper in a mixing bowl.

8. In a small skillet melt the 2 tablespoons
of butter. Add the shallots and garlic and

cook for 3 minutes or until soft and transparent. Add them to the mixing bowl.

9. Add the bread slices, sage and allspice. Knead the mixture with your hands until it is well blended. Correct the seasoning.

The veal:
10. Preheat the oven to 325°.

11. Dry the veal scallops well on paper towels. Season with salt and pepper.

12. Place a spoonful of the stuffing on each slice and roll up the slices. Either tie the veal birds with string on each end or fasten each end with a toothpick.

13. Lightly dredge the veal birds in flour and reserve.

14. In a large skillet heat the 4 tablespoons of butter and the oil. Add the veal birds, a few at a time, brown them lightly on all sides, then transfer them to the baking dish.

15. To the fat remaining in the pan add the meat glaze and wine. Bring the mixture to a boil, scraping the bottom of the pan well and reduce the liquid by 1/2.

16. Add the reserved sauce, bring it to a boil and pour it over the veal birds. Cover the baking dish with foil and place it in the preheated oven for 25 to 30 minutes.

17. Remove the dish from the oven. Carefully remove the veal birds to a serving platter. Discard the string or toothpicks.

18. Place the dish over high heat and slightly reduce the sauce. If it seems too thin (it should have the consistency of heavy cream) add the cornstarch mixture and cook the sauce until it is rich and glossy.

19. Pour the sauce over the veal birds and serve garnished with Poached Mushrooms.

The poached mushrooms

Ingredients

3/4 pound button mushrooms (reserve the stems for the sauce)
1 tablespoon lemon juice
4 tablespoons sweet butter
1 cup water
Pinch of salt

Preparation

1. Wipe the mushrooms well with damp paper towels, or run them quickly under cold water, drying them gently with a clean towel.

2. Place them in a bowl and sprinkle them with the lemon juice.

3. In a saucepan melt the butter, add the mushrooms and shake the pan to cover them well with the butter.

4. Add the water. Bring it to a boil. Reduce the heat. Add the salt and simmer the mushrooms covered for 3 to 5 minutes.

Remarks

The sauce can be prepared two or three days ahead of time. The veal slices can be stuffed and browned several hours in advance and placed in a baking dish. After baking, the finished dish can be kept warm for 30 to 40 minutes in a 200° oven. Serve the dish with a risotto flavored with freshly grated Parmesan cheese.

Souffle normand

Serves: 6
Preparation time: 35 minutes
Cooking time: 45 minutes

Here is a marvelous way to welcome the first chilly evenings of fall. Serve the souffle with cold Apricot Sauce (pages 119–120) or the Grand Marnier Sauce (pages 349–350). Without the addition of a sauce, Souffle Normand is still one of the best in the souffle repertory.

Ingredients

3   apples peeled, cored and sliced
2   tablespoons apricot preserves
Pinch of cinnamon
1   tablespoon water
3   tablespoons flour
¾ cup milk
½ cup sugar
2   tablespoons sweet butter
4   egg yolks
1   tablespoon vanilla
4   tablespoons rum or Calvados
6   egg whites at room temperature
Salt
3 to 4 crumbled toasted macaroons

Optional:
2   cups Apricot Sauce (pages 119–120)

Garnish:
Confectioners' sugar

Preparation

1. Preheat the oven to 350°.

2. In a heavy saucepan combine the apples, apricot preserves, cinnamon and water. Cook over low heat until the mixture becomes a thick puree. Stir from time to time to make sure the bottom of the pan does not get scorched. Cool the puree and meanwhile make the sauce base.

3. In a heavy saucepan combine the flour with a little cold milk. Stir the mixture until it becomes a smooth paste. Add the remaining milk and the sugar and cook over high heat, stirring constantly, until the sauce is very thick and smooth.

4. Remove the saucepan from the heat. Add the butter. One by one, add the egg yolks, incorporating each one completely into the souffle base before adding the next one.

5. Flavor the mixture with vanilla and 3 tablespoons rum and reserve.

6. Place the egg whites in a copper bowl, add a pinch of salt and whisk by hand until they form soft peaks.

7. Gently fold the apple puree into the souffle base and taste it for sweetness, adding more sugar if needed.

8. Add a little of the beaten whites to the souffle base and fold them in by hand. Now fold the souffle-base mixture gently into the remaining egg whites. Set aside.

9. Butter a 6-cup souffle dish and sprinkle lightly with sugar, shaking out the excess.

10. Pour ½ the mixture into the mold.

11. Sprinkle with the macaroon crumbs and the remaining rum. Top with the remaining souffle mixture.

12. Set the mold in the middle part of the hot oven and bake the souffle for 35 minutes.

13. Remove from the oven, sprinkle heavily with confectioners' sugar and serve immediately. Serve the Apricot Sauce on the side.

Risotto a la toscana

Serves: 4 to 6
Preparation time: 25 minutes
Cooking time: 30 to 40 minutes

A well-flavored risotto is one of the best fall dishes. It is hearty, yet, when well prepared, it can even be served at an elegant dinner party. The rice must be creamy with a slightly resistant core in each grain.
A risotto of this kind should not be served as an accompaniment to a main course but rather as an appetizer or as a light supper. It can be followed by veal scallopini or fish.

Ingredients

½ pound chicken livers
Salt and freshly ground white pepper
6 tablespoons sweet butter
2 shallots, finely minced
⅓ cup finely minced cooked ham
1½ cups Italian rice, thoroughly washed
½ cup white wine
3 to 4 cups Chicken Stock (page 404)
1 large sprig fresh sage
2 tablespoons finely grated fresh Parmesan cheese

Optional:
A bowl of freshly grated Parmesan Cheese

Preparation

1. Preheat the oven to 300°

2. Clean the chicken livers, removing any green spots. Dice them and season them with salt and pepper. Heat 2 tablespoons of butter in a heavy skillet and add the chicken livers. Cook until they are lightly browned.

3. Add the shallots and cook the mixture over high heat until the shallots are soft and lightly browned. Add the ham and just heat through. Reserve the mixture.

4. In a heavy saucepan, melt 2 tablespoons of butter. Add the rice and stir until it turns a milky white and is well covered with butter.

5. Add the wine and a pinch of salt and let it come to a boil. When the wine has been absorbed, add ⅓ of the Chicken Stock, lower the heat and cook the rice, uncovered, for 2 or 3 minutes, stirring a few times with a wooden fork. Bury the sprig of sage in the rice and as soon as the liquid has been absorbed, add more stock. Be sure the rice is cooking over very low heat and that the bottom of the pan does not get scorched. In about 20 to 25 minutes the rice should be creamy and almost tender. If you like it quite tender, cook it for 5 to 10 more minutes, adding a little more stock.

6. As soon as the rice is done, remove the sage. Add the chicken liver mixture, remaining butter and 2 tablespoons of grated Parmesan cheese. Cover the saucepan and place it in the warm oven for 5 minutes.

7. Serve as soon as possible, adding a little more salt and pepper if necessary, with a bowl of Parmesan on the side.

Remarks

Sage is an herb that retains its freshness well into the fall. If, however, you do not have fresh sage, sprinkle the chicken livers with ½ teaspoon of dry sage before sauteeing.

Shrimp baleares

Serves: 6
Preparation time: 35 minutes
Cooking time: 25 minutes

■ ◑

Here is a dish that originated in Mallorca. Catalan cooking, in spite of its heavy hand with garlic and hot peppers, is not without refinement. As prepared in Spain this dish is quite spicy and often includes a mixture of shellfish. You may substitute scallops for the shrimp.

Ingredients

3 tablespoons finely minced parsley (preferably Italian)
3 tablespoons wine vinegar
2 large garlic cloves, minced
6 anchovy filets, minced
½ cup olive oil
2 small hot chili peppers
1 onion, finely minced
½ cup dry white wine
6 to 8 ripe tomatoes, peeled, seeded and chopped
Salt and freshly ground white pepper
2 pounds fresh raw shrimp, peeled
1 tablespoon small well-drained capers
1 cup Greek black olives, pitted

Garnish:
1 teaspoon grated lemon rind
2 tablespoons finely minced parsley
2 garlic cloves, minced

Preparation

1. In a mixing bowl combine the parsley, vinegar, garlic and anchovies and reserve.

2. In a large heavy skillet, heat the olive oil. Add the chili peppers and onion and cook until the onion is soft and lightly browned.

3. Add the wine and bring to a boil. Reduce the liquid by half and add the tomatoes,

salt and pepper. Cook until most of the tomato juice has evaporated.

4. Add the shrimp and cook for 5 to 7 minutes or until they turn a bright pink. Do not overcook them or they will get tough.

5. Add the capers, olives and the parsley vinegar, garlic and anchovy mixture and heat through. Correct the seasoning and pour onto a serving platter. Garnish with the grated lemon rind and additional parsley and garlic.

Remarks

This dish is usually served as an appetizer, but you may use it as a main course on a bed of saffron rice.

Notes

Catalan vegetable potpourri

Serves: 4 to 6
Preparation time: 30 minutes
Cooking time: 40 to 45 minutes

Spain, Italy, France and most of the other countries bordering the Mediterranean have in some way adopted this ragout of vegetables. France has its famous Ratatouille, Italy the Caponata. This Spanish version is perfect for an appetizer or as an accompaniment to a roast or steak. You can make it more substantial by serving each person a poached egg sprinkled with Parmesan cheese and fried bread slices.

Ingredients

2   medium eggplants, unpeeled, cut into 1-inch cubes
2   small zucchini, cut into small cubes
Salt
5 to 6 large very ripe tomatoes, peeled
3   tablespoons olive oil
2   small onions, thinly sliced
2   green bell peppers, finely sliced
½ cup Italian rice, thoroughly washed under cold running water
Freshly ground white pepper
1   small hot red pepper (dry chili)
2   tablespoons sliced, roasted peppers or pimientos

Garnish:
3   tablespoons freshly grated Parmesan cheese

Preparation

1. Place the eggplant and zucchini in a colander. Sprinkle with salt and drain for at least 30 minutes.

2. Do not seed the tomatoes. Chop them coarsely and retain all their juice.

3. Heat the olive oil in a large saucepan.

Add the onions and cook them over low heat until very soft and lightly browned.

4. Add the tomatoes with their juice, the green peppers, zucchini and eggplants. Then add the rice and season with salt and pepper.

5. Bring this mixture to a boil. Add the hot pepper. Reduce the heat and simmer, covered, over very low heat, for 35 to 40 minutes or until the rice is tender. You may have to add a few tablespoons of hot water if the mixture becomes too dry. After about 25 minutes add the pimiento strips or roasted pepper.

6. As soon as the rice is tender fluff it with 2 forks. Sprinkle with grated Parmesan, and serve.

Remarks

One cup of spicy Spanish sausage, finely sliced, can be added during the last 15 minutes of cooking. In that case omit the hot red pepper.

Notes

Balkan bean soup

Serves: 8 to 10
Preparation time: 30 minutes
Cooking time: 2 hours 15 minutes

In all the Balkan countries, as well as Spain, Italy and France, dried beans are an important part of the soups and ragouts that make up peasant cooking. There are innumerable varieties of this soup, each region having its own. This version is slightly spicy and has a pleasant smoky taste. The soup can be made 2 or 3 days in advance and will not lose its flavor even when reheated several times.

Ingredients

2 cups dry white beans (preferably Turkish or Greek)
5 garlic cloves
3 tablespoons olive oil
1 large onion, finely chopped
1 carrot, finely chopped
1 cup celery, finely chopped
2 leeks, finely chopped (white part only)
1 large Bouquet Garni (page 397), including 1 sprig sage and 1 sprig rosemary
1 ham bone
1-pound piece of smoked pork shoulder
2 hot chili peppers (dried)
Salt and freshly ground white pepper

Optional:
2 cups Beef Stock (page 405)
A few pieces garlic sausage, thickly sliced

Garnish:
2 tablespoons minced parsley
Salt and freshly ground black pepper

Preparation

1. Soak the beans overnight in cold water.

2. Drop the garlic cloves into boiling water for 2 minutes. The skin will slip right off. Reserve.

3. In a large casserole heat the olive oil. Add the onion, carrot, celery, leeks and garlic and saute for about 10 minutes without letting them brown. Add the beans, Bouquet Garni, ham bone, smoked pork shoulder and chili peppers. Cover with water.

4. Season with salt and white pepper. Cover the casserole and simmer the soup over low heat for 2 hours.

5. Remove the meat and ham bone as well as the Bouquet and chili peppers. Let the soup cool, then puree it in the blender and return it to the casserole. Remove any meat from the ham bone and add it, finely chopped, to the soup.

6. If the soup seems too thick, add some fresh Beef Stock or canned bouillon. Season with additional salt and black pepper and garnish with parsley. If you can get a good garlic sausage, slice it and add to the soup.

7. Serve hot with black bread.

Remarks

The chili peppers will make the soup quite spicy. If you prefer a less spicy soup, use just 1 chili pepper. If you have any leftover roast lamb, you may chop it finely and add it to the soup. If you like garlic, add 1 finely chopped clove to the parsley for garnish.

Notes

Balkan fish soup

Serves: 6
Preparation time: 45 minutes
Cooking time: 1 hour 15 minutes

A large tureen of hot soup followed by a simple main course is a wonderful fall meal. This soup can become a kitchen staple as you can add or substitute all kinds of fish and shellfish.

Ingredients

3 pints small fresh mussels
2 cups white wine
2 onions, sliced
1 large Bouquet Garni (page 397)
10 peppercorns
2 tablespoons sweet butter
3 tablespoons flour
1 carrot, sliced
2 leeks, sliced
1 celery stalk, sliced
2 pounds trimmings and fish heads
6 cups water
2½-pound bass or other firm white fish, cut into serving pieces
Salt and freshly ground white pepper
½ pound small raw fresh shrimp, peeled
3 egg yolks
2 tablespoons lemon juice
½ cup cream
1 tablespoon finely chopped parsley
2 tablespoons finely chopped fresh dill

Optional:
1 large lemon, unpeeled and cut into thin slices

Preparation

1. Clean the mussels thoroughly under cold running water. Scrub well in order to eliminate as much sand as possible.

2. Place the washed mussels in a large kettle. Add the wine, the onions, the Bouquet Garni and the peppercorns. Cover the kettle, bring the wine to a boil and steam the mussels for 5 to 10 minutes.

3. Strain the mussel stock through 2 layers of cheesecloth and set it aside. Remove the mussels from the shells and reserve.

4. In the same kettle melt the butter. Add the flour and cook without browning for 2 more minutes. Add the carrots, leeks and celery and cook for 3 to 5 minutes.

5. Add the fish trimmings and the reserved mussel stock together with the 6 cups of water and let this simmer for 45 minutes. Strain the stock and return to the pot.

6. Season the fish pieces with salt and pepper. Add them to the stock and simmer for 10 to 12 minutes, or until the fish flakes easily.

7. With a slotted spoon remove the fish pieces to a serving tureen. Add the shrimp to the stock and cook for 5 minutes. Then remove them to the tureen.

8. In a bowl beat the egg yolks with 2 tablespoons of lemon juice and the cream. Gradually add a little of the hot stock, beating constantly. Off the heat pour the egg-cream mixture into the hot soup. The soup should get slightly thicker. You may put it back over a low heat, but make sure it does not boil or it will curdle. Correct the seasoning and add more lemon juice if you like.

9. Add the reserved mussels and pour the soup over the fish in the tureen.

10. Sprinkle with parsley and dill and garnish with optional lemon slices.

Catalan cabbage soup

Serves: 4 to 6
Preparation time: 30 minutes
Cooking time: 2 hours 15 minutes

Most of the soups from the Pyrenees region make use of cabbage. Some are more refined than others. All are hearty and filling. It is of great importance, when making any vegetable soup, that all ingredients should be of the utmost freshness. The smell of good soup cooking should permeate the house.

Ingredients

2 tablespoons olive oil
2 large onions, thinly sliced
5 garlic cloves, finely minced
4 leeks, thinly sliced (white parts only)
4 large tomatoes, peeled and chopped
1 head Savoy cabbage, cut into chunks
2 to 3 beef shank bones
1 large Bouquet Garni (page 397), including the green of the leeks
1 red bell pepper, cut into strips
Salt and freshly ground white pepper
1 hot red pepper
10 cups White Stock (page 405)

Optional:
10 to 12 thin slices Italian pepperoni or other good garlic sausage

Garnish:
Thin French bread fried in olive oil with garlic

Preparation

1. In a casserole, heat the olive oil. Add the onions and garlic and cook for 5 minutes until the onions are soft but not browned.

2. Add the leeks and cook for 5 more minutes, stirring with a wooden spoon to be sure the onions are not browning.

3. Add the tomatoes, cabbage, bones, Bouquet Garni and bell pepper. Season with salt, pepper and the hot pepper.

4. Add the stock. Bring the soup to a boil. Skim the top and reduce the heat. Simmer covered, for 2 hours, skimming occasionally.

5. Before serving, remove the Bouquet and leek greens, and correct the seasoning. If there is any meat on the bones, remove it and add to the soup.

6. Add the optional garlic sausage and heat through. Serve with thin slices of French bread sauteed in olive oil and garlic. These can be made several days in advance and must be very crunchy. Serve them either on a separate plate or floating in each individual soup dish.

Remarks

This soup is best made a day or two ahead of time and reheated. The garlic sausages, if used, should be added just before serving.

Notes

Yugoslav stuffed-pepper soup

Serves: 6 to 8
Preparation time: 30 minutes
Cooking time: 2 hours 15 minutes

Here is a hearty dish that can be served as a meal by itself, or simply followed by a salad and cheese.

Ingredients

Salt
½ cup white Italian rice (not converted)
3 pounds ripe unpeeled tomatoes, coarsely chopped
6 tablespoons cooking oil
½ onion, finely minced
¾ pound ground beef (preferably chuck)
Large pinch oregano
Freshly ground black pepper
1 garlic clove, mashed
6 to 8 green peppers, cleaned and tops removed
4 tablespoons flour
2 tablespoons tomato paste
3 cups water
1 large Bouquet Garni (page 397)
1 tablespoon sugar
2 small hot chili peppers (dried)

Optional:
1 to 2 cups Beef Stock (page 405)

Garnish:
2 cups cooked white rice
  or 6 to 8 new potatoes cooked until tender

Preparation

1. In a small saucepan bring 1½ cups of water to a boil. Add a pinch of salt and the rice and simmer over low heat, without stirring, for 20 minutes or until tender. Cool the rice and reserve.

2. Put the tomatoes in a blender and puree at high speed. Then pass the tomato puree through a sieve and reserve.

3. In a small skillet, heat 1 tablespoon of oil. Add the finely minced onion and cook until it is soft but not browned. Reserve.

4. In a bowl combine the ground meat, onions, salt, oregano, pepper, cooked rice and garlic.

5. Correct the seasoning, then fill the peppers with the mixture. If there is meat left over, form into small meatballs to be added to the soup.

6. In a large casserole heat the remaining oil. Add the flour. Cook, stirring constantly, until it turns a light hazelnut brown.

7. Add the tomato puree, the tomato paste, 3 cups of water and the Bouquet Garni. Stir well to blend with the flour and bring to a boil.

8. Add the sugar, chili peppers, salt and pepper. Reduce the heat.

9. Carefully place the stuffed peppers and meatballs (if any) in the soup. Cover the casserole and over low heat simmer the soup for 1 hour and 30 minutes to 2 hours, skimming off the fat from time to time. If the soup thickens too much, add Beef Stock. Be sure to cook the soup over very low heat so as not to scorch the bottom of the casserole.

10. When the soup is ready, correct the seasoning. If you wish, whisk in 1 or 2 more tablespoons of tomato paste for a deeper color. Serve the soup right out of the casserole, with the rice (or potatoes) on the side, or put the rice in the bottom of a soup tureen and pour the soup over it. Serve with black bread.

Fresh tomato soup with creme fraiche and dill

Serves: 6
Preparation time: 25 minutes
Cooking time: 35 to 45 minutes

I am especially enamored with the tomato. I was once told that in Bulgaria people eat tomatoes as we would an apple and often carry an extra one around for a mid-afternoon snack. I often wonder if I am not a Bulgarian at heart.

Ingredients

3   pounds very ripe fresh tomatoes
4   tablespoons sweet butter
1   tablespoon olive oil
1   onion, finely minced
3   tablespoons flour
4   cups boiling water
1   large Bouquet Garni (page 397), including 1 teaspoon fresh marjoram
Salt and freshly ground white pepper
6   tablespoons Creme Fraiche (page 398) or sour cream
2   tablespoons finely chopped fresh dill

Optional:
1 or 2 cups cooked rice
1   cup Chicken Stock (page 404)

Preparation

1. Drop the tomatoes into boiling water for 1 minute. Drain and peel. Chop coarsely and reserve.

2. In a large saucepan, heat 1 tablespoon of butter and the oil. Add the onion and cook over low heat until lightly browned. Add the remaining butter.

3. When the butter is melted, add the flour and cook until it is golden brown. Be careful not to burn it!

4. Add the chopped tomatoes stirring constantly. Then add the boiling water, Bouquet Garni, salt and pepper. Cover and simmer the soup for 35 minutes.

5. Remove the soup from the heat. Remove the Bouquet. Cool the soup and puree it in the blender. If it seems too thick, thin it out with a little Chicken Stock or water.

6. Serve the soup in individual bowls, each topped with 1 tablespoon Creme Fraiche and a sprinkling of dill.

Remarks

For a more hearty soup, omit the Creme Fraiche (or sour cream) and substitute 1 or 2 cups of cooked rice.

Notes

Spaghettini
a la provencale

Serves: 4 to 6
Preparation time: 20 minutes
Cooking time: 20 minutes

Rather than the all-famous Spaghetti with Tomato Sauce, I find this version more refreshing. The tomatoes are left almost uncooked and the sauce retains the freshness of the ingredients. Fresh tuna, whiting, or any other firm fish, sauteed in olive oil, can be substituted for the canned tuna.

Ingredients

3   red peppers
3   tablespoons finely minced parsley
1   tablespoon fresh oregano or 1 teaspoon dried oregano
3   large garlic cloves, finely minced
1   tablespoon tiny capers
4 to 6 anchovy filets
1   pound spaghettini (Ronzoni No. 9)
3   tablespoons olive oil
1   onion, finely minced
10 to 12 Italian plum tomatoes, peeled and sliced
Salt and freshly ground white pepper
1   tablespoon tomato paste
6   ounces of tuna, preferably in olive oil

Optional:
3   tablespoons lightly sauteed pine nuts

Preparation

1. Preheat the broiler.

2. Place the red peppers on a cookie sheet and broil until they are well charred on all sides. Peel them under cold running water. Slice them in half and remove all white membrane and seeds. Cut the peppers into thin strips and reserve.

3. Combine the parsley, oregano, garlic, capers and anchovies in a bowl. Reserve.

4. Bring 4 quarts of salted water to a boil in a large casserole. When the water is at a rolling boil, add the spaghettini and cook over high heat for 8 to 9 minutes, or until barely tender.

5. While the spaghettini is cooking, heat the olive oil in a large skillet. Add the onion and cook until soft but not brown.

6. Add the tomatoes and red peppers. Season with salt and pepper. Add the tomato paste and cook the mixture for 3 to 5 minutes. The tomatoes should still retain their shape and freshness.

7. Add the tuna and just heat through. Reserve.

8. When the spaghettini is done, drain and put into a serving bowl.

9. Add the parsley and anchovy mixture to the tomatoes. Pour the mixture over the spaghettini. Toss lightly and garnish with the optional pine nuts.

Notes

Chicken a la mallorquina

Serves: 6
Preparation time: 25 to 30 minutes
Cooking time: 45 minutes to 1 hour

Ingredients

2 chickens (2½ to 3 pounds each), cut into serving pieces (reserve giblets and backs for stock)
Salt and freshly ground white pepper
6 to 8 tablespoons olive oil
2 onions, finely sliced
3 garlic cloves, minced
1½ red peppers, finely sliced
1½ green peppers, finely sliced
¼ to ½ teaspoon saffron
Pinch of hot red pepper (or two dried chili peppers)
½ cup finely cubed prosciutto
4 large ripe tomatoes, peeled, seeded and very finely chopped
½ cup white wine
1 Bouquet Garni (page 397)
1 cup Brown Chicken Stock (page 404)
12 shrimp (raw and peeled)
2 tablespoons finely minced parsley
Freshly ground black pepper

Optional:
1 teaspoon tomato paste
2 teaspoons cornstarch mixed with a little white wine

Garnish:
French bread slices fried in olive oil and garlic
2 additional tablespoons minced parsley

Preparation

1. Dry the chicken pieces thoroughly with paper towels. Season with salt and pepper.

2. In a large skillet or chicken fryer, heat 4 tablespoons of olive oil. Add chicken pieces a few at a time and brown them on all sides over medium heat, partially covered. Remove each piece as finished and reserve. Add a little more olive oil if necessary.

3. When all the chicken has been removed from the pan, reduce the heat and add the onions and 1 teaspoon of minced garlic. Cook until the onions are soft and very lightly browned.

4. Add the sliced peppers, saffron and hot red pepper or chili peppers. Cover the pan and continue cooking until the peppers are soft.

5. Add the prosciutto, the tomatoes and tomato paste, if desired. Bring to a boil and cook, uncovered, over high heat until most of the tomato juice has evaporated.

6. Add the wine, Bouquet Garni and Chicken Stock. Bring to a boil and return chicken pieces to the pan. Season again.

7. Cover the pan and simmer on top of the stove over low heat for 45 minutes or until the chicken is tender.

8. While the chicken is cooking, heat 2 tablespoons of olive oil in a small skillet. Add the shrimp and cook them for 3 to 5 minutes or until they turn bright pink. Season them with salt and pepper and sprinkle them with 2 tablespoons of minced parsley and the remaining minced garlic. Reserve.

9. When the chicken is done, remove it with a slotted spoon to a serving platter.

10. Raise the heat and reduce the sauce until it is thick enough to coat a spoon.

11. Add the shrimp, garlic and parsley mixture. Reduce the heat and cook the sauce for 2 minutes more.

12. Beat in the cornstarch mixture if the sauce seems too thin.

13. Season the sauce with salt and plenty of black pepper and pour it over the chicken. Garnish with more minced parsley and the fried bread.

Remarks

In Spain unpeeled shrimp are cooked in the sauce together with the chicken. This gives the sauce a stronger and rather unusual flavor which I personally prefer. Try it both ways. A Parmesan-flavored risotto is an excellent accompaniment.

Notes

Chicken a la meridionale

Serves: 4 to 6
Preparation time: 1 hour
Cooking time: 1 hour

Because of its marvelous versatility, chicken can be used with almost every seasonal vegetable. Here is a chicken "ragout" that has some of the elements of the famous French Ratatouille. It is good either hot or cold and is perfect for a large buffet.

Ingredients

2½ to 3 pounds of chicken cut into serving pieces (reserve back, necks and giblets for Brown Chicken Stock, page 404)
Salt and freshly ground white pepper
2 tablespoons sweet butter
½ cup plus 2 tablespoons olive oil
2 garlic cloves, finely minced
2 onions, finely sliced
4 large ripe tomatoes, peeled, seeded and chopped
½ cup dry white wine
1 Bouquet Garni (page 397)
1½ cups Brown Chicken Stock (page 404)
2 small unpeeled zucchini, cut into cubes, sprinkled with salt and drained for 30 minutes
1 small unpeeled eggplant, cubed, sprinkled with salt and drained for 30 minutes
1 green pepper, roasted, peeled and sliced into strips
1 tablespoon cornstarch mixed to a paste with a little stock
3 tablespoons minced fresh herbs (parsley, chives and marjoram)
½ cup pimiento, cut into thin strips

Preparation

1. Dry the chicken pieces thoroughly on paper towels. Season with salt and

pepper. Heat the butter and 2 tablespoons of oil in a large chicken fryer or skillet and saute the chicken pieces a few at a time until evenly browned on all sides. Remove the pieces to a side dish, regulate the heat so as not to burn the fat and continue sauteeing.

2. When all the chicken has been browned, add the garlic and onions to the skillet and cook until soft and lightly browned.

3. Add the tomatoes and wine and bring the mixture to a boil, scraping the bottom of the pan well.

4. Season the mixture with salt and pepper; add the Bouquet Garni and the Chicken Stock and return the chicken pieces to the pan. Cover the skillet and simmer the chicken for 40 to 50 minutes.

5. While the chicken is cooking, dry the zucchini and eggplant cubes well with paper towels. Heat 4 tablespoons of olive oil in a large skillet and saute the eggplant until lightly browned. Remove the cubes to a thick layer of paper towels to drain. Add more oil to the skillet and saute the zucchini pieces until they are lightly browned. Remove them to a side dish and quickly saute the green pepper strips for 3 to 5 minutes. Combine the eggplant, zucchini and pepper strips and reserve.

6. When the chicken is done, remove it with a slotted spoon to a side dish.

7. Strain the pan juices, pressing down well on the vegetables to extract all their juice. Return the juices to the pan and place the skillet over high heat.

8. Beat in the cornstarch mixture and add the eggplant, zucchini, and pepper mixture. Correct the seasoning.

9. Add the mixed herbs or parsley and pimiento. Pour the sauce over the chicken and serve.

Remarks

Buttered noodles are an excellent accompaniment to this dish. You may also serve additional sauteed eggplant slices garnished with minced parsley and garlic. Cubed veal can be substituted for the chicken. In that case use 2 to 3 cups of Brown Stock (page 403)—it must cover the meat—and braise the meat in the oven for 1 hour and 30 minutes to 1 hour and 45 minutes.

Notes

Duck a la catalane

Serves: 4
Preparation time: 45 minutes
Cooking time: 2 hours 15 minutes

In spite of the duck's natural affinity for fruits, I like to get away from the traditional and prepare it in a more hearty way such as this Catalan version. In Spain a duck is usually cut into serving pieces, but the presentation of the whole duck seems more appealing and suitable for the larger ducks of the United States.

Ingredients

1 5-pound duck, cleaned
Salt
Freshly ground white pepper
½ teaspoon paprika
½ teaspoon rosemary
1 large garlic clove, mashed
5 tablespoons sweet butter
2 tablespoons olive oil
¼ cup cognac
1 Bouquet Garni (page 397)
2 whole onions
2 tablespoons minced shallots
6 large tomatoes, peeled, seeded and chopped
1 teaspoon dry oregano or 2 tablespoons fresh
1 teaspoon dry basil or 2 tablespoons fresh
¼ teaspoon saffron diluted in 1 tablespoon of hot water
1 cup green pitted olives, parboiled for 5 minutes and drained
½ cup dry white wine
1½ cups Brown Duck Stock (page 405)

Optional:
1 tablespoon cornstarch mixed to a paste with a little white wine

Garnish:
Parsley sprigs or fresh watercress

Preparation

1. Preheat the oven to 350°.

2. Dry the duck thoroughly both inside and out with paper towels. Season with salt, pepper, paprika and rosemary. Rub the duck with the garlic. Prick the duck around the thighs and bottom part of the breast.

3. In a large flameproof casserole heat 3 tablespoons of butter with the olive oil.

4. Saute the duck over low heat on all sides until it is nicely browned.

5. While the duck is browning, warm the cognac in a little saucepan and ignite it. Pour the flaming cognac over the browned duck and shake the casserole until the flames subside.

6. Add the Bouquet Garni and the whole onions to the casserole. Cover it and place it in the oven. Braise the duck for 1 hour and 45 minutes to 2 hours, or until the juices run pale yellow.

7. While the duck is braising, heat the remaining butter in a skillet. Add the shallots and cook until they are soft but not browned.

8. Add the tomatoes, herbs and saffron. Cook for 10 minutes or until the mixture is reduced to a thick puree.

9. Add the parboiled olives and heat through. Season the mixture with salt and pepper. Add the salt with caution since the olives may still be slightly salty. Reserve the mixture.

10. When the duck is done, remove it to a baking sheet and keep it warm in the oven while finishing the sauce.

11. Place the casserole on top of the stove. Remove the onions and the Bouquet Garni. Cook the pan juices over high heat for 2 or 3 minutes until the drippings coagulate and the pure fat rises in the pan. Be careful not to burn the drippings. Pour all the fat out of the casserole and add the white wine. With a wooden spoon scrape the coagulated juices and cook until the wine is reduced to ¼ cup.

12. Add the Brown Duck Stock and reduce the stock by ⅓. Add the tomato and olive mixture and heat the sauce through. Add the cornstarch mixture if the sauce does not seem thick enough. Remove from the heat and reserve.

13. Place the duck under a hot broiler for 5 minutes or until the skin is nicely crisped.

14. Place the duck on a serving platter and pour the sauce around it. Serve immediately garnished with parsley sprigs or fresh watercress.

Remarks

You may serve glazed onions, sauteed mushrooms or a curry risotto as an accompaniment to this dish.

Notes

Pheasant a la basquaise

Serves: 6
Preparation time: 35 minutes
Cooking time: 1 hour 20 minutes

■ ◈

Ingredients

The pheasant:
½ pound slab bacon
7 tablespoons sweet butter
2 pheasants (2 to 2½ pounds each)
Salt and freshly ground white pepper
6 slices blanched bacon
1 onion, finely sliced
1 carrot, finely sliced
1 Bouquet Garni (page 397)
2 whole garlic cloves, peeled
1 cup Brown Stock (page 403)

The rice:
1½ cups Italian rice, thoroughly washed
3 cups water or light Chicken Stock (page 404)
2 tablespoons olive oil
1 cup diced fresh red pepper (if not available use a good brand of pimientos)
1 teaspoon crushed hot red pepper (or a good imported paprika)
4 medium tomatoes, peeled, seeded and chopped
Salt and freshly ground white pepper

Optional:
1½ cups thinly sliced Chorizo (Spanish sausage)
1 Beurre Manie (page 397)

Preparation

1. Preheat the oven to 375°.

2. Remove the rind and cut the bacon into 1-inch cubes. Drop the cubes into simmering water, cook for 5 minutes and drain.

3. In a large flameproof casserole, saute the bacon cubes in 2 tablespoons of butter until lightly browned. Remove the bacon and reserve.

4. In the same fat, brown the pheasants on all sides. Remove them from the casserole, season them with salt and pepper, and tie the bacon strips over the breasts and thighs of each bird.

5. Discard all but 1 tablespoon of fat from the casserole and add 3 more tablespoons of sweet butter. Saute the onion and carrot for 2 or 3 minutes.

6. Add the pheasants, bacon cubes, Bouquet Garni, garlic and the Brown Stock. Cover the casserole and place in the oven. Braise the pheasants for 50 minutes or until tender. While the birds are cooking, prepare the rice.

The rice:
7. Melt the remaining butter in a saucepan. Add the rice and stir to cover it well with butter. Add 3 cups of water or Chicken Stock. Bring to a boil and lower the heat. Simmer covered for 20 to 25 minutes.

8. While the rice is cooking, heat the olive oil in a skillet. Add the red pepper, hot pepper and the tomatoes and cook until the mixture is a thick puree. Season.

9. When the rice is tender, add the tomato puree and the Spanish sausage (if used). Cover the saucepan and place it in the oven for another 10 minutes. When the rice is done, pour it onto a serving platter.

10. Remove the pheasants from the casserole, discard the bacon slices, carve the birds into serving pieces and place on the rice. Surround with the bacon cubes.

11. Strain the sauce and skim off the fat. Discard the Bouquet Garni, reduce the sauce by half and thicken it, if necessary, with a little Beurre Manie.

Calves' liver portugaise
Serves: 4
Preparation time: 25 minutes
Cooking time: 10 minutes

Ingredients

6 slices calves' liver, cut ¼ inch thick
1 large sprig fresh sage
Juice of 1 lemon
Olive oil
½ cup flour
Salt and freshly ground white pepper
2 eggs, lightly beaten
2 cups homemade bread crumbs
½ cup sweet butter
3 tablespoons oil

The sage butter:
8 tablespoons softened sweet butter
3 tablespoons finely minced fresh herbs
   (1 tablespoon fresh sage, parsley, chives)
1 tablespoon lemon juice

Garnish:
Quartered lemons
Watercress sprigs

Preparation

1. Place the calves' liver in an enamel dish. Bury the sage among the slices.

2. Sprinkle the liver slices with lemon juice and dribble with olive oil. Marinate for 1 to 2 hours in the bottom part of the refrigerator.

3. Dry the liver slices with paper towels.

4. Dip the slices in flour seasoned with salt and white pepper, then in the beaten eggs and then into the bread crumbs until they are well coated.

5. Place the breaded slices on a large platter and return to the refrigerator for 30 minutes to 1 hour.

6. Meanwhile, make the herb butter by whipping the softened butter in a bowl and adding the finely minced herbs and lemon juice. Taste the butter; you may like a stronger flavor of sage. If you do, add an additional teaspoonful. Chill the herb butter until serving time.

7. Just before serving melt the ½ cup of butter together with the oil in a large skillet. Add the calves' liver slices and saute them over medium heat for 2 or 3 minutes. Turn them and saute them on the other side until they are nicely browned. They should still be somewhat rare in the center. Test one slice by making a small incision in it with a sharp knife. As soon as the liver is done, remove it to a serving platter.

8. Place a little of the sage butter on each slice of liver. Decorate the platter with quartered lemon and fresh watercress.

Remarks

Sauteed mushrooms are an excellent accompaniment to this dish. Chicken livers can be prepared in the same way and served with a Parmesan-flavored risotto.

Notes

Saute of calves' liver normand

Serves: 4
Preparation time: 20 minutes
Cooking time: 15 to 20 minutes

■ ○

This is an excellent recipe for last-minute entertaining. It is also well suited for a family dinner when you feel like having something light yet a little unusual. I find the combination of calves liver, bacon and apples to be just that.

Ingredients

8 slices calves' liver, cut ¼ inch thick
Flour for dredging
1 cup finely cubed bacon
8 tablespoons sweet butter
2 large onions, finely sliced
2 large tart apples, peeled and cut into ½-inch wedges
Freshly ground white pepper
1 tablespoon vegetable oil
Salt
2 tablespoons minced parsley

Preparation

1. Dry the calves' liver slices well with paper towels, then flour them, shaking off the excess.

2. In a large heavy frying pan, saute the bacon until lightly browned. Don't let it get too crisp. Remove it to paper towels. Pour out all but 1 tablespoon of the bacon fat and add 3 tablespoons butter.

3. When it is very hot, add the onions. When they are soft and transparent, add the apple wedges. Season with white pepper, cover the pan and cook the apples over low heat for 5 minutes. They should be soft but not mushy. Add the bacon cubes. Cover the pan again and braise the apples for 2 or 3 more minutes. Remove from the heat.

4. Melt 3 tablespoons of butter together with the oil in a heavy skillet. When very hot, add the calves' liver. Do not crowd your pan. Saute the liver for 2 or 3 minutes on one side and 2 minutes on the other. Be sure not to burn the butter.

5. As soon as the liver is done, season it with salt and pepper. Remove it to a serving platter. Pour all the fat from the pan. Add the remaining butter, and the parsley. Just melt the butter and pour it over the liver. Surround the liver with the apple mixture and serve immediately.

Remarks

The apples combine well with a simple roast loin of pork. Garnish the platter with braised chestnuts and sauteed apples.

Notes

Hamburgers aux fines herbes

Serves: 6
Preparation time: 15 minutes
Cooking time: 10 minutes

This is an inexpensive supper dish that I often make late into the fall.
In the summer I frequently broil the hamburgers over an open fire, then top them with the herb butter. A side dish of Basil and Tomato Sauce (page 400) also goes well with these hamburgers.

Ingredients

2 tablespoons sweet butter
1 medium onion, finely minced
2 pounds ground beef (preferably chuck)
1 egg
1 tablespoon finely minced fresh sage
2 teaspoons salt
½ teaspoon freshly ground black pepper
Pinch of cayenne pepper
Flour for dredging
4 tablespoons Clarified Butter (page 398)
1 tablespoon olive oil
¾ cup concentrated Brown Stock (page 403), thickened with 1 teaspoon cornstarch
The herb butter:
6 tablespoons sweet butter, softened
1 tablespoon finely minced parsley
1 small shallot, finely minced

Optional:
1 tablespoon finely minced mixed herbs (tarragon, chervil, savory)

Garnish:
Sprigs of watercress
Sauteed cherry tomatoes

Preparation

1. In a small mixing bowl combine the butter with parsley, shallot and optional

Ragout of lamb danois

Serves: 6
Preparation time: 45 minutes
Cooking time: 2 hours 45 minutes

herbs. Season with salt and freshly ground black pepper. Set aside.

2. Place the meat in a mixing bowl and reserve. In a small skillet melt 2 tablespoons of butter. When it is hot, add the onion. Cook until it is soft and lightly browned, then add it to the ground meat together with the egg, sage, salt, black pepper and cayenne. The meat mixture should be very light. Add 1 to 2 teaspoons water if it seems too heavy.

3. Shape the meat into oval hamburgers. (If cooked on a grill, form it into cylinders.)

4. Just before cooking, dredge the hamburgers lightly with flour. Shake off the excess.

5. In a large skillet, melt the Clarified Butter and the oil. When very hot, add the hamburgers and cook until nicely browned on both sides. Remove to a serving platter.

6. Pour all the fat out of the pan. Add the Brown Stock and reduce it to 2 tablespoons.

7. Remove the pan from the heat and add the herb butter. When it is melted, pour it over the hamburgers. Season with additional black pepper and serve garnished with watercress and Sauteed Cherry Tomatoes.

Remarks

If you are going to grill the hamburgers on an open fire or over charcoal, add to the meat mixture 1 small hot red chili pepper, crushed well with mortar and pestle. Serve the herb butter in little bits over each hamburger.

This is an ideal main course for a large dinner party or buffet. It is a mild ragout highly flavored with dill and quite lovely for fall dining. Fresh dill is a must in this recipe.

Ingredients

4   pounds shoulder of lamb, cut
    into 1½-inch cubes
5   cups cold water
2   pounds lamb bones
2   carrots
2   celery stalks
2   leeks
1   Bouquet Garni (page 397)
1   tablespoon salt
6 to 8 peppercorns

The vegetables:
18 small white onions
2   tablespoons sweet butter
½ pound quartered mushrooms (or whole
    button mushrooms)
Salt and freshly ground white pepper

The sauce:
5   tablespoons sweet butter
3   tablespoons flour
1 to 2 tablespoons lemon juice
1 or 2 teaspoons sugar
3   tablespoons minced fresh dill

Garnish:
Sprigs of fresh dill

Preparation

1. In a large casserole combine the water, lamb bones, carrots, celery, leeks, Bouquet Garni, 1 tablespoon salt and peppercorns. Let the stock come to a boil. Skim off the gray scum and simmer the stock for 45 minutes to 1 hour, partially covered.

2. Strain the stock and return it to the casserole. Add the lamb and simmer, partially covered, for 1 to 1½ hours or until the meat is tender when pierced with the tip of a knife. Add the onions 15 minutes before the lamb is done.

The vegetables:
3. In a 10-inch skillet, melt 2 tablespoons butter. Add the mushrooms, seasoned with salt and white pepper, and saute them for 3 to 5 minutes over high heat, constantly shaking the pan. Remove from the heat and reserve.

4. When the meat is done, remove it and onions with a slotted spoon to a side dish and keep warm in a 200° oven while you make the sauce.

The sauce:
5. Strain the stock from the casserole into a saucepan and reduce it over high heat to 2 cups.

6. In a large casserole (one in which you can serve the lamb) melt the 3 tablespoons of butter, add the flour and cook for 2 or 3 minutes. Do not let it brown. Add the hot stock all at once and cook the sauce, whisking it constantly, until it is very smooth and thick.

7. Add the lemon juice, sugar, and dill. Correct the seasoning. Return the lamb to the casserole. (Be careful not to include any juices that may have accumulated around the meat.)

8. Add the mushrooms and simmer the ragout covered for 5 more minutes. Serve garnished with additional sprigs of fresh dill.

Remarks

This dish can be made a day or two in advance and reheated in a 300° oven for 1 to 1½ hours.

Notes

Ragout of lamb grecque

Serves: 6
Preparation time: 45 minutes
Cooking time: 2 hours 15 minutes

■ ✦

Lamb has a natural affinity for eggplant.
In this recipe the meat is slowly
braised with cubed eggplant and tomatoes.
It should be prepared a day ahead of time
since ragouts are at their best the second
day. This is the perfect fall meal, gutsy
and flavorful with the last touch of
summer vegetables.

Ingredients

4 medium eggplants
Salt
3 pounds boneless shoulder of lamb,
   cubed
Freshly ground white pepper
1 cup salt pork, blanched and cubed
2 large onions, finely chopped
2 garlic cloves, finely minced
3 tablespoons tomato paste
1 teaspoon cumin
½ teaspoon turmeric
6 large tomatoes
¾ cup olive oil
Freshly ground black pepper
½ cup fine homemade bread crumbs
2 tablespoons finely minced parsley
1 teaspoon finely minced basil
1 teaspoon finely chopped oregano

Optional:
1 tablespoon cornstarch mixed to a paste
   with a little water

Preparation

1. Preheat oven to 375°.

2. Peel 2 eggplants and cut them into 1-inch
cubes. Leave the other two unpeeled and
cut them into ½-inch slices. Sprinkle both
cubes and slices with salt and place them

in two separate colanders for at least 2
hours.

3. Season the lamb with salt and pepper.

4. In a large casserole, saute the salt pork
over medium heat. When crisp, remove
to a side dish. In the fat remaining in the
casserole saute the lamb, a few pieces
at a time until all the cubes are nicely
browned. Remove them to a side dish.

5. Remove all but 2 tablespoons of fat from
the casserole. Add the onions and garlic.
Saute them until soft but not browned.

6. Add the tomato paste, cumin, turmeric,
and 4 tomatoes, peeled, seeded and
chopped. Cook this mixture for 2 or 3 minutes, then return the lamb to the casserole and reserve.

7. In a large heavy skillet heat 4 tablespoons of olive oil. Dry the eggplant cubes
well on paper towels and saute them in
the hot oil until nicely browned.

8. Add the eggplant cubes and salt pork to
the lamb. Set the casserole in the middle of
the preheated oven and braise the lamb
for 1 hour and 45 minutes or until the meat
is tender when pierced with a fork.

9. A few minutes before the lamb is done,
drain the eggplant slices. Dry well on paper
towels.

10. Heat 2 tablespoons of olive oil in a
frying pan and saute the eggplant slices
until lightly browned, adding more oil to the
pan when needed.

11. Slice the remaining unpeeled tomatoes
into thick slices. Sprinkle with salt and
let them drain for a few minutes.

12. Remove the casserole from the oven. Skim off all the fat. (There will be quite a lot as the eggplant will have released much of the frying oil.) Place the casserole on top of the stove and beat in the optional cornstarch mixture until the sauce is thick and smooth.

13. Pour the ragout into an oval baking dish. Place the eggplant and tomato slices in an overlapping pattern on top of the lamb. Season with salt and black pepper.

14. In a small skillet heat 2 tablespoons of olive oil. Add the bread crumbs and herbs. Saute for 2 or 3 minutes, then sprinkle the bread-crumb mixture on top of the eggplant and tomato slices.

15. Run the dish under the broiler for 3 to 5 minutes. Serve immediately.

Remarks

If you cook the lamb the day before, reheat it in the oven. The eggplant and tomato slices should be prepared at the last moment.
Serve the ragout with a tossed green salad and crusty French bread. No other vegetable is necessary.

Notes

Oxtail ragout bonne femme

Serves: 4 to 6
Preparation time: 50 minutes to 1 hour
Cooking time: 3 hours 45 minutes

Oxtails are an inexpensive but very tasty cut of beef. They are at their best when braised slowly in wine with vegetables. This ragout should be prepared one or two days ahead of time to give the meat and vegetables time to blend well. It is a perfect dish for the first cold days of fall.

Ingredients

4 pounds oxtails, cut into 2-inch pieces
Salt and freshly ground white pepper
Flour for dredging
4 tablespoons cooking oil
5 tablespoons sweet butter
2 celery stalks, finely minced
2 leeks, finely minced
1 large carrot, peeled and finely minced
2 large onions, finely minced
2 large garlic cloves, minced
2 tablespoons tomato paste
2 cups dry red wine
4 cups Brown Stock (page 403)
1 Bouquet Garni (page 397)
1 tablespoon cornstarch mixed with
    ⅓ cup of Brown Stock

The vegetables:
2 cups tiny new potatoes, peeled
2 cups carrots, peeled and cut into 2-inch matchsticks
18 small white onions
½ pound fresh mushrooms, quartered
Freshly ground black pepper

Preparation

1. Preheat the oven to 350°.

2. Remove some of the fat from the oxtail pieces. Dry them well on paper towels and season with salt and pepper. Dredge the

pieces in flour, shaking off the excess.

3. In a large flameproof casserole, heat the oil. Add the oxtail pieces a few at a time; brown them on all sides, regulating the heat so as not to burn the oil.

4. When all the pieces have been browned, remove them to a side dish, discard the oil, and add 3 tablespoons of butter to the casserole, then add the minced vegetables, including the garlic, and cook over low heat for 5 minutes or until they are soft, but not browned. Add the tomato paste and the wine and bring it to a boil.

5. Return the oxtail pieces to the casserole and cover them with 3 cups of Brown Stock. If the liquid does not cover the oxtails, add the remaining stock.

6. Bury the Bouquet Garni among the oxtails and add a large pinch of salt and pepper. Cover the dish and place it in the oven. Braise for 2 hours and 45 minutes to 3 hours or until almost tender.

7. Remove the casserole from the oven. With a slotted spoon remove the oxtail pieces to a side dish. Discard Bouquet.

8. Strain the sauce and skim off the fat. There will be a great deal of fat so before skimming let the sauce "rest" for 30 minutes to allow the fat to rise to the top.

9. Return the oxtails to the casserole and add the potatoes, carrot sticks and onions.

10. Cover the meat and vegetables with the strained sauce and return the casserole covered to the oven. Cook the ragout for 45 more minutes or until both the oxtails and vegetables are tender.

11. While the ragout is braising, heat the remaining butter in a small skillet. Add the mushrooms and brown them over high heat for 2 or 3 minutes. Season them with salt and pepper and set aside.

12. Remove the casserole from the oven. With a slotted spoon remove both the oxtails and the vegetables to a deep serving platter.

13. Set the casserole over high heat and reduce the sauce by $1/3$. Correct the seasoning and skim off any remaining fat.

14. Beat the cornstarch mixture into the sauce and cook it for 2 more minutes or until it heavily coats the spoon.

15. Add the sauteed mushrooms to the sauce and a large sprinkling of black pepper; pour the sauce over the oxtails and vegetables and serve very hot with crusty bread followed by a green salad and a platter of interesting cheeses.

Remarks

This dish is often served in deep soup plates. If you plan to do that, do not reduce the sauce too much. It should have the consistency of light cream. Do not serve any additional vegetable. When the ragout is made in advance, reheat it in a 350° oven for 45 minutes before serving.

Notes

Pork chops abazia

Serves: 6
Preparation time: 15 minutes
Cooking time: 50 to 55 minutes

Yugoslav cuisine is full of good gutsy food. It is peasant fare at its best, and reflects understanding of the value of fresh fruits and vegetables in their seasons. Here is a sample of Yugoslav cooking.

Ingredients

6 center-cut pork chops, 1 inch thick
Salt and freshly ground white pepper
1 sprig rosemary
3 tablespoons olive oil
4 shallots, finely chopped
1 teaspoon finely minced garlic
1 teaspoon hot Hungarian paprika
6 large very ripe tomatoes, seeded, peeled, coarsely chopped
½ cup dry white wine
1 dry red hot chili pepper
1 tablespoon tomato paste
2 small green peppers, sliced
½ cup roasted red peppers (pimientos), coarsely chopped

Garnish:
2 tablespoons finely chopped parsley

Preparation

1. Dry the chops with paper towels. Season with salt and pepper.

2. In a large heavy skillet heat 3 tablespoons of olive oil until it is almost smoking. Brown the chops for 2 or 3 minutes on each side and remove them to a plate.

3. Pour out all but 2 tablespoons of the fat. Lower the heat. Add the shallots and garlic and cook until soft. Make sure not to burn them.

4. Add the paprika, tomatoes and wine. Bring the mixture to a boil and lower the heat. Add the hot chili pepper, tomato paste, green pepper and rosemary.

5. Return the chops to the pan. Cover it tightly and let them simmer for 45 minutes. Five minutes before they are ready, add the roasted red peppers.

6. Remove the chops to a serving dish. If the sauce seems a little thin, raise the heat and reduce it until it heavily coats the spoon. Discard the rosemary. Correct the seasoning and pour the sauce over the chops. Garnish with parsley and serve immediately.

Remarks

This dish can be cooked in a 350° oven for 45 to 50 minutes. Pork has a tendency to dry out and should therefore be served as soon as possible. In Yugoslavia the chops are placed on top of a pilaf of rice. It makes a hearty and filling meal. Several kinds of sauteed vegetables go well with this dish—mushrooms or eggplant.

Notes

Medallions of pork in mustard and caper sauce

Serves: 4 to 6
Preparation time: 50 minutes
Cooking time: 1 hour 30 minutes

■ ✦

Ingredients

The sauce:
4   tablespoons Clarified Butter (page 398) or cooking oil
2   shallots, finely minced
2   tablespoons finely minced carrots
2   tablespoons finely minced celery
3   tablespoons flour
2½ cups concentrated Brown Stock (page 403), heated
1   small Bouquet Garni (page 397)
1   teaspoon tomato paste
Pinch of salt and pepper
2   tablespoons small capers
2   tablespoons minced parsley
Freshly ground black pepper

The mustard butter:
4   tablespoons sweet butter, softened
2   tablespoons Dijon mustard
Pinch of English dry mustard
1   teaspoon of lemon juice

The pork:
2   tablespoons sweet butter
2   tablespoons cooking oil
16 to 20 filet-of-pork medallions, cut ¾ inch thick, or 12 boned loin-of-pork medallions, cut ½ inch thick
Salt and freshly ground white pepper
2   tablespoons finely minced shallots
1   garlic clove, finely minced
1   teaspoon meat glaze
½ cup dry white wine

Optional:
1   Beurre Manie (page 397)

Garnish:
Small glazed turnips
Potato balls

Preparation

1. Preheat the oven to 325°. Butter a large flameproof baking dish and set aside. Start by making the sauce.

2. In a heavy saucepan melt the Clarified Butter. Add the minced vegetables and cook them over low heat for 5 to 8 minutes or until they are very soft but not browned.

3. Add the flour and stir it until it is well blended with the vegetables. Raise the heat a little and cook, stirring constantly, until the mixture becomes a hazelnut brown. Do not burn or scorch the bottom of the saucepan.

4. As soon as the flour mixture has turned nutty brown, add the hot Brown Stock all at once and stir until the mixture is smooth and lightly thickened.

5. Add the Bouquet Garni, tomato paste, salt and pepper. Do not oversalt as the sauce will become saltier as it reduces. Partially cover the pan and simmer for 1 hour, stirring it from time to time.

6. Strain the sauce and reserve.

7. While the sauce is cooking, make the Mustard Butter. In a small bowl place the softened butter. Add the Dijon and dry mustard and blend the mixture well with a wooden spoon. Add the lemon juice and chill.

The pork:
8. In a large skillet melt the 2 tablespoons of butter and oil.

9. Season the pork medallions with salt and white pepper. When the butter and oil

are very hot, add the pork medallions,
a few at a time, and brown them on both
sides. As the medallions brown, remove
them from the pan and set them aside.

10. Add the shallots and garlic to the pan
and cook them over low heat until they
are soft but not browned.

11. Add the meat glaze and the wine. Bring
it to a boil and scrape the bottom of the
pan well. Reduce the wine to 2 tablespoons.

12. Add the strained sauce and bring it
to a boil.

13. Place the pork medallions in the buttered baking dish and pour the sauce over
them. Cover the dish with foil and set it in
the oven. Braise the pork for 25 to 30
minutes.

14. Remove the baking dish from the oven
to the top of the stove. With a slotted
spoon remove the pork to a serving platter.

15. Raise the heat and reduce the sauce
slightly, skimming off the fat. If it does not
coat the spoon heavily, beat in the Beurre
Manie, bit by bit, until the sauce reaches
the right consistency.

16. Add the minced capers and parsley and
heat through.

17. Remove the sauce from the heat and
whisk in the Mustard Butter little by little
until it is well incorporated into the sauce.

18. Correct the seasoning, adding a good
dash of black pepper.

19. Spoon the sauce over the medallions
and serve garnished with tiny glazed turnip
and potato balls.

Ragout of veal galicia

Serves: 6
Preparation time: 30 minutes
Cooking time: 1 hour 45 minutes

Spain is not known for its veal, but northern Spain has some very similar in quality
to that found in the United States. In this
dish of Spanish origin, the veal is
casserole-cooked in the oven, then mixed
with white beans. It is a hearty dish that
needs no accompaniment other than a
well-seasoned salad and good bread.

Ingredients

4 pounds boneless veal, cut into 1-inch
  cubes
Salt and freshly ground white pepper
6 tablespoons olive oil
1 cup finely chopped onions
½ cup finely chopped carrots
½ cup finely chopped celery
1 leek (white part only), finely sliced
2 garlic cloves, minced
½ cup white wine
1½ pounds ripe tomatoes, peeled, seeded
  and chopped
1 cup Chicken Stock (page 404)
1 large Bouquet Garni (page 397)

The beans:
1½ cups dried white beans (preferably the
  Greek or Turkish kind)
1 large Bouquet Garni (page 397)
1 tablespoon salt

Optional:
1 Beurre Manie (page 397)

Preparation

1. Soak the beans overnight.

2. Preheat oven to 350°.

3. Dry the veal well on paper towels and
season with salt and pepper.

4. In a large flameproof casserole heat the olive oil. When it is very hot, add the veal a few pieces at a time and brown them well on all sides. Remove them from the casserole and continue browning until all the meat is done.

5. Add the vegetables (except the tomatoes) to the casserole and cook them over low heat for about 3 to 5 minutes. Add the wine and bring to a boil, scraping the bottom of the casserole well.

6. Add the tomatoes and Chicken Stock. Return the veal to the casserole together with the Bouquet Garni and place the casserole in the oven. Cook the ragout for about 1 hour or until the meat is almost tender.

7. In the meantime, drain the beans. Place them in a casserole with the tablespoon of salt, water to cover and a Bouquet Garni. Cook for 25 to 30 minutes or until the beans are almost done. Drain them and reserve.

8. Add the beans and continue cooking the ragout for 30 more minutes or until both the beans and veal are tender.

9. During the last 15 minutes of braising, uncover the casserole to reduce the juices and brown the top. If the sauce seems too thin, beat in the Beurre Manie. Serve directly from the casserole.

Remarks

The pan juices may be reduced on top of the stove. If you do that, remove the veal and beans with a slotted spoon to a serving dish. Add the Beurre Manie and season with additional salt and pepper.
Another variation is to saute, in 2 table- spoons of olive oil, ½ cup of bread crumbs together with 2 tablespoons of finely chopped parsley, basil and a touch of oregano. Sprinkle the bread-crumb mixture on top of the veal and beans and cook, uncovered, in the oven for the last 15 minutes.
Two or 3 veal knuckle bones can be added to the casserole. They add a great deal of flavor and body to the sauce. Discard the bones before adding the beans.

Notes

Veal scallops
a la piperade

Serves: 6
Preparation time: 35 minutes
Cooking time: 1 hour

■ ◓

The "piperade" is a famous Basque specialty made of sweet peppers, tomatoes, garlic and onions, which are then scrambled with eggs. There are numerous recipes for this dish, some including ham and others made with mushrooms. The vegetable mixture is excellent cold and I often use it for filling crepes.
Here the Piperade is used in combination with veal scallops and cheese.

Ingredients

5 tablespoons sweet butter
6 to 8 large veal scallops, cut ⅛ inch thick
Salt and freshly ground white pepper
Flour for dredging
2 eggs, lightly beaten
1½ to 2 cups fresh homemade white bread crumbs
5 tablespoons olive oil
2 shallots, finely minced
1 garlic clove, minced
2 green peppers, finely cubed
1 red pepper, finely cubed
4 large ripe tomatoes, peeled, seeded and chopped
1 tablespoon finely minced fresh basil or 1 teaspoon dry
½ teaspoon oregano
6 slices Gruyere or imported Swiss cheese

Optional:
½ cup minced prosciutto

Preparation

1. Preheat the oven to 350°.

2. Butter a baking dish (large enough to hold the meat in 1 layer) with 2 tablespoons of butter and then reserve.

3. Dry the veal scallops thoroughly on paper towels, season with salt and pepper, and dredge in flour, shaking off the excess. Dip the veal scallops into the beaten eggs and then into the bread crumbs, coating each one thoroughly. Place on wax paper and refrigerate for 1 to 2 hours.

4. In a large skillet, heat 3 tablespoons of olive oil, add the shallots and garlic and cook until tender but not browned.

5. Add the peppers and continue cooking until they are soft, for 3 to 5 minutes.

6. Add the tomatoes, salt, pepper and herbs and continue cooking over high heat until the mixture becomes very thick.

7. Add the optional prosciutto, heat through, remove the skillet from the heat and reserve.

8. Heat the remaining butter and oil in another large skillet. Add the veal scallops a few at a time and saute them on both sides until they are nicely browned. Carefully remove them to the baking dish.

9. Top each veal scallop with 1 heaping tablespoon of the pepper and tomato mixture, top with a slice of cheese and place in the oven. Bake the veal for 25 minutes or until the cheese has melted and is lightly browned. Serve at once directly from the baking dish.

Remarks

Braised white onions are an excellent accompaniment to this dish. They can be added just before serving. Serve a Curry Risotto (page 384) on the side.

Halibut steaks marengo

Serves: 4 to 6
Preparation time: 25 minutes
Cooking time: 1 hour

Ingredients

½ pound small mushrooms
1½ cups Fish Stock (page 406)
½ cup Greek pitted olives (black)
4 to 6 halibut steaks, cut into ¾-inch-thick
   slices
Milk
Salt and freshly ground white pepper
Flour for dredging
4 tablespoons sweet butter
4 tablespoons olive oil
3 tablespoons finely minced shallots
6 large tomatoes, peeled, seeded and
   finely chopped
1 Bouquet Garni (page 397)
1 teaspoon oregano
2 tablespoons tomato paste
¾ pound small mushrooms
1 Beurre Manie (page 397)
Freshly ground black pepper

Garnish:
2 tablespoons finely minced parsley
1 teaspoon finely minced fresh garlic
1 teaspoon finely grated lemon rind

Optional:
12 to 16 new potatoes, cooked and buttered

Preparation

1. Wipe the mushrooms with damp paper
towels. Remove the stems and add them to
the Fish Stock. Heat the stock, simmer
it for 15 minutes, and reserve.

2. Poach the olives in boiling water over
low heat for 5 minutes. Drain on paper
towels and set aside.

3. Dip the halibut steaks into milk for
2 or 3 minutes. Dry them with paper towels.

4. Season the fish steaks with salt and
pepper and lightly dredge them in flour,
shaking off the excess.

5. In a large deep skillet melt the butter
and 2 tablespoons of oil. Add the fish
steaks and brown them well on one side.
Turn them carefully with a large spatula
and brown them on the other side. Carefully remove the fish to a side dish.

6. To the fat remaining in the pan add the
shallots. Cook over low heat until they are
soft but not browned.

7. Add the tomatoes, salt, pepper, Bouquet
Garni and oregano. Bring the mixture to
a boil and add tomato paste and the Fish
Stock.

8. Return the fish steaks to the skillet.
Cover it tightly and simmer on top of the
stove for 20 to 25 minutes, or until the fish
flakes easily. Carefully remove the steaks
to a serving platter.

9. While the fish steaks are cooking, heat
remaining oil in a skillet. Add the mushrooms and cook them over high heat until
they are nicely browned. Do not overcook.
Remove the skillet from the heat and
reserve.

10. When the fish steaks are done, remove
them carefully to a serving platter. Strain
the sauce, pressing down well on the
tomato pulp to extract all the juice.

11. Return the sauce to the pan and reduce
it by ⅓ over high heat. Add a Beurre Manie,
a little at a time, whisking constantly
until the sauce heavily coats a spoon.

12. Add the mushrooms and olives, salt

and black pepper. Remove the sauce from the heat.

13. Remove any accumulated juices around the fish steaks with paper towels. Pour the sauce over the fish steaks, and keep them warm until serving time.

14. Combine the parsley, garlic and lemon rind and sprinkle the mixture over the fish steaks just before serving.

15. Serve the fish steaks with the optional buttered new potatoes.

Notes

Paella a la basquaise
Serves: 6
Preparation time: 45 minutes
Cooking time: 1 hour

Every region in Spain has its own way of preparing the paella and, of course, each region claims that its way is the only right one. Some restaurants solve this problem by having two or three types of paella on the menu. Personally, I am very partial to the Basque Paella that is lightly spicy and does not use chicken.

Ingredients

2 cups raw long-grain rice
1 pound fresh mussels
18 small hard-shell clams, thoroughly rinsed and scrubbed
2 pounds fresh halibut, or other firm white fish, cut into bite-sized cubes
Salt and freshly ground white pepper
½ cup olive oil
1 pound fresh shrimp, peeled, with tails left on
1 large onion, finely minced
1 teaspoon finely minced garlic
1 red pepper, finely sliced
4 large ripe tomatoes, peeled, seeded and chopped
¼ pound cubed prosciutto
2 small hot dry chili peppers
½ teaspoon saffron
1 teaspoon oregano or 1 sprig fresh oregano
1 teaspoon basil
3 to 4 cups hot Chicken Stock (page 404)
½ pound finely sliced Chorizo (Spanish sausage) or substitute garlic sausage
1 cup shelled peas (blanched in boiling water for 5 minutes)

Garnish:
Pimiento strips
2 lemons, quartered

Preparation

1. Preheat the oven to 350°.

2. Wash the rice thoroughly under cold running water and drain. Reserve.

3. Wash both the mussels and clams thoroughly until all sand has been removed. Do not soak them in cold water.

4. Dry the fish pieces thoroughly with paper towels and season with salt and pepper.

5. In a large skillet, heat ¼ cup of olive oil. When it is very hot add the fish cubes and brown them on all sides. Remove them to a side dish and reserve.

6. To the fat remaining in the skillet add the shrimp and cook them over medium heat until they turn bright pink. Season with salt and white pepper. Remove the cooked shrimp to a side dish and reserve.

7. Add 2 tablespoons olive oil to the skillet. Add the onion, garlic and red pepper slices and cook until the onions are very soft and lightly browned. Be sure not to burn the mixture. Add the tomatoes and prosciutto, chilies and saffron. Season the mixture with salt and pepper, oregano and basil. Bring to a boil and cook, stirring constantly, scraping the bottom of the pan well, until most of the tomato juice has evaporated.

8. Add the rice and 3½ cups of Chicken Stock. Bring the mixture to a boil again and cook over medium heat until ½ of the broth is absorbed.

9. Pour half the rice mixture into an earthenware casserole. Make a layer of fish cubes and Chorizo and top with the remaining rice. Cover the casserole and bake the rice for 25 minutes.

10. Uncover the casserole and fold the shrimp and peas lightly into the rice. Cover again and continue baking for 10 to 15 minutes or until the rice is tender and all the broth has been absorbed. If the rice seems dry, yet still too crisp, add the remaining Chicken Stock.

11. Uncover the casserole and bury the clams and mussels in the rice. Cover the casserole again and cook for another 10 to 15 minutes or until the shells of both mussels and clams have opened. Discard any mussels or clams that have not opened.

12. Garnish the paella with pimiento strips and lemon quarters. Serve directly from the casserole.

Remarks

For a more elaborate paella, you may add a small lobster, cut into serving pieces without removing its shell. The lobster pieces are cooked in olive oil until they turn bright pink, then added to the rice together with the fish and sausages. A paella is an excellent summer dish as it usually is cooked on an open fire. Make sure you have good control of your heat since the rice must not scorch. An "open" paella is cooked like a risotto insofar as the stock is added slowly after each addition is absorbed. You will need up to 6 cups of stock.

Coquilles saint-jacques savoie

Serves: 6
Preparation time: 25 minutes
Cooking time: 30 minutes

■ ◘

There are any number of exciting ways to prepare scallops. Unfortunately we seem to fall back on the few popular recipes used in most French restaurants. Scallops are an excellent cold hors d'oeuvre. They are also lovely in combination with other fish. You can serve this dish in scallop shells, on fried bread slices or, as often done in certain regions of France, as a main course surrounded by boiled potato balls and buttered carrots.

Ingredients

1 cup dry white wine
1 onion, stuck with a clove
1 large Bouquet Garni (page 397)
6 to 8 peppercorns
½ teaspoon salt
1½ pounds bay scallops

The sauce:
1 tablespoon Dijon mustard
½ teaspoon dry English mustard
1 teaspoon tomato paste
Juice of ½ lemon
4 egg yolks
10 tablespoons sweet butter
Salt and freshly ground white pepper
1 tablespoon finely chopped parsley
2 teaspoons small capers, well drained

Garnish:
1 tablespoon finely chopped chives
2 lemons, quartered

Preparation

1. In a large saucepan combine the wine, onion, Bouquet Garni and peppercorns. Season with salt and simmer, covered, for 20 minutes.

2. Add the scallops. Cover the saucepan and simmer for 5 minutes. Remove the pan from the heat. Drain the scallops and keep them warm.

3. In a bowl beat the mustards, tomato paste and lemon juice into a smooth paste.

4. Add the egg yolks to the mustard mixture and beat until it is light and creamy.

5. Melt the butter in the top part of the double boiler over hot water. The butter should be warm, *not* hot. Keep the water simmering and slowly whisk the yolk mixture into the melted butter. The sauce should get thick and creamy. Be sure not to let it come to a boil or the yolks will curdle. Remove the sauce from the heat. Season it with salt and pepper.

6. Add the parsley, capers and finally the warm well-drained scallops. Serve immediately, garnished with chives and lemon quarters.

Notes

Red snapper a la mexicaine

Serves: 6
Preparation time: 25 to 30 minutes
Cooking time: 35 minutes

■ ◆

When cooking this dish, I usually make enough to have some leftovers as it is delicious cold. The fish is fileted in this recipe, but you may make it with whole fish. It will look more attractive, but is harder to serve.

Ingredients

6 fresh red snapper filets
Salt and freshly ground white pepper
Flour for dredging
4 tablespoons olive oil
3 large shallots, finely minced
3 large garlic cloves, finely chopped
6 to 8 ripe tomatoes, peeled, seeded and
    chopped
2 tablespoons finely chopped fresh herbs
    (oregano, thyme and chervil)
1 ripe avocado
1 to 2 teaspoons lime juice
Dash of Tabasco

Optional:
1 Beurre Manie (page 397)
1 tablespoon tomato paste

Garnish:
Avocado slices
Lime slices
Fresh mint leaves

Preparation

1. Preheat oven to 350°.

2. Season the fish filets with salt and pepper and dredge them lightly with flour, shaking off the excess.

3. Heat the olive oil in a large skillet and saute the filets over high heat for 2 or 3 minutes on each side. Remove them carefully to a flameproof baking dish large enough to hold the fish in one layer.

4. In the same oil, saute the shallots and 2 cloves of garlic. When the shallots are lightly browned, add the tomatoes and cook the mixture for 2 minutes.

5. Pour the mixture together with the herbs on top of the fish and cover the dish with buttered wax paper. Bake in the oven for 25 to 30 minutes.

6. While the fish is baking, mash the avocado in a small mixing bowl, adding lime juice, salt, pepper, a little Tabasco, and the remaining clove of garlic. Do not mash it too fine; it should have some small chunks left in it.

7. When the fish is ready, lift it out carefully onto a platter. Place the baking dish over direct heat and reduce the juices by 1/3. If a Beurre Manie is used for thickening, add it bit by bit before adding the avocado puree. Add the optional tomato paste. Lower the heat and beat in the mashed avocado. Once the avocado puree has been added, do not let the mixture come to a boil. Correct the seasoning and pour the sauce over the fish. Garnish with avocado slices, lime slices and mint leaves.

Notes

Filets of sole riviera

Serves: 6
Preparation time: 45 minutes
Cooking time: 15 to 20 minutes

Ingredients

3 large tomatoes
Salt
12 4-inch filets of sole
Milk
½ cup flour
Freshly ground white pepper
3 eggs, lightly beaten
2 cups homemade white bread crumbs
6 or 7 tablespoons oil
3 large green peppers, roasted, seeded
   and cut into strips
3 large red peppers, roasted, seeded and
   cut into strips
Freshly ground black pepper
4 tablespoons sweet butter

The anchovy butter:
8 tablespoons sweet butter, softened
2 teaspoons to 1 tablespoon anchovy
   paste
1 tablespoon lemon juice

Garnish:
6 rolled anchovy filets
Quartered lemons
Finely minced parsley

Preparation

1. Do not peel the tomatoes; cut them into thick slices and sprinkle them with salt. Let them drain on a large plate for 30 minutes.

2. Dip the filets in milk. Dry them lightly with paper towels.

3. Season the flour with salt and white pepper; dip the filets in the seasoned flour; transfer them to the beaten eggs and cover them well, then coat them thoroughly with

bread crumbs. Place the filets on a large platter and refrigerate for 1 hour.

4. Twenty minutes before you plan to serve, heat 3 tablespoons of olive oil in a large skillet; add the roasted pepper strips. Cook for 2 or 3 minutes over high heat. Season them with salt and black pepper. Transfer them to a serving platter and keep them warm. Set the pan aside.

5. In another skillet heat the 4 tablespoons of butter with 2 tablespoons of oil. Add the filets, two at a time, and saute them over medium heat for 3 minutes. Turn them over carefully without breaking through the coating and saute for 3 to 4 minutes more. Regulate the heat so as not to burn the fat.

6. While the sole is sauteeing, add a little more olive oil to the pan in which you sauteed the peppers. Add the tomato slices and cook them quickly until they are heated through (about 2 minutes). Remove the pan from the heat.

7. As soon as the filets are done, place them on the bed of peppers.
Top the filets with the tomato slices, decorated with the anchovy filets. Surround the platter with quartered lemons and sprinkle with parsley.

8. In a small saucepan melt the softened butter over very low heat; add the anchovy paste and lemon juice. Pour the anchovy butter over the sole and tomatoes and serve immediately.

Beets a la creme

Serves: 6
Preparation time: 15 minutes
Cooking time: 45 minutes to 1 hour
■ ●

Beets often are ignored as a warm vegetable. It is a pity as they are a tasty
complement to roasted or grilled meats.

Ingredients

6 to 8 medium-sized beets
Salt
4 tablespoons sweet butter
1½ cups heavy cream
Freshly ground black pepper

Garnish:
2 tablespoons finely chopped parsley

Preparation

1. Wash the beets thoroughly in cold water
and remove the greens.

2. In a large casserole bring salted water
to a boil. Add the beets and cook, covered,
over medium heat until tender when
pierced with a fork. Drain the beets and
peel them. The skin will come off very
easily. Cut the beets into ¼-inch-thick
matchsticks.

3. In a large skillet melt the butter. Add
the beets and saute them for 2 minutes,
constantly shaking the pan to coat the
beets evenly with butter. Season with salt.

4. Add the heavy cream and continue cooking until it is reduced to a glaze just coating the beets.

5. Sprinkle heavily with black pepper and
parsley. Serve immediately.

Remarks

The beets may be cooked one or two days
in advance and sauteed at the last moment.

Brussels sprouts a l'indienne

Serves: 4 to 6
Preparation time: 25 minutes
Cooking time: 45 minutes
■ ●

A well-prepared vegetable can add
importance to the simplest main
course such as sauteed pork chops or
braised veal cutlets.

Ingredients

4 to 5 tablespoons sweet butter
1 medium onion, finely minced
1 to 2 teaspoons curry powder
3 tablespoons flour
2 cups hot Chicken Stock (page 404)
1 Bouquet Garni (page 397)
Salt and freshly ground white pepper
Pinch of freshly grated nutmeg
2 quarts Brussels sprouts

Optional:
4 tablespoons Creme Fraiche or heavy
    cream with a dash of lemon juice

Preparation

1. In a heavy saucepan, melt 4 tablespoons
of butter. Add the minced onion and cook
it over low heat for 5 minutes without
browning.

2. Add the curry and blend it well. Add the
flour and cook, stirring, for 3 to 5 minutes
without letting the mixture brown.

3. Pour the hot Chicken Stock all at once
into the pan and whisk over medium heat
until the sauce thickens.

4. Add the Bouquet Garni. Cover the pan
and cook over very low heat for 20 minutes,
stirring occasionally.

5. Strain the sauce through a fine sieve
and whisk in the optional cream and seasoning. Film with a little additional
butter and reserve.

6. Trim the Brussels sprouts and remove any wilted leaves. Drop the sprouts into fast-boiling salted water. Reduce the heat and cook 15 to 20 minutes according to size. Test for doneness by piercing with a fork.

7. When the sprouts are done, drain them and run them quickly under cold running water to stop further cooking. Pour them into a serving dish.

8. Reheat the sauce and completely cover the Brussels sprouts with it.

Remarks

The dish may be made in advance, putting the Brussels sprouts and sauce into an au gratin dish and reheating them in the oven. Or the sprouts can be partially cooked in advance and finished just before serving time.

Notes

Spaghettini with eggplant

Serves: 4 to 6
Preparation time: 35 minutes
Cooking time: 25 minutes

There are many ways to serve pasta—traditional ones and whimsical ones. Everything goes, as long as you keep in mind that there is nothing worse than overcooked spaghetti accompanied by bottled Parmesan cheese.

Ingredients

2 small eggplants, peeled and finely diced
Salt
6 medium tomatoes, peeled and finely chopped
½ to ¾ cup good olive oil
Freshly ground white pepper
1 pound thin spaghettini (Ronzoni No. 9)
1 cup finely diced prosciutto
1 red onion, thinly sliced
2 garlic cloves, finely minced
1 tablespoon oregano
2 tablespoons fresh marjoram, finely minced, or 1 teaspoon dry marjoram

Garnish:
Freshly ground black pepper
Grated Parmesan cheese

Preparation

1. Peel the eggplants and cut into 1-inch cubes. Place them in a colander. Sprinkle them with salt and let them drain for 2 hours.

2. Put the chopped tomatoes in a large sieve. Sprinkle them with salt and let them drain for 2 hours.

3. Dry the eggplant cubes on paper towels. In a large skillet heat 4 tablespoons of olive oil. When it is very hot, brown the eggplant cubes on all sides. (You may need more oil.) Then season them with salt and pepper and reserve.

Gratin catalan

Serves: 4 to 6
Preparation time: 45 minutes
Cooking time: 45 minutes

4. Bring 4 quarts salted water to a fast boil in a large casserole. Add the spaghettini and cook it over high heat until it is just tender (8 to 10 minutes).

5. While the spaghettini is cooking, saute the prosciutto in 1 tablespoon oil for 1 or 2 minutes. Remove it from the pan and reserve.

6. Remove all but 2 tablespoons of fat from the skillet. Add the onion and garlic and cook until the onion is soft but not browned.

7. Add the well-drained tomatoes, oregano, marjoram, eggplant and prosciutto. Cook for 3 to 5 minutes. Season with salt and pepper.

8. When the spaghettini is done, drain it well and return to the casserole.

9. Pour the tomato and eggplant sauce over the spaghettini and toss lightly. Sprinkle with black pepper and grated cheese. Serve additional grated cheese on the side.

In the summer you may vary this dish by adding ½ cup of freshly pureed basil to the tomato mixture together with 2 additional cloves of minced garlic.

Notes

Ingredients

3 medium eggplants
Salt
6 peppers (red and green)
¾ cup olive oil
3 tablespoons pine nuts
¾ cup fresh homemade bread crumbs
Freshly ground white pepper
Pinch of oregano
2 tablespoons parsley
2 tablespoons tiny capers
6 anchovies
2 large whole pimientos, cut into strips
½ cup pitted black olives

Preparation

1. Preheat the broiler.

2. Cut the unpeeled eggplants into ¼-inch-thick slices. Sprinkle with salt and place in a colander over a bowl for 1 hour.

3. Brush the peppers with olive oil. Place them in the broiler and broil on all sides. They should be well scorched but do not burn them. Run them under cold water and remove the skins. Slice the peppers in half, remove the seeds, then cut the peppers into thick strips. Reserve.

4. In a small skillet heat 2 tablespoons of olive oil. Add the pine nuts and cook them until they are lightly browned. Add the bread crumbs. Saute the mixture for a few minutes, then season with a pinch of salt and pepper. Add the oregano and parsley.

5. Drain the eggplant slices and dry well on paper towels. In a large skillet heat 4 tablespoons of olive oil. Saute the eggplant slices, adding more oil as you need it, until they are nicely browned.

6. In an oval baking dish make a layer of eggplant. Top with a layer of peppers. Sprinkle with a few capers and repeat the layers. Top with bread-crumb mixture.

7. Make a lacing of anchovies and optional pimiento strips with the black olives in between in a decorative pattern. Dribble olive oil over the vegetables and bread crumbs.

8. Bake the gratin for 10 to 15 minutes in a 350° oven. Serve warm or at room temperature.

Remarks

This is an excellent accompaniment for a roast leg of lamb, lamb chops, or shish kebabs. Avoid using canned black olives. They have no taste whatsoever. The best olives are the ones called "Greek olives."
Always taste anchovies. If they are too salty, soak them in a little milk for 10 to 15 minutes. Dry on paper towels and add to the dish.

Notes

Green beans in basil sauce

Serves: 4 to 6
Preparation time: 30 minutes
Cooking time: 25 minutes

In the fall I puree a great quantity of basil, cover it with olive oil, seal it and refrigerate. I can then use it in recipes where the fresh herb is necessary, as in this, one.

Ingredients

1½ pounds fresh green beans
6 tablespoons olive oil
2 medium onions, sliced thinly
4 ripe tomatoes, peeled, seeded and chopped
Salt and freshly ground white pepper
1 Bouquet Garni (page 397)
½ cup finely chopped basil
2 garlic cloves
¼ cup chopped parsley

Optional:
3 anchovy filets
½ cup whole black olives

Preparation

1. Snap off the tips of the green beans. Bring a large casserole of salted water to a boil. Add the beans and cook for 10 minutes or until barely tender. Drain immediately and run under cold water. This retains their freshness and color.

2. In a large skillet, heat 4 tablespoons of olive oil. Add the onions and cook them for 10 minutes, covered, over low heat until they are soft but not browned.

3. Add the tomatoes, salt, pepper and Bouquet Garni. Cook the mixture for 10 to 15 minutes over fairly high heat until it is very thick. Remove the bouquet.

4. Add the drained green beans to the skillet and simmer covered for 5 minutes

Peppers andalouse

Serves: 4 to 6
Preparation time: 15 minutes
Cooking time: 15 minutes

■ ●

5. Puree the basil, garlic, parsley, and the remaining olive oil in the electric blender. Add the puree to the tomato and bean mixture. Correct the seasoning. Heat through and serve.

Remarks

You may, if you like, add minced anchovies to the basil mixture. Add the black olives a few minutes before serving. They should be just heated.
For a light supper, serve the beans with grilled or sauteed shrimp.

Notes

3 green bell peppers
3 red sweet peppers
18 small white onions
½ pound finely cubed bacon
Salt and freshly ground black pepper
2 tablespoons finely minced parsley
2 garlic cloves, finely minced

Preparation

1. Cut the tops off the peppers and remove the seeds and thin white membrane. Cut each pepper into fine strips.

2. Peel the onions and drop them into simmering water. Cook for 5 minutes, drain and reserve.

3. In a large frying pan, saute the bacon cubes until almost crisp. Remove them to a side dish.

4. Remove all but 2 tablespoons of bacon fat from the skillet. Add the onions and roll them in the fat until they are nicely browned. Add the peppers and cook the mixture over high heat for 10 minutes. Add the bacon cubes and season.

5. Do not overcook the peppers. They should still be somewhat crisp. Sprinkle with parsley and garlic and serve.

Remarks

This is an excellent "bed" for a simple casserole-roasted chicken or duck. I often serve the peppers with a roast leg of lamb, adding, in that case, 2 cups of cooked white beans to the pepper mixture, making a lovely and colorful vegetable for a buffet table.

Cauliflower salad

Serves: 4
Preparation time: 15 minutes
Cooking time: 25 to 30 minutes

Cauliflower is another staple of the super-market that is rarely prepared with any imagination. It is, however, a versatile vegetable and makes one of the most delicious salads.

Ingredients

1 cup milk
1 large cauliflower
2 tablespoons red wine vinegar
3 to 5 tablespoons olive oil
1 small garlic clove, crushed
½ cup heavy cream or ½ cup Creme
    Fraiche (page 398)
Juice of ½ lemon
Salt and freshly ground white pepper
1 teaspoon Dijon mustard
1 tablespoon finely chopped fresh chives

Garnish:
1 hard-boiled egg
1 tablespoon finely chopped fresh parsley
Black olives (preferably Greek)

Preparation

1. In a 3-quart saucepan bring salted water to a boil. Add the milk and the cauliflower broken into small flowerets. Cook over medium heat until just tender. Drain im-mediately and run under cold water to stop further cooking. Place the pieces in a mixing bowl.

2. Combine the vinegar, olive oil and garlic. Pour this dressing over the cauliflower while it is still warm. Chill for at least 2 hours.

3. Meanwhile combine the cream and lemon juice in a small bowl and let the mixture stand for 2 hours.

4. Add salt and pepper. Beat in the mus-tard and chives.

5. Drain the cauliflower thoroughly. Put it into a serving bowl and toss it lightly with the cream and lemon dressing. Taste for seasoning and add salt and pepper if needed.

6. Separate the egg yolk from the white and chop both very finely. Sprinkle the cauliflower with an outside circle of egg white and inside circle of yolks. Sprinkle with parsley and decorate with black olives.

Notes

Fresh mushroom salad a la dijonnaise

Serves: 4 to 6
Preparation time: 15 minutes
Cooking time: none

■ ○

A fresh mushroom salad is one of the most memorable fall salads. You may add finely sliced raw Belgian endives dressed with a little lemon juice and olive oil and serve the salad as an hors d'oeuvre.

Ingredients

¾ to 1 pound fresh mushrooms
Salt and freshly ground white pepper
2 to 3 tablespoons white wine vinegar
1 cup Creme Fraiche (page 398)
1 tablespoon lemon juice
2 tablespoons finely minced scallions
2 teaspoons Dijon mustard

Optional:
2 Belgian endives, finely sliced lengthwise
   and dressed in Lemon Vinaigrette
   (page 408)

Preparation

1. Do not wash the mushrooms. Remove the stems and reserve for soup or stock. Wipe the mushroom caps with a damp paper towel and slice them thinly. Place them in a serving bowl and sprinkle with salt, pepper and vinegar. Marinate for 30 to 40 minutes.

2. Mix the Creme Fraiche, lemon juice, salt and pepper, scallions and Dijon mustard in a small bowl.

3. Drain the mushrooms and pour the cream and mustard sauce over them. Blend well and correct the seasoning. Chill for 2 to 4 hours before serving.

4. Put the mushrooms in the center of a serving bowl and surround by the optional endives.

Mushroom and pepper salad

Serves: 4 to 6
Preparation time: 25 minutes
Cooking time: 20 to 30 minutes

■ ○

Here is an irresistible salad that I serve as an appetizer with a platter of sliced prosciutto. It is a welcome change from the popular prosciutto and melon, and is also good with lamb or steak.

Ingredients

3 green peppers
3 red peppers
½ pound fresh mushrooms
1 tablespoon lemon juice
3 tablespoons wine vinegar
6 tablespoons olive oil
Salt and freshly ground black pepper
1 garlic clove, finely minced
2 tablespoons fine chopped parsley

Garnish:
2 tablespoons finely sliced pimiento strips

Preparation

1. Preheat the broiler.

2. Place the peppers on a baking sheet and broil them until the skin blackens and blisters, turning them over to broil evenly. When they are ready, scrape the skin off under cold running water and cut off the tops. Cut the peppers in half and remove the seeds and membrane. Cut into thin strips and place in a salad bowl.

3. Do not wash the mushrooms. Wipe them with wet paper towels, remove the stems and reserve for soup or stock. Slice the mushrooms thinly and add to salad bowl.

4. Mix the lemon juice, vinegar and olive oil. Pour over the mushroom and pepper mixture. Season with salt and black pepper. Sprinkle with minced garlic and parsley.

5. Toss the salad. Garnish with pimiento strips. Chill for 1 or 2 hours. Bring the salad back to room temperature before serving.

Remarks

If you cannot find red peppers, substitute 2 more green ones. Garnish with ½ cup finely sliced pimientos. Rolled anchovy filets and quartered hard-boiled eggs can also garnish the salad. Many Italian groceries carry both yellow and red pimientos, which make a lovely color combination with the green pepper and white mushrooms.

Notes

Mediterranean potato salad

Serves: 4 to 6
Preparation time: 25 minutes
Cooking time: 15 to 20 minutes

A potato salad can be interesting and, when well prepared, is an excellent accompaniment to a cold roast, shish kebabs or as a luncheon salad together with a platter of assorted sausages. Seasonal vegetables —such as fresh green peas or diced green beans, both cooked until barely tender—can be added to the salad.

Ingredients

4 to 6 medium-sized new potatoes
Salt
1 red bell pepper
1 green bell pepper
6 to 8 tablespoons olive oil
2 tablespoons red wine vinegar
1 small garlic clove, mashed
1 red onion, very finely sliced
1 cup diced cooked green beans
2 French cornichons, finely sliced, or 2 dill gherkins
1 7-ounce can tuna fish
2 tablespoons tiny capers
Freshly ground black pepper

Garnish:
2 tablespoons finely chopped fresh basil
Rolled filets of anchovies
Quartered tomatoes
Black olives

Preparation

1. Cook the potatoes in their skins in plenty of salted water.

2. While they are cooking, place the peppers under the broiler until their skins are completely blistered and lightly charred. Then run them under cold water and peel off the skin. Cut the peppers in half and

remove the seeds. Cut the peppers into thin slices and reserve.

3. Drain the cooked potatoes. Peel and slice while still hot. Place the slices in a serving bowl.

4. Combine the olive oil, vinegar and garlic and pour the dressing over the still-warm potatoes.

5. Add the onion, peppers, green beans, sliced cornichons, broken-up tuna and capers to the bowl, then toss the salad lightly with two spoons.

6. Season the salad with salt and pepper. Sprinkle with basil and garnish with anchovy filets, tomatoes and olives.

7. Chill the salad for 1 hour, then bring back to room temperature before serving.

Remarks

If you cannot get a fresh red pepper, use a good brand of canned pimientos. Some Italian groceries have both red and yellow pimientos. These make a nice color combination. If you like a stronger basil flavor, puree 3 tablespoons of basil together with 2 cloves of garlic in the blender, then add the olive oil and vinegar and pour the dressing over the potato salad.

Notes

Salade bernoise
Serves: 4 to 6
Preparation time: 15 minutes
Cooking time: 25 minutes

■ ●

The Belgian endive, with its delicate color and slightly bitter flavor, is a marvelous vegetable that I like to use as much as possible during the winter months. Here it is combined in a hearty hors d'oeuvre salad. It can also be served as an accompaniment to grilled or poached fish.

Ingredients

4   medium-sized all-purpose potatoes
¼ cup hard cider (or white wine vinegar)
2   eating apples
12 small shrimp, cooked, peeled and finely chopped
1   cup smoked ham (preferably Westphalian), cut into strips
2   tablespoons shallots, finely minced
2   Belgian endives
1   teaspoon Dijon mustard
Juice of ½ lemon
¾ cup Creme Fraiche (page 398)
Salt and freshly ground white pepper

Optional:
½ cup Vinaigrette (pages 408–409)

Garnish:
2   hard-boiled eggs, quartered
Finely minced parsley

Preparation

1. Boil unpeeled potatoes in salted water until tender. Peel them and when cool enough to handle cut them into small cubes. Place the cubes in a salad bowl and sprinkle with hard cider or vinegar while they are still warm.

2. Peel and core the apples. Cut them into small cubes and add to the potatoes.

3. Add the shrimp to the salad bowl together with the ham strips and the shallots.

4. Trim the endives. Peel off any wilted leaves and wash the endives quickly under cold running water. Dry them thoroughly, cut them into strips lengthwise, and add them to the salad bowl.

5. In a mixing bowl, beat the mustard together with the lemon juice until the mixture is smooth and creamy. Add the Creme Fraiche and let the dressing stand for 30 minutes. If it seems too thick, thin it out with the Vinaigrette.

6. Pour the dressing over the salad. Toss very carefully so as to not break the potato and apple cubes. Season with salt and pepper.

7. Garnish with hard-boiled eggs and parsley.

Remarks

If you cannot get hard cider, sprinkle the potatoes lightly with white wine vinegar. Endives should never be soaked in water as this accentuates their bitter flavor.

Notes

Apple crepes with rum and apricot sauce

Serves: 6 to 8
Preparation time: 30 minutes
Cooking time: 45 minutes

Ingredients

12 to 14 Dessert Crepes (page 399), flavored with rum

The sauce:
1 cup dried apricots
2 cups water
1 cup sugar
1 3-inch piece vanilla bean
Dash of lemon juice
½ cup apricot brandy
Confectioners' sugar

The filling:
3 tablespoons white raisins
3 tablespoons rum or cognac
2 to 2½ pounds cooking apples, peeled and coarsely chopped
½ cup apricot jam
½ cup sugar
Large pinch of cinnamon
1 teaspoon grated lemon rind
Confectioners' sugar

Optional:
2 tablespoons pine nuts

Preparation

The sauce:
1. In a small heavy saucepan, combine the dried apricots, water, sugar, and vanilla bean. Bring the mixture to a boil, reduce the heat and simmer, covered, until the apricots are very soft.

2. Cool the apricots in their syrup and then puree with all the cooking juice in the blender at high speed.

3. Pass the sauce through a fine sieve. Add lemon juice to taste and the apricot brandy. Chill the sauce. If, after chilling, it seems

Crepes hongroises

Serves: 6 to 8
Preparation time: 45 minutes
Cooking time: 15 minutes

to lack sweetness, add a little confectioners' sugar.

The filling:
4. In a small bowl combine the raisins and pine nuts (if used). Sprinkle them with the rum and marinate for 2 hours.

5. Place the apples mixed with apricot jam and sugar in a heavy casserole. Cook, covered, over medium heat, for 15 or 20 minutes, stirring from time to time. Uncover the casserole, raise the heat and cook the apples, stirring often, until they are reduced to a very thick puree. Taste the puree for sweetness and add more sugar if necessary.

6. Add the cinnamon, lemon rind and the raisin and pine nuts mixture. Let the apple puree cool.

7. Fill the warm crepes with the apple-puree mixture and place them in a buttered baking dish.

8. Sprinkle the crepes heavily with confectioners' sugar and run them under the broiler until the sugar is lightly caramelized. Serve the crepes right out of the baking dish with the apricot sauce on the side.

Remarks

The crepes can be flambeed with a mixture of 3 tablespoons of apricot brandy and 3 tablespoons of rum just before serving. Other purees—such as pears, chestnuts or peaches—make excellent fillings for crepes.

Ingredients

12 to 14 Dessert Crepes (page 399)
1 ½ cups ground walnuts
½ cup sugar
¾ cup milk
2 tablespoons raisins
½ teaspoon cinnamon
½ teaspoon lemon rind

The sauce:
6 ounces semisweet chocolate
¼ cup sugar
¾ cup strong coffee
2 tablespoons rum
3 tablespoons sweet butter
1 cup heavy cream, whipped

Preparation

1. In a small saucepan, combine the walnuts, sugar, milk, raisins, cinnamon and lemon rind. Cook over low heat for 5 minutes. Let the mixture cool completely. It should be very thick.

2. Put 1 tablespoon of the walnut mixture on each crepe and roll them up.

3. Place the crepes on a serving platter. Top with the chocolate sauce and serve a bowl of whipped cream on the side.

The sauce:
4. In a saucepan, combine the chocolate, sugar, and coffee. Cook over low heat until the chocolate is completely dissolved and the sauce is smooth. Add the rum.

5. Off the heat, beat in the butter and when the sauce is smooth and shiny, taste it for sweetness, adding more sugar if needed. Pour it over the crepes. Serve with a bowl of unsugared whipped cream.

Baked apples grandmere

Serves: 6
Preparation time: 10 minutes
Cooking time: 45 minutes

Fresh apples in early fall are a treat. A large bowl of apples served with cheese and wine make a perfect dessert. Here is another way that is popular around the French and Italian countryside.

Ingredients

¾ cup raisins
2 tablespoons white rum
6 tart baking apples
¼ teaspoon lemon rind
4 tablespoons sugar
2 tablespoons butter
1 cup white wine
½ cup boiling water
2 tablespoons apricot preserves

Preparation

1. Preheat oven to 375°. Soak the raisins in the rum for ½ hour.

2. Wash and core the apples. Be careful not to break through the bottoms of the apples. Peel a strip ½ inch wide off of each stem end; place in a baking pan.

3. Stuff the cavities of each apple with the raisins; sprinkle with lemon rind and sugar. Dot with butter and spoon wine over them.

4. Add the boiling water to the pan. Cover with foil and bake for 25 minutes. Uncover and continue baking for 15 to 20 minutes more. Baste with the pan liquid.

5. Remove the apples to a serving platter. Add the apricot jam to the pan juice. Heat and spoon over the apples.

6. You may present this more elegantly with whipped cream flavored with Calvados on the side.

Mont blanc au caramel

Serves: 8 to 10
Preparation time: 40 minutes
Cooking time: 45 minutes to 1 hour

Here is a variation of a famous chestnut dessert. It is rich and will therefore go a long way. It is best served after a simple light main course. Chestnuts are no fun to peel, but the result is worth the effort.

Ingredients

1 quart milk
1 2-inch piece vanilla bean
2 pounds chestnuts, peeled (page 397)
2 cups sugar
¼ cup water
¼ cup boiling water
2 tablespoons sweet butter
2 tablespoons cognac

The cream:
1½ cups heavy cream
3 tablespoons confectioners' sugar
1 teaspoon vanilla extract
Chocolate Sauce (page 397)

Optional:
Macaroon Crumbs (page 401)

Preparation

1. In a large saucepan combine the milk, 1½ cups sugar and the vanilla bean. Add the chestnuts. If the milk does not cover them, add a little water. Cover the pan and cook the chestnuts for 40 minutes or until very tender.

2. While the chestnuts are cooking, make the caramel by combining the remaining sugar and ¼ cup of water in a small saucepan. Cook until it turns a light nutty brown color. Do not burn.

3. Add the boiling water. Cook the syrup for 2 or 3 minutes and reserve.

4. Puree the well-drained chestnuts in a food mill or blender. Add the caramel, butter and cognac. Cool.

5. Put the chestnut puree into a pastry bag fitted with a star tube. Pipe the puree onto a round platter in a circle, leaving a center opening the size of a grapefruit. Chill completely.

The cream:
6. Whip the cream. Add the confectioners' sugar and the vanilla. Put the whipped cream in a pastry bag and fill the center of the chestnut puree with it.

7. Pour a little Chocolate Sauce around the chestnut ring and sprinkle the whipped cream with Macaroon Crumbs. Serve the rest of the sauce on the side.

Notes

Pears in chocolate sabayon

Serves: 4 to 6
Preparation time: 10 minutes
Cooking time: 20 to 30 minutes
■ ●

Pears and chocolate have had a long and happy "relationship." I find, however, that pure chocolate sauce overpowers the flavor of the pears. This version is more delicate!

Ingredients

4 to 6 Bartlett or other large pears
3 cups water
1 cup sugar
1 piece lemon peel
1 stick cinnamon (2 inch)

The sauce:
3 ounces semisweet chocolate
¾ cup coffee
4 tablespoons sugar
8 egg yolks
2 tablespoons cognac

Garnish:
1 cup whipped cream sweetened with 2 tablespoons verifine sugar and 2 tablespoons brandy

Preparation

1. Peel the pears, leaving 1 inch of the stem. Leave the pears whole.

2. In a saucepan, combine the water, sugar, lemon peel and the cinnamon stick.

3. When the sugar is dissolved, add the pears and poach them covered over low heat until tender. (The cooking time varies a great deal, depending on the ripeness of the fruit.)

4. When the pears are tender, remove the saucepan from the heat. Let the pears cool completely in the syrup. Refrigerate until serving time. Just before serving make the sauce.

5. In a small saucepan, combine the chocolate and 2 tablespoons of coffee. Cook over low heat until the chocolate is completely melted and smooth.

6. In the top of a double boiler, combine the sugar and egg yolks. Add the remaining coffee. Whisk the mixture over simmering water with a hand beater or a balloon whisk until the mixture is creamy and thick. Do not let it come to a boil or the sauce will curdle. Remove from the heat and add the cognac.

7. Drain the pears. Place them in a serving dish and pour the warm sauce over them. Serve the whipped cream on the side or pipe it in a decorative pattern around the pears.

Remarks

For a lovely presentation place a pear in the bottom of a tall parfait glass. Top with the sauce and then with whipped cream. Beautiful-looking but hard to eat.
To serve the sauce cold, incorporate the whipped cream into the chilled sauce and top the pears just before serving. The sauce, in that case, can be made well in advance.

Notes

Chestnut meringue tart

Serves: 8 to 10
Preparation time: 50 minutes
Cooking time: 45 minutes

Fall is the time when we are ready to spend more time in the kitchen and entertaining becomes more elaborate. A chestnut tart is a delicious fall dessert and well worth the effort of peeling fresh chestnuts.

Ingredients

1 Tart Shell (page 407)
1 pound chestnuts, peeled (page 397)
2 cups milk
¾ cup sugar
¼ cup water
1 tablespoon vanilla extract
4 ounces sweet chocolate
2 tablespoons strong coffee
2 tablespoons rum

The topping:
3 egg whites
½ cup sugar
2 tablespoons finely slivered almonds

Preparation

1. Preheat the oven to 350°.

2. Combine the peeled chestnuts with the milk and, if necessary, add enough water to cover them. Cook them over low heat, partially covered, for 45 minutes or until they are very tender. Drain the chestnuts and puree them in the blender.

3. In a heavy saucepan, combine the sugar and ¼ cup of water. Cook until the syrup forms a soft ball when dropped into the cold water (or 238° on the candy thermometer).

4. Add the vanilla, then add the syrup mixture to the chestnut puree. Incorporate it thoroughly.

Viennese almond torte

Serves: 4 to 6
Preparation time: 20 minutes
Cooking time: 45 minutes

5. In a small saucepan combine the chocolate and coffee. When the chocolate is dissolved, add it to the chestnut puree together with the rum.

6. Fill the tart shell with the chestnut mixture.

7. For the topping, beat the egg whites, adding the sugar gradually, until they are stiff and stand up in soft peaks.

8. Spread the meringue on top of the chestnut puree. Sprinkle with slivered almonds and bake the tart for 10 minutes or until the meringue is delicately browned.

Notes

Ingredients

4   eggs
¾ cup sugar
½ pound blanched almonds, finely ground
¼ teaspoon almond extract
1   tablespoon kirsch
½ cup sifted cake flour
¼ teaspoon baking powder
¼ cup sweet butter, creamed
½ cup apricot preserves

Garnish:
¾ cup apricot preserves
3 or 4 tablespoons confectioners' sugar
½ cup finely slivered blanched almonds

Preparation

1. Preheat oven to 375°. Butter and flour an 8-inch cake pan.

2. In a mixing bowl, beat the eggs and gradually add the sugar. Continue beating until the mixture doubles in volume and is pale yellow.

3. Add the almonds to the egg mixture together with the almond extract and kirsch.

4. Add the cake flour and baking powder to the eggs, folding them in carefully until they are perfectly blended.

5. Add a little of the egg mixture to the butter, then reverse the process and beat until the mixture is perfectly blended.

6. Pour the batter into the cake pan. Set it in the middle of the oven and turn the heat down to 350°. Bake the cake for 30 to 40 minutes. It should puff slightly and be lightly browned. Test it with a toothpick which, if the cake is done, should come out dry. Remove the cake from the oven.

Walnut torte

Serves: 8 to 10
Preparation time: 45 minutes
Cooking time: 30 minutes

7. Let the cake cool for 10 minutes, then run a knife around the edges and turn it out onto a plate. Immediately reverse the cake so that the browned side faces up.

8. Slice the cake in two horizontally. Spread the bottom half with ½ cup of apricot preserves and top it with the other half of the cake.

9. In a small saucepan combine ¾ cup of apricot preserves with 2 tablespoons of confectioners' sugar. Heat until the sugar has dissolved completely. Pass the mixture through a sieve and glaze the top and sides of the cake with it.

10. Toast the almonds in the oven for 3 to 5 minutes or until lightly browned. Sprinkle them on top of the glaze and on the sides of the cake. Just before serving, sprinkle the cake with the remaining confectioners' sugar.

Notes

Here is a dessert that requires some work, but it is perfect for a buffet party when you have to serve a large number of people.

Ingredients

The cake:
6 eggs
¾ cup sugar
1¼ cups sifted flour
1 teaspoon baking powder
¾ cup finely grated walnuts

The filling:
1 cup finely sliced almonds
4 egg yolks
½ pound sweet butter, softened
1½ cups sugar
½ cup water
1 tablespoon instant coffee

Preparation

1. Preheat oven to 375°.

2. Toss the almonds on a baking sheet and place in the oven until they are lightly browned. Set aside.

3. For the cake separate the 6 eggs. Beat the yolks together with the sugar until they double in volume and are pale yellow.

4. Mix the flour, baking powder and walnuts. Add to the yolks and blend the mixture well.

5. Beat the egg whites until stiff but not dry. Add them to the above mixture. Blend by hand. This will help to keep the batter light.

6. Butter and flour two 8-inch round cake pans. Pour half the batter into each pan and

bake for 30 minutes or until a toothpick comes out dry.

7. Cool the cakes on a rack. Remove them from the pans and slice each in half horizontally.

8. In a mixing bowl beat the 4 egg yolks until they are pale yellow. Reserve.

9. Whip the butter until it is light and fluffy.

10. Combine the sugar and water in a small saucepan and cook until the sugar is dissolved. Cook until the candy thermometer is at 238°. If you do not have a candy thermometer, test by dropping a little of the syrup into cold water. It should form a soft ball.

11. Add the hot syrup in droplets to the egg yolks, beating continually until the mixture is thick and cool.

12. Slowly add the butter and the coffee. The butter cream should be very thick and smooth. Refrigerate it until it reaches a spreading consistency.

13. Spread about ¼ of the butter cream on a cake layer. Top with another layer and continue until all four layers have been generously covered. Frost the top and sides and press the toasted almonds on the side of the cake. Decorate the top with small rosettes of the butter cream (or whipped cream) pressed through a pastry bag. Chill until serving time.

Notes

8

In winter a knowledgeable cook's opportunity to prove her skill starts with careful shopping and an awareness of seasonal pitfalls. It is a great mistake to think that out-of-season strawberries or asparagus, for instance, will be flavorful.

They are certainly expensive and sometimes it is fun to have a luxury fruit or vegetable out of season, but on the whole you can do marvels with more readily available produce that you can compare in quality with that of other markets.

With the passing of fall, I automatically reach for my winter "treasures." Classic dishes such as choucroute, cassoulet or Tuscan bean soup became centerpieces for the winter dinner table. There is a heartiness in winter foods unequaled at any other time of the year. The Winter Kitchen is really a working kitchen, one that challenges you into cooking creatively with simple ingredients such as cabbage, white beans, carrots and celery.

the winter kitchen

Symbols

Inexpensive　　**Moderate**　　**Expensive**

Easy　　**Intermediate**　　**Difficult**

Mushrooms a la campagnarde
Poulet flamand
Oranges sevillane

This menu is composed of light dishes that
do not require very much preparation and
are therefore suitable for last-minute
entertaining. For a more elaborate presentation, fill entree crepes with the mushrooms and top them with an herb butter.
As an accompaniment to the chicken, serve
curry-flavored risotto or buttered noodles.
For a variation, serve the oranges simply
marinated in a sugar syrup flavored with
Grand Marnier or Triple Sec. Toward spring
add a few choice whole strawberries to
the fruit bowl.

Mushrooms
a la campagnarde

Serves: 4
Preparation time: 15 minutes
Cooking time: 50 minutes

■ ○

This dish, in one version or another, can be found all through France, Spain and Italy in the fall when field mushrooms are in season. In Catalonia it is often accompanied by grilled blood sausage or other country sausage. Field mushrooms are not available commercially in the United States, but the dish is still delicious when prepared with our cultivated ones. Serve it by itself as an appetizer or as an accompaniment to roasts, sauteed veal or eggs.

Ingredients

½ ounce imported dried mushrooms
1½ pounds fresh mushrooms
1½ cups Brown Stock (page 403)
4 to 6 tablespoons sweet butter
2 tablespoons finely minced shallots
2 garlic cloves, finely minced
4 tablespoons finely minced parsley
  (preferably the flat Italian parsley)
1 Beurre Manie (page 397)
Salt and freshly ground black pepper
8 thin slices French bread, rubbed with
  garlic and fried in olive oil

Garnish:
2 tablespoons minced parsley

Preparation

1. Wash the dried mushrooms thoroughly under cold running water and break them into tiny pieces.

2. Place the dried mushroom pieces and the fresh mushroom stems in a saucepan together with the Brown Stock. Bring to a boil. Reduce the heat and simmer, covered, for 40 minutes.

3. While it is simmering, clean the mushroom caps well with wet paper towels. Do not wash them. If they are large, cut them into quarters.

4. In a large heavy skillet melt 4 tablespoons of butter. Add a few mushrooms at a time and cook them over high heat for 2 or 3 minutes or until they are well browned. Be sure not to crowd your pan or the mushrooms will steam. Remove the browned mushrooms to a side dish and continue sauteeing until all are done. Add more butter if necessary.

5. While the mushrooms are browning, strain the stock and reserve 1 cup.

6. When all the mushrooms are done, put more butter in the pan. Add the shallots, garlic and parsley and cook for 2 minutes or until the shallots are soft but not browned.

7. Add 1 cup of the stock, reduce the sauce over very high heat, and whisk in little bits of Beurre Manie till the sauce is thickened. Return the mushrooms to the skillet. Season with salt and black pepper. Heat the mushrooms through but do not cook further. Pour them onto a serving platter and garnish with the fried bread and additional minced parsley.

Notes

Poulet flamand

Serves: 4
Preparation time: 20 minutes
Cooking time: 1 hour 45 minutes

A chicken properly roasted and well seasoned is, in my opinion, as elegant as a
complicated ragout. It gives the cook an
opportunity to be creative with her choice
of vegetables and salads.

Ingredients

1 roasting chicken (3 to 3½ pounds)
Salt and freshly ground white pepper
½ teaspoon imported paprika
1 garlic clove, mashed
6 tablespoons sweet butter
2 tablespoons cooking oil
1 large Bouquet Garni (page 397)
2 small whole onions
3 cups Brown Chicken Stock (page 404)
8 small Belgian endives
Juice of 1 lemon
¾ cup heavy cream
1 teaspoon Dijon mustard
1 Beurre Manie (page 397)

Garnish:
Minced parsley

Preparation

1. Preheat the oven to 375°.

2. Season the chicken with salt, pepper,
paprika and garlic. Rub the cavity with salt
and rub the entire chicken well with butter. Truss the chicken.

3. Melt 2 tablespoons of butter and the oil
in a large flameproof baking dish. Add
the Bouquet Garni and onions. Place the
chicken on its side in the baking dish and
roast it for 1 hour and 30 minutes. Baste
it every 10 minutes with the warm Chicken
Stock. Turn the chicken once to brown on
the other side.

The endives:
4. While the chicken is roasting, clean the
endives with a damp paper towel. If possible, avoid washing them. Trim off any
wilted outer leaves. Season with salt and
pepper and sprinkle with lemon juice.

5. Melt 2 tablespoons of butter in a baking
dish large enough to hold the endives in
one layer. Place them in the dish, add ½
cup of Chicken Stock and cover with buttered wax paper. Place them in the oven
(below the chicken) and cook for 45 minutes to 1 hour or until tender (but not
falling apart).

6. While the endives are cooking, combine
the cream and mustard in a small mixing
bowl and reserve.

7. When endives are done, remove them
from the oven and reserve.

8. When the chicken is done, remove it
from the baking dish and cut it into 4 serving pieces. Keep warm.

9. Place the baking dish on top of the
stove, add ½ cup of stock and deglaze the
pan juices over high heat.

10. Add the endives and simmer them in
the sauce for 2 or 3 minutes. Slice them
in half lengthwise and place them on a
serving platter. Top with the chicken
pieces.

11. Pour the cream and mustard mixture
into the pan juices and continue to cook
the sauce for about 3 minutes. Add the
Beurre Manie, bit by bit, until the sauce
heavily coats a spoon. Correct the seasoning. Pour the sauce over the chicken,
garnish with parsley and serve at once.

Oranges sevillane

Serves: 4
Preparation time: 10 minutes
Cooking time: 10 minutes

Oranges are at their best when prepared very simply. Here is a dessert that is an excellent complement to a hearty dish such as a choucroute or a cassoulet.

Ingredients

½ cup white raisins
¼ cup Curacao
4   medium navel oranges
½ cup sugar
⅓ cup water

Optional:
½ cup sliced pitted dates for garnish
2   tablespoons Curacao

Preparation

1. Soak the raisins in ¼ cup Curacao for 1 hour.

2. With a sharp knife or vegetable peeler, remove the skin from 4 oranges, keeping the pieces as long as possible. Be sure not to include any white membrane while peeling. Cut the peel into very thin strips (called "julienne") and place them in a saucepan with boiling water. Blanch them for 10 minutes, then run under cold water. Drain and dry them on paper towels. Add them to the raisins.

3. Remove the remaining white membrane from the oranges. Cut them crosswise (horizontally) into thick slices. Place the slices in a glass serving bowl.

4. Drain the raisins and orange strips, reserving the liqueur, and sprinkle the oranges.

5. Place the sugar and ½ cup water in a small saucepan over high heat. Boil, stir-ring occasionally, until the syrup turns a light nutty brown. (If it turns dark brown, discard it as it will have a bitter taste.) As soon as it reaches the nutty brown color, remove the saucepan from the heat.

6. Add ¼ cup of hot water, the drained liqueur from the raisins and the orange strips. Let the syrup cool completely and pour it over the oranges. Sprinkle them with additional Curacao if you wish and refrigerate until serving time. Garnish with dates if desired.

Remarks

Caramel syrup is good with all fruits and ice creams and will keep well for a few weeks in a covered jar in the refrigerator.

Notes

Canapes bertil
Ragout of beef ticino
Marble bavarian cream

This menu is somewhat Scandinavian in feeling. The light spinach-and-smoked-salmon appetizer is appropriately followed by a rich ragout of beef flavored with dill. Serve with simply cooked rice and small glazed white onions. A salad dressed in a Lemon Vinaigrette is a "must" to set the stage for the Bavarian Cream. The ragout and the dessert can be made one or two days ahead of time. The canapes, however, must be prepared at the last minute.

Canapes bertil

Serves: 6 to 8
Preparation time: 10 minutes
Cooking time: 10 minutes

This Scandinavian specialty is the fulfill-ment of the hostess' dream. It takes only minutes to prepare and the result is both imaginative and elegant. The entire success of this appetizer depends on freshly cooked spinach and excellent smoked salmon.

Ingredients

2 pounds fresh spinach
Salt
2 tablespoons sweet butter
Freshly ground black pepper
Pinch of nutmeg
½ cup Clarified Butter (page 398)
6 to 8 slices of day-old white bread, cut
    into ½-inch-thick slices, crust removed
½ pound smoked salmon

Garnish:
1 tablespoon of capers
2 lemons cut in quarters

Preparation

1. Wash the spinach thoroughly. Remove the stems and discard any wilted or yellow leaves. Place the spinach, drained, in a large casserole. Do not add water. Season it with a pinch of salt and cook, covered, over low heat until it is just wilted. Drain it again in a colander and squeeze it lightly to extract all of the moisture.

2. Melt the butter in a skillet. Add the spinach and saute it for 2 or 3 minutes. Season with black pepper and nutmeg and keep warm.

3. Melt the Clarified Butter in a 10-inch skillet and saute the bread slices until crisp and lightly browned. Place them on a serv-ing platter. Top each with 2 tablespoons of spinach.

4. Chop the smoked salmon. Form it into 1-inch balls. Place them on the spinach and sprinkle with a few capers. Garnish the platter with lemon quarters and serve immediately.

Remarks

Bread sautes better in Clarified Butter, but if you do not have time to prepare it, add 2 tablespoons of vegetable oil and 2 table-spoons of sweet butter to the pan and saute the bread slices over low heat until lightly browned on both sides.
To save time the salmon can be placed in slices on top of the spinach.

Notes

Ragout of beef ticino

Serves: 6 to 8
Preparation time: 30 minutes
Cooking time: 2 hours 30 minutes

A well-prepared ragout has no resemblance to "stew." Here are a few rules: the meat has to be browned carefully, then braised slowly, and the sauce carefully seasoned and thickened to the right consistency. When these rules are followed the result is marvelous.

Ingredients

3   pounds beef chuck, cut into 2-inch cubes
3   tablespoons sweet butter
2   tablespoons cooking oil
Salt and freshly ground white pepper
3   large onions, finely minced
2   garlic cloves, finely minced
1   teaspoon imported paprika
2   tablespoons tomato paste
1   teaspoon marjoram
2   pounds fresh mushrooms, sliced (stems included)
2   tablespoons chopped fresh dill
1   cup sour cream

Garnish:
Whole poached mushrooms
Sprigs of fresh dill

Preparation

1. Preheat oven to 350°.

2. Wipe the meat well with paper towels.

3. In a large flameproof casserole, melt 2 tablespoons of butter and add 1 table-spoon cooking oil. Season the meat with salt and pepper and saute a few pieces at a time until they are evenly browned. Do not crowd your pan. You may need more butter and oil. Do not burn the fat.

4. Remove all the meat from the casserole. Add the onions and garlic and cook until they are tender but not browned. Add the paprika, tomato paste and marjoram.

5. Return the meat to the casserole, coating it well with the onion mixture. Add the mushrooms. Do not add any liquid; the mushrooms will release enough juice to braise the beef. Cover the casserole tightly. Place in the preheated oven and cook for 2 hours or until the meat is just tender when pierced with a fork.

6. Place the casserole on top of the stove. If there seems to be too much liquid, remove the meat with a slotted spoon and reduce the sauce over high heat. When the sauce has reached the right consistency (it must heavily coat a spoon), return the meat to the casserole.

7. Mix the chopped dill with the sour cream and swirl it carefully into the ragout. Correct the seasoning. Serve garnished with whole poached mushrooms and sprigs of dill.

Remarks

This dish may be made a day ahead of time, but the sour cream and dill should be added only at the last minute. Because most of the mushrooms will disintegrate during the cooking, reserve a few choice ones for garnish. Poach them in a saucepan with ½ cup of water, a dash of lemon juice and 2 tablespoons of butter. Cook them over low heat for 3 to 5 minutes. The poaching liquid can then be added to the ragout.

Marble bavarian cream

Serves: 8
Preparation time: 45 minutes
Cooking time: 15 to 20 minutes

Bavarian creams are often too gelatinous and therefore are often disappointing in spite of their visual effect. A good Bavarian Cream requires work, but it is certainly worth the effort, especially since it can be prepared well in advance and can be served for a large buffet party. This particular dessert is best made in a deep ring mold.

Ingredients

¾ cup sugar
¾ cup water
¾ cup hot milk
4 egg yolks
1 tablespoon gelatin
4 egg whites

The chocolate custard:
3 ounces semisweet chocolate
¾ cup milk
3 egg yolks
½ cup sugar
1 tablespoon vanilla extract
1 tablespoon gelatin
¼ cup strong coffee
1½ cups heavy cream

Optional:
2 tablespoons dark rum

Preparation

1. Lightly oil a mold with an unflavored oil.

2. In a small saucepan put ½ cup of sugar and ¼ cup water. Boil the mixture over high heat just until it turns a brown nutty color. Remove the saucepan immediately from the heat. Do not burn the caramel. Avert your face and pour ¼ cup of hot water into the caramel, turning it into syrup. Stir in the hot milk.

3. Cream the yolks with ¼ cup sugar in the top of a double boiler. Add the warm caramel milk and stir constantly until the custard coats the spoon. Remove it from the heat. (If you see any lumps, strain the custard through a sieve.)

4. In a small saucepan over low heat dissolve the gelatin in ¼ cup of water. As soon as it is dissolved, pour it into the caramel custard and beat well. Chill the custard.

5. In a saucepan, melt the chocolate. Add ¾ cup of milk and blend until the chocolate is completely dissolved.

6. In the top of the double boiler whisk the yolks with ½ cup of sugar until light and creamy. Add the chocolate milk and beat the custard over medium heat until it coats a spoon. Remove it from the heat and add the optional rum and the vanilla.

7. Dissolve the gelatin in the coffee in a small saucepan over medium heat. When completely dissolved add it to the custard.

8. Beat the egg whites until they form soft peaks. Add ½ the beaten egg white to the caramel custard, incorporating it well. Add the other ½ to the chocolate custard.

9. Whip the cream until it doubles in volume. Add ½ of it to the caramel custard and the other ½ to the chocolate custard. Let both custards thicken in the refrigerator for 1 to 2 hours, whisking them from time to time.

10. Now pour both custards simultaneously into the oiled mold. Swirl a knife through them to give a marbled effect. Chill for at least 4 hours or until firm.

11. When ready to serve, run a sharp knife around the edge of the Bavarian Cream and unmold it onto a serving platter, or serve from a pretty crystal bowl.

Remarks

You may present this dessert more elaborately by serving a Chocolate Sauce (page 397) on the side.

Notes

Stuffed smelts la gavina
Veal chops in sauce moutarde
Cafe "espresso" sabayon

In this menu the dishes are highly flavored and somewhat "earthy." Both the appetizer and main course are country dishes with a great deal of character. Following the main course serve a well-seasoned endive salad and 2 or 3 interesting dessert cheeses. The coffee Sabayon is a light dessert that must be made at the last minute and will give the meal a rich finale. It can also be served cold.

Stuffed smelts la gavina

Serves: 6
Preparation time: 30 minutes
Cooking time: 45 minutes

Ingredients

12 medium-size smelts
10 ounces spinach
Salt
½ cup cooked Italian rice
1 egg yolk
1 tablespoon freshly grated Romano cheese
Freshly ground white pepper
2 tablespoons sweet butter
1 tablespoon pine nuts
4 tablespoons olive oil
½ cup fresh white homemade bread crumbs
2 tablespoons finely chopped parsley
½ teaspoon oregano
1 garlic clove, finely minced
⅓ cup white wine
Freshly ground black pepper

Garnish:
Fresh watercress
6 slices of lemon

Preparation

1. Have the fishmarket clean the smelts and remove the center bones, leaving the heads on.

2. Preheat oven to 375°.

3. Rinse the spinach well under cold running water. Remove the stems and put the spinach in a saucepan with a pinch of salt. Do not add any water. Cook the spinach over low heat until it is completely wilted. Drain it and as soon as it is cool enough to handle, squeeze it between your hands into a firm ball. Chop it finely.

4. In a bowl combine the rice, spinach,

egg yolk, cheese, salt and pepper.

5. In a small skillet heat the butter. Add the pine nuts and saute them until they are lightly browned, then add them to the spinach and rice mixture.

6. Season the smelts with salt and pepper. Stuff each with a little of the rice mixture.

7. Put 2 tablespoons of olive oil in a rectangular baking dish. Place the smelts in the dish.

8. In a skillet heat the remaining olive oil. Add the bread crumbs, parsley, oregano and garlic. Saute for 1 or 2 minutes and sprinkle the smelts with this mixture. Dribble the wine over them.

9. Season the smelts with black pepper and bake for 25 to 30 minutes.

10. Serve garnished with watercress and slices of lemon.

Remarks

If you want to make this dish during the summer, substitute an equal quantity of fresh sorrel for the spinach and use fresh herring instead of the smelts.

Notes

Veal chops in sauce moutarde

Serves: 6
Preparation time: 35 to 40 minutes
Cooking time: 40 to 50 minutes

■ ◑

Here is an excellent way to prepare veal that is not of the best quality. The slow braising and the highly flavored sauce enhance the veal greatly.

Ingredients

6 veal chops, cut ¾ inch thick
Salt and freshly ground white pepper
¾ cup heavy cream plus 2 tablespoons
1 tablespoon Dijon mustard
5 to 7 tablespoons sweet butter
2 shallots, finely minced
¼ pound fresh mushrooms, finely minced, including some stems
Flour for dredging
2 tablespoons oil
2 medium-sized onions, very finely sliced
2 garlic cloves, finely minced
½ cup white wine
½ cup Brown Stock (page 403)
1 Bouquet Garni (page 397)
Dash of lemon juice

Optional:
1 Beurre Manie (page 397)

Garnish:
Braised Belgian endive

Preparation

1. Have the butcher prepare a small pocket in each chop or cut one yourself with a small sharp paring knife. Season the chops with salt and pepper and reserve.

2. In a small bowl, combine ¾ cup cream and mustard and reserve.

3. Preheat the oven to 325°.

4. In a small skillet, melt 2 tablespoons of butter. Add the minced shallots and cook over medium heat until they are soft but not browned.

5. Add the mushrooms and cook them over high heat until all the liquid has evaporated.

6. Add 2 tablespoons cream and continue cooking until the mixture is very dry. Season with salt and pepper.

7. Stuff a little of the mixture into each chop pocket and sew the opening with heavy thread. Lightly dredge the chops in flour, shaking off the excess.

8. In a large skillet heat 3 tablespoons of butter with the oil. Add the chops and brown them over medium heat on both sides. Do not crowd your pan. Remove the chops to a side dish as soon as they are done and reserve. If the fat in the pan is burnt, discard it, and add fresh butter to the pan.

9. Add the onions and garlic to the pan and cook until lightly browned. Add the wine, raise the heat and cook until it is reduced to 2 tablespoons, scraping the bottom of the pan well. Add the Brown Stock. Bring it to a boil and return the chops to the pan together with the Bouquet Garni. Cover the pan with foil and then with a lid and place in the oven. Braise the chops for 30 minutes.

10. Remove the pan from the oven and with a slotted spoon remove the chops to a serving platter.

11. Place the pan over high heat and add the cream and mustard mixture. Cook the sauce over high heat until it is reduced by ⅓ and coats the spoon heavily. If needed, add little bits of Beurre Manie to thicken

the sauce. Add a dash of lemon juice. Taste the sauce and season with additional salt and pepper if needed. Pour the sauce over the veal chops and garnish the platter with Braised Belgian endives.

Remarks

The entire dish can be prepared 30 to 40 minutes in advance and kept warm in a 200° oven.

Notes

Cafe "espresso" sabayon

Serves: 6
Preparation time: 5 minutes
Cooking time: 5 to 7 minutes

■ ●

Coffee Sabayon is a light and easy dessert, ideal for last-minute entertaining. It can easily be turned into a mousse by chilling for 2 to 4 hours and then combining it before serving with 2 cups of whipped cream.

Ingredients

8 egg yolks
6 tablespoons sugar
¾ cup strong coffee (preferably espresso)
¼ cup cognac

Garnish:
Shaved chocolate
Champagne biscuits

Optional: (for mousse)
2 tablespoons confectioners' sugar
2 cups whipped cream

Preparation

1. In the top of a double boiler combine the egg yolks and sugar and beat until the mixture is pale yellow and forms a ribbon when dropped from a spoon.

2. Add the coffee. Place the pan over simmering water and whisk, preferably with an electric hand beater, until the mixture doubles in volume and is creamy and thick. Do not let it come to a boil. To be sure of the right consistency, keep a spoon at hand. If the cream coats the spoon heavily, the Sabayon is ready.

3. Incorporate the cognac. Pour into individual china coffee cups, top with shaved sweet chocolate. Place a champagne biscuit or two on each saucer or serve them on a separate plate. Serve immediately while warm.

Remarks

You may combine the egg yolks, sugar and coffee well in advance and have the water ready at simmer. The cooking of the Sabayon *has* to be done at the last minute if the dessert is to be eaten warm.
For a cold coffee mousse you may need additional sugar. Combine 2 tablespoons confectioners' sugar with 2 cups of whipped cream and add it to the coffee cream.

Notes

Viennese shrimp toast
Alsatian pork chops
Brazilian flambeed bananas

Even though many people do not consider
pork chops "important" enough for an
elegant dinner party, they are an excellent
main course when well prepared.
The shrimp toast can be made well in advance and reheated in the oven while the
chops are braising.
The flambeed bananas do require last-
minute preparation but their marvelous
affinity to pork and the delicious result
make the effort worthwhile. If possible,
flambe the bananas at the table in
front of your guests.

Viennese shrimp toast

Serves: 6 to 8
Preparation time: 20 minutes
Cooking time: 5 minutes

Shrimp are available year-round but, unfortunately, because of the popularity of two or three tired recipes their marvelous potential is seldom realized. Here is a fresh way to serve shrimp as an appetizer. You may substitute poached mussels or crabmeat for the shrimp or even mix two or three different shellfish.

Ingredients

The shrimp toast:
6 to 8 slices white bread
4   tablespoons Clarified Butter (page 398) melted
5   tablespoons sweet butter
2   large onions, finely chopped
Salt and freshly ground black pepper
Dijon mustard
1½ pounds fresh-cooked shrimp, peeled
1   cup unflavored white bread crumbs
2   tablespoons parsley (flat-leaf kind if possible)
1   garlic clove, finely minced

The sauce:
10 tablespoons sweet butter
2   chicken bouillon cubes dissolved in 6 tablespoons boiling water
Few drops Worcestershire sauce
2   tablespoons shallots, finely minced
Juice of ½ lemon
Salt and freshly ground white pepper

Garnish:
Quartered lemons
Fresh watercress or parsley sprigs

Preparation

The shrimp toast:
1. Preheat oven to 375°.

2. Remove the crusts from the bread slices and saute them lightly in Clarified Butter until nicely browned on both sides. Place them on a cookie sheet when done.

3. Melt the 2 tablespoons of sweet butter in a skillet and saute the onions until soft but not brown. Then put them in an electric blender and puree for 1 or 2 minutes. Season with salt and pepper.

4. Coat the toast slices with a layer of Dijon mustard, then a layer of the onion puree.

5. Place 4 or 5 shrimp in a decorative pattern on each slice of toast. Try to use small shrimp as they look more delicate and attractive. If you must use large shrimp, cut them in half lengthwise.

6. In a separate skillet melt 3 tablespoons of butter and add the bread crumbs, parsley and garlic. When the bread crumbs are well coated, remove and reserve.

7. Spread a little of this bread-crumb mixture on each slice of shrimp toast. Sprinkle with salt and freshly ground black pepper. Bake in the oven for 5 to 10 minutes. Place the toast on a serving platter and garnish with quartered lemons and watercress or parsley sprigs.

The sauce:
8. Melt the ¼ pound of butter in a heavy-bottomed saucepan.

9. Add remaining sauce ingredients and heat thoroughly. Place the sauce in a sauceboat and serve on the side. Garnish the platter or individual plate with watercress and slices of lemon.

Alsatian pork chops

Serves: 6
Preparation time: 45 minutes
Cooking time: 1 hour 45 minutes

Pork chops are often served broiled or fried in the United States. They are frequently overcooked and dry. There are many exciting ways to prepare pork. Slow braising, as in the following recipe, brings out the fullest flavor. I find pork particularly good in winter when we feel ready for a hearty meal. This particular recipe can be put together well ahead of time and is especially good for entertaining.

Ingredients

6   pork chops, cut 1 inch thick
Salt and freshly ground white pepper
1   cup cubed salt pork or lean bacon
3   tablespoons Clarified Butter (page 398)
1   tablespoon cooking oil
12 small white onions
3   baking apples
1½ cups Brown Stock (page 403)
1   large head of Savoy cabbage, cut into thick slices
2   tablespoons sweet butter
½ cup heavy cream
1   tablespoon currant jelly

Optional:
1   teaspoon cornstarch dissolved in 1 tablespoon of stock or water

Preparation

1. Preheat oven to 375°.

2. Dry the pork chops well with paper towels. Season with salt and pepper.

3. Drop the salt pork into boiling water for 5 minutes and drain on paper towels. This takes the excess fat out of it. If you cannot get good quality salt pork, use bacon,

which should also be parboiled for 5 minutes and drained.

4. In a 12-inch skillet melt the Clarified Butter. Saute the salt-pork cubes, then remove them to a flameproof casserole. Add the chops to the skillet 2 or 3 at a time and brown on both sides. Do not crowd your pan or the chops will not brown properly. When all the chops are done, remove them from the skillet to the casserole.

5. Pour out all but 2 tablespoons of fat from the skillet. Add the oil and brown the onions lightly for 5 to 6 minutes. Remove them to the casserole.

6. Peel, core and quarter the apples and add them to the casserole.

7. To the fat remaining in the skillet add the Brown Stock. Raise the heat and scrape the bottom of the skillet to loosen the crusty particles of the meat. Pour this juice over the chops. Braise in the oven for 1 hour and 15 minutes.

8. In the meantime put the cabbage into boiling salted water and cook for 10 minutes or until just tender. Drain immediately and run under cold water.

9. Heat the 2 tablespoons of sweet butter in a large skillet and saute the cabbage for 5 minutes. Season and keep warm.

10. When the chops are done, place the cabbage on a serving platter and arrange the chops on top of it. Place the onions, apples and salt-pork around the chops.

11. Degrease the pan juices. Place the casserole on top of the stove over high heat and reduce the sauce.

12. Mix the cream with the currant jelly and add this to the sauce. Correct the seasoning. If the sauce seems too thin, add the cornstarch and cook the sauce until it heavily coats a spoon.

13. Spoon the sauce over the chops and serve.

Notes

Brazilian flambeed bananas

Serves: 6
Preparation time: 10 minutes
Cooking time: 5 to 8 minutes

Bananas are one of the "fresh fruits" available in winter at a reasonable price. We seem to use them almost always in fruit salads and fail to give them a chance to hold their own as a lovely dessert. Flambeed bananas are easily and quickly prepared and offer a welcome change from the chocolate mousse and Bavarian creams so often served in winter.

Ingredients

4   tablespoons sweet butter
3   tablespoons brown sugar
1   teaspoon vanilla
½ teaspoon cinnamon
½ cup fresh orange juice
Juice of 1 lemon
6   bananas, peeled
½ cup banana liqueur

Garnish:
Grated rind of 1 orange
Grated rind of 1 lemon

Preparation

1. In a large heavy-bottomed skillet melt the butter over low heat. Add the brown sugar and stir for 2 or 3 minutes until it melts. Add vanilla, cinnamon, orange and lemon juice.

2. Cut a ¼-inch slice off each banana. Place the bananas in the skillet cut side down and heat for 2 or 3 minutes. Make sure they are just warmed through and not "mushy."

3. Transfer the bananas to a serving platter. Increase the heat under the skillet and reduce the pan juices until they become syrupy and heavily coat a spoon.

4. Warm the banana liqueur, add it to the
skillet and ignite it (or, if you prefer,
do the actual flambeeing at the table).

5. Pour the sauce over the bananas and
sprinkle with grated orange and lemon rind.
Serve immediately.

Remarks

This may be served with plain vanilla
ice cream or with vanilla ice cream mixed
with equal amounts of whipped cream and
flavored with 2 tablespoons of rum.

Notes

Westphalian rolls remoulade
Soup au farci
Swiss baked pears

This is a simple supper or Sunday lunch menu. Winter is the time when hearty soups are more appreciated and they can be meals by themselves. The Soup au Farci fills this need and can be made a day or two ahead of time. The Westphalian Rolls are filled with the traditional Celeri Rave Remoulade, a favorite in French cuisine and one of the best winter salads. For variation use it as the filling for artichoke bottoms marinated in vinaigrette. You can also substitute finely sliced baked ham for the Westphalian ham or simply serve the salad with a well-flavored country pate. Follow the soup with the baked pears, a light and pleasant dessert, one that will add an appropriate finishing touch to a cozy supper or Sunday lunch.

Westphalian rolls remoulade

Serves: 8 to 10
Preparation time: 35 minutes
Cooking time: none

Ingredients

2 large celery knobs
Juice of 1 lemon
1 cup Mayonnaise (page 402)
2 teaspoons Dijon mustard
1 tablespoon white wine vinegar
Salt and freshly ground black pepper
¼ pound small fresh mushrooms
½ cup Vinaigrette (pages 408–409)
2 tablespoons finely minced chives
1 tablespoon finely minced parsley
8 to 10 thin slices Westphalian ham,
    prosciutto or excellent cooked ham

Garnish:
1 bunch fresh watercress
Black olives

Preparation

1. Peel the celery knobs and immediately drop them into a large bowl of cold water, acidulated with the juice of ½ lemon. When all the knobs have been peeled, remove them one by one, grate them as finely as possible and place them in a bowl. Sprinkle with the remaining lemon juice.

2. Combine the Mayonnaise with the mustard and vinegar and fold it into the grated celery. Season the mixture with salt and pepper and marinate for at least 2 hours.

3. Remove the mushroom stems and reserve them for soup or stock. Wipe the mushrooms with a damp paper towel and cut them into very thin slices.

4. Place the mushrooms in a separate bowl, sprinkle them with the Vinaigrette, chives and parsley. Season with salt and pepper and marinate for 2 hours.

5. Just before serving, drain the mushrooms thoroughly and fold them into the celery-knob salad.

6. Spoon a little of the mixture into each slice of ham, roll them up and place them on a serving platter.

7. Garnish with fresh watercress and black olives.

Remarks

The salad can also be filled into well-seeded and drained cucumber boats or artichoke bottoms. Do not use canned ones.
You may serve additional Vinaigrette on the side to be used on the watercress. A bowl of sweet butter and thinly sliced black bread go well with this winter hors d'oeuvre.

Notes

Soup au farci

Serves: 8
Preparation time: 45 minutes to 1 hour
Cooking time: 1 hour 30 minutes

I cannot think of a better winter soup: earthy, hearty, a culinary treasure. It is found in many French farmhouses. The stuffing in the cabbage leaves varies according to what is available, since it is often made with leftovers.

Ingredients

16 to 18 cabbage leaves (preferably Savoy cabbage)
2 tablespoons sweet butter
2 tablespoons finely chopped onion
1 garlic clove, minced
½ pound ground beef (preferably chuck)
¾ cup finely chopped smoked ham
1 cup cooked Italian rice
Salt and freshly ground white pepper
Pinch of ground bay leaf and pinch of thyme
1 egg
1 tablespoon finely chopped parsley
10 to 12 cups concentrated Beef Stock (page 405)

Preparation

1. Preheat the oven to 325°.

2. Drop the cabbage leaves into boiling water for 2 minutes. Drain immediately and put on paper towels to dry. Place the leaves on a cutting board and cut a thin wedge from the core end of each leaf. Reserve the prepared leaves.

3. In a skillet, heat the butter. Add the onion and garlic and cook for 3 minutes until tender but not browned.

4. Add the ground meat and break it into small pieces with a fork. Brown it lightly. Remove the meat and onion mixture to a mixing bowl.

5. Add the ham, cooked rice, salt, pepper and the rest of the seasonings. Add the egg and parsley and work the mixture with your hands until it is well blended.

6. Put 1 to 2 tablespoons of the mixture on each cabbage leaf and roll the leaves up, starting at the core and tucking in the sides to seal as you go along. The stuffing must be completely enclosed.

7. Place the cabbage leaves, sealed side down, in a large casserole. Add 2 cups Beef Stock and cook the cabbage, covered, over low heat for 45 minutes.

8. After 45 minutes, add the remaining Beef Stock and continue cooking over low heat for 30 to 40 minutes more.

9. Serve each person 1 or 2 stuffed cabbage leaves together with one or two ladles of the bouillon. Serve with black bread and a bowl of sweet butter.

Remarks

The soup is sometimes topped with finely chopped parsley. Carrots, cut into cubes, or 1 or 2 cubed potatoes can be added during the last 40 minutes of cooking. Personally, I do not find any additions necessary.

Notes

Swiss baked pears

Serves: 8
Preparation time: 10 minutes
Cooking time: 10 to 15 minutes

This is a perfect dessert when you are faced with last-minute entertaining. You can make it more elaborate by using the pears as a filling for dessert crepes. You can also serve them on top of coffee ice cream in parfait glasses. For another variation the pears can be put into prebaked small tart shells.

Notes

Ingredients

8   baking pears, peeled, cored and quartered
6 to 8 tablespoons sugar
8   tablespoons butter
1½ cups heavy cream
3   tablespoons kirsch

Garnish:
¾ cup finely sliced toasted almonds, or 2 tablespoons Praline Powder (page 402)

Preparation

1. In a heavy-bottomed skillet, place the pears in one layer and sprinkle heavily with sugar and little bits of butter. Cook them, uncovered, over high heat, shaking the pan until the sugar turns light brown and the pears are caramelized.

2. Pour in the cream mixed with kirsch and cook for a few minutes longer until the cream heavily coats a spoon.

3. Pour the pears into a serving dish and sprinkle with toasted almonds or Praline Powder.

4. Serve the dessert warm accompanied by champagne biscuits and a sweet white wine.

Artichoke bottoms en souffle

Serves: 6
Preparation time: 1 hour
Cooking time: 45 minutes

Ingredients

6   large fresh artichoke bottoms, poached
    and then sauteed in 2 tablespoons sweet
    butter (page 71) or 12 small artichoke
    bottoms, poached and then sauteed in
    2 tablespoons sweet butter

The souffle:
5   tablespoons sweet butter
2   finely minced shallots
1   cup finely minced fresh crabmeat
2   teaspoons lemon juice
Salt and freshly ground white pepper
1   cup milk
1   small Bouquet Garni (page 397)
3   tablespoons flour
4   egg yolks
½   teaspoon dry mustard
½   cup finely grated cheese (Gruyere mixed
    with freshly grated Parmesan)
5   egg whites at room temperature

Preparation

1. Preheat the oven to 375°.

2. In a large baking dish place the sauteed
artichoke bottoms. Reserve.

3. In a small skillet melt 2 tablespoons of
butter. Add the shallots and cook until
they are soft and not browned.

4. Add the crabmeat and lemon juice.
Season with salt and pepper and cook over
very low heat until the mixture is just
heated through. Reserve.

5. Heat the milk with the Bouquet Garni.
Let the bouquet steep in simmering milk
for 10 to 15 minutes, then remove it.

6. In a heavy-bottomed saucepan, melt the
remaining butter. Add the flour and cook
for 2 minutes, stirring constantly, without
letting it brown.

7. Add the hot milk all at once and keep
stirring until the mixture gets very thick
and smooth.

8. Remove the saucepan from the heat, add
the egg yolks one at a time. Incorporate
each yolk completely into the sauce before
adding the next one.

9. Season the mixture with salt, pepper and
dry mustard.

10. Return the saucepan to the heat and
whisk the sauce until it is well heated
through. Do not let it come to a boil.

11. Remove the saucepan from the heat and
fold in the crabmeat mixture.

12. Add the grated cheese and reserve.

13. Beat the egg whites in a copper bowl
with a wire whisk, adding a pinch of salt.
Beat until the whites form soft peaks.

14. Fold a little of the beaten egg white into
the souffle base. Then pour the mixture
into the remaining whites, folding it with
your hands.

15. Pour the souffle mixture on top of the
artichoke bottoms. Do not try to fill each
one, just cover the whole dish with the
mixture.

16. Place the baking dish in the oven and
cook the souffle for 12 to 15 minutes or
until well puffed and lightly browned. Do
not overcook. This souffle does not need
as much cooking time as one cooked in a
deep mold.

Coquilles saint-jacques bellevue

Serves: 8
Preparation time: 15 minutes
Cooking time: 35 minutes

Cold scallops make a wonderful appetizer. In this particular recipe you may use large sea scallops which are usually less expensive than bay scallops. Serve in individual shells lined with a leaf of Bibb lettuce or fill it into cold artichokes.
You may even be a little creative and add some mussels and tiny fresh shrimp for variation.

Ingredients

1½ pounds of sea scallops, cut in half or, if very large, in quarters

The bouillon:
1 cup dry white wine
1 cup water
6 peppercorns
1 teaspoon salt
1 large Bouquet Garni (page 397)
1 large sprig of dill or a few dill seeds
1 large onion, stuck with a clove

The sauce:
¼ cup white vinegar
Juice of 1 large lemon
5 tablespoons olive oil
3 tablespoons mustard
¼ cup very fine minced green onions or chives
1 tablespoon minced dill
2 tablespoons finely chopped parsley
2 to 3 tablespoons sugar
Salt
A pinch of cayenne pepper
Freshly ground black pepper
⅓ cup Creme Fraiche (page 398)

Garnish:
A few tiny capers
1 large lemon cut into wedges

Preparation

1. In a heavy saucepan combine all the bouillon ingredients. Bring the mixture to a boil. Reduce the heat and simmer, covered, for 30 minutes.

2. Add the scallops and poach them, covered, for 5 minutes. Drain them and let cool. You may reserve the poaching liquid for another use.

3. For the sauce, combine the vinegar, lemon juice, olive oil, mustard, onions or chives, dill, parsley, sugar and salt in a jar. Cover the jar and shake vigorously. You will obtain a mayonnaise-like dressing. Correct seasoning and add a dash of cayenne and black pepper to taste. Whisk in the Creme Fraiche. Pour the sauce over the scallops and refrigerate for at least 2 to 4 hours before serving.

4. Garnish the scallops with capers and lemon wedges.

Remarks

If you are making this appetizer in the summer, add 1 tablespoon of finely minced fresh tarragon to the sauce. The reserved poaching liquid can be used to poach filets of sole or as a base for a scallop soup.

Notes

Frito misto a l'indienne

Serves: 6
Preparation time: 25 minutes
Cooking time: 5 minutes

This Frito Misto is actually an appetizer, but you can fry larger fish, such as whole trout or perch, in the same way and serve them as a main course.

Ingredients

12 small whole smelts, cleaned (heads left on)
12 small whole shrimp, raw and peeled with tail left on
12 to 16 bay scallops
Juice of 2 lemons
Salt
Vegetable oil for deep frying
Flour for dredging

The batter:
1 cup sifted all-purpose flour
1 cup warm water
1 teaspoon salt
2 tablespoons olive oil
2 to 3 egg whites

The sauce:
2 cups Mayonnaise (page 402)
1 to 2 teaspoons curry powder
2 tablespoons finely minced chives or finely minced scallions
1 garlic clove, mashed
1 teaspoon anchovy paste
2 tablespoons tiny well-drained whole capers
Lemon juice

Optional:
2 tablespoons minced fennel tops

Garnish:
Deep-fried whole scallions
Deep-fried parsley sprigs
3 lemons, quartered

Preparation

1. Preheat the oven to 200°.

2. Place the fish and shellfish in a bowl and sprinkle with lemon juice and salt. Let mixture stand for 1 or 2 hours in the refrigerator.

The batter:
3. In a large bowl combine the 1 cup of flour and the water. Stir the mixture until it is quite smooth but do not overstir. It should have the consistency of very heavy cream. Add the 1 teaspoon of salt and let the mixture stand for 2 hours. Do not refrigerate.

4. While the batter is standing make the sauce. To the mayonnaise add the curry powder, chives, garlic, anchovy paste, capers and optional fennel tops. Blend well. Check the seasoning, adding a little lemon juice to taste. Chill until serving time.

5. Dry the fish and shellfish thoroughly with paper towels. Lightly dredge them in flour, shaking off the excess. Heat the oil (3 inches deep) in your deep fryer. It should be hot enough to sizzle when a drop of batter comes in contact with it.

6. Fold the egg whites into the batter, then dip the fish and shellfish into it a few at a time and proceed to deep-fry them, regulating the heat of the oil so that the fish gets cooked through without burning.

7. With a slotted spoon carefully remove the deep-fried fish and shellfish to a clean towel and sprinkle with a little salt. Place the bowl of sauce in the middle of a round serving platter surrounded by the Frito Misto.

8. With the remaining batter coat the scallions and fry these as well. At the very last, drop large sprigs of parsley into the hot fat for just a second. Place them on top of the fish, garnish the platter with the lemon quarters and serve immediately.

Remarks

Keep the deep-fried fish and shellfish in a 200° oven while proceeding with the rest of the frying. Another beaten egg white can be added to the batter if, after a little time, it seems to lack fluffiness.
In summer, add a tablespoon of finely minced fresh tarragon or summer savory to your sauce.

Notes

Mushrooms in sauce moutarde

Serves: 4 to 6
Preparation time: 20 minutes
Cooking time: 30 minutes

■ ○

Mushrooms, poached and covered with a good sauce, make an exciting appetizer. Serve them in toasted bread cases or use them as a filling for crepes for a more formal presentation.

Ingredients

1½ pounds small button mushrooms
¾ cup water
Salt
1 tablespoon lemon juice
2 tablespoons sweet butter

The sauce:
4 tablespoons sweet butter
3 tablespoons flour
2 cups warm Chicken Stock (page 404)
1 teaspoon dry mustard
1 teaspoon Dijon mustard
1 Bouquet Garni (page 397)
Salt and freshly ground white pepper
4 tablespoons Creme Fraiche (page 398)
   or heavy cream
A few drops of lemon juice

Garnish:
2 tablespoons finely minced dill or parsley, or a mixture of the two

Preparation

1. Wipe the mushrooms with wet paper towels. Avoid washing them. Remove the stems and reserve for soup or stock.

2. In an enamel saucepan combine the water, salt, lemon juice and 2 tablespoons of butter. Bring to a boil and add the mushrooms. Cover the pan and simmer over low heat for 5 minutes. Remove the pan from the heat. Leave the mushrooms in their liquid while making the sauce.

Shrimp salad rovigo

Serves: 4 to 6
Preparation time: 20 minutes
Cooking time: none

■ ◉

3. In a heavy saucepan, melt the 4 tablespoons butter. Add the flour, and cook for 3 minutes, stirring constantly, without letting it brown.

4. Add the warm Chicken Stock all at once and whisk constantly until the sauce is smooth and thick.

5. Make a paste out of the dry and Dijon mustards with a little water. Beat the mustard mixture into the sauce. Add the Bouquet Garni, salt and pepper and cover the pan. Simmer the sauce for 20 minutes over a very low flame.

6. Remove the Bouquet and add the Creme Fraiche and lemon juice.

7. Drain the mushrooms and add them to the sauce. Heat the mushrooms through, but do not let the sauce come to a boil. Pour into a serving dish.

8. Sprinkle with dill or parsley and serve.

Remarks

This is also an excellent brunch dish as an accompaniment to poached eggs. You may sprinkle the dish with grated Parmesan and quickly run it under the broiler.

Notes

A cold salad is not necessarily a summer dish. I often serve a cold hors d'oeuvre on a winter night, followed by soup and sauteed veal scallops.

Ingredients

¼ pound fresh mushrooms
2 tablespoons tarragon vinegar
Salt and freshly ground white pepper
1 pound fresh small shrimp, cooked and peeled
Juice of 1 lemon
Olive oil
1 sprig parsley
2 bay leaves
1 cup Mayonnaise (page 402)
2 tablespoons chili sauce
1 mashed garlic clove
2 tablespoons finely chopped scallions (white part only)

Garnish:
Quartered hard-boiled eggs
Pimiento strips

Preparation

1. Do not wash the mushrooms; simply wipe them with a damp paper towel. Remove the stems and reserve for another use. (They are always good for stock and stuffing.) Slice the mushrooms finely and place in a bowl. Sprinkle with the vinegar, a pinch of salt and pepper and marinate for at least 1 hour.

2. Place the shrimp in another bowl and sprinkle with lemon juice and a few drops of olive oil. Add the sprig of parsley and the bay leaves. Let the shrimp marinate, covered, for at least 2 hours.

3. To the Mayonnaise add the chili sauce, garlic and scallions. Taste for seasoning.

4. Drain both the shrimp and the mushrooms. Remove the parsley and bay leaves and combine the shrimp and mushrooms in a glass serving dish.

5. Add the Mayonnaise and carefully blend it into the salad. Be sure not to break the mushroom slices. Refrigerate the salad for 1 or 2 hours before serving. Correct the seasoning.

6. Garnish with hard-boiled eggs and pimiento and serve cold.

Remarks

For a more elegant presentation, serve this salad on fresh artichoke bottoms. These should be cooked well in advance, chilled and marinated in a well-seasoned Vinaigrette (pages 408–409). Serve with thinly sliced, buttered pumpernickel.

Notes

Spinach toast a l'italienne

Serves: 6 to 8
Preparation time: 20 minutes
Cooking time: 30 minutes

This light appetizer takes only minutes to prepare. You may also serve it as an accompaniment to roasts, grilled meats and fish, or as a brunch dish topped with poached eggs.

Ingredients

1 pound fresh spinach
Salt
4 tablespoons sweet butter
½ pound finely sliced fresh mushrooms (reserve stems for soup or stock)
½ cup to ¾ cup finely cubed prosciutto
Freshly ground black pepper
4 to 6 tablespoons Clarified Butter (page 398)
6 to 8 slices white bread, crust removed

Optional:
¾ cup finely grated fresh Parmesan cheese

Preparation

1. Wash the spinach thoroughly under cold running water. Do not soak it. Remove the tough stems and place the spinach in a wire salad basket or a colander. Let drain over a bowl for 30 minutes.

2. In a large casserole bring 3 quarts salted water to a boil. Add the spinach and cook for 3 to 5 minutes. Strain it immediately and cool in a colander.

3. In a large skillet heat the 4 tablespoons of sweet butter, add the mushrooms and cook over high heat until they are nicely browned.

4. Add the spinach and cook the mixture over low heat for 3 minutes or until all the moisture has evaporated.

Avocado veloute soup

Serves: 6
Preparation time: 25 minutes
Cooking time: 45 minutes

■ ●

5. Add the prosciutto. Cover the skillet and cook the mixture for 2 or 3 more minutes or until the prosciutto is heated through.

6. Season with salt and black pepper. The mixture must be very "dry." Set aside.

7. In a large skillet melt the Clarified Butter and brown the bread slices on both sides. Remove the toast to an ovenproof platter.

8. Top each piece of toast with the spinach mixture and sprinkle with grated cheese (if used). Place the dish under a hot broiler for 1 or 2 minutes or until the cheese is lightly browned. Serve very hot.

Remarks

You may prepare both the toast and the spinach mixture ahead of time, but do not combine them until the last minute or the bread will get soggy.

Notes

Ingredients

6 tablespoons sweet butter
1 cup finely minced scallions (green part only)
2 garlic cloves, mashed
1½ ripe avocados
Juice of 1 lemon
4 tablespoons flour
6 cups Chicken Stock (page 404)
Salt and freshly ground white pepper
3 egg yolks
1 cup heavy cream
Few drops of Tabasco

Garnish:
Finely minced fresh chives
½ cup heavy cream, whipped and slightly salted

Preparation

1. In a small heavy saucepan melt 2 tablespoons of butter. Add the scallions and garlic and cook, covered, over low heat for 5 minutes or until the scallions are very soft but not browned. Remove them to the top part of a blender.

2. Add the coarsely mashed pulp of 1 large avocado. Sprinkle with ½ of the lemon juice and blend the mixture at high speed until it becomes a smooth puree. Set aside.

3. In a large saucepan melt the remaining butter. Add the flour and cook the mixture, stirring constantly, for 2 minutes without browning.

4. Add the hot Chicken Stock and whisk until the soup becomes slightly thick and very smooth.

5. Season the soup with salt and pepper

and let it simmer, partially covered, for 30 to 40 minutes.

6. In a mixing bowl combine the egg yolks, Tabasco and cream and blend them well. Fold the avocado puree into the cream and yolk mixture.

7. Pour the mixture into the soup and, stirring constantly, heat the soup through without letting it come to a boil. Correct the seasoning and keep the soup warm.

8. Peel the remaining ½ avocado and cut it into tiny cubes. Sprinkle them with remaining lemon juice and add them to the soup just before serving.

9. Serve the soup garnished with chives and a spoonful of whipped cream.

Remarks

This is actually a year-round soup. You may serve it cold in summer and vary it by substituting Creme Fraiche for the whipped cream and fresh chervil for the chives.

Notes

Celeriac soup

Serves: 6 to 8
Preparation time: 25 minutes
Cooking time: 1 hour

Soups are an essential part of the Winter Kitchen. They should be hearty and well flavored. Celeriac, or celery knob as it is often called, is one of the best winter vegetables. It has a unique flavor and makes a delicious soup, which can be frozen successfully.

Ingredients

4   tablespoons sweet butter
2   large onions, sliced
3   medium-sized potatoes, peeled and cubed
4   celery knobs, peeled and cubed
2   parsnips, peeled and cubed
Salt and freshly ground white pepper
8   cups Chicken Stock (page 404)
1   large Bouquet Garni (page 397)
1   cup heavy cream (approximately)

Garnish:
1   tablespoon finely minced parsley

Optional:
1 to 2 tablespoons sweet butter

Preparation

1. In a large casserole, melt 4 tablespoons of sweet butter. Add the onions and cook for 2 or 3 minutes without browning.

2. Add the potatoes, celery cubes, and parsnips. Season with salt and pepper and cover with the Chicken Stock. Add the Bouquet Garni. Bring to a boil. Cover partially and simmer for 45 minutes or until the vegetables are very tender.

3. Uncover the soup and cool completely. Puree it in an electric blender or pass it through a food mill.

4. Thin the soup with cream. You may not need a whole cup, depending on how thick the puree is.

5. Correct the seasoning and, if desired, beat in the additional 1 or 2 tablespoons of butter just before serving. Sprinkle the soup with finely minced parsley.

Notes

Flemish soup of winter vegetables

Serves: 6
Preparation time: 30 minutes
Cooking time: 35 minutes

■ ●

Here is a soup that brings to the table all that is good in winter vegetables. You may add or omit any vegetable you like. The homemade Chicken Stock is a must, but the rest is up to you.

Ingredients

2 carrots
2 leeks (white part only)
2 cups fresh spinach
1 head Boston lettuce
6 cups Chicken Stock (page 404)
1 parsnip, peeled, cut in half lengthwise, then cut into 1-inch pieces
2 small potatoes, peeled and cubed
3 small turnips, peeled and cubed
4 tablespoons sweet butter
4 tablespoons flour
Salt and freshly ground white pepper
1/2 cup heavy cream

Garnish:
2 tablespoons minced parsley and chives

Preparation

1. Peel the carrots and cut them into 1-inch strips lengthwise. If they are very young and tender, leave them whole.

2. Wash the leeks thoroughly under cold water to eliminate all sand.

3. Wash and trim the spinach. Wash and cut the lettuce into large chunks.

4. Heat the Chicken Stock and add the carrots, leeks, parsnips, potatoes, and turnips. Cook until the vegetables are just tender or for about 20 minutes. Be careful not to overcook. Strain the stock and keep warm. Reserve the vegetables.

5. In a large casserole, melt the butter. Add the flour and cook for 2 or 3 minutes without browning. Add the warm stock all at once and whisk until the soup gets slightly thicker and is very smooth.

6. Add the spinach and lettuce. Season with salt and pepper and add the reserved vegetables. Cook for 5 minutes.

7. Just before serving, add the cream and heat the soup without letting it come to a boil. Sprinkle with parsley and chives and serve from a large tureen.

Remarks

For a change you may add tiny pieces of chicken to the soup by simmering 1 or 2 extra chicken breasts for 30 minutes in the stock before making the soup. Drain the chicken breasts and reserve. Just before serving cut them into little strips and add to the soup.

Notes

Cream of shrimp and dill soup

Serves: 4 to 6
Preparation time: 35 minutes
Cooking time: 50 minutes

■ ●

This is a lovely Danish soup, usually made with crayfish but equally good with shrimp. It can be served cold in summer with fresh mint or chervil substituted for the dill.

Ingredients

1½ pounds uncooked shrimp
5 cups Fish Stock (page 406)
5 tablespoons sweet butter
1 onion, minced
1 carrot, minced
1 celery stalk, minced
2 small leeks, white parts only, finely sliced
1 Bouquet Garni (page 397)
3 tablespoons flour
½ cup heavy cream (or more if desired)
Juice of ½ lemon
Salt and freshly ground white pepper
2 tablespoons finely chopped fresh dill

Preparation

1. Peel the raw shrimp, reserving the shells. Dice the shrimp and reserve.

2. In a large saucepan, combine the Fish Stock and shrimp shells and simmer for 30 minutes. Strain the broth and reserve.

3. In another saucepan, melt 3 tablespoons of butter. Add the vegetables and simmer, covered, for 10 or 15 minutes or until they are quite tender.

4. Add all but 2 tablespoons of shrimp, the Fish Stock and Bouquet Garni and bring to a boil. Then lower the heat and simmer for 10 more minutes.

5. Cool the soup. Puree in the blender.

6. Melt the remaining butter in a heavy saucepan. Add the flour and cook without browning for 2 to 3 minutes.

7. Add the pureed soup and stir constantly until it is smooth. Thin it out with the cream. Add the reserved shrimp and simmer for 5 more minutes. You may add more cream according to how you like the soup.

8. Add the lemon juice, salt, pepper and dill.

Remarks

If you serve the soup cold, it may need additional thinning out with cream. Finely diced crabmeat makes an attractive garnish for this soup. Serve it with slices of black bread and sweet butter.

Notes

Crepes toscana

Serves: 6
Preparation time: 45 minutes
Cooking time: 40 minutes

◼ ⚪

The filling in this recipe is a traditional northern Italian ravioli stuffing. But I found it to be a perfect filling for crepes, which are much easier to prepare and somewhat lighter. I decided to combine in this recipe the fine cuisine of France and the peasant cooking of Italy.

Ingredients

1 calf's brain
12 tablespoons sweet butter
10 ounces fresh spinach
Salt
Freshly ground white pepper
Pinch of nutmeg
1 egg
¼ cup freshly grated Parmesan cheese
12 Entree Crepes (page 398)
¼ cup parsley, finely minced
1 teaspoon lemon juice
1 teaspoon finely minced garlic
2 shallots, finely minced
¼ pound fresh medium-sized mushrooms, sliced
Freshly ground black pepper

Preparation

1. Carefully remove the membrane from the calf's brain. Soak the brain in iced water for 1 or 2 hours. Dry it well on paper towels.

2. In a skillet heat 2 tablespoons of butter. Add the calf's brain and saute on both sides over low flame for about 10 minutes. Remove from the flame and reserve.

3. Remove the stems from the spinach and wash it thoroughly under cold running water. Place it in a casserole without water and cook over low heat until the spinach

releases all its juices and it is completely wilted. Remove it from the flame and drain it thoroughly.

4. Pass the spinach together with the calf's brain through a food mill or meat grinder. Season with salt, white pepper and nutmeg.

5. Add the egg and Parmesan and beat until the mixture is thoroughly blended.

6. Place 1 tablespoon of the mixture on each crepe. Roll them up, tucking in the ends, and place them seam side down in a rectangular buttered baking dish.

7. Soften 8 tablespoons of butter at room temperature and beat in the parsley, lemon juice, garlic and shallots. Place bits of this herb butter on top of each crepe and place them in the oven for 25 minutes or until heated through.

8. While the crepes are in the oven melt the remaining butter in a large skillet and saute the mushroom slices for 2 or 3 minutes. Season with salt and black pepper. Shake the pan 2 or 3 times to cover them evenly with butter.

9. Five minutes before you take the crepes out of the oven, sprinkle them with the mushroom slices. Return the pan to the oven for a few more minutes and serve.

Notes

Spaghettini ticino

Serves: 4 to 6
Preparation time: 20 minutes
Cooking time: 25 minutes

Ingredients

¾ pound mushrooms
7 tablespoons sweet butter
2 tablespoons finely minced scallions
  (both white and green parts)
1 small garlic clove, mashed
Salt and freshly ground white pepper
1 cup diced prosciutto
1 pound thin spaghettini (Ronzoni No. 9)
1½ cups heavy cream
½ cup freshly grated Parmesan cheese
Freshly ground black pepper

Preparation

1. Do not wash the mushrooms. Wipe them with a damp paper towel and slice them, reserving the stems for stock or soup.

2. In a large skillet heat 3 tablespoons of butter. When it is hot, add the mushroom slices and cook them without browning for 2 or 3 minutes.

3. Add the onions and garlic and cook the mixture for 2 or 3 minutes. Season with salt and white pepper. Remove from the heat and reserve.

4. In a small skillet, heat 2 tablespoons of butter. Add the prosciutto, cover the skillet and cook for 5 minutes over low heat. Remove from the heat and reserve.

5. In a large casserole bring 4 or 5 quarts of salted water to a boil. Add the spaghettini and cook it over high heat until barely tender (8 to 10 minutes).

6. While the spaghettini is cooking, add the cream to the mushroom mixture and cook it rapidly until the mixture is reduced by ⅓.

7. Lower the heat, add the prosciutto and correct the seasoning. Remove from the heat and reserve.

8. When the spaghettini is done, drain it well. Pour it back into the casserole and add the remaining butter. Pour the mushroom and prosciutto mixture over the spaghettini. Toss lightly and sprinkle with the Parmesan and a good dash of black pepper. Serve immediately.

Notes

Chicken breasts a la bernoise

Serves: 6
Preparation time: 20 minutes
Cooking time: 25 minutes

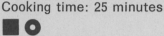

Ingredients

6 chicken breasts (lightly pounded)
½ teaspoon salt
Freshly ground white pepper
1 cup flour
2 eggs, beaten
1½ to 2 cups fresh homemade bread crumbs
4 tablespoons Clarified Butter (page 398)
1½ cups heavy cream
1 Bouquet Garni (page 397)
Juice of 1 lemon
6 slices Swiss cheese

Preparation

1. Preheat the broiler.

2. Season the chicken breasts with salt and pepper. Dredge them in flour, shaking off the excess. Dip them into the beaten eggs, coat the chicken pieces with bread crumbs, place them on a platter and refrigerate for 1 or 2 hours.

3. Melt the Clarified Butter in a large skillet and saute the chicken breasts over medium heat 2 or 3 minutes until they are lightly browned on both sides.

4. Place the chicken breasts in a large buttered baking dish.

5. In a small saucepan, heat the cream together with the Bouquet Garni. Reduce the cream by ¼ and remove it from the heat. Discard the bouquet. Add the lemon juice and season with salt and pepper.

6. Place a slice of Swiss cheese on each chicken breast. Pour the cream around the chicken pieces and place the dish in the oven for 10 to 12 minutes or until the

cheese is completely melted and the sauce bubbles. Serve immediately.

Remarks

If the chicken breasts are sauteed well in advance, the whole dish can be ready for the oven hours ahead of time. Serve whole stuffed mushrooms and the Estouffade of Carrots (page 379) with this dish.

Notes

Poulet a la vasca

Serves: 4 to 6
Preparation time: 15 to 20 minutes
Cooking time: 45 to 50 minutes

This is a dish which originated in northern Spain. It is usually prepared with a local fish called Rape. I found that translating the dish into "chicken" was quite successful. Of course, you must be a garlic lover, but even for those who do not like garlic, the subtle flavor of this dish will come as a surprise.

Ingredients

1   large head of garlic (about 15 cloves)
2   2½-pound chickens, cut into serving
     pieces
Salt and freshly ground white pepper
3   tablespoons sweet butter
1   tablespoon cooking oil
2   cups heavy cream
½ cup dry white wine
1   Bouquet Garni (page 397)
1   tablespoon cornstarch mixed to a paste
     with a little cream

Optional:
1   cup cooked fresh peas
2   tablespoons finely minced parsley

Garnish:
12 small sauteed mushroom caps

Preparation

1. Drop the garlic cloves into fast-boiling water for 1 minute, then drain. The skin will slip right off. Reserve the cloves.

2. Dry the chicken pieces well on paper towels and season with salt and pepper. In a large frying pan, melt the butter and oil. Add the chicken pieces and cook, covered, for 10 minutes over low heat without browning.

3. While the chicken is cooking, heat the cream in a saucepan and reserve.

4. After 10 minutes, add the wine to the frying pan. Bring it to a boil and cook it over high heat until it is almost completely evaporated. Add the cream, garlic and Bouquet Garni. Simmer the chicken, partially covered, for 35 to 40 minutes or until tender. Remove it to a serving platter and keep it warm.

5. Strain the sauce through a fine sieve, pressing down on the garlic cloves to extract all their juice. Return the sauce to the pan, cook it over high heat to reduce it by $1/3$ and whisk in the cornstarch mixture a little at a time. Continue whisking until the sauce is thick and smooth.

6. Pour the sauce over the chicken. Sprinkle with parsley and the optional green peas, and surround with sauteed mushrooms.

Notes

Duck a la martinique

Serves: 4 to 6
Preparation time: 1 hour 15 minutes
Cooking time: 2 hours

■ ●

Several fresh fruits, such as peaches, oranges and cherries, take to duck the way a duck takes to water. The combination of duck and pineapple is somewhat more unusual yet equally harmonious.

Ingredients

2 ducks (4 to 4½ pounds each)
Salt and freshly ground white pepper
1 onion, finely minced
1 carrot, peeled and finely minced
1 large celery stalk, finely minced
1 Bouquet Garni (page 397)
2½ cups Brown Duck Stock (page 405)
2 tablespoons sweet butter
2 tablespoons brown sugar
1 ripe pineapple, peeled, cored and sliced
¼ cup sugar
¼ cup red wine vinegar
1 tablespoon cornstarch
⅓ cup unsweetened pineapple juice
¼ cup cognac
1 Beurre Manie (page 397)

Optional:
2 to 4 tablespoons sweet butter

Preparation

1. Preheat the oven to 350°.

2. Thoroughly dry the ducks with paper towels, both inside and out. Season them with salt and pepper. Truss the ducks and reserve.

3. In a large baking dish, place the minced vegetables and the Bouquet Garni. Place the ducks on their side in the dish. Prick their fatty parts—thighs and the lower breast—and add ½ cup of Brown Duck Stock to the pan. Place the ducks in the

oven and roast for 1 hour and 45 minutes, turning them once. Do not baste them. If the vegetables seem about to burn, add a little more stock to the pan. With a bulb baster, remove some of the accumulated fat from the pan several times during the roasting time.

4. In a large skillet, heat the butter and brown sugar. When the mixture is very hot and the sugar is dissolved, add the pineapple slices, a few at a time, and saute them on both sides until they are lightly browned. Place on a plate and reserve.

5. To make the sauce: In a heavy saucepan, combine the sugar and vinegar. Cook over low heat until the mixture becomes a caramel-colored syrup. Immediately add 1½ cups of stock to the caramel and bring the mixture to a boil.

6. Reduce the heat. Mix the cornstarch and pineapple juice and beat the mixture into the sauce. Cook until it becomes thick and glossy.

7. Keep the sauce warm over very low heat.

8. When the ducks are done, transfer them to a baking sheet and return them to the oven.

9. Place the roasting pan over high heat. Cook the pan juices for 2 or 3 minutes and then carefully remove the remaining fat from the pan, reserving the dark coagulated juices.

10. Add the cognac to the pan with 1 cup of stock. Bring the mixture to a boil, scraping the bottom of the pan well and reducing the pan juices to ½ cup. Strain the pan juices into the prepared sauce.

11. Beat the Beurre Manie into the sauce and correct the seasoning, adding a good dash of white pepper. Enrich the sauce with the optional butter.

12. Turn the broiler on and run the ducks under it to crisp their skin. Remove them to a serving platter. Carve them into four pieces each and spoon a little sauce over them.

13. Garnish the platter with the sauteed pineapple slices, spoon the remaining sauce over the fruit and serve.

Remarks

The sauce can be started several hours ahead and finished an hour before serving. Keep the duck warm in the oven for 30 to 45 minutes. You may heat the pineapple slices in the sauce instead of sauteeing them. They will, however, thin out your sauce a little and the slices will turn a little sour if they are brought to a boil. The sauteed pineapple slices may be kept warm in the oven together with the ducks. The pineapple leaf tops should be reserved to garnish each end of the serving platter.

Notes

Stuffed guinea hen menagere

Serves: 4
Preparation time: 45 to 50 minutes
Cooking time: 1 hour to 1 hour 15 minutes

■ ◆

A guinea hen is a delicious little bird that requires short cooking and makes an excellent meal for two. It has been completely domesticated in the United States and has, therefore, no "gamey" flavor to speak of. It is important to keep the meat of the guinea hen moist. If you cannot get guinea hens, you may use squabs.

Ingredients

2 guinea hens (2 to 2½ pounds)
1 teaspoon crushed juniper berries
1 to 2 teaspoons cognac
Pinch of powdered thyme
Pinch of rosemary
½ cup olive oil
4 to 6 large slices blanched bacon
4 tablespoons sweet butter
2 medium-sized onions, cut in half
1½ to 2 cups hot Brown Chicken Stock
    (page 404)

The stuffing:
4 tablespoons sweet butter
3 tablespoons scallions, finely minced
4 large chicken livers, cleaned and cut into
    small cubes
Salt and freshly ground white pepper
Pinch of nutmeg
2 cups mushrooms, finely minced
4 tablespoons cream cheese
2 eggs
1 garlic clove, mashed
2 tablespoons minced parsley
½ to ¾ cup unseasoned white bread
    crumbs
1 teaspoon cornstarch mixed with a little
    stock

Optional:
2 tablespoons sweet butter

Garnish:
Sprigs of watercress

Preparation

1. Preheat the oven to 350°.

2. Place the guinea hens in a porcelain or enamel dish. Rub the cavities with the juniper berries, cognac, thyme and rosemary. Sprinkle them with olive oil and marinate for 1 or 2 hours. Wipe the guinea hens well with paper towels.

3. To make the stuffing: In a skillet melt 2 tablespoons of butter. Add the scallions and the chicken livers. Season the mixture with salt, pepper and nutmeg, and cook over high heat until nicely browned.

4. Remove the chicken livers and scallions to a bowl and add 2 more tablespoons of butter to the pan. Quickly saute the mushrooms until they are lightly browned. Add them to the bowl.

5. Add the cream cheese, eggs, garlic and parsley to the bowl and blend the mixture well with a wooden spoon.

6. Add enough bread crumbs to make a thick stuffing. It should not be dry.

7. Correct the seasoning and fill the cavities of the guinea hens with the stuffing. Truss the birds. Season with salt and pepper.

8. Cover the breast of each bird with 2 slices of blanched bacon and tie it in place with kitchen string.

9. In a large flameproof baking dish, melt 4 tablespoons of butter. Place the guinea hens in the baking dish and place the onion

halves around them. Cover the dish with foil and set it in the oven. Roast the guinea hens for 1 hour, basting them every 10 minutes with the hot Chicken Stock. After 40 minutes, remove the bacon slices and continue basting the birds. When they are done (the juices must run pale yellow when the birds are tested with a fork), remove them to a serving platter.

10. Degrease the sauce and place the baking dish on top of the stove.

11. Remove the onions, raise the heat and add the remaining stock. Stir in a little of the cornstarch mixture and cook the sauce until it heavily coats a spoon.

12. Remove the pan from the heat and beat in the optional butter. Correct the seasoning, spoon a little of the sauce over the birds and serve the rest on the side.

13. Garnish the guinea hens with fresh watercress and tomatoes.

Notes

Filet of beef en casserole
Serves: 6
Preparation time: 45 minutes
Cooking time: 1 hour 50 minutes

The idea that a roasted filet of beef is automatically elegant and tasty has always mystified me. The cut is certainly expensive and tender, but because of its blandness extra care and preparation are needed

Ingredients

7 tablespoons sweet butter
1 onion, thinly sliced
1 carrot, thinly sliced
1 small celery stalk, sliced
2 whole garlic cloves
½ ounce imported dried mushrooms, diced (plus fresh mushroom stems)
2 cups Brown Stock (page 403)
1 tablespoon cooking oil
3- to 3½-pound filet of beef
Salt and freshly ground black pepper
1 large thin piece of pork fat or 6 slices of blanched bacon
¼ cup Scotch whisky
1 large Bouquet Garni (page 397)
2 tablespoons finely chopped shallots
½ pound fresh mushrooms (whole button mushrooms or larger ones, quartered)
Freshly ground white pepper
1 or 2 Beurre Manies (page 397)
2 to 4 tablespoons cold sweet butter

Preparation

1. Preheat the oven to 375°.

2. In a saucepan melt 2 tablespoons of butter. Add the onion, carrot, celery and garlic. Cook over low heat for 5 minutes until the vegetables are soft but not browned.

3. Add the diced dried mushrooms and Brown Stock. Cover the saucepan and simmer the mixture for 1 hour.

4. In a casserole, heat 3 tablespoons of butter and the oil. When very hot, add the filet and brown it well on all sides over medium heat. Remove it to a side dish. Season it with salt and pepper. Tie the pork fat or bacon slices around the filet. Remove all but 2 tablespoons of the fat.

5. Pour the Scotch, warmed, into the casserole. Ignite and when flames have subsided, scrape the bottom of the pan well. Reduce the whisky to 1 to 2 tablespoons.

6. Return the filet to the casserole, with the Bouquet Garni, and pour the stock and vegetable mixture around it. Cover the casserole and place in the oven for 45 to 50 minutes.

7. While the beef is braising, melt the remaining butter in a small skillet. Add the shallots and cook for 2 or 3 minutes without browning.

8. Add the fresh mushrooms and cook over high heat until they are lightly browned. Remove them from the heat, season with salt and white pepper. Reserve.

9. When the meat is done, remove it to a serving platter. Remove the pork fat or bacon slices and keep the filet warm while making the sauce.

10. Strain the pan juices through a fine sieve. Press down on the vegetables to extract as much of their juices as possible. Carefully degrease the sauce. Return it to the casserole and cook over high heat to reduce it by ⅓.

11. Add the Beurre Manie bit by bit until the sauce reaches the consistency of heavy cream and coats a spoon heavily.

Off the heat beat in the cold butter.

12. Add the mushrooms and cook the sauce for 2 or 3 more minutes.

13. Slice the filet into ½-inch-thick slices, then spoon a little of the mushroom sauce over the meat and serve the remaining sauce on the side.

Remarks

Braised endives are a delicious accompaniment to this dish. Place them in a buttered baking dish and braise them in 1 cup of Brown Stock and 2 tablespoons of butter for 40 minutes.

Notes

Filet of beef helsinki

Serves: 4 to 6
Preparation time: 30 minutes
Cooking time: 15 to 20 minutes

Here is a dish that is somewhat like the famous Stroganoff but with a touch of Scandinavian flavor. It demands last-minute preparation to ensure the right texture and taste.

Ingredients

1 teaspoon dry mustard
1 teaspoon Dijon mustard
½ cup cold water
Pinch of sugar
2 tablespoons flour
1 cup Creme Fraiche (page 398), or 1 cup heavy cream
½ pound fresh mushrooms
6 tablespoons sweet butter
Salt and freshly ground white pepper
1 tablespoon vegetable oil
2 pounds tenderloin strips, 2 inches long, 1 inch thick
¾ cup finely minced scallions (white part only)
1 teaspoon minced garlic
½ cup Concentrated Brown Stock (page 403)
2 tablespoons finely minced dill
Freshly ground black pepper

Preparation

1. In a small bowl combine the dry mustard and Dijon mustard with the water and sugar. Let the mixture stand for 30 minutes to develop flavor.

2. Add the flour and blend it well with the mustard.

3. Add the Creme Fraiche and reserve.

4. Clean the mushrooms with a damp paper towel. Reserve the stems for soup or stock and then slice the mushrooms thinly.

5. Melt 2 tablespoons of butter in a small skillet. When it is hot, add the mushrooms and season with salt and pepper. Cook the mushrooms over high heat for 2 or 3 minutes and reserve.

6. In a heavy 12-inch skillet, melt the remaining butter with the oil. When very hot, saute the tenderloin strips, a few at a time, over very high heat. Do not crowd your pan. The strips have to saute quickly so as to remain a little rare on the inside. As they are done, remove them from the skillet and reserve. Continue sauteeing until all the meat is done. Season it with salt and pepper.

7. Add the scallions and garlic to the skillet and cook over medium heat until they are soft but not browned.

8. Add the Brown Stock and reduce it by ⅓.

9. Pour the cream and mustard mixture into the skillet and cook the sauce until it is thick enough to coat a spoon heavily.

10. Return the steak strips to the skillet, add dill and the sauteed mushrooms. Shake the pan to cover the strips evenly with the sauce. Do not cook anymore, for the meat must not be overdone.

11. Taste for seasoning and add a dash of black pepper. Serve right out of the pan or pour into a serving dish.

Remarks

Dry dill cannot be used for this dish. If you cannot get fresh dill, which is grown in hothouses all year round, omit it.

Calves' liver in mustard and caper sauce

Serves: 4 to 6
Preparation time: 25 minutes
Cooking time: 8 to 10 minutes

■ ●

When you start your winter meal with a hearty soup, sauteed calves' liver accompanied by a garniture of seasonal vegetables, such as sauteed Brussels sprouts or mushrooms, will make an excellent main course.

The liver requires last-minute preparation, but since it takes only a few minutes it is certainly worth the effort.

Ingredients

1 teaspoon dry hot mustard
4 tablespoons sweet butter, softened
1 teaspoon Dijon mustard
6 slices of calves' liver, cut ½ inch thick
Salt and freshly ground white pepper
Flour for dredging
3 tablespoons sweet butter
1 tablespoon cooking oil
2 tablespoons minced shallots
½ cup dry white wine
1 cup Concentrated Brown Stock (page 403)
½ cup heavy cream
1 to 2 tablespoons capers

Garnish:
3 tablespoons minced parsley

Preparation

1. Dissolve the dry mustard in 1 tablespoon of water and let it stand for 10 minutes to develop flavor.

2. In a small mixing bowl combine the softened butter with the Dijon mustard and dry mustard mixture. Blend the mixture thoroughly with a wooden spoon and reserve.

3. Season the liver slices with salt and pepper and dredge them lightly in flour, shaking off the excess.

4. Heat the 3 tablespoons of butter with the oil in a large heavy 12-inch skillet, or better use two skillets at the same time. When the butter and oil are very hot, saute the calves' liver on both sides until well browned. The center should still be pink. Test one slice by cutting a tiny slit in it with a very sharp knife.

5. When the liver is done, remove it to a serving platter and keep it warm.

6. Remove all but 2 tablespoons of fat from the skillet. Add the shallots and the wine and cook the mixture over high heat (scraping well the coagulated cooking juices) until the wine is reduced to 3 tablespoons.

7. Add the Brown Stock and cream and continue cooking the sauce over high heat until it is reduced by ⅓.

8. Remove the skillet from the heat and beat in the mustard butter, whisking the sauce until it is well blended. Add the capers and correct the seasoning.

9. Pour the sauce over the calves' liver and sprinkle with the minced parsley. Serve immediately.

Remarks

Chicken livers can be prepared in the same manner and served on top of a Parmesan-flavored risotto.

Lamb chops en cocotte

Serves: 4
Preparation time: 25 minutes
Cooking time: 45 minutes

Here is a change from the usual broiled lamb chops—a French country dish that is both hearty and flavorful. Serve it with a well-seasoned salad and a Broccoli Puree (page 334).

Ingredients

6   tablespoons sweet butter
1   tablespoon cooking oil
8   loin lamb chops, cut ¾ inch to 1 inch thick
Salt and freshly ground white pepper
4   onions, sliced
2   pounds new potatoes, peeled and sliced
1   teaspoon thyme
2   tablespoons finely chopped parsley
2   garlic cloves, finely minced
2   bay leaves
1   cup Concentrated Brown Stock (page 403)

Preparation

1. Preheat oven to 375°.

2. In a large skillet melt 4 tablespoons butter together with the oil. When very hot, add the chops, a few at a time, and quickly brown them on each side. It is better to use two pans than to crowd the skillet. Remove the chops and season them with salt and pepper.

3. Discard all but 1 tablespoon of fat from the skillet. Add the remaining butter. When it is hot, add the onions and saute them until they are soft but not browned.

4. While the onions are cooking, drop the potato slices into boiling water. Cook them for 5 minutes and drain them on paper towels.

5. Butter a large baking dish and place a layer of potatoes on the bottom. Top it with a layer of onions seasoned with salt and pepper. Place the chops on the onions and sprinkle them with thyme, parsley, garlic, and bay leaves. Cover with another layer of onions and finish with the potatoes. Season with salt and pepper again and pour the Brown Stock around the chops.

6. Cover the baking dish with foil and bake for 35 to 40 minutes or until the potatoes are quite tender and most of the stock has been absorbed. Uncover the dish for the last 5 minutes of cooking to brown the top layer of potatoes. Serve directly from the baking dish.

Remarks

Anchovies go extremely well with lamb and this dish changes character completely with the addition of 4 anchovies, finely minced, and added to the parsely and garlic mixture.

Notes

Roast lamb duchesse

Serves: 6
Preparation time: 25 minutes
Cooking time: 2 hours 30 minutes

This is a wonderful country recipe usually prepared with a very small young leg of lamb, which is braised rather than roasted. Since this kind of lamb is not available in the United States, I have adapted the recipe to the roasting method. This dish is usually served with a puree of potatoes highly flavored with garlic and fresh herbs, but you can substitute or add other seasonal fresh vegetables such as broccoli or Brussels sprouts.

Ingredients

1   4-pound leg or shoulder of lamb, boned and rolled
Salt and freshly ground white pepper
2   garlic cloves, mashed
1   teaspoon marjoram
Flour
3   tablespoons sweet butter
1   tablespoon oil
2 to 2½ cups Lamb Stock (page 406), or Brown Stock (page 403)
1   carrot, scraped and left whole
2   whole celery stalks with tops
2   whole onions
1   large Bouquet Garni (page 397)
1½ pounds small white turnips, peeled and quartered, or cut into ovals
1   Beurre Manie (page 397)

Garnish:
Watercress

Preparation

1. Preheat oven to 375°.

2. Dry the lamb well with paper towels.

3. Season the lamb with salt, pepper, garlic and marjoram. Sprinkle it with flour.

4. Heat the butter and oil in a large baking dish and brown the roast on all sides. Remove the lamb from the baking dish and pour out all but 2 tablespoons of the fat. Add 1 cup of stock, bring it to a boil, scraping the brown particles from the bottom of the pan.

5. Return the roast to the dish together with the carrot, celery stalks and onions. Bury the Bouquet Garni among the vegetables. Cover well with foil. Place the dish in the oven and roast the meat for 1 hour and 30 minutes, basting it with additional stock (1 cup) every 10 minutes.

6. While the roast is in the oven, drop the turnips into boiling water for 5 minutes and drain. Add them to the pan and continue roasting the lamb for 30 more minutes.

7. Remove the roast to a carving board. Let it rest for 10 minutes.

8. With a slotted spoon remove the turnips to a serving platter. Strain the pan juices, discarding the vegetables and the Bouquet.

9. Add the remaining stock and reduce the sauce over very high heat, adding the Beurre Manie, bit by bit, until the sauce heavily coats a spoon. Correct the seasoning.

10. Carve the lamb into thin slices and place them in a center row on the serving platter. Surround with turnips and garnish with watercress. Spoon some of the sauce over the lamb. Serve the rest on the side in a sauceboat.

Pork medallions with fennel butter

Serves: 4 to 6
Preparation time: 20 minutes
Cooking time: 50 minutes

Ingredients

18 filet of pork medallions, cut ¾ inch thick,
   or 6 to 12 boned loin pork chops
2 tablespoons fennel seed, crushed in a
    mortar and pestle
Salt and freshly ground white pepper
Flour for dredging
3 tablespoons sweet butter
2 tablespoons oil
Juice of 1 lemon
1½ cups Brown Stock (page 403)
1 Beurre Manie (page 397)
½ cup heavy cream
Freshly ground black pepper

The fennel butter:
4 tablespoons sweet butter, softened
1 garlic clove, mashed
2 tablespoons finely minced fennel leaves

Preparation

1. Preheat the oven to 325°. Butter a large flameproof baking dish and set it aside.

2. Roll each medallion in the fennel seeds.

3. Season the medallions with salt and pepper and dredge them lightly in flour, shaking off the excess.

4. In a heavy 12-inch skillet melt the butter and oil. When very hot, add the medallions, a few at a time and brown them on both sides. Remove the browned medallions to the buttered baking dish and reserve.

5. Add ½ the lemon juice to the pan and 1 cup Brown Stock. Bring to a boil, scraping the bottom of the pan well. Reduce the liquid by ⅓ and pour it over the medallions.

6. Cover the dish with foil and place in the middle part of the oven. Braise the medallions for 25 to 30 minutes.

7. While the medallions are cooking, combine the softened butter with the garlic and fennel leaves and chill.

8. When the meat is done, remove it with a slotted spoon to a serving dish.

9. Place the baking dish over high heat, add the remaining stock and reduce the sauce by ¼; adding a little Beurre Manie until the sauce reaches the consistency of heavy cream.

10. Add the remaining lemon juice and the cream. Continue cooking the sauce for 2 or 3 minutes. Correct the seasoning, adding a good dash of black pepper.

11. When the sauce is done, remove the baking dish from the heat and beat in the fennel butter. As soon as the butter has melted, spoon the sauce over the pork medallions and serve with White Bean Puree (page 341).

Notes

Roast pork a la canelle

Serves: 6
Preparation time: 1 hour
Cooking time: 3 hours

Ingredients

The cabbage:
2 tablespoons sweet butter
1 onion, minced
1 tablespoon sugar
1 cup Brown Stock (page 403)
2 pounds red cabbage, finely shredded
Salt and freshly ground white pepper
2 tablespoons red wine vinegar
2 cloves
3 tart apples, peeled, cored and quartered
½ to 1 tablespoon lemon juice
2 tablespoons cooking oil
2 tablespoons flour

The roast:
1 3-pound boneless loin of pork
Salt and freshly ground white pepper
1 teaspoon cinnamon
2 garlic cloves
½ teaspoon powdered rosemary
2 tablespoons sweet butter
2 tablespoons olive oil
1 minced onion
1 minced carrot
1 celery stalk, minced
¾ cup white wine
1 cup Brown Stock (page 403)
1 Beurre Manie (page 397)
1 large Bouquet Garni (page 397)

Optional:
12 to 18 chestnuts, peeled and boiled in
    stock until almost tender
6 Baked Apples (page 346)

Preparation

The cabbage:
1. Preheat the oven to 350°.

2. In a large casserole melt 2 tablespoons of butter. Add the minced onion and cook until it is very soft but not browned. Add the sugar and cook the mixture until the sugar is lightly caramelized.

3. Add ½ cup of Brown Stock. Bring it to a boil and add the shredded cabbage, salt, pepper, vinegar and cloves. Cover the casserole, place it in the oven and cook for 2 hours, stirring from time to time.

4. After 2 hours, add the quartered apples and the optional chestnuts. Cover the casserole again and simmer the cabbage for 1 hour longer. Correct the seasoning. It may need a little more sugar and a dash of lemon juice to give it the right sweet and sour taste.

5. In a small saucepan heat the cooking oil. Add the flour and cook until it turns a light nutty brown. Add the remaining ½ cup of stock. Bring it to a boil and add to the cabbage. Cook for 10 more minutes and reserve.

The roast:
6. While the cabbage is cooking, dry the meat thoroughly on paper towels and season it with salt, pepper and cinnamon.

7. Cut the garlic cloves into tiny slivers, roll them in the powdered rosemary and insert them into the roast.

8. Heat the butter and olive oil in a large casserole. Saute the roast in it over medium heat until nicely browned on all sides. Remove the roast to a side dish.

9. Add the vegetables and cook until they are tender but not browned.

10. Return the meat to the casserole together with the wine, ½ cup of stock and

the Bouquet Garni. Bring the liquid to a boil, cover the casserole and place it in the oven. Cook the roast without basting for 1 hour.

11. After 1 hour, uncover the roast and baste it every 10 minutes for 1 hour.

12. When the roast is done, cut into thin slices, place it on a serving platter and surround it with the red cabbage.

13. Degrease the pan juices. Strain the sauce through a fine sieve pressing down well on the vegetables to extract all their juice.

14. Discard the Bouquet and add the remaining stock. Bring the sauce to a boil and thicken it with bits of Beurre Manie. You may not need a whole "ball," for the sauce should just be thick enough to coat a spoon. Correct the seasoning and spoon the sauce over the meat and serve the optional baked apples on the side.

Remarks

The cabbage will be more flavorful if it is prepared a day ahead of time and reheated in the oven while the roast is cooking.

Notes

Roast of pork vouvray

Serves: 6 to 8
Preparation time: 35 minutes
Cooking time: 2 hours 15 minutes

Ingredients

¾ cup white wine (preferably Vouvray)
2 dozen pitted prunes
1 3½- to 4-pound boned loin of pork
Salt and freshly ground white pepper
3 to 6 tablespoons sweet butter
2 tablespoons oil
1 cup Brown Stock (page 403)
1 Bouquet Garni (page 397)
¾ cup heavy cream
2 tablespoons currant jelly
1 teaspoon lemon juice
1 tablespoon cornstarch mixed with
  1 tablespoon stock

Optional:
2 to 4 tablespoons sweet butter
1 teaspoon orange rind

Preparation

1. In a bowl combine the wine and the prunes and marinate for 2 to 4 hours at room temperature.

2. Preheat the oven to 375°.

3. With a sharp knife make a pocket in the pork by cutting a slit the length of the roast to within 1 inch from each end. Stuff the loin with 8 to 10 prunes. Sew up the opening and tie with kitchen string at 1-inch intervals. Season the loin with salt and pepper.

4. Melt the butter and oil in a large casserole. When hot, brown the loin evenly on all sides over medium heat. As soon as it is well browned, remove it from the casserole.

5. If the fat in the pan is burned, discard it and add 3 tablespoons of fresh butter to

Steak a la polonaise

Serves: 2 to 4
Preparation time: 10 minutes
Cooking time: 10 minutes

■ ◕

the casserole. Add the Brown Stock and bring it to a boil.

6. Drain the wine from the prunes and add it to the casserole.

7. Bring the liquid to a boil and return the loin to the pan together with the Bouquet Garni. Cover the casserole tightly and place in the oven.

8. Roast the loin for 1 hour and 45 minutes to 2 hours. When it is done, remove it to a baking sheet.

9. Place the roast under the broiler for 5 minutes while you finish the sauce. Watch the meat carefully so it does not burn.

10. Degrease the pan juices. Place the casserole on top of the stove and reduce the juices over high heat by 1/3.

11. Add the cream and currant jelly and continue cooking until the jelly is completely dissolved.

12. Correct the seasoning. Add the lemon juice and the remaining prunes. The sauce should have a sweet and sour taste.

13. Whisk the cornstarch into the sauce and cook until the sauce heavily coats a spoon.

14. Remove the casserole from the heat and beat in the optional cold butter and orange rind.

15. Remove the roast from the broiler and slice it thinly, placing slices on a platter. Slice just enough for 1 serving per person and leave the rest to be carved later as pork has a tendency to dry. Coat the slices with the sauce and prunes and serve the rest of the sauce in a sauceboat.

A pan-fried steak with sauteed mushrooms takes only a few minutes to prepare and the result is both elegant and delicious. If you are making the dish for more than two people, work with two skillets at the same time, finishing the sauce in one skillet. Potatoes Aioli (page 383) make an excellent accompaniment to these steaks.

Ingredients

4 tablespoons Clarified Butter (page 398)
2 to 4 shell steaks, cut 3/4 inch thick
2 to 4 tablespoons sweet butter
1/2 pound mushrooms, quartered
3 tablespoons minced shallots
Salt and freshly ground black pepper
2 tablespoons cognac
1 cup Concentrated Brown Stock (page 403)

Optional:
1 Beurre Manie (page 397)

Garnish:
Stewed Italian Tomatoes (page 386)

Preparation

1. Heat the Clarified Butter in a large skillet. When it is very hot, almost smoking, add the steaks and cook them for 4 minutes on each side.

2. While the steaks are cooking, melt 2 tablespoons of butter in another skillet. Add the mushrooms and cook them over high heat until they are lightly browned.

3. Add the shallots and cook for 2 more minutes until they are soft but not browned. Season with salt and pepper and reserve.

4. When the steaks are done, remove them

to a serving platter and season with salt and pepper.

5. Pour out all but 1 tablespoon of fat from the steak skillet. If the butter has burned, discard it and replace it with 2 tablespoons butter.

6. Add the cognac and cook until it is almost entirely evaporated.

7. Scrape the bottom of the skillet, add the Brown Stock and reduce it over high heat until it lightly coats a spoon.

8. Add the mushrooms to the sauce. Simmer for 2 more minutes and beat in the optional Beurre Manie, bit by bit, until the sauce heavily coats a spoon. Correct the seasoning and pour the sauce over the steaks. Garnish the platter with watercress and stewed Italian tomatoes.

Remarks
Filet steaks can be substituted for the shell steaks.

Notes

Scallops of veal vaudoise
Serves: 6
Preparation time: 35 minutes
Cooking time: 40 minutes

This is a recipe with a touch of Italy, France and Switzerland, all combined into one rich and lovely dish. The meat should be of excellent quality, but even lesser veal will be tender and tasty due to the final baking.

Ingredients

½ pound fresh mushrooms
7 tablespoons sweet butter
1 tablespoon finely minced shallots
2 tablespoons heavy cream
Salt and freshly ground white pepper
12 very thin squares veal scallops, cut ¼ inch thick
6 thin slices cooked ham
Flour for dredging (about 2 tablespoons)
2 tablespoons cooking oil
6 thin slices Gruyere or imported Swiss cheese

The sauce:
1½ cups heavy cream
1 Bouquet Garni (page 397)
Juice of ½ lemon

Preparation

1. Preheat the oven to 375°.

2. Wipe the mushrooms with wet paper towels. Remove the stems and reserve for stock. Slice ¼ pound of mushrooms and reserve. Mince the remaining ¼ pound and set aside.

3. Heat 2 tablespoons of butter in a small skillet. Add the minced mushrooms and shallots and cook them over high heat until lightly browned. Add the cream and continue cooking the mixture for 3 minutes until the moisture has evaporated.

4. Season the above mixture with salt and pepper, and puree it.

5. Season the veal with salt and pepper. Place a little of the mushroom puree on 6 of the slices and top with a slice of ham. Top each with another slice of veal and pound the edges with a cleaver to seal them or seal with toothpicks. Dredge the veal "cases" lightly in flour, shaking off the excess.

6. Heat 3 tablespoons of butter and the cooking oil in a large skillet. Saute the veal cases over medium heat 3 to 5 minutes until they are lightly browned on both sides. Carefully transfer them to a buttered rectangular baking dish and reserve.

7. For the sauce, simmer the 1½ cups of cream together with the Bouquet Garni over low heat for 5 minutes. Remove the Bouquet, season the cream with salt and pepper, and add the lemon juice.

8. Top each veal case with one slice of cheese. Pour the lemon cream around the veal. Place the dish in the oven and bake for 25 to 30 minutes or until the cheese is melted and the sauce is bubbly and lightly reduced.

9. While the veal is baking, melt the remaining butter in the small skillet and quickly saute the sliced mushrooms over high heat for 2 or 3 minutes, or until lightly browned. Season with salt and pepper.

10. When the veal is done, sprinkle with the sliced mushrooms and serve immediately.

Roast veal in lemon sauce

Serves: 6 to 8
Preparation time: 45 minutes
Cooking time: 2 hours

■ ✛

A well-flavored veal roast is an elegant dish suitable for a small dinner party. It demands top-quality veal and excellent stock.

Ingredients

1 boned veal roast (3 to 4 pounds)
Salt and freshly ground white pepper
Paprika
Marjoram
2 garlic cloves, finely mashed
4 tablespoons sweet butter
2 to 4 tablespoons oil
5 medium onions, finely sliced
2 teaspoons sugar
Juice of 1½ lemons
½ cup dry white wine
1¼ cups Brown Stock (page 403)
1 Bouquet Garni (page 397)
1 cup diced prosciutto
1 tablespoon cornstarch mixed with a little Brown Stock
2 to 3 tablespoons minced parsley

Optional:
1 teaspoon meat glaze

Preparation

1. Preheat the oven to 350°.

2. Dry the meat thoroughly with paper towels. Season with salt, white pepper, paprika, marjoram and garlic.

3. In a large casserole, heat the butter and oil.

4. When the butter and oil are very hot, brown the veal roast on all sides over medium heat. Remove it from the pan.

5. If the fat has burned, discard it and add more butter. Add the onions and cook them

until they are lightly browned. Add the sugar and continue cooking the onions until they are well glazed. Do not burn them.

6. Add the optional meat glaze, ⅔ of the lemon juice and the wine. Bring to a boil and over high heat reduce the liquid by ⅓.

7. Add the Brown Stock and return the veal roast to the casserole. Add the Bouquet Garni, cover the casserole with foil and place it in the oven. Roast the veal for 1 hour and 30 minutes to 1 hour and 45 minutes.

8. Remove the roast to a serving platter and keep it warm while finishing the sauce.

9. Place the casserole over high heat. Add the remaining lemon juice and the pros-ciutto.

10. Heat the prosciutto through and add just enough of the cornstarch mixture to thicken the sauce. It should coat a spoon heavily.

11. Add the parsley to the sauce and cor-rect the seasoning. Slice the veal. Place the slices on a serving platter. Spoon the the sauce over them and serve.

Remarks

You may substitute for the minced pros-ciutto ¼ pound of button mushrooms sauteed in 2 tablespoons of butter until they are nicely browned. Add them to the sauce together with the minced parsley.

Veal scallops
a la fermiere

Serves: 4 to 6
Preparation time: 35 minutes
Cooking time: 50 minutes

Here is a simple dish that can easily be part of a year-round repertory. It is prefer-able to use carrots with greens attached, but fresh, packaged, trimmed carrots will do. Other vegetables such as turnip balls or small white onions can be added to the dish for a variation.

Ingredients

2 to 3 medium-sized carrots
12 veal scallops, cut ⅛ inch thick
Salt and freshly ground white pepper
Flour for dredging
5 tablespoons sweet butter
2 tablespoons oil
3 tablespoons finely minced scallions
  (white part only)
1 tablespoon sugar
1 cup Chicken Stock (page 404)
½ pound mushrooms, quartered, stems
  removed
1 teaspoon lemon juice
4 tablespoons Creme Fraiche (page 398),
  or ½ cup heavy cream
1 Beurre Manie (page 397)

Preparation

1. Preheat the oven to 350°.

2. Peel the carrots with a vegetable peeler. Slice them lengthwise and cut them into 1- to 1½-inch-long matchsticks. (If pack-aged carrots are used, first remove the hard core, which is often woody and tough.) Drop the carrots into boiling water for 8 minutes. Drain and reserve.

3. Dry the veal well on paper towels. Season with salt and pepper and dredge lightly in flour, shaking off the excess.

4. In a large skillet heat 3 tablespoons of butter and the oil. When very hot, brown the veal on both sides and remove it to a buttered baking dish.

5. Add the scallions to the skillet and cook until they are soft but not browned.

6. Add the carrots and sprinkle them with sugar and salt. Shake the pan and lightly glaze the carrots for 2 or 3 minutes.

7. Add the Chicken Stock. Bring it to a boil, scraping the bottom of the pan well. Pour the mixture over the veal. Cover the baking dish with foil and set in the oven. Braise the veal and vegetables for 30 minutes.

8. While the veal is cooking, melt the remaining butter in a small skillet. Add the mushrooms, salt, pepper and lemon juice and quickly brown the mushrooms, shaking the pan. Reserve.

9. When the veal is ready, remove it to a warm serving platter.

10. With a slotted spoon, remove the carrots and place them around the veal.

11. Place the pan over high heat and reduce the pan juices for 2 or 3 minutes.

12. Add the Creme Fraiche and continue cooking the sauce over high heat. It should heavily coat a spoon. If it seems to lack the right consistency, beat in the Beurre Manie.

13. Add the mushrooms to the skillet and just heat through. Remove from the heat, correct the seasoning and pour the sauce over the veal slices. Serve immediately.

Remarks

If the carrots are not tender enough after braising, continue cooking them for a few minutes in the sauce before reducing it. Veal chops can be prepared in the same manner but should be braised for 45 minutes.

Notes

Coquilles saint-jacques a la lyonnaise

Serves: 4 to 6
Preparation time: 40 minutes
Cooking time: 1 hour

■ ◕

Without doubt fresh Long Island bay scallops deserve the most elaborate preparation. Here is a lovely winter dish, elegant and subtle in taste. Follow it with a simple roast veal and a light dessert. You can serve this also as a main course, accompanied by buttered rice and followed by an endive salad.

Ingredients

1   cup dry white wine
1   cup water
1   large Bouquet Garni (page 397)
1   onion, stuck with a clove
1   teaspoon salt
6   crushed peppercorns
1½ pounds bay scallops

The sauce:
2   egg yolks
¾ cup heavy cream
2   teaspoons Dijon mustard
½ teaspoon dry mustard
3   tablespoons sweet butter
3   tablespoons flour
Dash of lemon juice
2   tablespoons cold sweet butter

The vegetables:
2   tablespoons sweet butter
2   small carrots, cut into 1½-inch-long matchsticks
2   leeks, white part only, cut into 1½-inch-long matchsticks
2   small tender celery stalks, cut into 1½-inch-long matchsticks
4   large mushrooms, stems removed (reserve for stock), cut into matchsticks
½ cup dry white wine
Salt and freshly ground white pepper

Preparation

1. For the sauce, combine in a small mixing bowl the yolks, cream and both mustards. Whisk the mixture until well blended and then reserve.

2. Melt 2 tablespoons of butter in a heavy skillet. Add the carrots, leeks and celery. Cover the pan and simmer the vegetables until they are tender but not falling apart.

3. Add the mushrooms and ½ cup of white wine. Let the mixture come to a boil and cook, uncovered, over high heat until the wine has completely evaporated. Season lightly with salt and pepper and reserve.

4. While the vegetables are cooking, combine in a 3-quart enamel saucepan 1 cup of wine, water, Bouquet Garni, onion, 1 teaspoon of salt and the peppercorns. Bring the mixture to a boil, reduce the heat and simmer, covered, for 30 minutes.

5. Add the scallops, cover the saucepan and simmer for 5 minutes. Remove the scallops with a slotted spoon and keep them warm.

6. Strain the broth into another saucepan and reduce to 1 cup.

7. Melt 3 tablespoons of butter in a heavy saucepan. Add the flour and cook for 3 minutes without browning, stirring constantly. Add the hot scallop broth all at once and whisk constantly until the sauce is smooth and thick. Correct the seasoning and add the lemon juice. Cook the sauce over very low heat for 20 minutes.

8. Add the cream and egg yolk mixture. Heat the sauce but do not let it come to a boil or it will curdle.

Risotto of scampi

Serves: 8
Preparation time: 20 minutes
Cooking time: 35 minutes

■ ◑

9. Remove the sauce from the heat, beat in the cold butter, add the stewed vegetables and correct the seasoning. Pour the sauce over the scallops and serve at once.

Remarks

The dish may be garnished with additional finely sliced mushrooms sauteed in butter and a few thin carrot matchsticks also sauteed in butter.
Poach the scallops well in advance and keep them warm over a pan of hot water. When making the coquilles in the late spring, add 1 tablespoon of finely minced fresh herbs such as chives, chervil, and tarragon to the vegetable mixture.

Notes

A good risotto makes an excellent appetizer or even a main course. I often serve this one accompanied by a fresh spinach salad for a simple dinner. The secret of a good risotto is the quality of the rice, which should remain creamy with the grains retaining their shape. Risotto cannot be made with converted rice.

Ingredients

4 to 5 cups Fish Stock (page 406)
8 tablespoons sweet butter
1 small onion, finely minced
2 cups Italian or Carolina rice
½ cup dry white wine
1 large Bouquet Garni (page 397)
2 tablespoons olive oil
1 pound small fresh shrimp, raw and peeled
Salt and freshly ground white pepper
¼ cup brandy
2 shallots, finely chopped
1 garlic clove, finely chopped
1 tablespoon finely minced parsley

Optional:
½ cup freshly grated Parmesan cheese

Preparation

1. Preheat the oven to 300°.

2. Bring the Fish Stock to a boil and keep it warm over low heat.

3. In a saucepan, melt 2 tablespoons of butter. Add the onion and cook, without browning, for 5 minutes.

4. Stir in the rice and saute it for 2 or 3 minutes until it is well covered with butter. Raise the heat and add the wine. Cook

until the wine is completely absorbed by the rice. Add 2 cups of stock and the Bouquet Garni. Cover the saucepan partially and cook the rice over low heat, stirring it occasionally with a fork.

5. While the rice is cooking, melt 2 tablespoons of butter with the olive oil in a 10-inch skillet.

6. Add the shrimp, season with salt and pepper and cook over high heat for 5 minutes until the shrimp turn a bright pink. Sprinkle with the brandy and cook until it is completely evaporated.

7. Add the shallots, garlic and parsley. Cook the mixture for 2 or 3 more minutes, coating the shrimp well with the herbs. Turn off the heat. Keep them warm.

8. Check the rice and when most of the stock is absorbed add 2 more cups. Continue to simmer, partially uncovered, for another 10 minutes, stirring from time to time.

9. When the rice is soft and creamy, add the shrimp mixture and the remaining butter. Stir it carefully, cover the saucepan and place it in the oven for 8 to 10 minutes. Serve immediately with a side dish of grated Parmesan cheese.

Remarks

This is a hearty dish, well suited to winter dining. I also like to make it in summer for supper, adding a sprig of fresh rosemary and a few unshelled mussels during the last 10 minutes of cooking.

Fresh broccoli puree
Serves: 4
Preparation time: 15 minutes
Cooking time: 35 to 40 minutes

Ingredients

1 bunch broccoli (about 2 pounds)
Salt
¼ cup Italian rice (unconverted)
½ cup to ¾ cup Creme Fraiche (page 398)
4 to 6 tablespoons sweet butter
Freshly ground black pepper
Pinch of freshly ground nutmeg

Preparation

1. Cut an inch off each stalk of broccoli and remove all the leaves. Cut the stalks in half lengthwise and scrape each one with a vegetable peeler. Wash thoroughly under cold running water and reserve.

2. In a 1-quart saucepan bring 1 cup of water to a boil, add ½ teaspoon of salt and the rice. Bring the water back to a boil, reduce the heat, and cover the saucepan. Cook until the rice is tender (about 20 minutes). Drain and reserve.

3. In a large casserole bring 5 or 6 quarts of salted water to a boil, add the broccoli stalks and cook uncovered, until tender (about 15 minutes). Drain. Chop coarsely.

4. Puree the broccoli in a food mill or blender together with the rice. Season the puree with salt and pepper and return it to the saucepan.

5. Cook the puree for 2 or 3 minutes, stirring constantly, until it is "dry." There should be no liquid in the bottom of the saucepan.

6. Remove the puree from the heat and beat in the Creme Fraiche and butter.

7. Season with a good dash of black pepper and a pinch of nutmeg and serve.

Brussels sprouts
a la catalane

Serves: 4 to 6
Preparation time: 15 minutes
Cooking time: 35 minutes

■●

Northern Spain makes great use of Brussels sprouts as a winter vegetable. They are usually sauteed in lard with finely smoked ham or prosciutto. Spanish cooks believe that the first water used for poaching Brussels sprouts should be discarded to insure proper digestion. Serve this dish as an accompaniment to a roast duck or a roast loin of pork.

Ingredients

2   quarts fresh Brussels sprouts
½ pound slab bacon, cut into lardons
4   tablespoons sweet butter or lard
2   small white onions, each stuck with 1 clove
Salt and freshly ground white pepper
¾ cup concentrated Chicken Stock (page 404)
⅓ cup finely grated fresh Parmesan cheese
2   tablespoons minced parsley

Preparation

1. Preheat the oven to 375°.

2. Trim the Brussels sprouts, remove any wilted leaves. Bring 4 to 5 quarts of salted water to a boil in a large casserole, and drop in the sprouts. Lower the heat, cook the sprouts for 10 minutes and drain.

3. Drop the lardons into boiling water and cook for 5 minutes. Drain on paper towels and reserve.

4. In a large flameproof baking dish, melt the butter, add the bacon and sprouts as well as the onions, salt and pepper. Cook over medium heat for 2 minutes.

5. Add the Chicken Stock and remove the dish from the heat.

6. Cover with foil and place the baking dish in the oven. Cook for 25 to 30 minutes or until the sprouts are tender. If by that time there are still juices in the baking dish, uncover it, place it over direct heat and reduce the pan juices to a glaze.

7. Sprinkle the sprouts with Parmesan and return to the oven until the cheese is melted. Sprinkle with parsley and serve.

Notes

Brussels sprouts a la suisse

Serves: 4 to 6
Preparation time: 30 minutes
Cooking time: 40 minutes

Ingredients

2 quarts Brussels sprouts
Salt
4 tablespoons sweet butter
Freshly ground white pepper
1 cup finely cubed ham
1 cup Creme Fraiche (page 398) or heavy
   cream
½ cup grated Gruyere cheese
Freshly ground black pepper

Preparation

1. Preheat the oven to 350°.

2. Clean the Brussels sprouts under cold running water, removing any wilted leaves.

3. Drop the sprouts into 5 quarts of fast-boiling salted water and cook over low heat for 10 minutes. Drain immediately.

4. Melt the butter in a large baking dish and add the sprouts (in one layer to insure even cooking). Sprinkle with pinch of salt and white pepper. Cover the dish with buttered foil or wax paper and bake for 15 minutes.

5. Uncover the dish and add the ham and Creme Fraiche.

6. Sprinkle with cheese and continue baking uncovered for 10 more minutes or until the sprouts are tender and the cheese melted. If the cream cooks down too much, cover the dish again with foil or wax paper.

7. Season the Brussels sprouts with freshly ground black pepper and serve right from the baking dish.

Celeriac a l'italienne

Serves: 4
Preparation time: 30 minutes
Cooking time: 30 minutes

Ingredients

2 pounds celery knobs, peeled and cut
   into small cubes
Salt
6 tablespoons sweet butter
1 cup heavy cream
Freshly ground white pepper
Pinch of fresh nutmeg
½ cup finely cubed prosciutto
2 tablespoons freshly grated Parmesan
   cheese
1 tablespoon finely minced parsley
Freshly ground black pepper
Dash of lemon juice

Preparation

1. Drop the celery-knob cubes into acidulated water.

2. Bring salted water to a boil in a large saucepan. Drop the cubes into the water and cook until tender. Drain and dry with paper towels.

3. In a large heavy skillet, melt the butter. Add the cream and season with salt, white pepper and nutmeg. Cook over high heat until the liquid is reduced by ½.

4. Add the celery cubes, reduce the heat, cover the skillet and simmer for a few minutes, shaking the pan to cover the cubes well with the cream. Add the prosciutto and Parmesan and just heat through.

5. Sprinkle with parsley and freshly ground black pepper. Correct the seasoning and add a dash of lemon juice. Serve.

Endive a la bernoise

Serves: 6
Preparation time: 10 minutes
Cooking time: 30 minutes

The Swiss make wonderful use of Belgian endive. Here is a dish that is both simple and useful for last-minute entertaining. Serve it as an accompaniment to a simple roast chicken, sauteed veal cutlets or calves' liver.

Ingredients

12 firm Belgian endives
Juice of ½ lemon
Salt
4 tablespoons sweet butter
Freshly ground white pepper
1 cup heavy cream, warmed
3 tablespoons finely grated Gruyere cheese or a mixture of Gruyere and Parmesan

Preparation

1. Preheat the oven to 350°.

2. Wipe the endives with a wet paper towel, or rinse quickly under cold running water. Do not soak in water. Trim any wilted leaves.

3. Put the endives in a casserole, cover with water and add the lemon juice and a pinch of salt. Bring the water to a boil, then reduce the heat and simmer for about 10 minutes or until the endives are almost tender but still firm. Carefully remove them to a paper towel and drain well.

4. In a baking dish (large enough to hold the endives in one layer) melt the butter, add the endives, season with salt and pepper.

5. Pour the warm cream around the endives and bake for 10 minutes or until the cream is reduced by ⅓. Baste 2 or 3 times with the cream.

6. Sprinkle with the grated cheese and continue to bake for 5 more minutes or until the cheese is melted. Serve right out of the baking dish.

Remarks

The endives may be poached in advance and baked at the last minute or you may run them under the broiler to brown for the last 3 minutes. You may serve the dish as an appetizer together with assorted sausages, smoked ham or sliced prosciutto.

Notes

Endive a la provencale

Serves: 6
Preparation time: 20 minutes
Cooking time: 1 hour

Even though Belgian endive is a northern European vegetable, it harmonizes perfectly with the highly flavored Provencale butter sauce. This is a delicious accompaniment to grilled or poached fish.

Ingredients

6 filets of anchovies
Milk
2 tablespoons finely minced parsley
2 garlic cloves, finely minced
2 finely minced shallots
Juice of 1 lemon
12 firm medium-sized Belgian endives
Salt and freshly ground white pepper
6 to 8 tablespoons sweet butter
½ cup warm Brown Stock (page 403)

Garnish:
1 tablespoon tiny capers
12 shrimp, raw and peeled, sauteed in
   butter
Freshly ground black pepper

Preparation

1. Preheat the oven to 350°.

2. Soak the anchovies for 5 minutes in a little milk. This will remove some of their saltiness. Drain and finely chop.

3. In a small bowl, combine the anchovies, parsley, garlic, shallots and half of the lemon juice. Reserve.

4. Wipe the endives with wet paper towels. Trim and remove any wilted outer leaves. Season with salt and pepper and sprinkle with the remaining lemon juice.

5. Melt 4 tablespoons of butter in a flame-proof baking dish. Place the endives in the dish in one layer and pour the warm Brown Stock around them. Cover with buttered wax paper and place in the oven. Turn the endives once or twice while baking for 45 minutes to 1 hour (or until tender when pierced with a fork).

6. When the endives are done, remove them to a serving platter.

7. Place the baking dish over high heat and add the anchovy-and-parsley mixture. Remove from the heat and whisk in 2 to 4 tablespoons of butter. As soon as it is melted, pour the sauce over the endives.

8. Garnish the dish with capers, shrimp and a large dash of black pepper.

Remarks

The dish can be cooked entirely on top of the stove, in which case endives will be done in much less time. Slow oven braising, however, gives them a better flavor.

Notes

Braised fennel polonaise

Serves: 4 to 6
Preparation time: 15 minutes
Cooking time: 40 minutes

■●

Fennel is a superb winter vegetable that has fortunately gained popularity in the United States. It has a slight aniseed flavor. Finely sliced raw fennel is an excellent addition to the winter salad bowl. Cooked fennel is a good accompaniment to a roast pork or sauteed calves' liver.

Ingredients

4 to 6 small fennel bulbs
4 tablespoons Clarified Butter (page 398)
2 tablespoons lemon juice
2 tablespoons minced parsley
Salt and freshly ground white pepper
2 tablespoons sweet butter
½ cup homemade white bread crumbs
2 tablespoons finely minced hard-boiled egg

Garnish:
Chopped parsley

Preparation

1. Trim the fennel bulbs of all the leaves and remove one layer of the tough outer stalks. Bring 3 to 4 quarts of salted water to a boil in a large casserole. Add the fennel bulbs and cook them, partially covered, over medium heat for 25 to 30 minutes or until they are tender. Drain the bulbs and cut them lengthwise into 2 or 3 slices, depending on their size.

2. In a small saucepan, heat the Clarified Butter over low heat until it turns light brown.

3. Add the lemon juice, parsley and the fennel slices and cook over very low heat for 5 more minutes. Season with salt and pepper.

4. Melt the 2 tablespoons of sweet butter in a small skillet. Brown the bread crumbs in the butter and add the minced egg.

5. Sprinkle the fennel with the bread crumb and egg mixture; add the chopped parsley. Serve immediately.

Remarks

The fennel bulbs can be cooked well in advance and slowly reheated. Endives and poached kohlrabies also lend themselves extremely well to this preparation.

Notes

Gratin of leeks aurora

Serves: 6
Preparation time: 30 minutes
Cooking time: 25 to 30 minutes

Ingredients

12 leeks of even size, about ¾ to 1 inch
    thick
Salt
5 tablespoons sweet butter
1 cup finely cubed cooked ham
3 tablespoons flour
2 teaspoons tomato paste
2 cups Chicken Stock (page 404)
Freshly ground white pepper
2 egg yolks
2 tablespoons Creme Fraiche (page 398)
½ cup grated Gruyere cheese

Preparation

1. Cut off some of the green, leaving the leeks about 4 to 5 inches long. Wash them thoroughly under cold running water, then soak them in cold water for 1 hour to remove all possible sand.

2. Place the leeks in a casserole and cover with salted water. Bring the water to a boil, reduce the heat and cook the leeks, partially covered, for 15 to 20 minutes or until tender. Test them several times as some stalks may be done before others.

3. Drain the leeks on paper towels and then place in one layer in a well-buttered baking dish.

4. In a small skillet heat 2 tablespoons of butter, add the ham and saute it for 3 minutes until coated with butter and heated through. Reserve.

5. In a heavy saucepan melt the remaining butter. Add the flour and cook for 3 minutes without browning. Add the tomato paste and blend it with the flour.

6. Add the Chicken Stock all at once and stir until the sauce has thickened and is very smooth.

7. Season the sauce with salt and pepper and remove it from the heat.

8. In a small bowl, beat the egg yolks and Creme Fraiche until well blended.

9. Add the cubed ham and the egg yolk mixture to the sauce.

10. Place the sauce over a very low flame to reheat, but do not let it come to a boil. Pour the sauce over the leeks, sprinkle with the grated cheese and run under the broiler until the cheese is melted and lightly browned.

Remarks

For a variation, wrap each cooked leek in a thin slice of ham and then coat with the sauce.

Notes

Puree of white beans

Serves: 4 to 6
Preparation time: 20 minutes
Cooking time: 1 hour

Ingredients

2 cups dry white beans
Chicken Stock (page 404) or water
1 carrot, peeled
1 onion, stuck with a clove
1 Bouquet Garni (page 397)
Salt
2 tablespoons sweet butter
2 tablespoons finely minced onion
1 cup heavy cream
Freshly ground white pepper

Optional:
2 to 4 tablespoons sweet butter

Preparation

1. Soak the beans overnight in cold water, which should cover them by 3 inches. Drain the beans the following day.

2. Place the beans in a large casserole and cover them with fresh water or a light Chicken Stock. Add the whole onion, carrot, the Bouquet Garni and a large pinch of salt. Bring the water to a boil, reduce the heat and simmer the beans, partially covered, for 45 to 50 minutes or until they are quite tender.

3. While the beans are cooking, melt the butter in a saucepan. Add the minced onions and cook until it is soft but not browned.

4. Add the cream and simmer for 15 to 20 minutes or until it is reduced by ⅓. Strain and reserve.

5. When the beans are done, strain them. Discard the Bouquet Garni and the whole onion.

6. Puree the beans in a food mill and add the cream.

7. Put the puree in a heavy saucepan and cook it over medium heat for a few minutes, stirring constantly, until it is very thick.

8. For enrichment add the optional butter and season with salt and lots of pepper.

Remarks

This is an excellent puree that can be served with innumerable dishes. In summer it can be flavored with 1 tablespoon minced fresh sage or rosemary.

Notes

winter vegetables

Celeriac salad
a la normande

Serves: 4
Preparation time: 15 minutes
Cooking time: 20 to 25 minutes

Ingredients

2 large celery knobs
Salt
1 crisp apple, peeled and finely cubed
2 tablespoons chopped walnuts
Freshly ground white pepper
¾ cup Mayonnaise (page 402)
4 teaspoons lemon juice
2 teaspoons Dijon mustard
3 tablespoons whipped cream
½ cup ham, cut into fine strips
1 tablespoon minced parsley

Garnish:
8 whole walnuts

Preparation

1. Peel the celery knobs and drop them into acidulated water to keep them from turning brown. Bring 4 or 5 quarts of salted water to a boil in a large casserole and poach the celery knobs for 20 minutes or until easily pierced with a sharp knife. They should still be slightly crisp. Drain them and cut them into small cubes and place them in a serving bowl.

2. Add the apple cubes to the serving bowl.

3. Add the chopped walnuts, a pinch of salt and pepper to taste.

4. Combine the Mayonnaise, 3 teaspoons of lemon juice, mustard and whipped cream in a bowl. Pour the mixture over the salad and toss lightly.

5. Sprinkle the salad with the ham strips and parsley and garnish with whole walnuts.

6. Chill the salad for several hours. Just before serving bring it back to room temperature and correct the seasoning, adding the remaining lemon juice if necessary.

Remarks

This salad goes well with a platter of Westphalian ham or prosciutto. Pascal celery, finely diced, can be prepared in the same manner. It is, however, no substitute for celery knobs which have a flavor all their own.

Notes

Celeriac salad a la viennoise

Serves: 6
Preparation time: 35 minutes
Cooking time: 30 to 35 minutes

Ingredients

2 pounds celery knobs, peeled
Salt
1 tablespoon Dijon mustard
1 teaspoon finely grated horseradish
2 small dill pickles, finely minced
1 tablespoon white vinegar
1 cup Mayonnaise (page 402)
2 tablespoons finely minced parsley
1 tablespoon finely minced chives
1 freshly ground white pepper

Optional:
⅓ cup finely cubed ham

Preparation

1. Drop the celery knobs, as peeled, into acidulated water to prevent them from turning brown. Bring salted water to a boil in a large casserole. It should cover the celery knobs by 2 inches. Cook until the celery knobs are tender when pierced with a fork (about 30 minutes). Drain them and when cool enough to handle, cut them into small cubes, place them in a serving bowl and sprinkle with lemon juice.

2. In a small mixing bowl, combine the mustard, horseradish, pickles and vinegar and blend well.

3. Add the Mayonnaise, mustard-vinegar mixture, and seasoning to the celery cubes.

4. Add the parsley and chives and the cubed ham if used.

5. Toss the salad carefully with 2 forks and chill for 2 hours before serving.

Winter fennel salad

Serves: 4 to 6
Preparation time: 15 minutes
Cooking time: none

Fennel is an excellent winter vegetable. It is good raw in various salads as well as cooked. Here is a salad that can be served as an appetizer or lunch salad together with a platter of assorted cheese and French bread.

Ingredients

2 large fennel bulbs
1 cucumber, peeled, seeded and thinly sliced
Salt
1 cup finely sliced radishes
Juice of 1 large lemon
1 teaspoon verifine sugar
1 teaspoon Dijon mustard
6 tablespoons olive oil
2 tablespoons finely minced scallions
Freshly ground black pepper

Optional:
2 or 3 quartered hard-boiled eggs
12 black olives

Preparation

1. Trim the fennel bulbs and wash thoroughly. Reserve some of the greens for soup or stock. Cut the bulbs into thin slices. Place them in a salad bowl and reserve.

2. Cut the cucumber in half lengthwise. With a melon-ball cutter or spoon, remove all the seeds. Cut the cucumber into thin slices and place them in a colander. Sprinkle with salt and drain for 30 minutes to 1 hour.

3. Dry the cucumber slices with paper towels and add them to the fennel together with the sliced radishes.

4. In a small bowl combine the lemon juice, sugar, Dijon mustard and olive oil. Whisk the dressing until it is smooth and creamy.

5. Add the scallions and pour the dressing over the salad.

6. Season the salad with salt and black pepper and toss lightly. Refrigerate for 30 minutes before serving.

7. Just before serving, garnish the bowl with hard-boiled eggs and black olives.

Remarks

If you are going to serve the salad as an appetizer, you may add 1 cup of crumbled Feta cheese or another fresh goat cheese. I particularly like the combination of fennel and Feta. If you find the taste of raw fennel a little overpowering, blanch the vegetable for 2 or 3 minutes. Drain immediately and run under cold water to stop further cooking.

Notes

Watercress salad a la bernoise

Serves: 4
Preparation time: 5 minutes
Cooking time: 8 to 10 minutes

This is an unusual and absolutely delicious salad that requires last-minute preparation. The dressing is served warm and takes only 5 minutes to prepare. Serve this as a light appetizer or following the main course. Other greens such as dandelion can be prepared in the same way.

Ingredients

2　bunches fresh watercress, trimmed and washed
4 to 6 slices bacon
2　eggs
1　teaspoon Dijon mustard
3　tablespoons lemon juice
2　tablespoons white vinegar
2　tablespoons sugar
Salt and freshly ground black pepper

Preparation

1. Place the well-washed watercress in a wire salad bowl or a colander. Chill until serving time.

2. In a skillet saute the bacon slices. When they are crisp, remove them and drain them on paper towels. When cool, crumble and reserve.

3. In a heavy-bottomed 1-quart enameled saucepan combine the eggs, Dijon mustard, lemon juice, vinegar and sugar. Whisk the mixture until it is well blended.

4. Just before serving, combine the watercress and bacon bits in a salad bowl. Season with salt and pepper.

5. Place the saucepan over high heat and cook the dressing, stirring vigorously, until it is thick and smooth. Do not let it

come to a boil. Immediately plunge the saucepan into a bowl of cold water to stop further cooking.

6. Spoon the warm dressing over the watercress and gently fold it in. Serve immediately.

Remarks

The dressing can be combined well ahead of time and kept warm by putting the saucepan in a pan of warm water. You may also make the dressing in the top part of a double boiler. Making it in a saucepan is a little more tricky, but takes only 3 to 4 minutes to prepare.

Notes

Baked apples in sauterne

Serves: 6
Preparation time: 10 minutes
Cooking time: 40 minutes

Baked apples are an excellent accompaniment to a roast pork or duck. They can also be served as a dessert and are at their best when served warm. A side dish of sweetened Creme Fraiche is a must!

Ingredients

6   pitted prunes
1   cup sauterne
6   McIntosh or Roman Beauty apples
2   tablespoons sweet butter
4   tablespoons sugar
1   2-inch piece cinnamon stick
½ cup apricot preserves
Lemon juice

Optional:
2   tablespoons rum or cognac

Preparation

1. Preheat the oven to 350°.

2. Soak the prunes in the sauterne for 30 minutes. Drain and reserve the sauterne.

3. Peel the apples and core them, being careful not to pierce through the bottom. Immediately sprinkle the apples with lemon juice or drop them into acidulated water to prevent them from turning brown.

4. Butter a large flameproof baking dish. Place the well-drained apples in the dish. Stuff each one with a drained prune. Top with a little bit of butter and sprinkle them with sugar. Pour the sauterne around the apples, add the cinnamon stick and cover the dish with buttered wax paper. Bake the apples for 40 minutes, basting them often with the sauterne in the dish. Be careful not to overcook them or they will burst. Discard the cinnamon stick and carefully remove the apples to a serving platter.

5. Place the baking dish on top of the stove and slightly reduce the pan juices.

6. Add the apricot preserves, rum or cognac, and continue cooking the sauce until the preserves are dissolved. Taste the sauce and, if you wish, add a dash of lemon juice.

7. Pour the sauce over the apples and serve them while they are still warm.

Remarks

When serving the apples as an accompaniment to roast, omit the rum or cognac from the sauce.

Notes

Crepes alaskine

Serves: 6
Preparation time: 25 minutes
Cooking time: 45 minutes

Ingredients

12 to 14 Dessert Crepes (page 399)

The sauce:
Juice of 1 large orange
Rind of 1 large orange
2 tablespoons confectioners' sugar
¼ cup white rum
¼ cup Grand Marnier
¼ cup cognac
6 tablespoons sweet butter
1 pint vanilla ice cream

Preparation

1. In a small saucepan combine the orange juice and rind. Add the sugar and cook the mixture over low heat until the sugar is melted.

2. Add the rum, Grand Marnier and cognac and heat. Add the butter and cook until the butter is just melted. Keep the sauce warm.

3. Fill 12 to 14 warm crepes with 1 table-spoon vanilla ice cream and place them on an oval serving dish. Spoon the warm sauce over the crepes and serve.

Remarks

You may flambe the crepes at the table with an additional ¼ cup of cognac. These crepes require last-minute preparation, though the sauce can be prepared in advance. If you do not have the time for the final assembly, omit the vanilla ice cream. Fold the crepes into triangles, dip them in the sauce and keep them warm until serving time.

Crepes au chocolat

Serves: 10
Preparation time: 35 to 40 minutes
Cooking time: 15 minutes

A most delicious combination—crepes and chocolate mousse. The crepes must be paper thin, the mousse made with the best chocolate available.

Ingredients

16 to 18 Dessert Crepes (page 399)

The filling:
4 ounces semisweet chocolate
2 tablespoons strong coffee
1 teaspoon vanilla extract
3 large eggs, separated
2 tablespoons verifine sugar
Pinch of salt
Confectioners' sugar

The sauce:
⅓ cup cognac
⅓ cup rum

Optional:
2 cups of sweetened whipped cream

Preparation

1. In the top of a double boiler, melt the chocolate in the coffee with the vanilla until the mixture is smooth.

2. In a mixing bowl, beat the egg yolks and the sugar until the mixture is light and lemon-colored.

3. Gradually beat the chocolate into the egg-yolk mixture and blend carefully.

4. Beat the egg whites with a pinch of salt until they form soft peaks.

5. Fold the beaten egg whites into the chocolate and egg yolk mixture. Refrigerate the chocolate mousse for 4 hours or until it is well set.

6. Place the crepes on an ovenproof plate with a sheet of wax paper between each two. Cover them with foil and warm them in a 200° oven.

7. Place 1 tablespoon of chocolate mousse on each crepe. Roll them up, place them on a serving platter and sprinkle them with confectioners' sugar.

8. Warm the cognac and rum in a small saucepan. Pour it over the crepes and ignite at the table. Serve the optional whipped cream on the side.

Notes

Crepes au mocha

Serves: 6 to 8
Preparation time: 45 minutes to 1 hour
Cooking time: 40 to 50 minutes

Ingredients

The mocha batter (for 12 to 14 crepes):
¾ cup all-purpose flour, sifted
1 tablespoon sugar
3 eggs
1½ cups milk
1 teaspoon instant coffee dissolved in
     1 tablespoon coffee
2 tablespoons cognac
½ teaspoon vanilla extract
⅛ teaspoon salt
¼ cup melted sweet butter

The custard filling:
3 egg yolks
½ cup sugar
3 tablespoons flour
1 cup warm milk
1 teaspoon vanilla extract
2 or 3 tablespoons cognac
4 or 5 tablespoons Macaroon Powder (page
     401)

Garnish:
1 cup heavy cream, whipped
1 tablespoon confectioners' sugar
2 to 3 tablespoons cognac

Preparation

1. Place all the batter ingredients except the butter in the top part of the blender.

2. Cool the melted butter and whisk it into the batter.

3. Let the batter stand for 1 or 2 hours before making crepes according to directions on page 398.

4. For the filling combine the egg yolks and sugar in a mixing bowl and whisk the mixture until it is fluffy and pale yellow.

Add the flour and warm milk and whisk the mixture until it is very smooth.

5. Pour the mixture into a heavy-bottomed 3-quart saucepan and cook the custard over medium heat, 5 to 7 minutes, stirring constantly, until it is very thick, being careful not to scorch the bottom of the pan. The custard must cook for 1 or 2 minutes. Do not stop stirring.

6. Pour the hot custard immediately into a bowl and add the vanilla, 2 tablespoons of cognac and 2 tablespoons of Macaroon Powder. Chill the custard for 2 or 3 hours.

7. Fill the crepes with a spoonful of the custard, roll them up and place them carefully in a rectangular, well-buttered baking dish.

8. Sprinkle the crepes with the remaining Macaroon Powder and confectioners' sugar.

9. Just before serving run the dish under a hot broiler to caramelize the sugar lightly. Serve directly from the dish with the following sauce on the side.

10. To the remaining custard add the whipped cream, confectioners' sugar and 2 to 3 tablespoons of cognac. Serve the sauce well chilled.

Remarks

The crepes may also be filled with vanilla ice cream and topped with warm Chocolate Sauce (page 397).

Fresh fruits in grand marnier sauce

Serves: 4 to 6
Preparation time: 35 minutes
Cooking time: 5 to 10 minutes

■ ●

Here is an excellent way to dress up the Good Old Fruit Salad. Personally, I never find a well-prepared fruit salad dull, as long as it is really fresh and the fruits have some affinity for each other. Watermelon should never be part of the fruit salad, its consistency being too watery. Pears do not take well to fruit salad either, as they turn brown quickly. Use oranges, apples, seedless grapes, bananas and a few ripe strawberries. Sprinkle the salad with 2 tablespoons of Grand Marnier just before serving.

Ingredients

The salad:
3 navel oranges, peeled and diced
1 large ripe banana, peeled and sliced
1 crisp apple, peeled and diced
1 cup white seedless grapes
1 cup small whole strawberries or large strawberries, halved
2 tablespoons sugar

Optional:
1 to 2 tablespoons kirsch

The sauce:
4 egg yolks
1 teaspoon cornstarch
½ cup sugar
1 cup warm milk
¼ cup Grand Marnier
1 teaspoon vanilla extract
1 teaspoon grated orange rind
½ cup of heavy cream, whipped

Preparation

1. Combine all the fruits in a serving bowl and sprinkle with sugar and the kirsch.

Cover the dish and refrigerate until serving time.

2. In the top part of a double boiler, combine the egg yolks, cornstarch and sugar. Beat the mixture until it is pale yellow. Add the warm milk and set over the simmering water. Whisk the mixture constantly until it gets thick and heavily coats the spoon. Do not let it come to a boil or the custard will curdle.

3. When the custard is done, immediately remove it from the heat. Strain it into a serving bowl and add the Grand Marnier, vanilla and orange rind. Let the custard cool completely and then refrigerate it covered for 2 to 3 hours.

4. Just before serving, whisk the whipped cream into the sauce and taste the sauce for flavor. You may like more liqueur or more orange rind.

5. Drain the fruit salad of any accumulated juice in the bottom of the bowl and pour the sauce over the fruit. Serve immediately.

Remarks

Other fruits, such as baked apples, pears, or a bowl of fresh strawberries, can be served with this sauce.

Notes

Flan au praline

Serves: 6 to 8
Preparation time: 25 minutes
Cooking time: 45 minutes to 1 hour

A caramel custard is an excellent dessert when well prepared. But as so often happens, simple dishes, well prepared, somehow are hard to find in either restaurants or private homes. Here the custard is flavored with Praline Powder which gives it a great deal of character. The dessert can be given a seasonal touch by filling the center with poached sliced pears in winter or with fresh strawberries in the spring.

Ingredients

The custard:
2 cups milk
2½ cups sugar
3-inch piece vanilla bean, or 2 teaspoons
    vanilla extract
3 eggs
3 egg yolks
⅓ cup water
2 tablespoons light rum
3 tablespoons Praline Powder (page 402)

Optional:
½ cup heavy cream
Confectioners' sugar
¼ cup Praline Powder (page 402)

Preparation

1. Preheat the oven to 325°.

2. In a saucepan heat the milk with ¼ cup sugar and the vanilla bean. Keep the milk warm, letting the vanilla bean steep in it for 30 minutes to impart its flavor.

3. In a mixing bowl combine the whole eggs, yolks and another ¼ cup of sugar. Whisk the mixture until it is well blended and reserve.

4. In a heavy-bottomed 1-quart saucepan heat the remaining sugar and the water. Cook the mixture, without stirring, until it starts to turn a light brown. Watch it carefully and remove the saucepan from the fire as soon as the caramel becomes a hazelnut brown.

5. Immediately pour the caramel into a ring mold, tipping the mold to coat it evenly with the caramel. Set the mold aside.

6. Pour the warm milk into the egg and sugar mixture, whisking constantly. (Discard the vanilla bean if you have used it. Otherwise, add the vanilla extract.) Add the rum.

7. Strain the mixture through a fine sieve into another bowl.

8. Add the Praline Powder and skim the foam off the mixture. Pour it into the prepared mold. Set the mold in a pan of hot water and bake the custard in the oven for 45 minutes to 1 hour or until a knife comes out clean.

9. Remove the custard from the oven and let it cool.

10. Chill the custard and when it is quite cold, run a knife around the edge and unmold it onto a serving platter.

11. If there is any caramel left in the mold, place the mold over a low flame, add a little hot water and melt the caramel. Cool the syrup and then pour it over the custard.

12. If you are using the heavy cream, whip it just before serving. Sweeten it with confectioners' sugar and place it in the center of the custard. Sprinkle with additional Praline Powder.

Macaroon mousse with chocolate sauce

Serves: 8 to 10
Preparation time: 25 minutes
Cooking time: none

■ ○

Here is a dessert that lends itself well to a dinner-party menu. It serves 8 to 10 people easily, is simple to prepare and can be done well in advance. It does not limit the hostess to any season since it uses kitchen staples. Macaroon Crumbs are easy to make and can be refrigerated for several weeks.

Ingredients

6 eggs
⅔ cup verifine sugar
2 teaspoons vanilla extract
6 tablespoons dark rum
1½ cups heavy cream, whipped
5 tablespoons Macaroon Crumbs (page 401)
1½ tablespoons plain gelatin
½ cup coffee

Garnish:
Chocolate shavings

The sauce:
½ pound sweet dark chocolate, broken into small pieces
1 cup coffee
4 tablespoons sweet butter
3 tablespoons dark rum

Optional:
2 tablespoons granulated sugar
1 to 2 teaspoons vanilla extract

Preparation

1. Fill a 2-quart saucepan with water, bring it to a boil, then reduce the heat until the water is barely at a simmer.

2. In a large mixing bowl—one that will fit on top of the saucepan—combine the eggs, sugar, vanilla and rum. Whisk the mixture

lightly and place the mixing bowl over the barely simmering water. Whisk the mixture from time to time, until it feels tepid when touched with a finger.

3. While the eggs are warming up, whip the cream and reserve.

4. When the egg mixture feels warm, remove the bowl from the heat and beat the mixture with an electric beater until it has tripled in volume and is pale yellow and very fluffy. Continue beating while you add the Macaroon Crumbs, a few at a time. Incorporate them well into the mixture.

5. Combine the gelatin with the coffee and heat in a small saucepan until it is completely melted.

6. Cool the gelatin slightly and then, whisking constantly, pour it, a few drops at a time, into the egg mixture.

7. Place the bowl over a larger bowl filled with ice cubes and whisk the mixture until it thickens and starts to set (about 3 to 5 minutes).

8. Fold the whipped cream into the egg and macaroon mixture. Pour into a crystal bowl and chill for 4 hours before serving.

9. Garnish the mousse with chocolate shavings. Serve the following warm chocolate sauce on the side.

The sauce:
10. In a heavy-bottomed saucepan combine the chocolate and coffee. Melt the chocolate over very low heat, stirring occasionally. Be careful not to burn it.

11. As soon as the chocolate is melted and the mixture is smooth, add the butter and rum.

12. Taste the sauce and add the optional sugar and vanilla extract to taste. The sauce should not be too sweet since the mousse itself is quite sweet.

Remarks

The sauce can be made a day ahead of time and reheated, preferably in the top of a double boiler. Additional butter can be added to it as well as more rum.
For this mousse the macaroons should not be ground into a powder. Rather place them in a plastic bag and roll them into coarse crumbs with a rolling pin.

Notes

Oeufs a la neige in grand marnier sauce

Serves: 6
Preparation time: 50 minutes
Cooking time: 25 minutes

Ingredients

4 egg whites at room temperature
Pinch of salt
¾ cup sugar
2 cups hot milk
½ cup plus 2 tablespoons sugar
2 teaspoons vanilla extract
6 egg yolks
1 teaspoon cornstarch
½ cup fresh orange juice
2 teaspoons orange rind, grated
¼ cup Grand Marnier or curacao

Garnish:
Strips of peel from 3 whole oranges
¼ cup Grand Marnier
Caramel Syrup: ½ cup sugar
           2 tablespoons water

Preparation

1. Place the egg whites in a copper bowl. Add the salt and beat the whites with a wire whisk. Slowly add the sugar, a little at a time, until the egg whites are stiff and glossy.

2. In a deep skillet heat the milk and the 2 tablespoons sugar. Bring the milk to a boil, then reduce the heat.

3. When the milk is at a simmer add the vanilla extract.

4. With 2 tablespoons shape the meringues into ovals and drop them into the hot milk. Poach each meringue for 2 minutes, then turn it carefully and poach for 2 more minutes on the other side. Do not overcook. Remove the cooked meringues with a slotted spoon to a thick layer of paper towels. Continue poaching until done.

5. Pass the milk through a fine sieve and reserve 1½ cups.

6. In the top part of a double boiler combine the yolks and the ½ cup of sugar. Beat the mixture until it is well blended and pale yellow.

7. Add the cornstarch and beat until it is completely incorporated into the yolks.

8. Add the orange juice and hot milk. Cook over simmering water until it thickens and lightly coats a spoon. Do not let it come to a boil.

9. Pour it into a serving bowl, add the orange rind and Grand Marnier. Taste the sauce and add a little more vanilla extract if desired.

10. Chill the sauce and when quite cool float the meringues in the sauce and refrigerate.

11. Remove the peel of 3 oranges, cut the peel into very fine strips. Drop them into boiling water and cook them over high heat for 10 minutes. Drain the strips and place them in a little bowl. Sprinkle with ¼ cup of Grand Marnier. Marinate until serving.

12. In a heavy 1-quart saucepan combine the sugar and water and cook, without stirring, until the mixture becomes a nutty brown. Do not burn the caramel. If it seems to be getting too dark, plunge the saucepan into cold water to stop further cooking.

13. Cool the caramel slightly and dribble it over the meringues, making a decorative pattern. Just before serving, drain the orange strips (the liqueur can be added to the sauce) and place them over the meringues. Serve very cold.

Pears andalouse

Serves: 6
Preparation time: 15 minutes
Cooking time: 25 minutes

Beziers poached pears

Serves: 6
Preparation time: 30 minutes
Cooking time: 30 to 35 minutes

Personally, I find pears to be the best and most versatile fall-winter fruit. They can be used in a great many ways. Here is one.

Ingredients

6 pears
1½ cups sugar
1 3-inch piece vanilla bean
3 cups water
½ lemon, quartered
2 oranges
½ cup fresh orange juice
½ cup red currant jelly
3 tablespoons curacao

Preparation

1. Peel the pears. Slice them in half lengthwise and carefully core them.

2. In a large saucepan, combine the sugar, vanilla bean and water. Add the lemon quarters and simmer the syrup for 5 minutes or until the sugar is dissolved.

3. Add the pears and simmer them in the syrup for 15 to 20 minutes or until tender.

4. While the pears are cooking, remove the skin of the oranges with a vegetable peeler. Cut into julienne strips, 2 inches long and about ⅛ inch wide. Drop them into boiling water and cook for 10 minutes. Drain and reserve.

5. Remove the pears to a serving bowl and sprinkle them with the orange strips.

6. Add the orange juice and the currant jelly to the pear syrup. Let the jelly melt and reduce the syrup until it lightly coats a spoon. Add the curacao and pour the syrup over the pears. Chill before serving.

Here are two delicious winter fruits, pears and oranges, combined in a delightful dessert. The pears can be stuffed with candied fruits, marinated for an hour in Grand Marnier, and served in their poaching syrup. In that case, substitute a 3-inch piece of vanilla bean for the cinnamon stick.

Ingredients

6 pears
2 cups water
1 cup sugar
1 cinnamon stick (2 inches long)

The custard:
6 small macaroons
½ to ¾ cup Grand Marnier
5 egg yolks
½ to ¾ cup sugar
1 cup orange juice
Grated rind of 1 orange

Preparation

1. Carefully peel the pears, cut them in half lengthwise and remove the core with a melon-ball cutter. Drop each peeled pear half into the acidulated water while you are peeling the rest.

2. In a shallow casserole combine the 2 cups of water, sugar and the cinnamon stick. Add the pear halves and simmer, covered, until they are soft, from 15 to 20 minutes. Test them often with the tip of a sharp knife as some may be ready before others. Be sure not to overcook them.

3. When all the pear halves are done, cool them in the poaching liquid. As soon as they are completely cooled, place them in

a serving bowl or slightly deep platter. Reserve the poaching liquid.

4. Soak the macaroons for a few seconds in ⅓ to ½ cup Grand Marnier until they are soft. Shape the macaroons into little domes and fill the pear cavities.

5. In the top of a double boiler combine the egg yolks and ½ cup of sugar and beat the mixture until the eggs are light and form a ribbon when falling off a spoon.

6. Add the orange juice and cook over simmering water until the mixture heavily coats the spoon, whisking it constantly and being careful not to let it boil or the yolks will curdle.

7. Remove the pan from the heat and add the remaining Grand Marnier and orange rind. Add 2 or 3 tablespoons of the poaching liquid and cool the custard.

8. When the custard is completely cooled, it may need a few drops of the poaching liquid to bring it to the consistency of heavy cream. Pour the sauce around the pears and refrigerate until serving time.

Remarks

Oranges vary greatly in sweetness, therefore be careful about adding too much sugar. If you have used ½ cup and the custard seems too sweet, add the juice of 1 lemon. If, on the other hand, it does not seem sweet enough, boil down the poaching liquid to a few concentrated tablespoons and add these to the custard.

Pineapple a la creole

Serves: 4
Preparation time: 10 minutes
Cooking time: 10 minutes

Ingredients

1 large ripe pineapple
½ cup sugar plus 2 tablespoons
¼ cup white rum
1½ cups tawny port
1 teaspoon grated lemon rind
Grated rind of 1 orange
Juice of 1 orange
1 stick of cinnamon, 3 inches long
½ teaspoon ground ginger
2 cloves
3 tablespoons red currant jelly

Optional:
Lemon juice

Preparation

1. Peel and slice the pineapple into thin slices. Carefully remove the hard core with a sharp knife. Cut each slice of pineapple into 4 pieces for easier serving and place the slices in a glass serving bowl. Sprinkle with 2 tablespoons of sugar and the rum and chill while making the sauce.

2. In a saucepan combine the port, lemon and orange rinds, the orange juice, ½ cup of sugar, cinnamon stick, ginger and cloves. Bring the mixture to a boil and cook over medium heat until slightly reduced or for about 8 minutes.

3. Add the currant jelly and continue cooking until the jelly is completely dissolved and the sauce lightly coats a spoon.

4. Cool and pour over the pineapple.

5. At serving time remove the cinnamon stick and cloves. Taste the sauce. If it seems too sweet, add a dash of lemon juice just before serving. Serve very cold.

Flambeed fresh pineapple

Serves: 4
Preparation time: 15 minutes
Cooking time: 10 minutes

Ingredients

1 large fresh pineapple
2 tablespoons granulated sugar
2 tablespoons curacao
4 tablespoons sweet butter
3 tablespoons brown sugar
½ cup orange juice
½ teaspoon ginger
¼ cup light rum

Optional:
1 tablespoon confectioners' sugar
Vanilla ice cream flavored with rum and
  raisins

Preparation

1. Peel the pineapple over a bowl in order to retain all the juices. Cut the pineapple into thin slices and carefully remove the hard core with a sharp knife. Place the pineapple slices in a shallow serving dish.

2. Sprinkle with the granulated sugar and curacao and marinate for 2 or 3 hours. Press all the juice out of the pineapple peel and reserve.

3. In a heavy skillet melt the butter over low heat. Add the brown sugar and cook until it is completely melted.

4. Add the orange juice, pineapple juice and ginger. Bring the sauce to a boil and reduce it over high heat until it heavily coats a spoon.

5. Reduce the heat and add the rum. Remove from the heat and taste the sauce for sweetness. If it is not sweet enough, add a little confectioners' sugar and return the sauce to very low heat until the sugar is dissolved.

6. Cool the sauce slightly and pour it over the pineapple slices. Serve immediately with the optional rum-flavored vanilla ice cream to which a few raisins, plumped up in a little hot water, have been added.

Remarks

In the summer, you can substitute freshly poached peaches for the pineapple, using some of the poaching syrup instead of the pineapple juice.

Notes

Almond caramel souffle with liqueur sauce

Serves: 4
Preparation time: 20 minutes
Cooking time: 30 to 35 minutes

■ ○

Here is a dessert for souffle lovers. Few realize that souffles are one of the simplest and least expensive desserts to make, requiring only kitchen staples.

Ingredients

The souffle (for a 6-cup souffle dish):
3 tablespoons flour
¾ cup milk
Sugar
4 eggs, separated, at room temperature
2 tablespoons sweet butter
1 tablespoon vanilla extract
3 tablespoons Praline Powder (page 402)
3 tablespoons white rum
2 egg whites, at room temperature
Salt

The sauce:
1 cup heavy cream
2 tablespoons confectioners' sugar
¼ cup cognac
¼ cup apricot brandy

Garnish:
Confectioners' sugar

Preparation

1. Preheat the oven to 400°.

2. In a saucepan combine the flour with a little milk to make a smooth paste. Add the remaining milk and the sugar and set the pan over medium heat. Whisk constantly until the mixture becomes very thick.

3. Remove the pan from the heat and beat in the egg yolks one at a time. Be sure to incorporate each yolk totally into the souffle base before adding the next one.

4. Set the saucepan over a very low flame and heat the mixture, but do not let it come to a boil or the yolks will curdle. Remove the mixture from the heat and cool for 2 or 3 minutes.

5. Whisk in the butter, vanilla extract, Praline Powder and rum. Reserve.

6. Beat the egg whites by hand with a large whisk. Add a pinch of salt and continue beating until the egg whites form soft peaks. Do not overbeat.

7. Fold the souffle base into the egg whites with your hands.

8. Lightly butter and sugar a souffle mold. Shake out the excess sugar.

9. Pour the souffle mixture into the mold and set it in the middle of the oven. Immediately reduce the heat to 375° and bake the souffle for 30 to 35 minutes.

10. Sprinkle the souffle with confectioners' sugar.

The sauce:
11. Whip the cream with 2 tablespoons of confectioners' sugar. Add the liqueurs and serve in a bowl on the side. This sauce can be prepared an hour before serving. Chill until serving time.

Remarks

A little trick for those who are afraid their souffle will not rise: Choose a mold that will just hold the souffle mixture. Make a collar of foil about 2 inches high, butter and tie it around the souffle dish. Pour in the souffle mixture. The souffle will rise above the rim of the mold. When ready, remove the collar and there is your perfect souffle!

The All-Seasons Kitchen is also a transitional and an "in between" kitchen. It offers a limited selection of fresh produce and uses supermarket staples such as carrots, potatoes and onions as well as dry vegetables such as white beans, chick peas and lentils. The All-Seasons Kitchen calls on the cook's creativity since it lacks the eye appeal of colorful fruits and vegetables. It requires gutsy, wholesome cooking in the tradition of European peasant food. Since the All-Seasons Kitchen relies heavily on starches like rice and pasta, the dishes demand the cook's ingenuity in combining the simplest ingredients to achieve a nourishing meal without resorting to frozen or canned foods.

the all-seasons kitchen

Symbols

● **Inexpensive**   ◉ **Moderate**   ✦ **Expensive**

■ **Easy**   ▫ **Intermediate**   ⊞ **Difficult**

Crepes aux fines herbes a la provencale

Serves: 6
Preparation time: 45 minutes
Cooking time: 20 to 30 minutes
■●

For years the crepe has been associated with la grande cuisine, yet a crepe is one of the simplest things to prepare. It is as versatile as pasta or rice and can be put together as elegantly or plainly as one desires. Here is an easy and delicious way to make crepes.

Ingredients

12 to 14 Crepes Fines Herbes (page 399)
10 tablespoons butter
2 tablespoons finely mashed anchovies
1 to 2 small garlic cloves, finely mashed
1 tablespoon finely minced parsley
1 teaspoon fresh tarragon
Freshly ground white pepper
Dash of lemon juice

Garnish:
Rolled filets of anchovies

Preparation

1. Preheat the oven to 325°.

2. In a mixing bowl cream the butter. Add the minced anchovies, garlic, herbs, a pinch of pepper and the lemon juice. Mix well and reserve.

3. Put a heaping teaspoon of the herb and anchovy butter on each crepe. Fold the crepes into triangles and place them, overlapping, in a well-buttered baking dish.

4. Heat the crepes in the oven for 15 to 20 minutes.

5. Garnish with rolled anchovy filets and serve warm.

Omelette savoyarde

Serves: 4 to 6
Preparation time: 20 minutes
Cooking time: 30 minutes

The open omelette is widely used in Mediterranean country cooking. Here is one that is perfect for a cold day. You may substitute or add anything you like, such as sauteed eggplant cubes, chives or cooked spinach.

Ingredients

1 cup finely cubed potatoes
¾ cup finely cubed bacon or ham
4 tablespoons sweet butter
2 leeks (white part only), cleaned and finely sliced
8 eggs
1 teaspoon salt
Freshly ground white pepper
2 tablespoons grated Gruyere or Swiss cheese
1 tablespoon olive oil

Preparation

1. Parboil the potatoes for 10 minutes in boiling salted water and drain.

2. In a heavy 10-inch skillet cook the bacon over low heat until it is almost crisp. Remove it to a side dish and discard all but 2 tablespoons of the fat. Add 2 tablespoons of butter to the pan.

3. When the butter is melted, add the leeks. Cover the pan and cook the leeks over low heat for 10 minutes or until they are very soft. Watch them so they do not brown. When the leeks are done, add the potatoes and cook the mixture for 5 more minutes.

4. In a bowl, beat the eggs with a whisk until frothy and light. Add salt and pepper and the grated cheese.

5. Add the leek and potato mixture and the bacon to the eggs.

6. Heat the remaining butter and oil in the skillet. Pour in the egg mixture and cook until the bottom is set and browned. Place another large skillet, oiled and hot, on top of the first skillet and reverse it. Cook the omelette in the second pan until the bottom is set and lightly browned. Serve immediately.

Notes

Alsatian vegetable soup

Serves: 8 to 10
Preparation time: 40 minutes
Cooking time: 2 hours

Almost every country in Europe has a great peasant soup, some of which are meals by themselves. This is one of them—marvelous for family dining or late Sunday suppers.

Ingredients

1   cup dry white beans
2   tablespoons sweet butter
2   onions, finely chopped
4   large garlic cloves, minced
3   carrots, peeled and quartered
4   leeks, sliced (white only)
2   celery stalks, cut into chunks
3   small white turnips, peeled and quartered
4   medium boiling potatoes, peeled and cut into chunks
1   large Bouquet Garni (page 397), including celery tops and 6 to 8 peppercorns
1   ham bone
1   pound lean blanched bacon (in one piece)
10 cups Beef Stock (page 405)
1   large cabbage, shredded (preferably Savoy cabbage)
Salt
6   peppercorns

Preparation

1. Soak the beans overnight in cold water. Drain them and parboil them for 15 minutes in salted water. Drain and reserve.

2. In a large casserole melt the butter. Add the onions and garlic. Cook for 2 or 3 minutes without letting them brown.

3. Add the carrots, leeks, celery, turnips, potatoes, beans and the Bouquet Garni.

Cover with 10 cups of Beef Stock, salt
and pepper and bring the mixture to a boil.

4. Add the ham bone and bacon. Cover the
casserole partially and cook the soup over
medium heat for 1 hour.

5. After 1 hour add the cabbage and continue cooking the soup for 1 more hour.
It should be very thick.

6. Remove the bacon and ham bone and
slice the bacon into serving pieces.
Return it to the kettle and serve the soup
either directly from the pot or in individual
earthenware dishes.

Remarks

Though grated Parmesan is not traditionally served with this soup, it is a very good
accompaniment. If you can get a good
smoked sausage or other smoked meat,
add it in the soup.
Always season it at the very end as the
bacon and ham bone usually salt the soup.

Notes

Cream of celery soup
a la francaise

Serves: 4 to 6
Preparation time: 25 minutes
Cooking time: 50 minutes

■ ●

The secret of all great soups is their base.
When using a homemade stock, even a
simple vegetable, such as Pascal celery,
can make a wonderful and delicate soup.

Ingredients

1   large bunch celery
2   carrots
1   parsnip
4   tablespoons sweet butter
5   cups Chicken Stock (page 404)
Salt
1   Bouquet Garni (page 397)
2   egg yolks
½ cup heavy cream
Freshly ground white pepper

Garnish:
1   cup freshly grated Parmesan cheese

Preparation

1. Wash the celery stalks well under cold
running water. Remove the tops and dice
the stalks.

2. Peel and dice the carrots and parsnip.
Melt 3 tablespoons of butter in a large casserole. Add the vegetables (except ½ cup
of diced celery) and cook over low heat
for 5 minutes.

3. Add the Chicken Stock, salt and pepper
and Bouquet Garni. Bring the stock to a
boil, cover, reduce the heat and cook for
40 minutes or until the vegetables are very
tender. Remove from the heat and cool.

4. In a small mixing bowl, combine the egg
yolks and heavy cream and blend them
well. Reserve.

5. Puree the soup in the blender until it is

very smooth. Return it to the casserole.

6. In a small skillet heat the remaining butter, add the reserved ½ cup of diced celery, cover and cook the celery until it is barely tender.

7. Add this celery to the soup with the egg yolk and cream mixture.

8. Reheat the soup over very low heat without letting it come to a boil, or the yolks will curdle. You can keep the soup hot over simmering water. Correct the seasoning. Serve with a side dish of grated Parmesan cheese.

Remarks

If the soup is too thick, thin it out with a little more cream.
For a variation, omit the egg yolks and pour the soup into individual bowls. Float a slice of sauteed French bread in each bowl and sprinkle heavily with grated Parmesan cheese. Place under the broiler to melt the cheese and serve.

Notes

Soupe gratinee genevoise

Serves: 4 to 6
Preparation time: 20 minutes
Cooking time: 1 hour 30 minutes

Ingredients

5 tablespoons sweet butter
3 tablespoons vegetable oil
6 large onions, finely sliced
2 garlic cloves, finely minced
3 tablespoons flour
½ cup dry white wine
6 cups Beef Stock (page 405)
1 large Bouquet Garni (page 397)
3 egg yolks
½ cup heavy cream
2 tablespoons dry sherry

Garnish:
12 pieces thinly sliced French bread (about ½ inch thick)
¾ cup grated Gruyere cheese

Preparation

1. Preheat oven to 350°.

2. In a large casserole melt the 2 tablespoons butter and 1 tablespoon oil. Add the onions and cook them, covered, over low heat until they are soft and lightly browned.

3. Add the garlic and cook for 2 or 3 minutes or until it is soft. Sprinkle the mixture with flour and stir with a wooden spoon for 2 or 3 minutes.

4. Add the wine and when it is slightly reduced, add the Beef Stock and the Bouquet Garni. Cover the casserole and cook the soup over low heat for 1 hour.

5. In the meantime, in 3 tablespoons butter and 2 tablespoons oil saute the bread slices until they are lightly browned and crisp. Reserve.

6. In a small mixing bowl beat the egg

yolks with the cream. Add the dry sherry. Whisk the mixture into the soup. Be sure not to let it boil once you have added the yolks or they will curdle.

7. Pour the soup into individual soup bowls or an earthenware tureen. Float the bread slices on top of the soup and sprinkle with cheese.

8. Place the soup bowls in a baking dish filled with hot water and bake in a 350° oven for 10 minutes or until the cheese is melted.

Remarks

The soup can be made well ahead of time up to the point of adding the egg yolks and cream. This is the kind of soup that is almost a meal and should be followed by a light main course. You can, for a variation, omit the bread and puree the soup before adding the egg yolks.

Notes

Tuscan white bean soup
Serves: 4 to 6
Preparation time: 25 minutes
Cooking time: 1 hour to 1 hour 15 minutes

This is an excellent winter soup that is quite filling. Serve it for Sunday brunch or for supper, followed by a light main course. If you have good boiled beef left over from the stock, you may add it, finely chopped, to the soup instead of the sausages.

Ingredients

1 cup dry white beans
2 tablespoons lard or sweet butter
1 large onion, finely minced
2 garlic cloves, finely minced
5 cups strong Beef Stock (page 405)
Salt
1 Bouquet Garni (page 397), including a
    small sprig of sage
1 cup heavy cream
Freshly ground white pepper
2 small spicy sausages, thinly sliced

Optional:
½ ounce dry mushrooms cooked until
    tender in 1 cup of stock

Preparation

1. Soak the beans overnight in cold water. Drain them the next day and reserve.

2. In a large casserole, heat the lard or butter. Add the onion and garlic and cook until the onions are soft but not browned.

3. Add the drained beans, the stock, a pinch of salt and the Bouquet. Bring the mixture to a boil and cook partially covered until the beans are very soft.

4. Cool the soup, remove the Bouquet and puree the soup in a blender until it is very smooth.

5. Return the soup to the saucepan and add the cream and season with salt and pepper.

6. A few minutes before serving add the sliced sausages, heat them through and serve the soup very hot accompanied by crusty bread and sweet butter.

Remarks

The mushrooms add an interesting flavor to this soup. If used, add them together with the sliced sausages before reheating the soup.

Notes

Basque poached country chicken

Serves: 4
Preparation time: 30 minutes
Cooking time: 1 hour 30 minutes

Here is a country dish in which all ingredients speak "loud and clear." The chicken, potatoes, onions and carrots must be fresh and not overcooked. The pepper sauce adds great character to this Basque specialty.

Ingredients

5 cups of Chicken Stock (page 404)
1 Bouquet Garni (page 397)
1 parsley root (optional)
1 parsnip, peeled and cut in half
2 celery stalks
1 plump whole chicken (3½ to 4 pounds)
Salt and freshly ground white pepper
6 small white turnips, peeled, cut in half
18 small new potatoes, peeled (shaped into balls)
2 small leeks, green parts included, cleaned and soaked in water
4 carrots, peeled, cut into 2-inch pieces

Optional:
1 parsley root

The red pepper sauce:
⅓ cup blanched and toasted almonds, slivered
½ cup well-drained chopped pimientos
4 tomatoes, peeled, seeded and chopped
2 hot fresh chili peppers or ¼ teaspoon cayenne
2 garlic cloves, crushed
¼ cup red wine vinegar
1 cup olive oil
1 teaspoon salt

Preparation

1. In a large casserole combine the Chicken Stock, Bouquet Garni, parsley root (if used), parsnip and celery stalks.

2. Season the chicken with salt and pepper. Truss it.

3. Bring the stock to a boil, reduce the heat and place the chicken in it. Cover the casserole and poach the chicken over low heat for 30 minutes.

4. Add the turnips, potato balls, leeks and carrots. The vegetables should fit tightly in the casserole. Cover it again and poach the chicken and vegetables for 45 minutes to an hour.

5. Test the chicken for doneness. It should be tender, but not falling apart. If the vegetables are tender before the chicken is done, remove them with a slotted spoon to a deep platter.

6. As soon as the chicken is done remove it carefully to the platter, add a little of the broth and keep the chicken and vegetables warm without further cooking until serving time. Strain the broth and serve a bowl of it to each person on the side together with the following sauce:

7. In the top part of the blender, combine the almonds, pimientos, tomatoes, chili peppers and garlic.

8. Blend the mixture at high speed for 1 or 2 minutes or until is is completely smooth.

9. Add the vinegar and enough oil to make a smooth red sauce. Taste the sauce; it should be very spicy. Correct seasoning and transfer sauce to a serving bowl.

Remarks

The garlic sauce Aioli (page 383) can also be served with the chicken and

in northern Spain it is often mixed with the Red Pepper Sauce.

Other meats, such as beef or tongue, can be cooked and added to the platter. This makes a much more interesting dish and I highly recommend it.

You may make a Veloute of Chicken out of the remaining broth. The recipe is on page 368.

Notes

Veloute of chicken

Ingredients

4 tablespoons sweet butter
4 tablespoons flour
5 cups chicken broth
½ cup heavy cream
Salt and freshly ground white pepper

Optional:
2 tablespoons finely minced mixed fresh
  herbs

Preparation

1. In a large heavy saucepan, heat the butter, add the flour and stir for 2 or 3 minutes without browning.

2. Add the hot chicken broth all at once and whisk the soup constantly until it is slightly thickened and smooth.

3. Add the heavy cream, salt and pepper and the optional herbs and serve very hot.

Notes

Poulet a la bresse

Serves: 4 to 6
Preparation time: 20 minutes
Cooking time: 45 minutes to 1 hour

The region of Bresse in France has always been famous for its chickens and many great chicken dishes originated in the peasant kitchens of the area. This dish, popular in Bresse, is good for an "in between" season as it makes use of the market staples.

Ingredients

2 2½-pound chickens, cut into eighths
4 tablespoons sweet butter
2 tablespoons vegetable oil
Salt and freshly ground white pepper
½ cup dry white wine
¾ cup strong Chicken Stock (page 404)
3 carrots, cut into large chunks
2 large onions, cut into large chunks
3 leeks (white part only), cleaned well
  and sliced in half lengthwise
1 large Bouquet Garni (page 397)
3 egg yolks
Juice of 1 lemon
1 cup heavy cream

Garnish:
2 tablespoons finely minced parsley
1 tablespoon finely minced chives

Preparation

1. Dry the chicken pieces on paper towels.

2. In a large skillet or chicken fryer melt the 3 tablespoons butter and 1 tablespoon oil. Add a few pieces of chicken at a time, skin side down at first, then turn to brown evenly on all sides. Remove finished ones from the pan and continue browning the rest of the pieces in the same way. (If the fat is burning, discard it and add 1 tablespoon of butter and 1 tablespoon of oil to the pan.)

3. Season the chicken pieces with salt and pepper.

4. To the fat remaining in the pan add the wine and Chicken Stock. Scrape the brown particles at the bottom of the pan in with the liquid. Lower the heat and return the chicken pieces to the pan.

5. Top the chicken with the vegetables. Add the Bouquet Garni.

6. Cover the pan tightly and cook for 45 to 50 minutes.

7. Remove the chicken pieces to an oven-proof serving platter and keep warm while you finish the sauce.

8. With a large slotted spoon, remove all the vegetables and the Bouquet from the pan—discard them. Raise the heat and reduce the sauce by ½. It should coat a spoon lightly. Keep an eye on the pan so the sauce does not reduce too much. Remove the pan from the heat.

9. In a small bowl beat the egg yolks until they are thick and creamy. Add the lemon juice and the cream. Whisk this mixture into the pan juices. Return the pan to the stove and cook over very low heat for 1 or 2 minutes. Do not let the sauce come to a boil or the egg yolks will curdle.

10. Correct the seasoning. Spoon the sauce over the chicken. Serve immediately or keep warm in a 200° oven for 20 or 30 minutes. Garnish the platter with parsley and chives.

Remarks

For a more "country" meal, serve the chicken surrounded by the cooked vegetables. In that case cut the carrots into 1½-inch-long pieces and instead of 2 large onions use 8 to 10 white onions or 6 to 8 whole peeled shallots. Both carrots and onions should be parboiled for 8 to 10 minutes before being added to the chicken.

Notes

Poulet au celeri

Serves: 4
Preparation time: 45 minutes
Cooking time: 2 hours 30 minutes

Ingredients

The stuffing:
1 cup fresh peeled chestnuts
    (page 397)
2 cups Chicken Stock (page 404)
2 tablespoons sweet butter
3 tablespoons finely minced onion
2 chicken livers
Salt and freshly ground white pepper
1 cup sausage meat, or a mixture of
    ground veal or pork
Pinch of allspice
1 garlic clove
1 egg
¼ cup bread crumbs, soaked in a little milk
    and squeezed dry

The chicken:
1 3½- to 4-pound roasting chicken
Salt and freshly ground white pepper
2 tablespoons sweet butter
1 tablespoon oil
2 cups Chicken Stock (page 404)
1 small Bouquet Garni (page 397)
2 onions, sliced in half
4 small celery hearts (2 inches wide and
    5 inches long)
1 Beurre Manie (page 397)

Optional:
2 tablespoons cold sweet butter

Preparation

1. Preheat the oven to 375°.

2. In a saucepan, combine the chestnuts and Beef Stock and cook, covered, for 45 to 50 minutes or until the chestnuts are tender. Drain and chop them coarsely. Reserve.

3. In a small skillet heat 2 tablespoons butter. Add the minced onion and the chicken liver. Season with salt and pepper. Cook until the liver is nicely browned. Remove from the heat, mince them finely, and reserve.

4. In a mixing bowl, combine the sausage meat, allspice, garlic, the chestnuts, the chicken liver, minced onion and the butter in which they were cooked. Add the egg and work the mixture with your hands to blend thoroughly.

5. Add the bread crumbs and mix well. Correct the seasoning.

6. Season the chicken with salt and pepper. Stuff it and sew the tail opening. Truss.

7. In a large baking dish, melt 2 tablespoons butter and oil. When it is very hot, brown the chicken on all sides. Do not burn the fat. Add a little Chicken Stock to the pan as well as the Bouquet Garni and the onion halves and place the chicken in the oven.

8. Clean the celery hearts under cold running water to remove all possible sand. Tie the pieces with kitchen string, drop them into boiling water and cook for 10 minutes.

9. Drain the celery and add to the chicken pan together with 1 cup of stock. Cover the pan with foil and braise the chicken for 1 hour and 15 minutes, basting often with pan juices. You may need a little more stock. If so, always add warm stock and baste the chicken with the hot juices.

10. After 1 hour and 15 minutes, remove the celery hearts to a side dish and keep warm.

11. Uncover the chicken and continue roasting for another 15 to 20 minutes or until the juices run pale yellow when tested with a fork. Keep basting the chicken and turn it to brown evenly on all sides.

12. Remove the chicken to the serving platter. Remove the strings from the celery hearts, cut each heart in two and place in a decorative pattern around the chicken.

13. Strain the pan juices into a small saucepan. Place the pan over low heat and beat in a Beurre Manie. When the sauce has reached the right consistency (it should heavily coat a spoon), remove it from the heat and beat in the optional 2 tablespoons of cold butter. Spoon the sauce over the celery and chicken and serve.

Remarks

The chicken can be carved in the kitchen. The stuffing is then placed in a little mound in the center of the platter, topped with the quartered chicken and garnished with the celery hearts. You may serve parslied potato balls and an endive salad with this dish.

Notes

Poulet piquant

Serves: 4 to 6
Preparation time: 40 minutes
Cooking time: 1 hour

■●

Ingredients

2 small chickens (2½ pounds each), cut into serving pieces
Salt and freshly ground white pepper
4 tablespoons olive oil
1 cup onions, finely minced
½ cup tomato puree
½ cup dry white wine
1 cup Chicken Stock (page 404)
Juice of 1 large lemon
1 tablespoon capers, finely chopped
2 small dill gherkins, finely chopped
2 tablespoons minced parsley
1 large garlic clove, finely minced
4 anchovies, finely minced
1 Beurre Manie (page 397)

Garnish:
2 quartered lemons
2 tablespoons minced parsley
Cherry tomatoes sauteed in 2 tablespoons of sweet butter

Preparation

1. Dry the pieces of chicken very well on paper towels. They must be as dry as possible, otherwise you will have a great amount of splattering when sauteeing in olive oil. Season with salt and pepper.

2. In a large frying pan heat 2 tablespoons of olive oil and add a few pieces of chicken. Saute them until they are very well browned on each side. Remove these pieces from the pan and continue until all the chicken is browned, adding a little more oil when needed. Make sure not to burn the oil.

3. Remove all but 2 tablespoons of fat from the pan. Add the onions and

cook over low heat until they are soft but not browned. Add the tomato puree and the wine. Let the mixture come to a boil and add the Chicken Stock. Bring to a boil. Lower the heat and return the chicken pieces to the pan.

4. Cover the pan tightly and simmer the chicken for 45 minutes or until tender. Don't overcook.

5. In the meantime, in a mixing bowl combine the lemon juice, capers, gherkins, parsley, garlic, and anchovies. Let this marinate for a few minutes.

6. When the chicken is done, remove the pieces to a serving platter. Raise the heat and reduce the pan juices by 1/3. Slowly, bit by bit, whisk in a Beurre Manie. The sauce will get thick and smooth.

7. Add the anchovy and parsley mixture. Lower the heat and simmer the sauce for 2 minutes. Correct the seasoning and pour the sauce over the chicken.

8. Garnish with lemon quarters, parsley and sauteed cherry tomatoes. Serve immediately.

Remarks

You can saute the chicken well in advance, and also prepare the anchovy and parsley mixture. The finished dish will keep warm in a 200° oven for 30 to 40 minutes but no more, as the chicken will dry out. Stuffed mushrooms or braised white onions are also perfect with this dish. Don't feel obliged to serve potatoes or rice.

Calves' liver savoyarde

Serves: 6
Preparation time: 10 minutes
Cooking time: 7 to 10 minutes

There are always days when we really do not feel like spending much time in the kitchen and yet would like a change in the menu. This recipe fills such a need. Serve the calves' liver for an informal dinner surrounded by a garniture of turnips and carrots sauteed in butter and arranged in an alternating pattern on the platter.

Ingredients

6 slices calves' liver, 1/2 inch thick
Salt and freshly ground white pepper
1 cup bacon, cut into 1/2-inch cubes
2 to 4 tablespoons sweet butter
4 to 6 leeks, white part only, sliced 1/4 inch thick
1 cup Brown Stock (page 403), mixed with 1 teaspoon cornstarch

Garnish:
2 tablespoons parsley minced
Sauteed turnips and carrots

Preparation

1. Cut the calves' liver into 1/2-inch-long strips and season with salt and pepper.

2. In a large heavy skillet saute the bacon cubes and when they are almost crisp remove them from the pan and reserve.

3. Remove all but 2 tablespoons of fat from the pan. In the same skillet melt 2 tablespoons butter. Cook the leeks, covered, over low flame until tender but do not let them brown. Remove them from the pan and reserve.

4. Add the remaining butter to the pan. Increase the heat under the skillet and add the calves' liver. Saute for 2 or 3 minutes.

The liver should remain pink inside. Make sure not to crowd the pan or the liver will "steam" instead of sauteeing. As soon as the liver is done, remove it to a serving platter.

5. Add the Brown Stock to the skillet and bring it to a boil. Add the bacon and leeks and heat through. Pour this mixture over the liver.

6. Serve immediately, garnished with parsley and surrounded with small turnips and carrots.

Notes

Sauteed turnips and carrots

Ingredients

1   teaspoon salt
2   cups of small white turnips, peeled and cut in half (or quarters)
2   cups carrots, cut into matchsticks
4   tablespoons sweet butter
Salt and freshly ground white pepper
1   tablespoon chopped parsley

Optional:
1   teaspoon chopped chives

Preparation

1. In a large saucepan bring 3 quarts of water to a boil. Add the salt and the turnips and carrots and cook for 10 minutes. Drain the turnips and run them under cold water. Place them on a double layer of paper towels and let them dry well.

2. In a large skillet heat the butter until it turns a light hazelnut color. Don't let it burn. Add the turnips and carrots and saute them over low heat until they are light brown and still slightly crisp. Season with salt and pepper.

3. Add the parsley and optional chives and arrange around the calves' liver.

Notes

Alsatian sausage potpourri

Serves: 4 to 6
Preparation time: 30 minutes
Cooking time: 1 hour 15 minutes

This is a flavorful country dish that calls for good sausages, such as the Kielbasa, which can be found at most German or Hungarian butchers. You may substitute smoked shoulder of pork or a meaty smoked ham bone for the sausages.

Ingredients

1 large head Savoy cabbage
1 pound slab bacon
8 to 10 garlic cloves
4 to 6 medium Kielbasa
2 carrots
4 medium potatoes
2 to 3 white turnips
2 celery stalks with leaves
8 whole shallots, peeled
1 large Bouquet Garni (page 397), including 2 celery stalks with their tops and 1 leek
2 to 3 cups Beef Stock (page 405)
Salt
Freshly ground white pepper

Preparation

1. Preheat oven to 375°.

2. In a large casserole bring 3 quarts of salted water to a boil.

3. Clean the cabbage, removing all wilted outer leaves. Cut the cabbage into quarters and blanch them for 8 to 10 minutes. Remove cabbage with a slotted spoon. As soon as the cabbage is cool enough to handle cut into large chunks.

4. Drop the bacon into the boiling water for 5 minutes. Then drop the garlic cloves into the same water for 1 or 2 minutes and slip off their skins.

5. Drain the bacon and cut it into bite-sized pieces.

6. Prick the sausages in several places. Cut the carrots, potatoes and turnips into large chunks.

7. Make a layer of cabbage in an earthenware casserole. Place the potatoes, shallots, sausages, turnips, carrots, bacon and Bouquet Garni on top. Strew the garlic cloves over them, then cover them with another layer of cabbage. Season with salt and pepper.

8. Add Beef Stock. It should come almost to the top of the vegetables.

9. Cover the casserole and bake for 1 hour or until the vegetables are tender but not mushy.

10. Remove the Bouquet. Serve directly from the casserole with Dijon mustard and dark bread.

Remarks

Garlic will lose its strong taste once cooked. Serve it on the side for mashing on dark bread.
The homemade stock adds a great deal of refinement to this otherwise very simple dish.

Notes

Shrimp in garlic and caper butter

Serves: 6 to 8
Preparation time: 15 minutes
Cooking time: 10 minutes

■ ●

Even though shrimp are at their best during the winter months, their year-round availability makes them an important standby for either a simple or an elegant meal. Here is a delicious way to prepare them—a welcome change from the unexciting shrimp cocktail.

Ingredients

2 pounds fresh shrimp
4 filets of anchovies, finely chopped
Juice of 1 lemon
2 to 3 garlic cloves, finely minced
2 tablespoons finely chopped parsley
2 tablespoons tiny capers
8 tablespoons sweet butter
2 tablespoons finely minced shallots
Salt and freshly ground black pepper

Optional:
1 to 2 dried hot red chili peppers

Garnish:
2 tablespoons finely minced parsley
2 tablespoons finely chopped pimientos
2 lemons, quartered

Preparation

1. Bring 3 quarts of salted water to a boil in a large saucepan. (If you have Fish Stock, by all means use that for poaching the shrimp.) When the water comes to a boil, add the shrimp and as soon as they turn bright pink, drain and peel them. It is not necessary to devein them.

2. In a small bowl, combine the anchovies, lemon juice, garlic, parsley and capers.

3. Heat the butter in a large skillet. Add the shallots and cook until they are soft but not browned.

4. Add the shrimp and shake the pan several times to coat them evenly with butter.

5. Add the parsley mixture and cook for 2 or 3 minutes more. Season with salt and pepper. Sprinkle with additional chopped parsley. Serve directly from the skillet with crusty bread.

Remarks

If you like a somewhat spicy touch, add the chilies when you saute the shallots and remove them just before serving. You may also garnish the dish with chopped pimientos and quartered lemons.

Notes

all-seasons main courses

Filets of sole
al vino bianco

Serves: 6
Preparation time: 25 minutes
Cooking time: 15 minutes

■ ○

There is a tremendous versatility to sole. It is not a fish which has to be masked in a white sauce. It lends itself well to year-round cooking and this particular recipe is good for those transitional cooking days when you feel like opening your refrigerator and finding in it most of the ingredients you need to prepare an elegant little meal in 30 minutes. Of course you may use other fish filets, such as red snapper or mackerel. If you add this dish to your summer repertory, add 1 or 2 tablespoons of minced herbs to the sauce.

Ingredients

2 large eggs
8 small filets of sole
Salt and freshly ground white pepper
Flour for dredging
2 cups fine homemade white bread crumbs
4 tablespoons Clarified Butter (page 398)
1 tablespoon oil

The sauce:
2 tablespoons olive oil
2 tablespoons shallots, finely minced
3 tablespoons finely minced parsley
1 tablespoon capers
2 garlic cloves, very finely minced
½ cup dry white wine
½ cup Fish Stock (page 406)
Freshly ground black pepper

Optional:
Pinch of oregano

Preparation

1. In a shallow bowl beat the eggs with 2 tablespoons of water.

2. Dry the filets well on paper towels.

Season with salt and pepper. Dip them into flour, shaking off the excess. Then dip them into the beaten eggs and then into bread crumbs. Place the filets on wax paper until you are ready to fry them. This can be done well in advance.

3. In a large frying pan heat the butter and 1 tablespoon of oil. Add the filets, making sure not to crowd the pan. Cook them over medium heat until they are golden brown. Turn them carefully with a spatula and brown on the other side. Make sure not to burn the butter.

4. In the meantime, heat 2 tablespoons of olive oil in a small saucepan. Add the shallots, the parsley, capers, garlic and anchovies. Simmer the mixture for 2 or 3 minutes. Add the wine and the stock. Reduce the mixture by half and pour it over the sole. Simmer the sole in the sauce for 2 or 3 minutes. Season with black pepper and the optional oregano and serve.

Remarks

For recipes that call for slow frying of breaded meats or fish I usually use Clarified Butter which does not burn as easily as unclarified butter. It is wise to clarify a large amount at one time and store it in a covered jar in the refrigerator (page 398).

Notes

Roast veal smitane

Serves: 6
Preparation time: 35 minutes
Cooking time: 2 hours

I always like to prepare this recipe at the very beginning of fall when I still have a good supply of fresh herbs. I find veal too delicate for dried herbs, especially tarragon, which tends to overpower if used in too large a quantity. Serve a garniture of simply cooked and buttered vegetables—carrots, glazed white onions and sauteed button mushrooms.

Ingredients

2 cups Chicken Stock (page 404)
4-pound veal roast, boned and rolled
1 garlic clove, mashed
Salt and freshly ground white pepper
½ teaspoon imported paprika
3 tablespoons Clarified Butter (page 398)
1 carrot, peeled and diced
1 celery stalk, peeled and diced
1 whole peeled onion
1 Bouquet Garni (page 397)

Sauce:
1 cup heavy cream
Juice of 1 lemon
2 shallots, finely chopped
2 tablespoons finely chopped herbs (tarragon, chervil, parsley)
1 cup dry white wine
Salt and freshly ground white pepper

Optional:
1 Beurre Manie (page 397)

Garnish:
2 tablespoons finely chopped tarragon and chives

Preparation

1. Heat the Chicken Stock in a saucepan and keep it warm on top of the stove.

2. In a mixing bowl combine the cream and lemon juice and let it stand at room temperature for 2 or 3 hours. It will thicken considerably.

3. Preheat oven to 350°.

4. In a small saucepan combine the shallots and herbs with the wine and cook the mixture over high heat until it is reduced to ¼ of a cup. Add the lemon and cream. Season lightly with salt and white pepper and set it aside.

5. Rub the veal with the garlic. Season it with salt, pepper and paprika.

6. In a large flameproof casserole, heat the butter on top of the stove. Add the roast and brown it well on all sides over medium heat. Remove it from the casserole.

7. Add the carrot, celery and onion to the casserole and cook for 2 or 3 minutes without browning.

8. Place the veal together with the Bouquet Garni on top of the vegetables. Set the casserole in the middle part of the oven and roast the veal for 1¾ to 2 hours. Baste every 10 minutes with warm Chicken Stock. Do not forget to baste or the meat will dry out. As soon as the meat is done, remove it to a platter. Discard the strings that tied the roast and keep the meat warm while you finish preparing the sauce.

9. Skim the fat off the juices remaining in the pan. Pass the vegetables through a sieve and press down hard with a spoon to extract all the juices.

10. Return these juices to the casserole. Add the lemon, cream and herb mixture.

Cook the sauce over high heat to reduce it by ⅓.

11. Add bit by bit the Beurre Manie (you may not need the entire "ball"), constantly stirring the sauce until it heavily coats a spoon. Correct the seasoning and remove from the heat.

12. Slice the veal and arrange it on a platter. Spoon a little of the sauce over the meat and sprinkle it with the tarragon and chives. Serve the rest of the sauce in a sauceboat.

Remarks

This kind of roast should not be "drenched" in sauce. You should be able to garnish the platter with a mixture of seasonal vegetables that do not float in sauce. Some cuts of veal tend to be very dry. Ask your butcher to place a stick of sweet butter in the center of the roll of meat. This will keep it extremely moist and tender.

Notes

Yugoslav white bean ragout

Serves: 6 to 8
Preparation time: 40 minutes
Cooking time: 1 hour and 30 minutes

Ingredients

3 cups dry white beans
Salt
6 peppercorns
1 Bouquet Garni (page 397)
1 whole onion, stuck with a clove
1 cup diced salt pork
1 pound spareribs, cut into small pieces
2 tablespoons sweet butter
1 onion, finely minced
2 garlic cloves, minced
2 green peppers, finely diced
2 red peppers, finely diced
4 to 6 fresh tomatoes, peeled, seeded and chopped
1 hot chili pepper (dried)
Freshly ground white pepper
2 small garlic sausages, sliced into ½-inch slices
2 tablespoons olive oil
2 tablespoons finely minced parsley
¾ cup bread crumbs

Preparation

1. Preheat the oven to 350°.

2. Soak the beans overnight. Drain and cover them with fresh water. Season with salt and peppercorns. Add the Bouquet Garni and the onion stuck with a clove.

3. Bring the water to a boil, reduce the heat and cook, partially covered, for 30 minutes until the beans are barely tender. While they are cooking, drop the salt-pork cubes into boiling water and cook for 5 minutes. Drain well on paper towels and reserve.

4. Season the spareribs with salt and pepper.

Carrots en estouffade

Serves: 6
Preparation time: 20 minutes
Cooking time: 30 minutes

■ ●

5. In a large skillet, heat the butter. Add the salt-pork cubes and cook them until almost crisp. Remove them to a side dish and reserve.

6. Add the spareribs to the fat remaining in the pan and brown them on all sides. Be sure not to burn the fat. Transfer the spareribs to a side dish and remove all but 2 tablespoons of fat from the skillet.

7. Add the minced onion and garlic and cook without browning for 3 minutes.

8. Add the peppers, tomatoes, hot chili pepper, salt and pepper.

9. Return the spareribs to the pan. Partially cover the skillet and cook the sauce for 40 minutes.

10. Drain the beans and pour them into a buttered baking dish. Discard the Bouquet Garni and whole onion. Add the salt-pork cubes to the beans.

11. After 40 minutes add the garlic sausages to the tomato sauce and cook it for 10 more minutes, uncovered, to heat the sausages through and reduce the sauce to a thick puree. Pour the tomato sauce over the beans and mix well.

12. In a small skillet heat 2 tablespoons of olive oil. When it is hot, add the parsley and bread crumbs and brown them lightly. Sprinkle the beans with this mixture.

13. Place the baking dish in the oven and bake the beans for 20 minutes. Serve directly from the dish.

Carrots are the most versatile of year-round vegetables, but they do vary in quality and for certain dishes fresh carrots (with their greens attached) are a must. For this recipe you may use packaged fresh carrots, although they, too, should be carefully examined for freshness.

Ingredients

2 pounds carrots, peeled
18 small white onions
4 tablespoons sweet butter
Salt
1 cup finely diced salt pork
1 teaspoon sugar
Freshly ground white pepper

Garnish:
2 tablespoons very finely chopped parsley

Preparation

1. Cut the carrots in half lengthwise. If they are very large, cut them in half lengthwise again and then into 1½-inch-long sticks. If you are doing this in advance, keep the carrots in cold water and refrigerated. They will keep this way for several days.

2. In a small saucepan bring 6 cups of salted water to a boil. Add the onions and cook them for 5 minutes. Drain and reserve.

3. In another 2-quart saucepan combine the carrots with 1 cup water and 2 tablespoons butter and a pinch of salt. Bring the water to a boil, cover the saucepan and cook the carrots over medium heat for 10 minutes or until they are barely tender. They should still be quite crisp. Drain and reserve.

Carrots royale

Serves: 6 to 8
Preparation time: 10 minutes
Cooking time: 20 minutes

4. In a heavy-bottomed 10-inch skillet saute the salt pork over low heat until it is crisp. Remove it from the skillet and pour out all but 2 tablespoons of the fat. Add the remaining butter to the fat.

5. When the butter is very hot, add the onions and the sugar. Cook for 2 or 3 minutes until the onions are lightly glazed.

6. Add the carrots and the salt pork. Shake the skillet to glaze the carrots. Cover the pan and simmer over very low heat for 10 to 15 minutes. Be sure not to overcook the carrots.

7. Correct the seasoning, adding a good pinch of pepper. Pour the vegetables into a serving dish and sprinkle with parsley.

Notes

This recipe calls for young tender carrots and in Europe it is usually made with whole baby carrots. Still, any fresh carrots will do, although the presentation may not be as pretty. If the carrots are large, cut them into 1½-inch matchsticks. When using young carrots, quarter them or even leave them whole.

Ingredients

2 pounds young carrots
8 tablespoons sweet butter
2 teaspoons sugar
Salt and freshly ground white pepper
¼ to ½ cup Brown Stock (page 403)
½ cup heavy cream
2 egg yolks
1 tablespoon finely chopped dill or mixed fresh herbs

Preparation

1. Trim the stems and scrape the carrots with a vegetable peeler. Cut them into matchsticks or slice them. Keep the pieces in a bowl of cold water until you are ready to use them.

2. In a heavy-bottomed 3-quart saucepan, melt the butter. Add the drained carrots, sugar, salt and white pepper. Cover the saucepan and simmer the carrots for 15 to 20 minutes. If they are very young, they may not take more than 10 minutes. Stir the carrots often and add the Brown Stock, a few drops at a time, to keep them from sticking.

3. In a small bowl, combine the cream and egg yolks until they are well blended. Add the herbs.

4. When the carrots are tender, uncover the pan, and continue cooking until only ½ cup of liquid is left in the pan. Remove the pan from the heat and swirl in the cream and herb mixture. Return the pan to the burner just long enough to heat the sauce. Do not let it boil or the yolks will curdle. Serve the carrots at once.

Remarks

The carrots can be prepared and cooked well in advance of serving, but the cream and egg yolks should not be added until just before serving.
Other herbs such as chervil, chives and mint can be substituted for the dill. Never substitute dill seed for fresh dill; rather use another fresh herb.

Notes

Cold leeks in sour cream

Serves: 4
Preparation time: 15 minutes
Cooking time: 10 to 12 minutes

■●

Leeks are a versatile, year-round vegetable, not just something used to flavor soups and stocks. They are good gratineed or simply poached and served with brown butter. Here is a way to serve them cold as an appetizer, as an accompaniment to cold poached fish or as part of your hors d'oeuvre table.

Ingredients

8 leeks
2 tablespoons sweet butter
1 teaspoon salt
1 cup Creme Fraiche (page 398) or sour cream
1 teaspoon Dijon mustard
1 small garlic clove, mashed
2 tablespoons prepared horseradish
2 tablespoons cider vinegar

Garnish:
Fresh watercress and whole radishes

Preparation

1. Trim the leeks and take off all but 1 inch of the greens. Remove the first one or two outer leaves. Cut a cross into the green part of the leeks and wash them thoroughly under cold running water to remove all the sand.

2. Place the leeks in a casserole with the butter and water to cover. Add salt and bring the water to a boil over high heat. Lower the heat, partially cover the casserole and simmer the leeks until barely tender. Test them frequently with the tip of a sharp knife. More often than not they are not equal in size, and some will therefore be done sooner than others. As the

leeks are done, remove them to paper towels and drain them well.

3. In a mixing bowl combine the Creme Fraiche, Dijon mustard, garlic, horseradish and vinegar. Be sure to squeeze the horseradish dry in a towel before adding it to the mixture.

4. Place the leeks on a serving platter and pour the dressing over them, coating them completely. Garnish the platter with watercress and radishes. Refrigerate the leeks for 2 to 4 hours before serving.

Remarks

You may, of course, poach the leeks a day ahead and make the sauce in advance too. If you have some very large leeks and others which are very thin, cut the large ones in half lengthwise.
If you want to serve leeks as a luncheon dish, place serving portions on individual plates and garnish with Boston lettuce, quartered hard-boiled eggs and a slice of prosciutto or other smoked ham.

Notes

Stuffed peppers venezia
Serves: 8
Preparation time: 15 minutes
Cooking time: 1 hour 15 minutes

Stuffed peppers with a mixture of raisins and pine nuts bring a change to your "traditional" kitchen. They take only minutes to prepare and require simple ingredients. You can serve them either hot or cold.

Ingredients

8 small bell peppers
Salt
¾ cup Italian rice
½ cup white raisins
2 tablespoons sweet butter
½ cup pine nuts
½ cup tuna fish (preferably packed in olive oil)
1 tablespoon finely minced capers
2 tablespoons finely minced parsley
Freshly ground black pepper
Large pinch of nutmeg
4 tablespoons olive oil

Preparation

1. Preheat oven to 375°.

2. Core and seed the peppers.

3. In a saucepan bring 2 cups of water to a boil. Add a large pinch of salt and the rice. Bring the rice to a boil, then lower the heat and simmer it, covered, for 20 minutes. Check once or twice, for it may need ¼ cup more water.

4. After 15 minutes add the raisins and continue cooking until the rice is tender. Remove the pan from the heat and cool.

5. In a small skillet melt the butter. Add the pine nuts and saute them for 2 or 3 minutes until lightly browned. Don't burn them.

6. Combine the pine nuts, tuna fish, capers, parsley, salt, pepper, and nutmeg with the rice. Taste the mixture. You may wish to add more parsley or capers. Fill the peppers with this mixture.

7. Pour 2 tablespoons of olive oil into a baking dish. Arrange the peppers in the dish and sprinkle with the remaining olive oil. Bake for 45 minutes. Serve the peppers warm or cold.

Remarks

You cannot use converted rice for this dish. If you cannot get Italian rice, use Carolina long grain. With the addition of the Tomato Sauce (page 400) you may easily serve these peppers as the main course for a light supper.

Notes

Potatoes aioli

Serves: 6
Preparation time: 10 minutes
Cooking time: 1 hour 15 minutes

■●

One of the simplest yet happiest marriages of American cooking with that of the French Provence is a well-baked potato topped with a tablespoon of Aioli sauce.

Ingredients

6 baking potatoes
2 tablespoons melted sweet butter

The sauce:
2 eggs
4 garlic cloves, peeled
1 teaspoon Dijon mustard
1 tablespoon tarragon vinegar
Good dash freshly ground white pepper
1 to 1½ cups olive oil
Dash of Tabasco
1 teaspoon salt

Preparation

1. Preheat the oven to 400°.

2. Scrub the potatoes, brush them with melted butter, and place them on a cookie sheet. Bake for 1 hour and 15 minutes or until tender when pierced with a fork.

3. In the meantime, break the eggs into the container of a blender.

4. Add the garlic, crushed into a paste with the salt in a mortar and pestle or with a garlic press (in that case you will lose some of the garlic juice!), the mustard, vinegar and pepper. Blend the egg mixture at high speed for 1 minute and then start adding the oil by drops. Be sure to add it very slowly at the beginning. As soon as the sauce begins to thicken, you may pour in the rest of the oil in an even stream.

5. Add the Tabasco, correct the seasoning and reserve.

Curry risotto

Serves: 4
Preparation time: 10 minutes
Cooking time: 25 minutes

6. When the potatoes are done, cut a slit in each one and let them cool slightly. Mash the potatoes in their skins and season with salt and pepper. Then top each one with 1 tablespoon of "Aioli" sauce. Serve the rest on the side.

Remarks

A platter of several cooked vegetables, such as cauliflower, carrots, leeks and turnips, served with a bowl of Aioli and crusty bread makes a marvelous first course or an excellent accompaniment to roast beef or whole grilled fish.
You may add 1 tablespoon of finely chopped fresh basil to the Aioli in summer and serve the sauce with grilled steaks and lamb chops.

Notes

This is a simple way to prepare rice, enhanced by the addition of cubed avocado or a few freshly cooked green peas. In summer you may change it with the seasonal addition of a roasted green pepper, finely chopped, and 1 tablespoon of minced chives.

Ingredients

½ teaspoon curry powder
1 tablespoon tomato paste
6 tablespoons butter
1 onion, finely chopped
1 cup Carolina rice
2 cups Chicken Stock (page 404)
Salt and freshly ground white pepper
1 small Bouquet Garni (page 397)

Optional:
Pimiento strips for garnish
1 ripe avocado, cubed

Preparation

1. Mix the curry and the tomato paste until smooth.

2. In a heavy-bottomed 2-quart saucepan melt 2 tablespoons butter. Add the onion and cook until tender. Add the rice, salt and pepper and mix it well with the butter and onion. Add the tomato-curry mixture and the Chicken Stock. Bring to a boil and lower the heat.

3. Add the Bouquet Garni and simmer the rice, covered, until it is tender (about 20 minutes). Remove the Bouquet.

4. Before serving beat the remaining butter into the rice. Garnish with avocado cubes and pimiento strips.

Sicilian rice with peppers

Serves: 4 to 6
Preparation time: 20 minutes
Cooking time: 35 to 40 minutes

■ ●

This well-flavored rice is an excellent accompaniment to a roast leg of lamb, sauteed chicken or calves' liver. It can be served as an appetizer by adding to it a lump of sweet butter and a handful of freshly grated Parmesan cheese before serving. You may also turn it into a hearty supper dish by placing the finished rice in a shallow oval baking dish, topping it with 4 to 6 slices of sauteed smoked ham and 4 to 6 eggs fried in olive oil.

Remarks

The rice will keep warm in a 200° oven for 30 to 40 minutes. If you prefer, it may also be cooked entirely in the oven at 350°. This will take about 40 to 50 minutes. For a variation, omit the curry and flavor the risotto with 1/3 to 1/2 cup freshly grated Parmesan cheese.

Notes

Ingredients

1 1/2 cups long-grain rice
3 tablespoons olive oil
1 onion, finely minced
1 large garlic clove, crushed
1 red bell pepper, finely minced, or 1 cup finely cubed pimientos
2 tablespoons finely minced parsley
2 large ripe tomatoes, peeled, seeded and chopped
Pinch of salt
Pinch of freshly ground white pepper
3 cups Chicken Stock (page 404) or water
1 Bouquet Garni (page 397), tied in a cheesecloth

Optional:
2 tablespoons sweet butter
1/2 cup finely grated Parmesan cheese

Preparation

1. Wash the rice thoroughly under cold running water and reserve.

2. In a heavy-bottomed saucepan, heat the olive oil, add the onion, garlic and bell pepper and cook the mixture over medium

heat until it is soft and lightly browned.

3. Add the parsley and tomatoes. Season the mixture with salt and pepper and cook it over high heat until all the tomato juice has evaporated and the mixture is thick.

4. Add the rice and cook it for 1 or 2 minutes, coating it well with the tomato mixture.

5. Add the Chicken Stock (or water), bring it to a boil and add the Bouquet Garni. Cover the saucepan tightly and cook the rice over very low heat for 20 to 25 minutes without stirring.

6. Just before serving remove the Bouquet and stir into the rice the optional butter and Parmesan. Fluff up the rice with two forks and serve immediately.

Notes

Tomatoes a l'italienne

Serves: 4
Preparation time: 10 minutes
Cooking time: 5 minutes

A simple accompaniment to grilled chops and steaks that is easy to prepare and gives a quick finishing touch to a platter.

Ingredients

8 to 12 ripe Italian plum tomatoes
4 tablespoons sweet butter
2 small garlic cloves, finely minced
2 tablespoons minced parsley
1 teaspoon oregano
Salt and freshly ground white pepper

Optional:
2 anchovy filets, finely minced

Preparation

1. Drop the tomatoes into fast-boiling water for 60 seconds. Drain them and peel.

2. In a large skillet melt the butter, add the tomatoes and cook over low heat until they are just heated through. Do not cook too long or they will disintegrate.

3. Add the garlic, parsley, oregano and optional anchovies and shake the pan to coat the tomatoes well with the herbs.

4. Remove the pan and season with salt and pepper. Serve immediately.

Remarks

When using the tomatoes as a garnish for lamb, add the minced anchovies to the garlic and parsley mixture. In the summer, you may add 2 tablespoons of finely minced basil, chives or a mixture of fresh herbs for the last two minutes of cooking.
The tomatoes can be served cold. If so, dribble them with olive oil and a little red wine vinegar before serving.

Cold carrot salad with fines herbes

Serves: 6
Preparation time: 15 minutes
Cooking time: 5 to 7 minutes

Tender young carrots make a lovely salad to serve with cold meats or as part of your hors d'oeuvre table. Carrots can be marinated at any time and I usually keep a large jar of them in the refrigerator. They are good for garnishing a cold poached fish or a mixed green salad.

Ingredients

6 to 8 young carrots
½ teaspoon salt
1 tablespoon sugar
6 tablespoons olive oil
2 tablespoons tarragon vinegar
¼ teaspoon powdered mustard
2 tablespoons finely chopped herbs (thyme, chives and chervil)
1 small garlic clove, crushed in a garlic press
Freshly ground white pepper
Juice of 1 large lemon

Preparation

1. Remove the green carrot tops. Scrape the carrots with a vegetable peeler and cut them in half lengthwise, then into 1½-inch-long sticks. Place them in a saucepan and cover them with water. Add the salt and sugar and cook the carrots over medium heat until they are barely tender (about 5 to 7 minutes). Drain and reserve.

2. In a small bowl combine the oil, vinegar, mustard and herbs. Whisk the dressing until it is very well blended. Add the garlic and pour the sauce over the carrots while they are still warm. Season with salt and pepper and refrigerate for at least 6 hours. Serve at room temperature, sprinkling the carrots with the juice of 1 lemon.

Remarks

You may, of course, use packaged carrots (not frozen or canned) if you cannot find fresh ones. In that case the cooking time will be longer. Also you may have to remove the hard core of the carrots and slice them into quarters instead of halves. The easiest way to prepare a very well-blended dressing is in a flour shaker or a small jar. Combine the ingredients indicated in the recipe (these can be doubled or tripled if you want to marinate various vegetables, such as beans, beets or poached zucchini) and shake the jar vigorously. You will have a lovely cream-like dressing that can be stored in the refrigerator for 2 or 3 days. Always bring the dressing back to room temperature and shake again before using.

Notes

Swiss potato and bacon salad

Serves: 6
Preparation time: 20 minutes
Cooking time: 20 minutes

This is a hearty appetizer salad, typical of Switzerland. It is usually served with a platter of "charcuterie" (various sausages), Dijon mustard, gherkins and black bread.

Ingredients

1   pound green beans
1   pound new potatoes
¾ cup Vinaigrette (pages 408–409)
2   tablespoons olive oil
½ pound slab bacon, cubed
1   red onion, finely sliced
2   tablespoons cider vinegar
2   tablespoons chopped parsley
Salt and freshly ground black pepper

Preparation

1. Break the tips off the beans and rinse them under cold water. Bring a large casserole of salted water to boil and drop the beans into it a few at a time. Cook uncovered over medium heat for 15 minutes or until just tender. Make sure not to overcook them. Test beans for doneness; they should always be slightly crunchy.

2. Drain the beans and run them under cold water to stop the cooking so that the beans will retain their crispness and fresh green color. Place them in a large bowl.

3. Wash the potatoes and cook them in salted boiling water until barely tender. Peel them as soon as they are cool enough to handle and slice them into ¼-inch-thick slices. Place the potatoes around the green beans. Pour the Vinaigrette over the warm potatoes and beans and toss lightly.

4. Heat the 2 tablespoons of olive oil in a large skillet. Add the cubed bacon and cook until just crisp. Remove the bacon cubes and drain on a paper towel.

5. Pour out all but 2 tablespoons of fat from the skillet. Add the finely sliced onions and cook them until they are tender and transparent. Be sure not to let them brown.

6. When the onions are done, add the vinegar. Let the mixture come to a boil and immediately pour over the potatoes and green bean salad. Sprinkle the salad with the bacon cubes and the chopped parsley. Season with salt and freshly ground black pepper. Serve at room temperature.

Remarks

There are many varieties of green beans. Some are flat and too large to prepare whole. In that case cut them into 2-inch pieces. A combination of green and wax beans looks very attractive and is delicious. This dish can also be served as an accompaniment to sauteed calves' liver or roasts.

Notes

Rice salad bagerette

Serves: 4 to 6
Preparation time: 25 minutes
Cooking time: 30 minutes

A cold rice salad is one of the most versatile dishes for year-round serving. You may add shellfish, such as finely diced fresh shrimp, crabmeat or mussels, or a combination of all three. The salad can be used for stuffing raw marinated mushrooms or poached artichoke bottoms. In the summer, stuff tomatoes with the salad.

Ingredients

1 cup raw Italian rice
2½ cups salted water
Juice of ½ lemon
3 tablespoons olive oil
½ cup heavy cream
1 teaspoon Dijon mustard
Salt and freshly ground black pepper
2 tablespoons finely minced scallions
2 tablespoons finely minced green pepper
2 tablespoons finely minced parsley
2 tablespoons finely minced pimiento
1 tablespoon finely minced dill gherkins

Optional:
½ pound lump crabmeat or
½ pound diced small shrimp

Garnish:
2 hard-boiled eggs, quartered
Sprigs of parsley

Preparation

1. Wash the rice thoroughly.

2. Bring the salted water to a boil and add the rice. Bring the water back to a boil, reduce the heat and simmer the rice, covered, for 25 to 30 minutes or until it is very tender and all the water has been absorbed. Sprinkle the rice with lemon juice and olive oil and chill for 2 to 4 hours.

3. Whip the cream lightly. It should not be stiff. Add the Dijon mustard, salt and pepper.

4. Mix the rice with the scallions, green pepper, parsley, pimientos and gherkins. Add the cream mixture. Correct the seasoning and refrigerate for 2 or 3 hours before serving or using for stuffing.

5. If you are adding any shellfish, shrimp or crab, these should marinate in ½ cup Vinaigrette (pages 408–409) for 2 hours. Drain and then add to the rice. Serve the rice in an earthenware bowl and garnish with eggs and sprigs of parsley.

Remarks

You cannot make this salad with converted rice. If you cannot get Italian rice, use Carolina long-grain rice.
You may need a little more whipped cream if the rice is refrigerated for more than 2 or 3 hours before serving.
When stuffing tomatoes or raw mushrooms, marinate them first in a well-flavored Vinaigrette.
When you make the salad in summer, a mixture of your favorite herbs will give the rice an individual flavor.

Notes

Swiss ham and gruyere salad

Serves: 4 to 6
Preparation time: 35 minutes
Cooking time: none

Salads can be a very creative outlet for every cook. Change one or two ingredients and the whole salad has a different taste and texture. Swiss cheese and ham are certainly supermarket staples which puts this salad into the all-seasons class. However, when made with Gruyere and excellent ham it is as elegant as any complicated concoction.

Ingredients

2   cups Gruyere cheese, cut into 2-inch-long matchsticks
2 cups cooked ham, cut into julienne matchsticks
1   teaspoon Dijon mustard
2   hard-boiled eggs (separated)
Juice of 1 lemon
1   teaspoon sugar
6   tablespoons olive oil
1 to 2 tablespoons Creme Fraiche (page 398) or heavy cream
Salt and freshly ground white pepper
2   tablespoons finely chopped parsley
3 to 4 small white onions, finely sliced

Garnish:
Whole radishes and black olives

Preparation

1. Combine the Gruyere and ham in a salad bowl.

2. In a small mixing bowl combine the mustard, hard-boiled egg yolks, lemon juice, sugar and oil. Whisk the mixture until it is smooth and very well blended. Add a little Creme Fraiche to give the dressing the consistency of a light mayonnaise.

3. Pour the dressing over the salad and toss. Season with salt and pepper.

4. Chill the salad for 2 or 3 hours. Remove the salad from the refrigerator 45 minutes to 1 hour before serving. Add the parsley and onions and sprinkle with the egg whites, finely diced. Garnish with the radishes and olives.

Notes

Banana, pineapple, grape potpourri

Serves: 4
Preparation time: 25 minutes
Cooking time: 8 to 10 minutes

Here is a light dessert that takes only minutes to assemble—that is if you have the sauce made in advance. The sauce will keep for several weeks in a covered jar in the refrigerator and can be used on other fresh fruit combinations, such as pears, plums, and peaches.

Ingredients

3   bananas, peeled and thinly sliced
1   tablespoon verifine sugar
2   teaspoons lemon juice
2   tablespoons banana liqueur
1   cup seedless white grapes
1   cup dark grapes, seeds removed
2   tablespoons kirsch
1   tablespoon sugar

Sauce:
3   egg yolks
½ cup sugar
3   tablespoons flour
1½ cups warm milk
2   tablespoons Praline Powder (page 402)
1   teaspoon vanilla extract
½ cup chopped walnuts

Garnish:
1   cup cubed fresh pineapple
½   cup grapes

Preparation

1. Place the bananas, sugar, lemon juice and liqueur in a bowl and marinate for 30 minutes.

2. Place the grapes in another bowl with kirsch and sugar and marinate for 1 hour.

3. To make the sauce combine the egg yolks and sugar in a bowl. Whisk the

mixture until it is light and fluffy and pale yellow.

4. Add the flour and whisk it in well.

5. Add the warm milk and whisk the mixture until it is very smooth.

6. Pour the mixture into a heavy-bottomed saucepan and cook over medium heat, whisking constantly until it comes to a boil and heavily coats a spoon. Be careful not to scorch the bottom of the casserole.

7. As soon as the sauce is thick, pour it through a sieve into a bowl.

8. Add the Praline Powder, vanilla extract and the liqueur drained from both the bananas and the grapes. Chill the sauce for 2 hours.

9. Just before serving combine the bananas, grapes, walnuts and sauce in a large crystal bowl. Garnish the bowl with cubed pineapple and additional grapes. Serve very cold.

Notes

Pineapple in kirsch cream

Serves: 4
Preparation time: 15 minutes
Cooking time: 10 to 12 minutes

Ingredients

1 ripe pineapple
½ cup sugar plus 2 tablespoons
⅓ cup kirsch plus 2 tablespoons
4 egg yolks
1 cup milk, warm
1 teaspoon vanilla extract
½ cup heavy cream

Preparation

1. Peel and core the pineapple and cut it into 1-inch cubes. Place the cubes in a bowl and sprinkle with 2 tablespoons of sugar and 2 tablespoons of kirsch. Chill until serving time.

2. In the top of a double boiler, combine the ½ cup sugar and egg yolks. Beat the mixture until it is pale yellow and smooth.

3. Add the warm milk. Place the mixture over simmering water and cook the custard, stirring constantly until it thickens and heavily coats a spoon.

4. Pour the custard into a bowl and flavor it with ⅓ cup kirsch and the vanilla. Chill the custard completely for 2 or 3 hours.

5. Whip the cream and beat it into the custard.

6. Just before serving, spoon a few tablespoons of the accumulated pineapple juices from the bowl into the kirsch cream to thin it out.

7. Place a few pineapple cubes in individual serving glasses (you may use clear wine glasses) and spoon the kirsch cream over them. Chill again until serving time.

Creole crepes

Serves: 4 to 6
Preparation time: 15 minutes
Cooking time: 10 minutes

There are many ways of serving crepes and with every season you can experiment with a different fruit in an unusual combination. Most important are the crepes themselves, which must be paper thin and perfectly cooked.

Ingredients

12 Dessert Crepes (page 399), warm

The filling:
3 tablespoons sweet butter
2 tablespoons brown sugar
Pinch of fresh nutmeg
3 small bananas, sliced
1 cup apricot preserves
1 teaspoon lemon rind
1 to 2 teaspoons lemon juice
3 tablespoons kirsch

Garnish:
3 tablespoons finely sliced almonds
⅓ cup warm banana liqueur and ⅓ cup rum
1 cup heavy cream, whipped, sweetened with 2 tablespoons confectioners' sugar

Preparation

1. Melt the butter over low heat in a large skillet. As soon as it is melted, add the sugar and nutmeg and cook for 2 or 3 minutes until the sugar is dissolved and lightly caramelized.

2. Add the sliced bananas together with the apricot preserves, lemon rind and juice. Heat the banana mixture thoroughly but do not overcook. The bananas should not be mushy.

Mocha creme brulee

Serves: 6 to 8
Preparation time: 15 minutes
Cooking time: 30 minutes

■●

3. Add the kirsch and taste the mixture. If it seems too sweet, add a little more kirsch and a little more lemon rind. Remove from the heat and reserve.

4. Sprinkle the almond slices on a cookie sheet and put into a 300° oven. Toast them lightly. Be careful not to burn them. Remove from the oven and reserve.

5. Fill the crepes with 1 to 2 tablespoons of the banana mixture, roll them up and place on a flameproof dish. Combine the banana liqueur and rum and pour over the crepes. Ignite and when the flames have subsided, sprinkle the crepes with the toasted almond slices and a dollop of whipped cream. Serve the remaining cream on the side.

Notes

This is an adaptation of the traditional Creme Brulee, which is a custard topped with sugar and run under the broiler to caramelize the sugar. I find this version with the addition of the coffee flavor more interesting.

Ingredients

1   cup milk
1   cup light cream
2   teaspoons instant coffee
6   egg yolks
1   teaspoon vanilla extract
1¼ cups sugar
¼ cup water

Preparation

1. Preheat the oven to 325°.

2. In a saucepan heat the milk and cream together with the instant coffee. When the milk liquid is hot and the coffee is completely dissolved, remove the saucepan from the heat and reserve.

3. In a bowl combine the egg yolks, vanilla and ½ cup of sugar. Whisk the mixture until it is pale yellow and fluffy.

4. Add the warm milk and coffee mixture and whisk again to blend well. Strain the mixture through a fine sieve and pour it into 6 or 8 porcelain ramekins.

5. Place the ramekins in a large baking dish, pour boiling water into the dish in the depth of 1 inch. Cover the ramekins with foil and place the baking dish in the oven. Bake the custards for 15 minutes.

6. Remove the ramekins from the oven and when the custards are completely cool, chill them for 1 hour. Remove them from the refrigerator and set aside.

7. Make the caramel: In a heavy saucepan combine ¾ cup of sugar and ¼ cup of water. Cook the mixture, uncovered, without stirring, until it begins to darken. Then continue cooking, stirring and watching it carefully until it becomes an amber-colored caramel.

8. Immediately remove the pan from the heat and dip it into cold water to stop further cooking.

9. Pour a little of the hot caramel over each custard and quickly turn the ramekins so as to cover the custard tops with the caramel.

10. If the caramel gets too thick before you have finished coating each ramekin, return the saucepan to medium heat until the caramel thins out again.

11. Return the coated ramekins to the refrigerator and chill until serving time.

Remarks

If you prefer a vanilla flavor, omit the coffee and add a 4-inch piece of vanilla bean to the milk. Steep the vanilla bean in the warm milk for at least 30 minutes before continuing with the recipe. Or you may substitute 2 teaspoons vanilla extract for the vanilla bean.

Notes

Mousse blanche

Serves: 6
Preparation time: 20 minutes
Cooking time: 5 minutes

Ingredients

5 egg whites, at room temperature
Salt
6 tablespoons sugar
1 tablespoon unflavored gelatin
¼ cup cold water
1 cup heavy cream
1 teaspoon vanilla
1 cup grated sweetened coconut

The sauce:
5 egg yolks
⅓ cup sugar
¾ cup sweet sherry
2 to 4 tablespoons white rum

Preparation

1. Beat the egg whites and salt until stiff but not dry. Gradually beat in the sugar a tablespoon at a time.

2. In a small saucepan dissolve the gelatin in the cold water and dissolve over medium heat. Fold the gelatin into the beaten egg whites.

3. Whip the cream until stiff and add the vanilla. Fold the cream into the egg whites. (Do this by hand to avoid breaking the air pockets of the meringue.)

4. Spoon the mousse into individual parfait glasses and chill.

5. When ready to serve sprinkle the top with the coconut and spoon a little warm sauce over each parfait.

The sauce:
6. In the top of a double boiler beat the egg yolks until they are slightly thickened and become pale yellow in color.

7. Beat in the sugar and the sherry. Cook the mixture, whisking constantly over low heat until the sauce doubles in volume and heavily coats a spoon. (The water in the bottom of the double boiler should remain at a simmer.)

8. Immediately remove from the heat. Stir in the rum and continue beating for 2 minutes off the heat. Serve warm.

Remarks

This sauce can be made an hour in advance and kept warm in the top of the double boiler off the heat. Just before serving, whip it again to make it smooth and fluffy.

Notes

Beurre manie

A Beurre Manie is used to thicken sauces in all fine cooking. These butter-and-flour balls can be made in advance and stored in a sealed jar in the refrigerator for 1 or 2 weeks.

Ingredients

1 tablespoon flour or 1 tablespoon potato starch
1 tablespoon sweet butter, softened

Preparation

Combine the butter and flour on a small flat plate and blend the mixture with a fork into a very smooth paste. Roll the paste into a ball and refrigerate. If to be used immediately, the paste does not have to be made into a ball or refrigerated. Just be sure that the flour and butter are completely incorporated.
A sauce will often need only a small Beurre Manie made out of 1 teaspoon of flour and I teaspoon of butter.

Bouquet garni

A Bouquet Garni is used for flavoring soups, stocks and sauces. When using fresh herbs, tie them together with a string. When dry herbs are used, tie them in a piece of cheesecloth for easy removal.

Ingredients

3 to 4 sprigs of parsley
1 bay leaf
½ celery stalk with leaves
½ teaspoon dry thyme or 2 small sprigs of fresh thyme

When fresh herbs are available, you may include a sprig of summer savory or fennel tops in the Bouquet.

Chestnut peelings

Yield: 1 pound

Preparation time: 45 minutes
Cooking time: 3 to 5 minutes

Preparation

1. With a sharp knife make an incision in the flat side of each nut.
2. Drop the chestnuts into boiling water and cook them for 2 or 3 minutes.
3. Remove 2 or 3 chestnuts at a time and take off both the outer coat and the inner skin of each. If a chestnut does not peel easily, return it to the boiling water for 1 more minute, then peel.

Remarks

Uncooked peeled chestnuts can be frozen for 1 or 2 months.

Chocolate sauce

An excellent chocolate sauce will enrich the simplest dessert. There is, though, one requirement—you must use the best possible chocolate.

Ingredients

8 ounces of semisweet chocolate
1 cup coffee
2 to 3 tablespoons sugar
4 tablespoons sweet butter
1 teaspoon vanilla extract

Optional:
¼ cup heavy cream

Preparation

1. In a small heavy saucepan, combine the chocolate, coffee, and sugar. Cook over very low heat until chocolate is dissolved.

2. Add the butter, bit by bit, and stir the sauce until it is smooth and shiny.

3. Add the vanilla extract and the optional cream. Keep warm over simmering water until serving time.

Clarified butter

The butter used in recipes throughout this book should be sweet (that is unsalted) butter.

There are several brands of butter on the market labeled "sweet butter" but with the label also reading "lightly salted." Use only butter that is labeled either just "sweet butter" or "unsalted butter."

To make Clarified Butter:

Melt any desired amount of sweet butter in a heavy saucepan over very low heat. As soon as the foam starts to subside, remove the pan from the heat and carefully skim off the foam with a spoon. Strain the yellow part of the heated butter through a fine sieve into a bowl. Be sure to leave all of the milky residue in the bottom of the pan to be discarded.

Clarified Butter is used for sauteeing bread or delicate meats such as chicken or calves' liver. It can be made in large quantities and stored covered in the refrigerator for 2 or 3 weeks.

Creme fraiche

Creme Fraiche is actually soured cream. It is far superior to commercial sour cream and is widely used in French cooking. Whereas sour cream may curdle in a hot sauce, Creme Fraiche will not and is therefore practical to have. Sugared Creme Fraiche is a delicious accompaniment to baked apples, poached pears and all berries. It can also be used in many salad dressings and as a garnish to cold poached vegetables.

Ingredients

4 cups heavy cream
3 teaspoons buttermilk

Preparation

1. Combine the cream and the buttermilk in a large jar.

2. Cover the jar and store it in a warm place away from drafts for 24 to 36 hours.

3. Refrigerate in a tightly sealed jar. It will keep for 2 to 3 weeks.

Remarks

In a warm kitchen the Creme will be ready for use in 24 hours.

Entree crepes

Yield: 16 to 18 crepes
Preparation time: 15 minutes
Cooking time: 35 to 40 minutes

Ingredients

1¾ cups sifted all-purpose flour
4 eggs
1 cup milk
1 cup water
Pinch of salt
Pinch of nutmeg
¼ cup melted sweet butter

Preparation

1. Combine all the ingredients except the butter in the top part of a blender, starting with the flour and eggs and finally adding the milk, water and seasonings.

2. Blend the mixture at high speed, scraping down from the sides of the jar any flour that has stuck to them.

3. Melt the butter in a small saucepan. Let it cool and then blend it into the crepe batter. Let the batter "relax" for 30 minutes to 2 hours.

4. Before using a crepe pan for the first time "season" it as follows: Sprinkle the pan with a thick layer of salt. Cover the salt with 1 inch of vegetable oil. Set the pan over high heat and while the oil is getting hot, tear off enough paper towels to make a large ball. As soon as the oil is very hot and begins to smoke, pour it out together with the salt. Quickly wipe the pan with the paper towels until the surface is smooth and not a grain of salt remains.

5. Brush the surface of the seasoned pan

with a little melted butter. Place the pan over medium to high heat and add a spoonful of batter, just enough to coat the bottom of the pan thinly. Pour out any excess batter.

6. Cook the crepe for 1 or 2 minutes, then loosen it with a sharp knife. Turn it over with your fingers or a spatula and lightly brown the other side. After the first crepe reduce the heat to medium. Slide finished crepes onto a plate, placing a sheet of wax paper between them.

Remarks

The first crepe often will not be successful and will probably have to be discarded, but it is a good way to test your batter. If the "test" crepe is too thick, add a little milk or water to your batter. After making two or three crepes, brush the pan again with melted butter. Cook the crepes over medium heat so as not to burn them. It will also make it possible for you to turn them with your fingers.
You can freeze crepes very successfully, placing wax paper between them and then wrapping them in foil. When needed, place the frozen crepes in their foil wrapping in a 200° oven for 1 hour and 30 minutes to 2 hours or until they are heated through.

Dessert crepes

For 12 to 14 crepes

Ingredients

1½ cups milk
4 eggs
1 cup sifted all-purpose flour
2 tablespoons cognac or Grand Marnier
1 tablespoon sugar
¼ cup melted sweet butter

Optional:
Pinch of finely grated lemon or orange rind

Preparation

See page 398.

Crepes fines herbes

For 20 to 24 crepes
Preparation time: 15 minutes
Cooking time: 45 minutes to 1 hour

Ingredients

1 cup milk
1 cup water
1½ cups sifted flour
4 eggs
Pinch of salt
Pinch of nutmeg
2 tablespoons finely minced fresh herbs (chervil, parsley, chives)
4 tablespoons melted butter

Preparation

1. Combine the milk, water, flour, eggs, salt and nutmeg in the top part of the blender and blend at high speed, scraping down any flour that sticks to the sides of the jar.

2. Pour the batter into a bowl. Add the minced herbs and melted butter and whisk to incorporate the butter and herbs. Let the batter stand for 2 hours before making the crepes (page 398).

Notes

Spinach crepes

For 20 to 24 crepes
Preparation time: 30 minutes
Cooking time: 45 minutes to 1 hour

Ingredients

2 cups fresh spinach
2 cups milk
1½ cups sifted flour
3 whole eggs
Pinch of salt
Pinch of nutmeg
4 tablespoons melted butter

Preparation

1. Place well-washed spinach in a saucepan and cook it over high heat until it is completely wilted. Drain the spinach and when it is cool enough to handle, squeeze it into a ball between your hands until all the liquid is removed.

2. Mince the spinach and place it in the top part of a blender. Add a little milk and puree until the mixture is completely smooth. Add the remaining milk and the rest of the ingredients except the melted butter and blend at high speed.

3. Pour the mixture into a bowl, add the melted butter and let the batter rest for 2 hours.

4. To make the crepes follow instructions on page 398.

Eggs mollets

Preparation time: 5 minutes
Cooking time: 6 minutes

Preparation

1. Eggs mollets are really soft-boiled eggs that can be used instead of poached eggs in many dishes.

2. Use eggs graded "Large." They must be at room temperature. Lower them into boiling water, reduce the heat and cook them over medium heat for 6 minutes.

3. Immediately run the eggs under cold water to stop further cooking. Peel them carefully and serve them as soon as possible. They may be kept warm over a pan of warm water for 5 to 10 minutes.

Remarks

Eggs Mollets can be coated with aspic or mayonnaise and served cold.

Fresh tomato sauce

Yield: 1½ to 2 quarts
Preparation time: 15 minutes
Cooking time: 1 hour 15 minutes

A good tomato sauce is a MUST in country cooking. It can be served simply as an accompaniment to sauteed veal or pork chops. It can be used as a base for fried or hard-boiled eggs or with vegetables such as sauteed eggplants or zucchini. It is at its best when made with fresh ripe tomatoes. Don't even try to make it with hothouse tomatoes.

Ingredients

3 tablespoons sweet butter
1 tablespoon olive oil
½ cup finely diced carrots
½ cup finely diced celery
½ cup finely diced onion
2 tablespoons flour
3 pounds tomatoes, peeled, seeded and drained
2 teaspoons sugar
Salt and freshly ground white pepper
1 Bouquet Garni (page 397)
1 large sprig of fresh basil or ½ teaspoon dried basil
1 sprig fresh oregano or ½ teaspoon dried
2 whole garlic cloves

Optional:
1 to 2 tablespoons tomato paste
½ to 1 cup Brown Stock (page 403)

Preparation

1. In a large heavy saucepan, heat the butter and oil. When it is hot, add the diced vegetables and cook them without browning for 5 minutes.

2. Add the flour and stir well. Cook it without browning for 3 minutes.

3. Force the tomatoes through a sieve or puree them in the blender. Add them to the saucepan together with the sugar and seasoning.

4. Add the Bouquet Garni, herbs and garlic. Simmer the sauce, partially covered, for 1 hour. Stir often. If it gets too thick, add a little Brown Stock. Beat in the tomato paste if the sauce lacks color.

5. Strain the sauce through a fine sieve, pressing down on the vegetables to extract all their juices.

6. Cool the sauce and refrigerate in sealed jars for 1 to 2 weeks or freeze for 2 or 3 months.

Remarks

For a Basil Tomato Sauce add ½ cup basil ground in a mortar with 1 tablespoon oregano to the finished sauce.

Notes

Macaroon crumbs

Yield: 1½ to 2 cups
Preparation time: 5 minutes
Cooking time: 1 hour

Ingredients

10 to 12 medium-sized almond macaroons

Preparation

1. Preheat the oven to 300°.

2. Place the macaroons on a cookie sheet and toast them in the oven for 45 minutes to 1 hour. Remove them from the oven and let them cool completely.

3. Put the macaroons in a plastic bag or paper bag and roll them into crumbs with a rolling pin.

Remarks

For Macaroon Powder (finer than the crumbs) place the toasted macaroons in the top part of the blender and grind for 1 minute at top speed. Refrigerate in a well-sealed jar for 2 to 3 months.
The Macaroon Powder can be used for topping ice cream, poached pears, souffles and crepes. It can sometimes be substituted for Praline Powder, but it has a very different flavor.

Notes

basics and sauces

Mayonnaise

Yield: 1½ to 2 cups
Preparation time: 5 minutes
Cooking time: none

Since the invention of the electric blender, I see no reason for using store-bought mayonnaise. It takes more time to "doctor up" a jar of commercial mayonnaise than it does to make one's own. The following ingredients make about 2 cups of delicious mayonnaise that will keep for 2 weeks in the refrigerator.

Ingredients

2 whole eggs
1 tablespoon lemon juice
Pinch of sugar
½ teaspoon salt
Pinch of freshly ground white pepper
1 teaspoon Dijon mustard
1½ cups of corn oil, or ½ corn oil and
    ½ olive oil

Preparation

1. Combine the eggs, lemon juice, sugar, seasoning and mustard in the blender. Blend at high speed for a few seconds.

2. Still at high speed, start adding the oil a few drops at a time. When the mayonnaise starts to thicken, add the oil in a thin stream until it is all absorbed.

3. If the mayonnaise gets too thick, add a little more lemon juice. Correct the seasoning and refrigerate in a well-sealed jar.

Praline powder

Yield: 1 cup
Preparation time: 10 minutes
Cooking time: 10 to 15 minutes

Ingredients

2 cups blanched slivered toasted almonds
1 cup sugar
2 tablespoons water

Preparation

1. Coat a baking dish lightly with vegetable oil and place the slivered almonds in it in one layer.

2. In a heavy saucepan combine the sugar and water. Cook over medium heat, stirring occasionally, until the mixture turns a light hazelnut brown. Do not let the caramel become dark brown as it will then have a burnt flavor.

3. Pour the hot caramel over the almonds in the pan.

4. In 2 or 3 minutes the caramel will harden. Break the caramel-almond mixture into small pieces and pulverize them in the blender. Refrigerate in a well-sealed jar for several weeks.

Hollandaise

Yield: about 1½ cups
Preparation time: 3 minutes
Cooking time: 3 minutes

Ingredients

4 egg yolks
1 to 2 tablespoons lemon juice
2 tablespoons heavy cream
¼ teaspoon salt
Pinch of freshly ground white pepper
1 cup Clarified Butter (page 398)

Preparation

Place the yolks, 1 tablespoon lemon juice and the cream in the blender. Turn to high speed, and slowly, a few drops at a time, add ½ cup of the warm Clarified Butter. The mixture will become quite thick. Pour the sauce into the top of a double boiler and set it over simmering water, slowly whisking in the remaining butter. Season the sauce with salt and pepper and the remaining lemon juice.

Remarks

The sauce can be made well in advance and can be kept warm in a bowl of warm water; if it separates, whisk in a tablespoon of cold water and beat vigorously until the sauce is smooth again.

Brown stock

Yield: 3 quarts
Preparation time: 30 minutes
Cooking time: 4 hours 30 minutes

Peasant, or country, cooking has few secrets. The steps and techniques are usually quite simple, but two things are of prime importance: the freshness of the ingredients used and the quality of the stock for soups and sauces.

Ingredients

2 pounds beef shank or brisket, cut into pieces
2 pounds beef bones
2 pounds veal bones, including a veal knuckle
2 carrots, scraped and diced
2 onions, diced
2 celery stalks, cleaned, including their tops
1 large Bouquet Garni (page 397)
2 large garlic cloves, whole
1 tablespoon tomato paste
2 teaspoons salt
4 quarts water

Preparation

1. Preheat the oven to 450°.

2. Place the meat, bones and diced vegetables in a large baking dish. Roast in the oven for 30 minutes. Shake the pan a few times to make sure that the vegetables are not burning. If any of the vegetables brown first, remove them with a slotted spoon to a stockpot and continue browning the rest with the meat and bones.

3. Transfer the browned vegetables, meat and bones to the stockpot. Add the celery stalks, Bouquet Garni, garlic, tomato paste and salt. Cover the mixture with water and bring it to a boil. Reduce the heat and simmer the stock very slowly, partially covered, for 4 hours. Continually remove any scum that may rise to the surface and

as much accumulated fat as possible. When the stock is done, cool it completely. Again remove all possible fat and store the stock in sealed jars in the refrigerator 2 to 3 weeks or it can be frozen for a couple of months. When refrigerated the stock must be brought back to a boil every 2 or 3 days to prevent it from spoiling.

Concentrated brown stock

Yield: 3 cups
Preparation time: 15 minutes
Cooking time: 50 minutes

Ingredients

½ cup Clarified Butter (page 398)
4 tablespoons flour
3 cups hot Brown Stock
1 Bouquet Garni (page 397)
1 cup white wine
1 tablespoon tomato paste
Salt and freshly ground white pepper

Preparation

1. Heat the butter in a 2-quart saucepan. Add the flour and cook over low heat, stirring constantly with a wooden spoon, until it turns hazelnut brown.

2. Add the Brown Stock all at once. Whisk the mixture until completely smooth. Lower the heat and add the Bouquet Garni.

3. Mix the wine with the tomato paste until it is well blended. Add the mixture to the stock and simmer, partially covered, for 40 minutes.

4. Strain the sauce and season it with salt and pepper. Cool the sauce completely and, when cold, cover it and refrigerate. It can be frozen for about two months.

Chicken stock

Yield: 3 quarts
Preparation time: 15 minutes
Cooking time: 3 hours

Ingredients

1   4½- to 5-pound chicken, quartered
1½ to 2 pounds chicken giblets (backs, necks and wings)
2   carrots, scraped
2   leeks (white part only), cleaned
2   celery stalks, including tops
1   parsnip, scraped
1   parsley root, scraped (including the green)
1   onion, stuck with 1 clove
1   large Bouquet Garni (page 397)
1   tablespoon salt
8   peppercorns
4   quarts of water (approximately)

Preparation

1. Place the chicken and the giblets in a large stockpot. Add the vegetables, Bouquet Garni, salt, peppercorns and water to cover the mixture by 2 or 3 inches.

2. Bring the stock to a boil and remove the scum carefully. Partially cover the pot, reduce the heat and simmer the stock for 3 hours. Skim off the fat several times.

3. Cool it uncovered and strain through a very fine sieve. Refrigerate overnight and the next day carefully remove all the hardened fat.

4. Heat the stock once more. Cool completely and refrigerate in sealed jars bringing it back to a boil every 2 or 3 days. It will keep for 2 weeks. It can be frozen for about 2 months.

Remarks

The chicken can be removed from the stockpot after 1 hour and 45 minutes (or when it is done) and used for salads or the fillings of crepes.

Brown chicken stock

Yield: 2½ quarts
Preparation time: 30 minutes
Cooking time: 3½ hours

Ingredients

2   tablespoons sweet butter
1   tablespoon oil
2   carrots, scraped and chopped
2   celery stalks, cleaned, including the tops
2   onions, coarsely chopped
3   whole leeks, coarsely chopped
3   pounds chicken trimmings (backs, necks and giblets)
5   large garlic cloves, whole, unpeeled
2   whole ripe tomatoes, unpeeled
2   teaspoons salt
1   large Bouquet Garni (page 397)
12 cups water (or more if needed)

Optional:
1   veal knuckle

Preparation

1. Preheat the oven to 375°.

2. Heat the butter and oil in a large baking dish. Add the vegetables and chicken and brown the mixture for 30 to 40 minutes. When the vegetables are browned (be careful not to burn them), transfer them with the chicken pieces to a large stockpot.

3. Add the garlic, tomatoes, salt, Bouquet Garni and water to the stockpot. Add the veal knuckle if used. This will give the stock a stronger flavor.

4. Bring the stock slowly to a boil. Partially cover the pot and simmer the stock for 3 hours. Carefully remove the scum several times during the cooking. If the stock is reducing too rapidly, add 2 cups of water.

5. When the stock is done, strain it through a fine sieve, cool it completely, then degrease it thoroughly. Refrigerate in sealed jars or freeze. It will keep up to 3 weeks refrigerated, up to 2 months frozen.

Brown duck stock

Yield: 3 cups
Preparation time: 30 minutes
Cooking time: 2 hours 10 minutes

Ingredients

1 tablespoon sweet butter
½ cup chopped onion
½ cup chopped carrot
1 celery stalk, minced
1 leek, green part included, well cleaned
  and cut in half
Giblets of 2 ducks, cut into small pieces
  (except the liver)
5 cups Chicken Stock (page 404) or water
1 Bouquet Garni (page 397)

Preparation

1. Melt the butter in a small casserole. Add the vegetables and giblets and brown for a few minutes.

2. Add the Chicken Stock and the Bouquet Garni and bring the mixture to a boil. Cover the casserole and simmer for 2 hours.

3. Strain the stock. Let it cool, then degrease it thoroughly and reserve. It will keep for several days in the refrigerator or in the freezer for 1 or 2 months.

White stock

Yield: 3 quarts
Preparation time: 20 minutes
Cooking time: 3 to 4 hours

White Stock is preferably made with veal. You may, however, add chicken giblets to it. This stock is used for soups and light sauces.

Ingredients

3-pound veal shank
2 pounds cracked veal bones, including
  1 veal knuckle
1 onion, peeled and stuck with 1 clove
2 celery stalks, including tops
1 parsnip, peeled
1 parsley root, peeled
1 Bouquet Garni (page 397)
2 carrots, scraped
2 leeks, green part included
4 quarts water

Preparation

1. Combine all the ingredients in a large stockpot and slowly bring the mixture to a boil. Reduce the heat and simmer partially covered for 3 to 4 hours. Skim the stock several times during the cooking.

2. Taste the stock: if the flavor is strong, it is ready. Strain it through a fine sieve, cool it completely, then remove accumulated fat from the top. If you cannot remove all the fat at once, refrigerate until the fat hardens. Then it is easy to remove.

3. Refrigerate in sealed jars or freeze. Refrigerated stock will keep for 2 weeks, but should be brought to a boil every 3 to 4 days. Frozen, it keeps up to 2 months.

Beef stock

The ingredients and preparation for Beef (Meat) Stock are the same as for White Stock except that you substitute beef shank for veal shank and cracked beef bones for veal bones.

Notes

Lamb stock

Yield: 1½ quarts
Preparation time: 15 minutes
Cooking time: 2 to 3 hours

A good Lamb Stock is made exactly like a well-flavored White Stock. If, however, you need only 2 to 3 cups of stock for a ragout or sauce, you can make a small quantity as follows.

Ingredients

2 to 3 pounds meaty lamb bones
2 carrots
2 celery stalks
3 leeks, green part included
1 large Bouquet Garni (page 397)
1 parsnip
Pinch of salt

Optional:
1 parsley root

Ingredients

1. Combine all the ingredients in a large casserole and cover with 8 cups of water. Bring to a boil and skim it carefully.

2. Cook the stock, partially covered, for 2 to 3 hours or until the liquid is reduced by ¼ and is well flavored.

3. Cool and strain.

4. Degrease thoroughly. Store in the refrigerator in a well-sealed jar for several weeks. It should be brought back to a boil every 2 to 3 days. It will keep frozen for about 2 months.

Fish stock

Yield: 1½ quarts
Preparation time: 20 minutes
Cooking time: 45 minutes

There are two versions of this stock. The first one requires sauteeing the vegetables for a few minutes in butter. The second simply combines the listed ingredients in a large casserole and simmers them for 30 to 40 minutes. Fish Stock can be frozen for a couple of months or refrigerated for 2 weeks. If refrigerated, it should be brought back to a boil every 2 or 3 days.

Ingredients

2 tablespoons sweet butter
1 tablespoon cooking oil
1 large onion, coarsely chopped
1 celery stalk, chopped
1 carrot, scraped and chopped
3 pounds lean fish trimmings (cod, whiting, halibut)
1 large Bouquet Garni (page 397), including celery tops and 1 whole leek, green part included
2 cups dry white wine
6 peppercorns
6 cups of water
Salt

Optional:
1 cup mushroom stems

Preparation

1. Heat the butter and oil in a large casserole. Add the vegetables and cook them without browning for 5 minutes.

2. Add the fish trimmings and the remaining ingredients and season with a pinch of salt. Bring the stock to a boil slowly, reduce the heat and simmer over low heat for 30 to 40 minutes.

3. During the cooking, remove the scum several times to insure a clear stock.

4. Strain the stock through a fine sieve lined with cheesecloth and cool completely before refrigerating.

Notes

Tart shell

Yield: 1 9- to 10-inch shell
Preparation time: 20 minutes
Cooking time: 25 to 30 minutes

Ingredients

2   cups sifted all-purpose flour (or more
     if needed)
1   egg
Pinch of salt
3 to 5 tablespoons cold heavy cream or
     ice water
1½ sticks cold sweet butter

Preparation

1. Place the flour in a large bowl and make
a well in the center. Put the egg and salt
in the well and work the mixture with your
hands.

2. Add the cold butter in little bits and
continue to work the mixture until it resembles corn flakes.

3. Gradually add the cream (or water) and
knead the dough just until it is smooth.
If it is sticky, add a little more flour, just
enough to produce a smooth ball.

4. Wrap the dough in floured wax paper
and let it stand for at least 2 hours before
rolling it out.

5. Roll the dough out to a thickness of
¼ inch. This quantity is enough for one
9- to 10-inch tart or for 6 to 8 individual
tarts.

Remarks

For individual tart shells replace the heavy
cream with ice water and add an egg white
to the mixture. Instead of lining the tart
shells with foil or wax paper for baking
(as described on page 408), place another
buttered tart mold in the shell and fill it
with dried beans or rice. The second mold
should be removed after 8 minutes, since
a tart shell needs only 15 minutes of baking
to be ready for filling.

Entree tart shells

Yield: 1 9- to 10-inch shell
Preparation time: 25 to 30 minutes
Cooking time: 30 minutes

Ingredients

2   cups sifted flour
1   egg
1   teaspoon salt
3 to 5 tablespoons iced water
1½ sticks cold sweet butter

Follow directions in Tart Shell.

Dessert tart shell

Yield: 1 9- to 10-inch shell
Preparation time: 25 to 30 minutes
Cooking time: 30 minutes

Ingredients

2   cups sifted all-purpose flour
1 to 3 tablespoons sugar
Pinch of salt
1   egg yolk
1½ sticks cold sweet butter
5   tablespoons ice water

Optional:
¼ teaspoon cinnamon, or ½ teaspoon
     finely grated lemon rind

Preparation

1. Put the sifted flour into a stainless steel
bowl. Add the sugar, salt and optional cinnamon or lemon rind. Make a well in the
center and add the egg yolk. Using your
hands, quickly combine the flour with
the egg.

2. Add the butter, broken into tiny pieces.
Work the flour and butter together with
your hands until the mixture resembles
corn flakes.

3. Add the ice water starting with 3 tablespoons, and quickly work the dough into
a ball. It will be slightly sticky and damp.
Sprinkle it lightly with flour and put it on a

floured board. Continue working the dough for 1 or 2 minutes until it is quite smooth. Do not overwork it.

4. Wrap the dough in floured wax paper and refrigerate for 1 to 1½ hours.

5. Place the dough on a floured board, and with a floured rolling pin, roll it into a 12-inch circle, ⅛ inch thick.

6. Lift the dough over the rolling pin into a 9- or 10-inch quiche pan. Press the dough gently against the sides of the pan.

7. Roll the rolling pin over the pan to remove the excess dough. Prick the bottom of the dough in 3 or 4 places. Make a decorative edge with the blunt edge of a knife and freeze the crust for 2 to 3 hours.

8. Preheat the oven to 350°

9. Line the pastry shell with foil or wax paper and fill it with rice or dried beans to keep the crust from puffing up during the baking time. Place the shell on a cookie sheet. Bake for 20 minutes or until set.

10. Remove the beans or rice and the wax paper or foil. Prick the bottom of the crust again and continue baking for 15 to 20 minutes or until it is lightly browned.

11. Cool the shell and when cool enough to handle, unmold it directly onto a cookie sheet and fill.

Herb vinaigrette

Yield: ¾ cup
Preparation time: 5 minutes
Cooking time: none

Ingredients

2 tablespoons tarragon vinegar
1 teaspoon Dijon mustard
1 teaspoon salt
1 garlic clove, mashed
2 tablespoons finely minced mixed herbs (chives, parsley, chervil, tarragon)
6 tablespoons olive oil

Preparation

In a wooden salad bowl, combine the vinegar, mustard, salt, garlic and herbs and blend the ingredients well. Let the mixture stand for 30 minutes to develop the full flavor of the herbs. Whisk in the olive oil a little at a time until the dressing is well blended. Makes ¾ cup of dressing, enough for a salad for 6 to 8.

Lemon vinaigrette

Yield: ¾ cup
Preparation time: 5 minutes
Cooking time: none

Ingredients

Juice of 1 lemon
1 teaspoon Dijon mustard
1 teaspoon granulated sugar
6 tablespoons olive oil
2 tablespoons minced green onion or chives
Salt and freshly ground white pepper

Optional:
2 tablespoons Creme Fraiche (page 398)

Preparation

1. In a small bowl, combine the lemon juice, Dijon mustard and sugar.

2. Whisk in the olive oil, a few drops at a time, until the sauce is smooth and well blended.

3. Beat in the optional Creme Fraiche and green onion.

4. Season lightly with salt and pepper and chill until serving time. Makes ¾ cup of dressing, enough for a salad for 6 to 8.

Notes

Provencale vinaigrette

Yield: ¾ cup
Preparation time: 5 minutes
Cooking time: none

Ingredients

1 teaspoon Dijon mustard
1 teaspoon salt
1 garlic clove, mashed
2 tablespoons good red wine vinegar
6 tablespoons olive oil
2 tablespoons finely minced green onions
Large pinch of freshly ground black pepper

Optional:
1 tablespoon tiny capers

Preparation

Combine the mustard, salt, garlic and vinegar in a small mixing bowl and blend into a paste. Whisk in the olive oil a little at a time to make a smooth dressing. Add the onions and pepper. If refrigerated, bring back to room temperature before serving and whisk again to blend well. Add the optional capers. Makes ¾ cup of dressing, enough for a salad for 6 to 8.

Vinaigrette a l'italienne

Yield: 1 cup
Preparation time: 5 minutes
Cooking time: none

Ingredients

1 teaspoon Dijon mustard
1 egg yolk (of a 2-minute soft-boiled egg)
1 large garlic clove, mashed
Salt and freshly ground black pepper
3 anchovy filets
2 tablespoons wine vinegar
6 tablespoons olive oil
1 tablespoon finely grated Parmesan
   cheese
½ medium red onion, very finely sliced

Preparation

In a wooden salad bowl, mix the mustard with the egg yolk, garlic, salt, pepper and anchovy filets. Mash the mixture until it is very smooth. Add the vinegar and slowly whisk in the olive oil. The dressing should be well blended. Add the Parmesan cheese and correct the seasoning. After tossing the salad greens in the dressing, add the onion.

Remarks

This dressing is particularly good with fresh spinach. Very thin slices of French bread fried in olive oil are an excellent accompaniment for this salad. Serve it either before or after a meal together with an assorted platter of cheeses.

Notes

Acidulated water: Water to which lemon juice has been added in proportions of 1 tablespoon of lemon juice to 1 quart of water. Acidulated water is used to keep fruits (such as pears or apples) and vegetables (such as celery knobs and artichokes) from turning dark.

Al dente: An Italian expression used to describe the degree to which pasta is cooked. Spaghetti should be cooked until barely done and somewhat chewy. Properly cooked spaghetti is considered "al dente."

Baking sheet: This can be either a regular cookie sheet or one that has low sides and is also called a jelly-roll pan. A baking sheet is useful for last-minute broiling of a whole duck or chicken.

Baste: To spoon fat or stock over a roast to prevent it from drying out. Basting is a must when roasting pork or veal or chicken. It is not necessary to baste a roasting duck.

Batter: The blended ingredients for crepes and some cakes.

Blanch: To cook partially fruits, vegetables, and some meats. Tomatoes, apricots and peaches are blanched to make it easier to remove their skins. Bacon and salt pork are often blanched to remove excess fat.

Blend: To mix together gently yet thoroughly various ingredients.

Bouquet garni:
See Basics, page 397.

Braise: To cook in a slow oven in a covered casserole or baking dish. Braising is the perfect method for preparing stews or

small fowl such as squabs and pheasants.

Clarify:
See Basics, page 398.

Coral: The roe, or eggs, found in female lobsters. Coral becomes red after cooking. It is a delicacy. Mash the coral with a little sweet butter and whisk it into a lobster or shrimp sauce.

Croutons: Tiny cubes of bread fried in butter or oil, sometimes with a clove of garlic. Croutons can also be browned in the oven. They are an excellent addition to soups, salads or scrambled eggs.

Cube: To cut into squares. Usually a cube is not as small as dice.

Deglaze: To add a little stock or wine to the coagulated drippings left in the roasting pan and to scrape with a wooden spoon until they are dissolved. Deglazing is the basic step in making a sauce for sauteed or roasted meats, fowl or fish.

Degrease: To remove the accumulated fat from pan juices, stocks, soups or sauces, preferably when they are cold. Degreasing a stock or sauce is extremely important and should be done thoroughly.

Dice: To cut into tiny squares.

Flambee: To pour heated liqueur over meats or desserts and then ignite it in order to evaporate the alcohol.

Fold: To blend delicately. Egg whites should be folded into a batter or food mixture so as not to break their air pockets.

Marinate: To place meats or fish in a liquid that is usually a combination of oil, wine and herbs. Marination often tenderizes a piece of meat and helps it develop flavor. Fruit is often marinated in a mixture of liqueurs and sugar so as to develop its full flavor.

Mince: To chop into very fine bits.

Parboil: To cook partially in boiling water, usually a little longer than when blanching.

Poach: To cook in barely simmering water. Delicate fruit and fish should be poached to keep them from falling apart.

Puree: To put cooked food in a blender or through a food mill to produce a paste-like consistency.

Reduce: To cook liquid such as stock or pan juices over high heat until it has evaporated to the desired consistency. This is the most important step in making sauce and in finishing all dishes that have been braised.

Saute: To cook meat, fish or vegetables in an open frying pan until brown. You may saute certain meats such as chicken breasts, pork chops or veal scallopine until they are done; other meats and fowl are sauteed until brown and then placed in the oven in a casserole to finish cooking. To saute, the food must be thoroughly dry, very little fat used and the pan never crowded.

Simmer: To cook in a liquid that is just below boiling point. Dishes such as rice are brought to a boil and then simmered until they are done.

Skim: To remove the scum that forms on the surface of stocks and soups during cooking. To obtain a clear stock it is extremely important to skim it often.

Truss: To tie meat or poultry with string so that it will keep its shape during cooking. Trussing chickens or ducks is important since it makes it easier to turn the birds during cooking.